Come On Down?

Come On Down? presents an introduction to popular media culture in Britain since 1945. It discusses the ways in which popular culture can be studied, understood and appreciated, and covers some of its most important forms and processes, and the key analytical issues they raise.

The contributors analyse some of popular culture's leading and most representative expressions: TV soaps, quizzes and game shows, TV for children, media treatment of the monarchy, pop music, comedy, advertising, consumerism and Americanization. The diversity of both subject-matter and argument is the most distinctive feature of the collection, making it a much-needed and extremely accessible, interdisciplinary introduction to the study of popular media culture.

The contributors, many of them leading figures in their respective areas of study, represent a number of different approaches which themselves reflect the diversity and promise of contemporary theoretical debates. Their studies encompass issues such as the economics of popular culture, its textual complexity and its interpretations by audiences, as well as concepts such as ideology, material culture and postmodernism.

The editors: Dominic Strinati is a lecturer in sociology at the University of Leicester. His previous work has been in the areas of political and industrial sociology, and he is the author of *Capitalism, the State, and Industrial Relations* (1982). He is currently working on a book on theories of popular culture. Stephen Wagg has taught sociology in further, higher and adult education since the mid-1970s and is currently tutor in sociology at the University of Leicester. He wrote *The Football World* (1984) and, with John Williams, edited *British Football and Social Change* (199
and compères comedy shows.

Come On Down?

Popular media culture in post-war Britain

Edited by
Dominic Strinati
and
Stephen Wagg

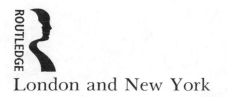

London and New York

First published 1992
by Routledge
11 New Fetter Lane, London EC4P 4EE

Simultaneously published in the USA and Canada
by Routledge
a division of Routledge, Chapman and Hall, Inc.
29 West 35th Street, New York, NY 10001

This collection © 1992 Routledge; individual chapters © 1992 individual
contributors

Typeset in 10 on 12 point Baskerville by
Witwell Ltd
Printed in Great Britain by
T.J. Press (Padstow) Ltd, Padstow, Cornwall.

British Library Cataloguing in Publication Data
Come on down?: popular media culture
  in post-war Britain.
  I. Strinati, Dominic
  302.2373

Library of Congress Cataloging in Publication Data
is also available

ISBN 0-415-06326-4
     0-415-06327-2 (pbk)

DS For my two sons, Adam and Jonathan

SW For Cassie
My daughter, friend and favourite comedian
With Love

Contents

Notes on contributors

Rosalind Brunt is Director of the Centre for Popular Culture at Sheffield City Polytechnic, where she teaches mass communications and women's studies. She is co-editor with Caroline Rowan of *Feminism, Culture and Politics* (Lawrence & Wishart, 1982) and was a member of the editorial board of *Marxism Today*.

Alan Clarke is a Principal Lecturer in the Centre for Leisure and Tourism Studies at the Polytechnic of North London. He previously worked at Sheffield University, where he began his research on police series, and was a member of the course team for the Open University's Popular Culture course. He has written on cultural studies, patterns of leisure and football.

Kathryn Dodd is a member of the Thomas Coram Research Unit at the Institute of Education currently working on the contemporary representations of adolescence. She spent several years as a researcher at Leicester University, and lectured in sociology and social policy at Coventry and Leicester Polytechnics. She has a book in press, *A Sylvia Pankhurst Reader*, and has also published on feminist writing in the inter-war years.

Philip Dodd is presently editor of *Sight and Sound*, was Deputy Editor of *New Statesman and Society*, and for many years was in the English Department at Leicester University. For five years he has also been a consultant to the Music and Arts Department of BBC television. He is co-author of *Relative Values*, a book on art and value, co-editor of *Englishness. Politics and Culture 1880–1920*, and author of numerous articles on television, film and art in journals from *Screen* to *Modern Painters*.

Christine Geraghty is a full-time trade union organiser for NALGO and a part-time lecturer in film studies for the University of London. She has been writing about soap operas since the 1970s, focusing in particular on the changing face of US and British prime-time soaps during that period.

Dick Hebdige is a Reader in the Communications Department of Goldsmith's College, University of London. He is the author of *Subculture: The Meaning of Style* (Methuen, 1979), *Cut 'n' Mix: Culture, Identity and Caribbean Music* (Routledge, 1987) and *Hiding in the Light* (Routledge, 1988), as well as numerous articles on cultural theory and popular culture.

Graham Murdock is a Reader in the sociology of culture in the Department of Social Sciences at Loughborough University and Professor of mass communications at Bergen University in Norway. He is the co-author of *Televising Terrorism* (Comedia, 1983), the co-editor of *Communicating Politics* (Leicester University Press, 1986) and the author of *The Battle for Television*, soon to be published by Macmillan.

Deborah Philips studied at the University of East Anglia and the University of Sussex, developing interests in feminist theory and cultural studies on the basis of a background in English/American Studies. She was a founder of *Women's Review* and worked on the Open University's innovative course "U203" on Popular Culture. She is currently Lecturer in English at the West London Institute of Higher Education.

John Street is Lecturer in politics and Director of the Centre for Public Choice Studies at the University of East Anglia. He is the author of *Rebel Rock: the Politics of Popular Music* and co-author of *Deciding Factors in British Politics*, the former published by Basil Blackwell in 1986 and the latter by Routledge in 1991. His latest book, *Politics and Technology*, will soon be published by Macmillan. He has written on popular music for *New Socialist, Marxism Today* and *The Times*.

Dominic Strinati is a lecturer in sociology at the University of Leicester. His previous work has been in the areas of political and industrial sociology, and he is the author of *Capitalism, the State, and Industrial Relations* (Croom Helm, 1982). He is currently working on a book on theories of popular culture.

Alan Tomlinson studied at the University of Kent and the University of Sussex, developing interests in sport and leisure studies on the basis of a background in historical/literary studies and the sociology of culture. He worked on the Open University course "U203" and has edited numerous collections on sport, leisure and cultural consumption. He is a Reader in the Chelsea School since 1975 and is now Reader in Sport and Leisure Studies in the Chelsea School Research Centre, at the University of Brighton. He edited *Consumption, Identity and Style* (Routledge 1990).

Stephen Wagg has taught sociology in further, higher and adult education since the mid-1970s and is currently tutor in sociology at the University of Leicester. He wrote *The Football World* (1984) and, with John Williams, edited *British Football and Social Change* (1991). He occasionally organizes and compères comedy shows.

Gerry Whannel is a Senior Lecturer in the Department of Sports Studies at Roehampton Institute. He has taught media and cultural studies and sports studies and worked as a researcher/consultant on a number of television documentaries. With Andrew Goodwin he edited *Understanding Television* (Routledge, 1990) and he has just written *Fields of Vision: Television Sport and Cultural Transformation*, also for Routledge.

Janice Winship has taught media and cultural studies at Wolverhampton Polytechnic and the University of Sussex, and is the author of *Inside Women's Magazines* (Pandora, 1987).

Introduction
Come on down? – popular culture today

Dominic Strinati and Stephen Wagg

It used to be the case that popular culture wasn't taken too seriously. Now the opposite seems to apply. Whereas once popular culture was dismissed and condemned as mass culture, without the specific characteristics of distinct and subtle forms being given their due and required consideration, now nearly every manifestation of popular culture, every nuance, every gesture, is made to bear an interpretational load it cannot always carry. Once popular culture was important enough to condemn but not important enought to take seriously. Now its importance is such that, on occasion, it may be taken too seriously.

As the study of popular culture has become more legitimate, and popular culture has become more central to modern western societies, the old distinctions upon which the old certainties rested have begun to be questioned or to break down. Culturally, it is increasingly difficult to distinguish satisfactorily between serious and trivial culture, between high and low culture, between popular and mass culture, between authentic and inauthentic culture, or between popular culture and art. Theoretically, it is increasingly difficult to analyse popular culture in terms of such conceptual distinctions as those between base and superstructure, reflection and autonomy, and production and consumption. So the invitation to 'come on down' no longer has the force it once had, partly because so many have been pleased to accept it, and partly because the topographical references are no longer so fixed and unambiguous. Hence the question mark in the book's title.

This situation has led to the emergence of a diversity of theoretical perspectives and re-evaluations which are reflected in this book. For one way of working through the problems and uncertainties, the lack of clear theoretical divisions and the absence of secure moral and evaluative positions, is precisely to work more consciously and consistently on popular culture itself. This obviously can't be done blind, as if history could reveal itself without theory. But it has to be done, and can be done, in terms of the theoretical diversity we know today – which in itself is no bad thing.

The articles in this reader can be seen in this light. Clearly they do not convey any sense of theoretical consistency or orthodoxy. Rather they show some of the range of interpretational issues and conceptual concerns at stake today. Some of the articles have more definite and coherent approaches to their subject matter than others. Indeed, one or two of the essays signal very clearly their sense of the virtues of diversity. Likewise, some of the articles draw more obviously on the old distinctions and certainties than others, while others more obviously question them. Some articles state more explicitly than others what informs their theoretical approach. But whatever the case for each writer, it is this relative openness, this promising uncertainty, this potentially productive diversity, rather than the simple injunction to take popular culture seriously or just to add to what has gone before, that provides one of the contexts for this volume.

The shift which is registered in this book has been from a conceptualization of popular culture as mass culture, via very theoretical and scientistic marxisms, to postmodernism and beyond (see O'Shea and Shwarz 1987). This transition has, of course, brought a number of refinements in the study of popular culture. Indeed, it has seen, through the coming together of different perspectives and preoccupations (literary, historical, sociological), the emergence of a new discipline called 'Cultural Studies'. In the USA this discipline seems about to be accorded academic institutional status. In Britain, however, it has continued to have a more unbounded and maverick formation and it has been this which has initiated and sustained interest and innovation in the study of popular culture. Moreover, although subjects like sociology and history, and even English literature, have had a somewhat varied and inconsistent interest in this field, cultural studies, despite – or perhaps because of – its lack of academic boundaries, its openness to ideas from Europe, its range of research methodologies, its lack of precise objects of enquiry, has been the most important focus of developments in Britain.

In this context, the Centre for Contemporary Cultural Studies at Birmingham University has been crucial, although other major influences, such as the pioneering writings of Raymond Williams (e.g. Williams 1963), must be acknowledged. Richard Hoggart's book *The Uses of Literacy*, while it tended to take an elitist and dismissive view of post-war popular culture, was, none the less, one of the works which inaugurated the sociological study of popular culture (Dyer 1973: pp. 39–40). Hoggart was the first director of the CCCS, and so many of the key contributors in the field of cultural studies today, including several of those who have written for this volume, taught and studied there. Related to this has been the importance of the Open University's (now unfortunately discontinued) degree in Popular Culture, the progenitors of which, again drawing upon the work of the CCCS, have been responsible for developing theory, research and key textbooks in the area (cf. Gurevitch *et al.* 1982 and O'Shea and Schwarz 1987).

One of the interesting things about all this is how – if we can put it in these terms – the study of popular culture has developed on the margins rather than in the centres of the British academic world. In this respect it is comparable with 'Women's Studies', and suggests how central notions of marginality may be to a theory of intellectual change and innovation. So although people who study popular culture will usually be aware that their field of endeavour doesn't carry the same academic *gravitas* as, say, the study of the economy, industrial relations or health, perhaps they should be wary of too great a degree of academic acceptance. For this field of endeavour still bears the traces of past condemnations, though this may be no bad thing if it allows students of popular culture to retain their critical edge. We hope that some sense of this edge is conveyed by the essays presented here.

One clear reason for the growing importance of the study of popular culture is the fact that popular media culture has become a more crucial and pervasive feature of our everyday lives. The TV set in 98 per cent and the video in almost two-thirds of British homes (*Guardian*, 20 September 1991: 6), the number of hours spent watching television, the mushrooming of pop culture and a popular press preoccupied with media celebrities all attest to this. Popular media culture, then, is increasingly central to the ways people live their lives, how they define those lives and how others may define those lives for them, how they come to construct and reconstruct their identities, and to their sense of time and place. This centrality, of course, lies behind the emergence of theories of postmodernism and provides one of their main points of attention, as well as forming an important focus for this book.

This book is also about politics in two senses. First, there are *cultural* politics which are clearly bound up with the evaluation of popular culture. These have been strongly influenced by the political movements of the 1960s, especially those concerned with civil rights and the 'politics of experience', by the development of subcultural studies, by the 'turn to Gramsci' (Bennett 1986), by more recent feminist perspectives and by the increasing importance of sexual politics more generally. The feminist perspective in the development of cultural politics is particularly interesting in this context since much popular media culture is consumed and enjoyed by – and sometimes directed at – women (think of the history of soap operas, for example). Feminists have thus sought to rescue such culture from male condescension (just as it has to be rescued from academic condescension), pointing out how popular or mass culture is often identified unfavourably with the social construction of the 'feminine' – the passive, the emotional, the consumer – while the 'qualities' of high culture or art – the active, the intellectual, the producer – are identified with the 'masculine' (Modleski 1986). These politics can also be associated with 'culturalist' approaches to the study of the media (Curran *et al.* 1982: 26–8).

Second, there are *party* and *parliamentary* politics. There was a time when leading political figures aligned themselves unambiguously with elite culture. Churchill, for example, was privately opposed to commercial television; Macmillan quoted Jane Austen in speeches. Since the 1960s, however, political leaders have paid regular homage to popular culture: Harold Wilson's award of MBEs to the Beatles springs immediately to mind, as does Margaret Thatcher's visit to the set of *Coronation Street* and her endorsement of the novels of Frederick Forsyth, and John Major's interview with Radio 1 disc jockey Steve Wright, early in 1991, during which he asked to hear a record by the country singer Marty Robbins. This phenomenon is also attested to by the fact that Boris Yeltsin, while holed up in the Russian parliament building in Moscow during the attempted coup in the Soviet Union, in the summer of 1991, listened to

Elvis Presley's recording of 'Are You Lonesome Tonight?', and asked his aides to get a message of support from Mick Jagger (*Guardian*, 26 August 1991 and 20 September 1991). As part of this redrawing of cultural boundaries and the gradual if informal legitimation of popular culture, reciprocal gestures have begun to emanate from the world of popular culture. Showbusiness celebrities are now, for example, a regular feature of British election campaigns (Grant 1991) – a pattern established in the United States since the 1930s.

Each writer here is concerned with politics at one level or the other, or, in some instances, at both levels. Moreover, their contributions reflect the growth of areas of interest generated by the development of the academic study of popular culture, another indication of the growing importance of popular culture, and we have tried to embody this as far as possible in the book. More specifically we have tried, taking the collection of essays as a whole, to cover: (a) the relationship between popular media culture and social difference – class, gender, ethnicity and race, and age (here embracing childhood and youth); (b) a diversity of popular cultural forms – the soap opera, the game show, the police drama, the women's magazine, the monarchy, the satirical comedy show, pop music, TV advertising; (c) popular cultural processes – consumption, Americanization, commercialization, cultural representations, audience interpretations, and ideological constructions; (d) the historical contexts provided by post-1945 British society.

As we have stressed, however, the perspectives adopted by the authors are various, reflecting the diversity of the area. The first two articles deal with general themes and aim to provide contexts for the discussion of popular culture. Deborah Philips and Alan Tomlinson consider changes in the patterns of cultural consumption, 'looking at some major recent trends in popular culture and leisure, and then focusing upon two cases – the phenomenon of media sport, and images of femininity in postwar women's fiction'. Dominic Strinati looks at the theme of 'Americanization', an issue at the centre of the debate between 'elitist' and 'populist' conceptions of popular culture, and one which attests to the complexity of cultural politics. He takes account of discourses about and audience responses to Americanization, as well as its political economy, and questions the extent to which domestic cultural identities have been eroded by American 'cultural imperialism'.

Next Janice Winship offers a novel interpretation of women's magazines which argues that the relationship between these popular cultural forms and their readers be conceived of in more active and creative terms. In particular, she views popular culture as material culture and makes use of the notion of discourses in order to challenge prevailing understandings of women's magazines, and their history.

Kathryn Dodd and Philip Dodd are concerned with identifying representations of the working class, and with determining which representations tend to predominate in popular culture. Looking at soap operas such as *EastEnders*, social surveys, and popular fiction they show how the working class is invariably framed and typified. Christine Geraghty also analyses soap operas but assesses them in relation to the family, and its popular cultural constructions. Since soaps are always about families, real or idealized – the community as family – she questions whether they can ever, as the makers of some of them claim, express radical or progressive ideas.

In the next contribution Stephen Wagg explores changing ideas of the child and of activity, passivity, and vulnerability, particularly in relation to children's television. Television is also the central concern of the next two writers. Garry Whannel provides a novel framework for understanding game shows, one which goes beyond existing theoretical interpretations. While taking gender as a major focus of attention, he looks at the history of the TV game show, and offers a more positive view of them than has been customary in cultural studies. Alan Clarke charts how police work has been depicted in TV fiction from the avuncular *Dixon of Dock Green*, wobbling on the balls of his feet in the 1950s, through the aggressive, fast-driving, plain-clothes hard men of *The Sweeney*, to the more conventional social realist police series such as *The Bill* in the 1980s and 1990s, which echo series in the early 1960s like *Z Cars*. In doing this, he points to the ways particular ideologies work in and through the TV police series.

Graham Murdock details the steady encroachment of advertising and commercial discourse in British popular media culture since the 1950s, taking into consideration such things as the rise of commercial TV, the role of sponsorship and product placement. He takes special pains to describe the erosion of distinctions between entertainment and advertising in a number of mass media. Looking also at a range of media Stephen Wagg offers a political reading of British satirical comedy since the 1950s and questions the depth of its subversiveness. Its most powerful thrust, he suggests, is an anti-political nihilism.

Political questions of a slightly different kind concern Rosalind Brunt who takes up the issue of the popularity of the British monarchy. In accounting for this, she looks at the changing role of the Royal Family, and shows how central it is to popular media culture, opening up the question of what the celebrity status of the monarchy may tell us about British culture and society.

In the penultimate contribution John Street outlines and examines a series of post-war 'moral panics' – 'shock waves' – about youth and popular music and links these to ideologies of youth and sexuality. Notably he avoids the pitfalls of seeing this history either in purely cyclical terms or as a process of decline. In his concluding assessment of these 'shock waves', he opens up new avenues of exploration in the analysis of responses to changes in popular music. Finally, Dick Hebdige uses postmodernist and 'excavatory' analytical and narrative techniques to interrogate shifting ideas of British ethnicity and nationality in popular culture. He does this by 'digging' into crucial 'moments' in the contestation and reconstruction of British identity. In his essay he suggests that identity is never made but is always being made and remade, and his concerns raise questions not only about how we may study popular culture, but how we may write about it.

REFERENCES

Bennett, T. (1986) 'The turn to Gramsci', in T. Bennett (ed.), *Popular Culture and Social Relations*, Milton Keynes: Open University Press.

Curran, J. *et al.* (1982) 'The study of the media: theoretical approaches', in M. Gurevitch *et al.*, *Culture, Society and the Media*, London: Methuen.

Dyer, R. (1973) *Light Entertainment*, London: British Film Institute.

Grant, L. (1991) 'Politics reaches for the stars', *Observer* magazine, 5 May 1991.

Gurevitch, M. *et al.* (1982) *Culture, Society and the Media*, London: Methuen.

Hoggart, R. (1958) *The Uses of Literacy*, Harmondsworth: Penguin.

Modleski, T. (1986) 'Femininity as mas(s)querade: a feminist approach to mass culture', in C. MacCabe (ed.), *High Theory/Low Culture*, Manchester: Manchester University Press.

O'Shea, A. and Schwarz, B. (1987) 'Reconsidering popular culture', *Screen* 28: 104-9.

Williams, R. (1963) *Culture and Society 1780-1950*, Harmondsworth: Penguin (originally published 1958).

Chapter 1

Homeward bound
Leisure, popular culture and consumer capitalism

Deborah Philips and Alan Tomlinson

LEISURE, POPULAR CULTURE AND EVERYDAY LIFE

Just a few years after the global defeat of fascism many aspects of popular culture in Britain continued to exhibit major features of pre-war British life. Everyday life in Britain remained class bound and gender specific, despite many dramatic changes set in motion during the war years, and prominent leisure activities of a collective and publicly experienced nature prospered. In the immediate post-war years many aspects of popular culture exuded a sense of stability and traditionalism; people engaged in established leisure activities and rituals in everyday life – the holiday outing, the night out at the dance hall – in ways that would have been instantly recognizable to their pre-war equivalents. Indeed, in the first years after the end of the war some established leisure activities achieved an all-time peak in their level of popularity.

In 1946, 1,635 million cinema admissions were recorded, a figure dwindling to 111 million by the end of the 1970s, on the eve of the home-video boom (Corrigan 1983: 30). Attendances rose again during the late 1980s, 'from fewer than one visit on average per adult in 1984, to 1.5 in 1989, when there were 88 million cinema visits in Britain' (Hughes 1991: 9). New multiplex cinemas, and a flexibility of usage of domestic tele-vision, encouraged such a growth. Attendances at top class professional soccer matches in the Football League had also peaked in the immediate post-war period: in the season 1946–7, the first after the war, attendances totalled 35.6 million. Two seasons later the attendance for the 1948–9 season was 41.2 million, a figure never reached again during the subsequent four decades of social and cultural change. The figure for the end of the 1950s was around 33 million; for 1969-70, 29.6 million; for 1979-80, 24.6 million; for 1984-5, 17.8 million; and by 1985-6, in the wake of the Bradford fire and the Heysel tragedy, the figure had slumped to an all-time low of 16.5 million (Mason 1989: 165; and figures provided by the Football League). Although the end of the 1980s saw some encouraging trends upwards (with the figure for 1989-90 standing at 19.46 million (HMSO, *Social Trends* 21)) and the high profile World Cup Finals in Italy in summer 1990 further rekindled enthusiasm for the game, by any comparison with the immediate post-war figures such increases remain marginal. Although the number of clubs affiliated to county football associations increased fourfold between the late 1930s and the mid-1980s – from around 10,000 to more than 40,000 (Mason 1989: 149) – the predominantly male public ritual of 'going to the match' was no longer the symbol that it had been of a community collectively at play.

By the 1980s, too, a key recurrent political theme had become intertwined with the fate of these two long-established cultural forms. Both became prominent targets for the law and order lobbies during the ascendancy of the New Right during the Thatcher years. Battle cries and rallying calls about the morality of the media and the safety of the streets indicated explicitly what has always been the case: that our everyday activities and popular cultural practices are not autonomous innocent worlds apart, but are constitutive of the social and political order. Just thinking about the movies and the football match, and their developemnt as cultural activities and leisure industries over the last forty years, directs us towards central questions about the nature of contemporary leisure and the conditions of its emergence. How does contemporary leisure represent new forms of consumption and ways of consuming? How has privatized consumerism affected forms of community life? To what extent is leisure a reflection of change, the index of change or a harbinger itself of important changes? If we are to move beyond mere descriptive histories and sociologies of the 'how many, where and when?' kind, these are the sorts of question that must be posed. The consideration of selected cases, informed by such questions and organized around key concepts, will provide the basis of an understanding of major influences upon popular culture in the post-war period.

One very important dichotomy becomes impossible to ignore: the public/private dimension. Much of contemporary leisure has inclined towards the expansion of ways of consuming in individualized and privatized forms *in the home*, and this has matched the rhetoric and ideology of the New Right/Thatcher years, as well as the marketing strategies of the new industrial barons of late twentieth-century Britain, the leisure retailers. In the cases which feature below (see pp. 21–5 and 25–41), the public/private dimensions of the consumption of sport and popular fiction are given some detailed consideration.

Everybody has a view on leisure and popular culture – on their ephemeral nature; or their inherent subjectivity; on their relevance to the realm of the personal; on their potential as expressions of freedom or individual choice; on their implicitly politicized and politicizing nature. Leisure is widely seen – both in the academic analysis and in the expressed views of people – as personal choice and *freely* chosen activity, and as a sign of widening freedoms. Defendants of liberal capitalism see modern industrial society as a world of golden opportunity for those willing to work, apply themselves and avail themselves of the goodies obtainable in the marketplace. While in previous phases of capitalism the class and status system was characterized by high degrees of rigidity, and conspicuous consumption was, to use Thorstein Veblen's term, the prerogative of the wealthiest classes and a handful of elite groups, modern consumer capitalism has enabled greater numbers to express themselves in the marketplace. In this context, as consumption becomes more and more targeted towards specialist segments of the market, people become encouraged to express their uniqueness and subjectivity as consumers. This, as much as the role that they might have as producers, becomes the source of their identity: consumer capitalism becomes in this sense enabling; people are seen as discriminating punters in the incessant commodity and credit stakes of the modern marketplace.

In the 1950s the combination of new techniques of mass production (of cars, fridges, washing machines, vacuum cleaners, for instance) with newly available forms of credit (hire purchase available at manageable rates of interest), produced an expanded consumer market. Social inhibitions were also breaking down, producing in Arthur Marwick's words 'the relatively free-wheeling society of the late 1960s and early 1970s (which) differed markedly from the tight and excessively traditionalist society of the late 1940s' (Marwick 1986: 19). In the United Kingdom the Conservative Prime Minister Harold Macmillan captured the spirit of the times with his claim that people had 'never had it so good'. Released from the austerity of the immediate post-war years, choosing between jobs available in the new and booming industries, encountering new types of domestic and leisure living, many at the time believed that here was the new Nirvana: full employment, lots of credit, affluence all round and a more open morality.

There was sufficient substance to these developments to constitute a real shift, a move into what Harry Braverman (1974) has called the phase of the emergence of the universal marketplace. Paradoxically, it is in this marketplace that the swing towards modes of individualized consuming intensifies; paradoxically because, as it penetrates more universally, everyday life becomes a more fully personalized construct. We are not talking here about a sudden and dramatic transformation from some idyllic collective culture to an individualized array of fragmented cultures: everyday life for some had for some time had been rooted in individualized modes rather than the collective. But the process certainly intensifies, and more and more aspects of everyday life become inextricably linked with new forms of commodity production which in turn generate new ways of consuming. Before looking at some major recent trends in popular culture and leisure, and then focusing upon two cases – the phenomenon of media sport, and images of femininity in post-war women's fiction – it is worth considering a little more fully the implications of this expansion of the universal marketplace.

THE UNIVERSAL MARKET

If there is any single idea that captures the essence of post-war developments in leisure and popular culture it is this notion of the universal market. Modern capitalism, for Braverman, revolves around a principle of monopoly, which extends the reach of the capitalist mode of production to the most private of spheres. All needs – 'the totality of individual, family and social needs' (Braverman 1974: 270) – become subordinated to the market. Such needs are actually reshaped 'to serve the needs of capital'. Although the social framework itself – capitalism – is here endowed with a sense of determinacy which can no doubt be questioned (in other words, some might accuse Braverman of a rather simplistic form of economic reductionism), the central point is an extremely persuasive one. Consider how much of our everyday life is lived in newly privatized forms in the last decade of this second millennium. Where individuals may have talked to each other in family and community settings in previous eras, they now have the choice of consuming alone in well-equipped consumer playgrounds in their own part of the increasingly fragmented home. Where young children may have played football on the streets, they now watch edited highlights of elite matches starring sponsored superstars whose wages have put the price of a spot or a seat at a live match way out of reach of many potential fans. It is not a question of being evaluative, or nostalgic, about this; rather, it is a matter of cultivating an adequately historicized understanding of the contemporary, one which will help us identify key recent trends, and which will therefore in turn highlight what is specific about the state of things in the here and now. It seems almost old fashioned now, if you are waged, salaried and buffeted against deprivation or hardship, to do anything which costs nothing; our patterns of leisure and the contours of popular culture have been redrawn by what Braverman calls 'one of the keys to all recent social history'.

This is the transformation by capitalism of 'all of society into a gigantic marketplace'. The source of our individual status – what we become known for – is not what we do, or what we can make, 'but simply the ability to purchase'. As modern urban society crams more and more people into less and less space, a central paradox of contemporary living emerges more and more clearly – the 'atomization of social life'. In such circumstances, life away from dehumanizing work and fragmented family becomes a search for some sociability; in Braverman's view this 'social artifice' is now only available in its marketable forms:

> Thus the population no longer relies upon social organiza-
> tion in the form of family, friends, neighbours, community,
> elders, children, but with few exceptions must go to market
> and only to market, not only for food, clothing and shelter,
> but also for recreation, amusement, security . . . the atrophy of
> community and the sharp division from the natural environ-
> ment leaves a void when it comes to the 'free' hours. Thus the
> filling of the time away from the job also becomes dependent

upon the market, which develops to an enormous degree those passive amusements, entertainments, and spectacles that suit the restricted circumstances of the city and are offered as substitutes for life itself. Since they become the means of filling all the hours of 'free' time, they flow profusely from corporate institutions which have transformed every means of entertainment and 'sport' into a production process for the enlargement of capital.

(Braverman 1974: 276, 277–8)

The embodiment of this form of activity, for Braverman, is an event such as a car-smashing derby which can draw large holiday or spare-time crowds. Some of us might remember, in Britain, similar spectactles in the late 1960s and early 1970s when piano-smashing competitions were held, often in seaside towns on Bank Holiday weekends. Not quite defined as old enough then to have antique value, these pianos were smashed out of existence, a subconscious preparation perhaps for the burgeoning market in home-based leisure goods – the portable television, the ghetto-blaster, the videocassette recorder, the personal stereo, the home-computer, the compact disc. All these resources were/are small, individualized, easily portable. The individual could now retreat more and more into privately defined worlds of consumption, where s/he could sample in peace the products of the booming consumer market. It is the central paradox of modern living that much of our subjectivity is constituted in response to the products of a mass market, whose products are often standardized objectively to cater for as large a public as possible. Braverman, admittedly coming close to a form of cultural elitism here, is scathing when talking of such products:

By their very profusion they cannot help but tend to a standard of mediocrity and vulgarity which debases popular taste, a result which is further guaranteed by the fact that the mass market has a powerful lowest–common-denominator effect because of the search for maximum profit. So enterprising is capital that even where the effort is made by one or another section of the population to find a way to nature, sport or art through personal activity and amateur or 'underground' inno-vation, these activities are rapidly incorporated into the market so far as is possible.

(Braverman 1974: 279)

Written on the eve of the explosion of punk rock into the consciousness of western youth, with its impact upon the recording industry, this pinpoints the central question about any sphere of popular culture. If the universal market reaches so far into all of our lives – in the third phase of its creation producing 'a "product cycle" which invents new products and services' (281) – what is the possibility of cultural initiative, intervention, autonomy? As punk rock became staple fare on the racks of high street fashion stores, and alternative comedians become stars and celebrities in the mainstream media, it is clear that the momentum of the popular does in so many cases give way to the force of the dominant. This looks silly sometimes, in the anachronistic punk styles of country youth in small town market squares – but it is profitable, and that is what counts. Incorporation remains the fate of many cultural challenges and innovations; it would be naive, overidealistic and romantically foolish to deny this.

There is, of course, more to it than Braverman recognizes. The act of consuming can be evaluative, critical, dynamic. Paul Willis's corpus of work on symbolic creativity in schools, leisure and everyday life is eloquent testimony to the capacity of young people to make products their own, or to dispute the taken-for-granted authority of institutional values, and impose upon them their own meanings (Willis 1977; 1990a; 1990b). He argues, for instance, that there is an 'unexpected life and promise of everyday grounded aesthetics in the ordinary life activities of young people' which is 'articulated . . . for the most part through the popular cultural products of the mainly commercial market' (Willis 1990a: 55). Ruth Finnegan, in a convincingly rigorous anthropological fashion, has demonstrated the deep-rootedness of cultural creativity in everyday life, in her study of music-making in the English new town of Milton Keynes in the early 1980s (Finnegan, 1989). And in the appropriate circumstances people are certainly attracted still to 'help each other to pleasure', in 'communal leisure groups (which) can be considered as organized forms of mutual aid' (Bishop and Hoggett 1986: 127). But socio-historically Braverman's central point holds. The market dominates contemporary forms of consumption, establishing the framework in which the act and renewed acts of consumption are possible. This is clear in the shifting patterns of leisure in post-war Britain.

RECENT TRENDS IN LEISURE AND POPULAR CULTURE

New technologies, and the social relations attributed to them, have been a formative influence upon modern leisure cultures. The impact of radio and the cinema on patterns of inter-war leisure was great, creating leisure opportunities in and out of the home. In the post-war period television displaced the radio as the central focus of domestic leisure, and the private motor car expanded people's out-of-home consumer horizons. As Ken Roberts put it at the beginning of the 1980s: 'Since the 1960s there has been no single leisure arrival as spectacular as the radio, cinema, television and private motor car' (Roberts 1981: 37). But ten years on from the time of Roberts's comment there have been some equally spectacular arrivals. Viewing patterns in the home have fundamentally changed with the arrival of time-shift viewing courtesy of videocassette recorders, now owned by nearly half the households in Britain (Tomlinson 1990); and with the advent of channel zapping, a technique which makes of all of us instant short-span armchair critics. Music no longer has to intrude upon everybody else's aural space, now that the personal stereo can reduce the scope of any musical genre to a background 'gnats' orchestra' (Williamson 1986: 209). Ways of consuming in the home can be fitted in with other more basic needs, such as eating. Deepfreeze food storage and microwave ovens make every member of the family into a fast-food gourmet. Extensive forms of fun and pleasure are available in these new modes of consuming: as John Clarke and Chas Critcher have put it, the 'incorporation of much of the new technology into family life, from computers to videocassette recorders, depends upon its convertibility into items of and for play' (Clarke and Critcher 1985: 173). One characteristic of these new forms of play stands out, though – the private and individual basis upon which much of such play takes place. And even out of the home the same essential pattern persists, as we look for novel consuming experiences in a state of what Raymond Williams has called 'mobile privatization' (Williams 1974), an 'ugly prase for an unprecedented condition' (Williams 1983: 188). Ugly or not, it captures the central dynamic of contemporary leisure:

What it means is that at most active social levels people are increasingly living as private small-family units, or, disrupting even that, as private and deliberately self-enclosed individuals, while at the same time there is a quite unprecedented mobility of such restricted privacies.

(Williams 1983: 188)

It is in the light of such a central theme that all talk of leisure participation rates must be understood. There are continuities in people's leisure – to dance, to walk, to watch television, to swim, to go on holiday – but there are also shifts in the ways in which these experiences are constructed and consumed.

Ken Roberts identifies 'four broad trends in British leisure in the 1980s' (1989: 52). First, *home-centredness* has been an important dimension in the privatization of leisure, the product of 'a more mobile population, the decline of local neighbourhood communities, and the rise of the relatively independent nuclear family'. For some, though, this home-centredness equates with new forms of deprivation: you can be trapped in a home-based lifestyle 'by poverty, and as a result of local communal facilities – cinemas, sports teams and pubs – either declining or disappearing completely'. The second trend identified by Roberts is *out-of-home recreation*: in, primarily, participant sport and tourism. But Roberts quite rightly emphasizes that this is a trend only for some, and for many people any out-of-home option remains very limited. A third trend is what Roberts refers to as *connoisseur leisure*: the leisure of the dedicated, committed expert; leisure cultures of an exclusive, excluding and minority kind. Though it is difficult to measure the scale of this, specialist forms of consumption (from the choice of your supermarket wine to the themed holiday which is targeted to you) have expanded in recent years; and specialist groupings in the form of voluntary associations might well have been in some senses strengthened by the growth of new technologies facilitative of networks and lines of communication. The final trend pointed to by Roberts is *the threat of the mob*. As Roberts puts it: 'Fears of the uncouth mob and of the devil making work for idle hands that have flickered throughout urban history have been rekindled and are settling on the young unemployed' (1989: 56). Such fears have also focused upon travelling people, peace protests and convoys, large gatherings at sports events, so-called rural lager louts, and non-conventional figures in policed urban settings: in Basingstoke in the late 1980s punk-style young people were banned from privately owned parts of retailing areas of the town centre.

Roberts's trends are important, with the primary one being home-centredness, for it is in the home that much of our connoisseur leisure is practised, away from the fear of the mob. And for those participating in out-of-home activities, many of the choices are newly individualized and packaged – sports participation is often little more than a form of narcissistic self-enhancement, now frequently geared to an appearance on the tourist circuit! How leisure is engaged in – not just what is done – is the key question. For where there seems to be a revived buoyancy in some leisure activities – the soccer match and the cinema is discussed above (see pp. 9-10), for instance – the increases remain relatively slight in comparison with earlier phases in the history of the forms; and, most importantly, any revival has been a reorientation of the activity itself, in the sense that the public culture of the stadium and the cinema is becoming a more integrated one in terms of the place of such sites in well-ordered leisure complexes.

In the 1980s 'people's leisure lives have been shaped by the spread into personal use of a wide range of new communication devices and household controls. This has produced a new flexibility in leisure that parallels a similar easing in the traditional routines of working life' (Leisure Consultants 1990: 16). The list compiled by Leisure Consultants Bill Martin and Sandra Mason shows the pervasiveness of the impact of such technologies upon our everyday lives:

Electronic publishing and printing
Teletext and videotext
Cable and satellite TV
Video recording and playing
Compact discs
Small personal and portable computers

Compact video cameras/recorders
Mini labs for rapid film processing

Microwave food processing

IMAX and other cinema innovations
Laser lighting systems
Health and fitness equipment

Audio animatronics
People moving systems
Interactive video

Intelligent cards
Computerized booking systems

Radio telephones
Fax machines

(Leisure Consultants 1990: 16)

Imagine – and some don't need to do that – flying in from your long-haul specialist activity short-break holiday, getting home and getting your slides in for one-hour processing; meanwhile popping something into the microwave whilst ringing all your friends on your mobile phone – if you hadn't checked their messages to you on your remote control ansaphone interceptor while waiting at baggage reclaim. Within minutes of arrival you could be sharing your home-and-away video and slideshow with your closest friends and neighbours. No wonder television viewing figures have fallen a little in recent years: the set is often lost under the rubble of all the other new technologies.

Yet despite the innovations of new technologies there are persisting patterns of participation in particular leisure activities in terms of class, age and gender characteristics both in and away from the home. Women's participation in sports activities, for instance, increased from around 32 per cent to 36 per cent between 1980 and 1986. But, most revealingly, women's participation in outdoor activities (including walking), having risen from 21 per cent to 25 per cent or so from 1977 to 1980, levelled out at 24 per cent in 1983 and 1986. It was in indoor activity that women's participation rose most dramatically – 12 per cent or so in 1977, 15 per cent in 1980, 18 per cent or so in 1983, and 21 per cent in 1986. Men continued to dominate outside sports, though with 40 per cent of men engaging in at least one outdoor activity; and 56 per cent of men participated in at least one activity, either indoor or outdoor. Generally speaking, then, twice as many men as women participated regularly in a sporting activity (figures from HMSO, *General Household Survey* 1986: Figure 13A and Table 13.11).

Some of the continuities in sport and leisure are deeply rooted in cultural inequalities. The most popular activities for women are often those which can be fitted in around the schedules and demands of the domestic role – an hour at bingo or keep fit; swimming with the kids. The public leisure culture of evening and weekend remains a male domain – pubs, clubs, sports leagues and other associational leisure forms continue to cater predominantly for men.

Newly individualized forms of leisure activity, for consumers of both sexes and all ages, have emerged. The leisure industries have moved swiftly to define newly fragmented markets in which discriminating categories of consumer seek through leisure a particular and desirable identity. Or, where large numbers gather – in, for example, indoor swimming centres – the whole complex has been redesigned to offer a multitude of experiences, a wide range of activities, rather than just the rectangular functionalism of the Victorian swimming bath. Whether people learn or reaffirm their swimming skills is not a concern in these developments – fun predominates in the 'leisure pool', profit depends on pleasure, and pleasure is linked in one way or another with exotic lifestyle. So you can swim up to cocktail bars in CentrePark's Tropicana Centre in Rotterdam, by the port's main river, and await the evening laser show over the main water area; or swim naked under the external wall of the Centre's health suite to glance at the outside world of dilapidated barges and dirty wharfside eyesores before gliding back in to the paratropical indoors of this water world. Here, in the family outing to the Centre (note how the terms 'baths' and even 'pool', has gone out of common usage), the family need not stay together: there are many options in the same facility.

When the bars are in the water itself swimming comes to take on new meanings. This is really what Raymond Williams was getting at – even where family groupings go, the ideal is for the individual in the family unit to go off on his or her own. Don't splash me on this side of the pool – you'll dilute my cocktail! In the Tropicana in June 1989 one of us sipped a lager by the poolside and at the next table a mother was knitting. How would you make sense of this in a survey on leisure participation? What was she actually doing – looking after the children, working freelance, engaging in leisure? The mobile and privatized consumer is a sophisticated beast, often up to many things at once – but, most important of all, s/he has some choices. In or out of the home the grip of privatization and individualization has become firmer and firmer in recent years.

SPORT AND MEDIA CONSUMPTION

For illustrative purposes, it is instructive to return to the case of sport. A recent survey has indicated that, at the end of the 1980s, football, so popular for a full century or so, is now less popular than athletics (see Table 1.1). The *Sunday Times* writer covering this piece of market research on 936 randomly selected adults (by Millward Brown market research agency) called this a revelation (Dighton 1989: A28). The scale of interest expressed in some major British sports was as follows:

Table 1.1 Interest in sports

	Men %	Women %	All %
Athletics	69	70	69
Football	64	30	47
Cricket	54	24	39
Rugby	43	21	32

Source: Sunday Times, 17 September 1989.

Fascinatingly, it is women who show slightly more interest than men in the boom sport of the 1980s. And of course such interest is generated by television coverage, just as Paul Gascoigne's lachrymose infantilism and Gary Lineker's sleek thighs feature in our popular culture from the media coverage of Italia 90. In the other sports – male team sports in their mainstream forms – well under half the number of women express an interest in the sport compared to the men. Such popularity stems from the high profile of athletics on television, quite as much as from the threefold increase (from a base of 1 in a 100) in participation in athletics between 1977 and 1986. General patterns of participation in sport remain very low, according to government studies such as the *General Household Survey*. In terms of 'physical pastimes', 'if walking is excluded, the propor-

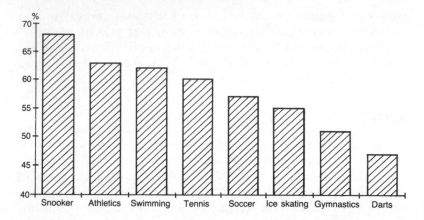

Figure 1.1 Interest in sport (percentage of population mentioning)
Source: Parker and Etherington 1989 for the Sports Council – Henley Centre, 1989.

tion of adults taking part in at least one outdoor activity is 18 per cent' (HMSO 1989: 214 and Table 13.7). Such findings are consistent across a range of studies, though there are variations according to seasonality and the frequency of participation recorded or asked for in the survey. Individual sport playing in early summer, for instance, might look high at 28 per cent of a sample, but this had dropped to 19 per cent by mid-winter 1988–9; and team sport playing (an indicator of more regular commitment) had dropped to a mere 14 per cent in the winter quarter of January – March 1989. This is a far from high rate of participation, particularly given that it records the levels 'on basis of participating at least once a quarter' (Henley Centre, summer 1989: 25).

Most people's experience of sport is now derived from the television screen. Despite some rises in participation rates, expressions of interest in sport are very much responses to what is available to the television viewer. Most people's experience of and interest in sport is of watching elite performers, from the comfort of their own armchairs. Another recent poll of people's interest in sport confirmed the ascendancy of athletics over soccer, but also noted that snooker outstripped them both (Figure 1.1).

'TV holds the key', as the Henley Centre notes. Sport, that great public spectacle, is now consumed in the most private of ways. Any rituals around it – mates round and cans of beer in for the Cup Final; late-night sessions jerking awake to the Superbowl – do not alter this fundamental fact. Indeed, television and the sponsorship that accrues to televisual sports with good media deals have become so important that they have challenged the basis of an older model of top class sport. A certain aspect of the 'play' or 'ludic' element is threatened by this process of commodification (Critcher 1989), and it is no exaggeration to describe the effects of this upon sport as a transformation or a remaking (Whannel 1986). The star syndrome (the Coe–Ovett story as a model, see Whannel 1983); product enhancement (Daley Thompson's ritzification of that boring old bedside drink, Lucozade); customer care (the search for the North American-style family audience as ideal consumer) – all these aspects of the uninhibited professionalization and commercialization of sport have swept aside the old models of first, the amateur as effortless expert and second, of a more regionally based participatory professional form. Sport is now revealed as big business and hard labour.

This has had some splendidly democratizing effects, with great talents now untainted by the stigma of professional effort: 'the complete amateur was one who could play several games extremely well without giving the expression of strain' (Holt 1990: 99–100). In the post-war years in Britain the prominent and privileged role of the amateur has been usurped in many sports from golf to cricket to athletics. And the rewards now unashamedly available in elite sports can attract a wider range of participants. The majority of the British squad for the late 1980s athletics World Cup Final in Barcelona was black. Despite depressing instances of racism in everyday life, among sports crowds and in some sports cultures (Maguire 1988a), Britain's world class sprinter Linford Christie has claimed that the athletics community itself shows no racist prejudice whatsoever. So one aspect of the remaking of British sport is its refreshing openness, its move towards a principle of equality of opportunity.

Yet the increasing dependence of sport upon media contracts, corporate sponsorship and marketing has turned many sport events into little more than encampments of the economic elite. Tented binges take place at Henley and at Wimbledon while the true fans, who were lucky enough to get in, watch this sideshow of capitalist gluttony. Seats remain empty in executive boxes or

VIP rows as that extra bottle of bubbly takes its toll. Most people don't see this, of course. They're at home watching the action on the box. That's where the sports administrators know the real market is. Any sport wanting to expand can't avoid this fact. Baseball and American football – two recent candidates for the big time – know this.

The National Basketball League was founded in England in 1972, and its formative features were those of the old amateur model: part-time administrators, slapdash organization, unevenness of playing standards. Three central changes have contributed to the sport's transformation: players have become workers; the game has been developed as a marketable commodity; and it has been constructed more and more as a spectacle, a grand event (Maguire 1988b: 309). The basis and the features of the game itself underwent changes. Rules of play were designed to accelerate action, obviate scoring and identify outright winners. Other norms of conduct began to stress 'display, "glitz" and entertainment' (308). And entrepreneurial owners, media interests and corporate sponsors have combined to undermine the authority and influence of the governing body. Competing interests have disputed the game's future, but the game was transformed by an 'Americanized influence' involving marketing strategies and the creation, construction and presentation of events. For a while the strategy was very successful, and basketball's mid-1970s half-hour slot on BBC's *Grandstand* was followed by a four-year contract with Channel 4 in the 1980s – a live match a week from October to April, twenty-six in all. When Channel 4 dropped the sport, attendance figures and sponsorship income dropped simultaneously (Barnett 1990: 112–13).

The impact made by American football in Britain owes little to the creative generation of an emergent culture in the lived rhythms of everyday life, and everything to the strategic planning of a USA-based multinational company – which is what the NFL (National Football League) really is. In association with Anheuser–Busch, makers of Budweiser beer, the NFL was aiming to reach a youngish, high earning and lucrative market. It did not take long to do this in the 1980s. James Connelly, the NFL's International Marketing Director, did not mince his words:

What you now have in the UK is a microcosm of the US NFL market with one major difference; business that took almost 20 years to develop in the USA has taken a fraction of that time in Great Britain. It is obviously a very receptive market for new ideas and products.

('Touchdown', *Sport and Leisure*, March/April 1987, cited in Maguire 1990: 213)

Connelly's strategy included four aims: the promotion of the game outside the USA; the creation and education of a new fan base; the generation of revenues; and the establishment and extension of NFL trademarks. The key to achieving all this was marketing via television placement of a 'strong programmed package' in a good slot. This would then generate interest and adequate exposure, at which point, as Connelly asserted to the Sports Council's National Recreation Management Conference, 'you can then go in and develop the resulting licensing businesses' (Maguire 1990: 225). They were developed so successfully in the UK that in the five years from 1982 to 1987 patterns of NFL overseas business were changed dramatically: Canada and Mexico had provided 60 per cent of NFL overseas business in 1982; the same year saw the first Channel 4/Cheerleader broadcast of the sport; by 1987 80 per cent came from Europe, where the UK was by far the biggest market.

Much more could be said, but the point is made. Whereas at a certain period in modern history the moving image industries were perceived as disseminating existing cultural forms, in contemporary consumer culture they are the source of the creation of cultural forms. A market has been constructed for a practice for which there was no established basis in the lived culture. Again, the spectactle is brought to us, packaged, pruned and highly commodified, in the domestic sphere. 'Interest in sport' means some degree of awareness of its presence on television. The main place of sport in contemporary popular culture – primarily through the rituals of domestic consumption – is as marketed product and media discourse.

THE CONSUMPTION OF POPULAR FICTION

Of all cultural commodities, books are those that are consumed most privately. But while the act of reading has always been, and by its very nature must remain, a private and largely domestic activity, the ideas and fantasies that popular fictional texts offer can provide insights into wider cultural aspirations and anxieties. By virtue of their popularity, bestsellers and widely read authors clearly touch a cultural nerve that goes beyond the individual reader. The act of choosing to buy or borrow and of reading a book may be a private experience, but the network of publishing hype, library categorization and criticism (both professional and that of friends' recommendations) within which those choices are made, belong to a broader cultural ideology.

The figures for the readership of popular fictional texts are very difficult to pinpoint with any kind of exactness; sales figures can only provide a rough indication of the actual readership of popular texts; books are commodities which are circulated, popular texts are borrowed from both friends and from libraries. Second hand book shops, book stalls at markets and charity shops have shelves full of battered and much-read paperbacks – indications of a circuit of readers beyond the initial purchaser. Sales figures are inevitably an underestimation of the number of the readers for each copy of a popular novel.

None the less, as Ken Worpole points out, 'Publishing in Britain, so long thought of as a cottage industry located in Bloomsbury, is now a billion pound business' (1984: chap. 1), and has become the largest manufacturing centre in London. Within this industry, fiction is the largest and most commercially successful category. In a 1982 survey of consumption, 45 per cent of respondents said that they were reading a book, and of those, two-thirds were reading fiction. And of those reading fiction, the large majority were women; about three-quarters of women's reading material is made up of novels, while half of books read by men are fiction. It is the publishing companies which market and distribute a specialized product which are now the most commercially successful, and of those in Britain, Mills & Boon, at the sign of 'the Rose of Romance' and now part of the Canadian Torstar Corporation (Philips: 1990), is the most stringently organized and perhaps the most aggressively marketed product of all. Mills & Boon spend more on advertising than any other publishing house, and they are unique as a publishing venture which hooks readers on the strength of its imprint and company profile, rather than on the names of individual authors. Of all fictional genres, it is the category of romance which is the best selling, and which now accounts for a third of paperback sales in the UK. Mills & Boon are the longest established company in this field, and can claim 65 per cent of the readership.

Mills & Boon represent (and have become a byword for) a paradigm of mass produced and standardized popular novels; but their marketing strategy and readership drive also construct the most privatized reading experience of all. Many readers not only read their romances in secret, but often do not even enter a shop to choose their books. Each volume carries a listing of the titles for the next month, all available from the 'Rose of Romance' club, and some of these titles are available exclusively from the 'Mills & Boon Reader Service'. This service, constructed as the membership of a community of romance readers, with a monthly newsletter is, in effect, a subscription service which now forms the basis of the company's approach to the marketing of its product. While its editor 'Sue' prefaces each newsletter with a personalized address to her readers, and the contents have helpful hints on handicrafts and exercise, there are in fact no contributions at all from readers. Competitions give prizes of free subscriptions to the Reader Service, while author profiles are all those from the Mills & Boon stable; clearly, the 'community' of romance readers has no focus but the brand name.

Subscription sales now dominate the romance market, a strategy first devised in 1971 by Lawrence Heisey, a soap salesman for Procter & Gamble who was hired by Harlequin (the Canadian arm of the company which owns Mills & Boon) to boost sales (Radway 1987: 39–42). It was Heisey who located paperback fiction in supermarkets, and who effectively devised the strategies still in place for constructing Mills & Boon and Harlequin as reliable brand names.

The establishing of a publishing company as a brand name and the history of Mills & Boon as a commercial organization is an image, although it may be extreme, of what was to happen to publishing companies as a new-found post-war popular readership, exacerbated by the discovery of a paperback market, was profoundly to alter the shape of the 'gentlemanly profession' of publishing.

BACHELOR GIRLS – WOMEN, WAR AND WORK IN POPULAR FICTION

Jenny Wren is the title of a wartime romance by the popular novelist Ursula Bloom, also a regular writer of short stories for women's magazines. In 1944, her heroine's experience of the war is represented in these terms: 'she had adored the life in the officers' mess. . . . She had thought that life has only begun when she had put on the wren's uniform, that the big war (which everybody thought to be such a catastrophe) had opened the gates to something like heaven for her' (Anderson 1974: 219).

Jenny was not alone as a heroine for whom the war represented less of a catastrophe than the opening up of a new world of possibilities. She is but one (if an unusually and naively honest example) of hundreds of fictional heroines in the magazine fiction and novels of the war period, who clearly articulate the new experiences and opportunities for women that the war had offered. A woman who trained and worked as a steel worker during the war years remembers her experiences in terms not dissimilar to those of the fictional Jenny: 'To be quite honest, the war was the best thing that ever happened to us. I was as green as grass and terrified if anyone spoke to me. . . . At work you did exactly as your boss told you and you went home to do exactly what your husband told you. The war changed all that. The war made me stand on my own two feet' (quoted in Lewis 1986: 147).

The incursion of women into war work represented an enormous shift in the numbers of women entering the workforce, and significant changes in the kinds of work that women undertook; a shift that could not be completely reversed. According to the 1931 census, there were 6 million working women, of whom 2 million were in domestic service; by 1951 the number of married women at work had trebled from the pre-war figures.

Although women were initially discouraged from volunteering for war work, by 1941, eighteen months into the war, it had become clear that the labour requirements for essential services and for civil defence were such that women had to be called upon. It was in March 1941 that Bevin, then Minister of Labour, appealed to the women of Britain in a radio broadcast summoning them to work: 'We must call for a great response from our women to run the industrial machine' (quoted in Lewis 1986: 113). From the end of 1941 women were actively recruited into war work; unmarried women from the ages of nineteen to thirty were conscripted into the women's services, into civil defence and industry, and those women with domestic responsibilities, up to the age of forty, were required to register at Employment Exchanges. From 1942, women were conscripted into the women's services or into other forms of war work. By 1943, there were 7.5 million women in paid employment; twice as many women were mobilized in the Second World War as had been active in the First.

The single, young woman who was then (and remains) the staple protagonist of popular romance fiction was of precisely the status and age group that the government was attempting to recruit into war work, and her fictional incarnations were rapidly pressed into service. The recruitment of women had its effect on the status and occupation of fictional heroines, and of their love objects, in the romantic fiction of such best-selling authors as Denise Robins, Ursula Bloom and Daphne du Maurier; heroes and heroines were now more likely to be garbed in uniform than in party dress, their love to bloom in the fields of battle. As the publicity material for the publishers Mills & Boon explains with pride, their authors made their own contribution: 'heroes were in the services, and heroines joined the war effort . . . uniformed officers embracing young sweethearts struck a chord with the women left at home' (Mills & Boon publicity leaflet 1985).

An expanded mass market for reading had been uncovered during the war years, and there was an increased availability for cheap editions of popular novels, despite the fact that paper rationing had its effect on the numbers of new fiction titles that could be published. Introduced in March 1940, the rationing of paper meant that while in 1939, 14,904 new titles were published of which 4,222 were novels, by 1945 the numbers were down to 6,747, and 1,179 novels. Although the war placed constraints on the production of new fiction, nevertheless the demand for novels went up. The Mills & Boon account of history explains in their publicity material that 'World War II presented Mills & Boon with a dilemma. Paper rationing meant fewer books could be published, but demand for romantic fiction was stronger than ever. . . . Every novel that could be printed was sold.' It was in the 1940s that the familiar Mills & Boon logo of a cupid, bearing his placard inscribed with the legend 'A Mills & Boon Love Story' made his first appearance on the front cover, and the 1940s Mills & Boon slogan, despite the effects of paper rationing, could state 'there is always a new Mills & Boon'. There was an organized supply of reading materials to those involved in war work, a policy which seemed to establish a widespread habit for reading; by 1949 17,034 new titles were published, and consumer spending on books had increased to £24 million in 1949, from a figure of £7 million in 1939. It has been argued that: 'The need to furnish abundant cheap reading matter for millions of American soldiers scattered throughout the world was probably what caused the American publisher to become seriously interested in the paperback' (Greenfield 1989: 204). And it was the American publishing market that really laid the groundwork for the paperback fiction market to become an industry in the post-war years.

But the 'blockbuster' phenomenon is not as recent as is sometimes assumed. The centralization and specialization of publishers and their categorizations of fictional texts may have reached a peak in the 1980s, but the mergers and conglomerates which have made that possible are part of a process that dates back to the immediate post-war period. With the introduction of the paperback, publishing houses entered into newly aggressive marketing policies, in order to survive.

During the war years, women's magazines also came to play a crucial part in the campaign to recruit women into wartime service. The importance of magazines in the strategy to mobilize women workers is indicated in a report published by the Ministry of Labour Advisory Committee, which stated that: 'the women's press is above all other media best fitted to translate to women the role they must fill in increasing numbers' (Ferguson 1983: 21). Mary Grieve, editor of the then bestselling *Woman*, became an adviser to the War Office. The concept of the working woman did not stop with editorials or patriotic articles, but came to permeate all aspects of the popular woman's magazine. From 1941, covers of *Woman* and *Woman's Realm* invariably depict glamorous uniformed women in work situations; as land girls, factory workers, nurses and in the services.

As the war progressed, increasingly the heroines of magazine short stories were uniformed workers, and the objects of their romantic attention were men in the forces. The services, farms and canteens where women worked became recurrent sites for fictional romances. Cookery columns sported such titles as 'Potatoes on parade', and discussed how to make rations stretch, while agony aunts advised on the etiquette of uniforms, and on how married women whose husbands were away could resist the new temptations offered by male colleagues. As a 1985 anniversary issue of *Woman* put it, magazine editors saw their readers as 'the women who had to summon up every ounce of strength to continue without their partners, put on a cheery face for their children, and be brave in spite of their fears. They found yet another way of making carrots and haricot beans into something special and restitched that pair of slacks for maybe the third time' (*Woman*, 4 May 1985: IPC Publications).

While women's magazines promoted an image of the glamour of working women, the advertising campaigns devoted to recruiting women into active war service promised not only the satisfaction of rallying to Britain in her hour of need, but also offered training skills and opportunities that they claimed would persist after the war. As the ATS (Auxiliary Territorial Service) advertisement stated: 'You can make a vocation of this war work . . . now and in the future'. The Women's Land Army promised a 'healthy happy job' and, indeed, the opportunities and training offered by war work did open up new possibilities for working women.

Many women were trained as drivers and mechanics within the services, and, after 1939, women were trained to fly Spitfires, if only to ferry them within Britain. Women pilots of the Air Transport Auxiliary were employed to deliver and to fly operational aircraft. By 1943, women ferry pilots were paid the same rates as men, although women were not allowed to carry ammunition. Under the auspices of the Women's Land Army, by 1944, 80,000 women workers were organizing the nation's agriculture; 100,000 women worked on the railways, 10,000 in the Post Office. Women also took over the skilled work of essential domestic services, as plumbers, electricians and gas fitters.

While women were effectively taking over the work of men to keep the country running, they were kept well away from combat. 'Total war' required that women's work was also essential to civilian defence, which, in support operations, employed 375,000 women. Within civil defence, most women initially worked as unpaid volunteers, but were paid from 1943, when civil defence work became compulsory. Such 'voluntary' work was categorized as essential war work. The majority of air raid ambulance drivers were women, and 2,600 women worked in the fire service, some driving fire engines. And it was the Women's Voluntary Services which provided the immediate welfare support necessary after the damage inflicted by air raids. Founded in 1938, the WVS workers were given no pay or rank, but none the less rallied and organized a million voluntary women workers with the motto: 'If it should be done, the WVS will do it.' It was delegated to the WVS to run centres, providing both food and information on behalf of local authorities, for those bombed out. They organized and staffed hostels, canteens and, perhaps most importantly, nurseries, essential for enabling other women to work.

By 1942, over a million and a half women workers had joined trade unions, and by 1948 there was an increase of 350,000 in the number of insured women workers over pre-war figures. Although the legislation structures for equal pay for equal work for women were still a long way ahead, discussions of it were already beginning; a 1942 Mass Observation survey had found that 95 per cent of women workers were in favour of equal pay. In 1944 the Eduction Bill was amended in order to allow for equal pay for women teachers. Even Churchill, who had vociferously protested over that amendment, later appointed a Royal Commission to discuss the social and economic implications of 'equal pay for equal work'. Although the commission had arrived at no conclusions by the time of its published report in 1946, and if that inconclusiveness was used to justify excuses for unequal pay for women, none the less, the issue was now on the agenda in a way that it had never been before.

By the end of the war the 'vocations' and training opportunities that the advertising campaigns had promised were not only forgotten, but actively withdrawn. The trade unions which women had joined were unable (or unwilling) to do anything when women workers were made redundant as the men returned after the war. The nurseries which had made it possible for women to work did not survive the end of the war. By 1946, 2 million women workers had already left factory work, and drifted away from the paid working population. In the immediate post-war period, the numbers of women in paid employment had risen to nearly 8 million, but by 1947 this figure had fallen to 6 million. Although the need for women workers continued, and there was now a drive to expand essential industries and services, the mood had changed considerably. Despite a government campaign to encourage women back to work, and a Central Office of Information film, *Women Must Work*, the heroines of contemporary romantic fiction were no longer inevitably active participants in national action. Among many other such fictional heroines is the protagonist of the 1947 Mills & Boon publication, *The House of Oliver*, Helen, a noble war widow (MacLeod 1947). She may have survived the rigours of a Japanese internment camp, but the novel clearly positions her as a wife, and her post-war future is mapped as a mother and as supportive companion to the hero.

If, during the war, magazines and popular romances had encouraged their readers to engage in the war effort – and the heroines of magazine stories were invariably engaged in public service – once the war was over, they now advised a return to the home front. As Mirabel Cecil points out in her survey of women's magazine fiction: 'There was a curious reversal among post-war heroines. The women's magazines of the 1940s and the 1950s retreated into the home, taking their heroines with them. After the upheaval of war, editors and writers decreed a return to the traditional roles of the sexes' (Cecil 1974: 189). The position of women's magazines as conveyers of social and economic policy which they had held during the war years carried over into the post-war period. While previously such popular magazines as *Woman* and *Woman's Own* had exhorted their readers, in articles, editorials, imagery and fiction, to contribute to the war effort, they now recommended a retreat into the home. Where once their advice had been to recycle and to make do and mend, in the national interest, now they celebrated a new consumerism, with newly elaborate recipes, dressmaking patterns and heroines who extolled the joys of 'setting up home' with all mod. cons. The new expansion of advertising in women's magazines saw a recurrent image of the hostess firmly advocating products from within the confines of her newly appointed home.

British magazine sales were booming in the post-war decade. *Woman* had reached a readership of 1 million immediately after the war, and by 1965 it could boast sales of 3 million and could claim that it was read by 40 per cent of the female population. But if the popular women's magazines were exhorting women to turn to the creation of homes fit for heroes and to return to the domestic front, women themselves and the heroines of popular novels were less acquiescent. Although the popular version of history (echoed by Cecil) is that those women who had worked during the war quietly went back to the home with the return of their men, and a look at the women's magazines of the period would suggest that this indeed was the case, the drift away from work was nothing like as sharp as it was in the image promoted by *Woman* and *Woman's Own*. For, whatever the problems, and despite the loss of 2 million women from the workforce immediately after the war, from 1950, the numbers of women working after the war had increased substantially from the pre-war years. Women were now firmly present in the kinds of work that previously would not have countenanced them: in engineering, car manufacture and transport, in the civil service and local government, there were now double the number of women that there had been before the war. The numbers of working women and the kinds of work that they engaged in are well documented in government reports, and to some extent the lived experience of women's working lives during the war is available from Mass Observation surveys, while the 1951 census demonstrates the long-term effects of shifts in the working population. The aspirations and possibilities for women were firmly on the agenda of the post-war period.

The war had seen the introduction of an Emergency Medical Service, in which the salaries of doctors and nurses were paid by the state; in 1944, a government White Paper shifted the payment of medical staff towards salaries. With the establishment of a National Health Service in 1948, voluntary nurses were transformed into paid workers as voluntary hospitals nationalized. The wartime recruitment of nurses, in a campaign which called for women to 'Train to be a nurse – a distinguished career for women' was one of the very few that sustained anything of its promise after the war. Nursing was the form of war work that had most easily accommodated the ideological positioning of women; while it allowed for women to undertake paid and professional work, it was none the less work that stayed within the 'feminine' qualities and boundaries of nurturing and caring. The American 'Sue Barton' series of nursing novels, which are thinly fictionalized career guidance books for girls, were actually a phenomenon of the war years, and recognize nursing as a valid career for girls. *Sue Barton: Student Nurse* (Dore Boylston 1942) was first published in Britain in 1942 and, reprinted in 1945 and 1947, was the first in a series of five novels which charted Sue's career from training through to her rise to *Sue Barton: Superintendent Nurse*. Full of technical detail and professional advice, the Sue Barton series set the agenda for a new genre of fictional career novels for women that flourished throughout the 1950s in both Britain and America, supported by serialized stories that appeared in popular girls' magazines, such as *Girl*, the female equivalent of the boys' *Eagle*.

While nursing had been a popular role for romance heroines, before the war years it had been seen largely as a noble calling which did not really carry the status of work, and often not even wages. However, with the establishment of the National Health Service in July 1948, nursing came to be a recognized area of (relatively) skilled labour for women. It was in the 1950s that the still popular hospital romance was established as a genre in its own right. Many of the new publishing paperback houses carried special hospital title imprints, among them Arrow, Fontana and Mills & Boon. Mills & Boon authors came increasingly to use the hospital as a setting for romance, their heroines still in uniform as nurses. As their publisher acknowledges: 'The injured heroes (of the war) set the scene for the Doctor and Nurse romances which were later to gain great prominence' (Mills & Boon publicity leaflet). Doctor and Nurse romances were to become the most successful genre for Mills & Boon, and the first of their publications to go into paperback forms; as the publishers explain, they 'built (the) paperback list on the Doctor and Nurse novels' (ibid.). It was for the Doctor and Nurse titles that Harlequin, the Canadian romance company who were to take over Mills & Boon in 1972, initially approached the company, thus setting up the structure for a hugely commercial enterprise in popular fiction.

Paperback publishing transformed the shape of book sales in the post-war period, in that paper-covered novels were the first books to have substantial sales outside bookshops. As the head of Harrap noted: 'It has become abundantly clear that more than three-quarters of the picture covered paperbacks are being sold outside the bookshops' (quoted in Greenfield 1989: 232). And it is clear from the sales sites for the marketing of books in corner shops that this new market for fiction was seen to consist of women. In 1948, Penguin entered into an agreement with Chatto & Windus, Faber, Hamish Hamilton, Heinemann and Michael Joseph to publish their hardcover titles in paperback under a joint imprint, and thus established itself as a major distributor for paper-covered fiction. Pocket Books was founded in America in 1952, and went into an agreement with Hodder Books. As Penguin and Pocket Books threatened to take over the market, other major publishers began to bring out their own paperback imprints: Collins responded with Fontana, Hutchinson with Arrow. All these paperback series met with great commercial success and, by 1957, were such an established fact of the book market that the Publishers' Association proposed a paperback group.

Such marketing and distribution successes drove popular consumption still more firmly into the domesticated privatized sphere. The 'paperback revolution' heralded the end of the commercial lending libraries, which had been the largest distributors of fiction; W. H. Smith closed their library in 1965, and Boots followed in the same year. Mills & Boon had originally sold most copies of their novels to lending libraries and had already begun to produce cheaply bound editions of their romance fiction for commercial libraries in the 1930s; with their demise came the need for Mills & Boon to launch its own paperback series. The book clubs which had thrived during the war were booming in the mid-1950s but competition with the paperback market finally sank most of them. However, by the early 1960s, the practice of buying books through mail order was an established cultural phenomenon; the book clubs had consolidated a market for books through the post, the means by which Mills & Boon continue to sell most copies. Book clubs work through selling what Greenfield has called a 'guaranteed popular choice' (Greenfield 1989: 238), a guarantee that has certainly led to a standardization in the genre and style of popular fiction.

But that standardization is less monolithic than many accounts of popular fiction will allow. Romance fiction has always been a site for an exclusively feminine discourse, and in order to achieve and sustain their enormous readership, such texts must address, at some level, experiences, aspirations and contradictions which are real for their women readers.

If mass market popular fiction, and Mills & Boon romances especially, do ultimately reaffirm the status quo, this may well explain their commercial success. The romance novel acts as a reassurance that happiness for women is achievable without fundamental change or disruption. The 'blockbuster' of the Jackie Collins mode offers its women readers the chimera of 'success', a version of 'feminist' achievement within the frames that are already in place, while the Mills & Boon romance, less financially ambitious, offers happy marriage as the pinnacle of female aspiration. Whatever the heroine may achieve within the events of such novels, her ultimate happiness can only be assured within these texts by the affirmation of a heroic male figure. But, for all this, these narratives are always instigated and propelled by conflict of some kind. Although these struggles are resolved within the terms of the dominant ideology, these are material conflicts (if less easily resolved) for their women readers, and would hardly be so widely read if this were not the case.

The new kinds of heroines that popular fiction had offered during the war years, whether the professional Sue Barton or the courageous servicewomen of wartime romances, could not be entirely withdrawn in the post-war years. The kinds of fiction directed at the new found market of women readers by no means endorsed the stay-at-home ideologies of the women's magazines of the early 1950s. A recurrent bestselling author, both during and for many years after the war, was Monica Dickens, whose work was (and still is) repeatedly reprinted in hard and paper covers. Her best known books are all accounts of working as a woman: *One Pair of Hands* (1939), *One Pair of Feet* (1942) and *My Turn to Make the Tea* (1951) were, respectively, accounts of her work as a cook–housekeeper, a nurse and as a journalist. Gina, the heroine of Mills & Boon's 1953 romance *Turn to the West* (Seale 1953), is first seen firmly located in a working environment in a large store, and is committed to her work as a sales girl and model. Although the kinds of work offered for women in romance narratives might not have great status, their heroines are financially independent, and are definitely seen to be working. The heroine is increasingly likely to meet romance through her work (as Gina does), and although her job is often one of service, it is one that nevertheless carries wages and some professional status.

The world of work features prominently in fictional romances throughout the 1950s and still more in the 1960s, and it has its effect on the characterization of heroes. The romance hero is much less likely to be a figure with inherited wealth than he was before the war, and is also much less likely to be a servant of the British Empire, thrashing the 'natives' in the 'colonies' (although the tradition still survives in a number of contemporary romances set in Canada, Australia or even South Africa, where the hero is likely to be engaged in quelling the landscape rather than the 'savages' – farming or 'ranching' features large in the contemporary romance). Instead, the hero comes to acquire status through his profession, and it is now more often than not that it is in the working environment that hero and heroine meet.

The career narratives that the Sue Barton series had initiated found their apogee in such texts as the *Book of Careers for Girls*, first published in 1955. In her introduction, Jean Heal, the editor, firmly advocates the need for young women to enter into the professions and cites a: 'new attitude to professional women (which) makes it possible for them to go on to new heights' (Heal 1955: 14). This handbook of careers advice is one of many published in the same period; Bodley Head, its publisher, also produced a range of fictionalized careers books, which offer advice on careers ranging from television and journalism to farming and teaching, and which also include narratives that are clearly British versions of the Sue Barton series, such as *Student Almoner*.

But despite this 'new attitude' towards women's work, romances continued (and continue) to perceive the role of women as one that was ultimately fulfilled through marriage and the family. Mills & Boon are now the most prolific publishers of fiction specifically for a female market, and their novels can be seen consistently to negotiate the conflicting demands of work and family. They constantly rework and re-present the double demands on woman of an ideology of femininity and one of domesticity. The woman is required to enter the floating work population when required (as during the war), but is presented primarily as homemaker and the linchpin of domestic labour.

One of the unwavering rules of the contemporary Mills & Boon romance is that the hero should be in a more powerful position than the heroine; the 1985 Mills & Boon advice sheet to potential authors suggests that the 'gentleman must be rich and/or powerful', and goes on to recommend that 'the hero is meant to be a man of authority, used to being obeyed, he should be shown as such and the other characters react to him accordingly'. The Silhouette – the American publishing company that now also embraces Mills & Boon – tipsheet (1985) is still more specific: 'The hero, 8 – 12 years older than the heroine, is a dynamic, virile, supremely masculine man. . . . Always wealthy and successful, he is also magnetically attractive.' This notional power is always translated narratively into a superior status at work for the hero. However independent the heroine may appear

to be, and however much her work may appear to have professional status, that position is always eventually undermined by
the authority of the hero. In contemporary Mills & Boon
romances the changing status of women at work is represented by
heroines who may now be lawyers, accountants, bank managers;
but the hero is inevitably in a position of superior professional
authority. The familiar work and gender relationships that were
established in the 1950s, of boss and secretary and of doctor and
nurse, may now have shifted to take account of the place of
women in the workforce; but the power relationship remains the
same. A random survey of recent Mills & Boon publications
produced the following work relations between hero and
heroine: if she is a journalist, he is the magazine publisher
(*Centrefold*); if she is a bank manager, he is the bank's most
important client (*Impulsive Attraction*); if she is a restaurateur,
he owns the syndicate that threatens to take her restaurant over
(*Bring Back Yesterday*). She may even be an airline pilot, but he
is the major stockholder in the airline company (*Prisoner of
Shadow Mountain*).

A straw poll of contemporary Mills & Boon romances also
reveals the extent to which they continue to draw on an ideology
of nursing which still sustains an image of an angel whose care
and work is a 'natural' extension of her maternity. Sophy, of
Capable of Feeling, is employed as a nurse to a group of children;
her inevitable marriage to their father represents a smooth and
uncontradictory transition from waged to unwaged labour, and
marriage is within the novel (as is customary in Mills & Boon
romances) unequivocally seen as a social step up for the heroine.
Similarly, *Plain Jane* begins her story as the gardening editor of a
local magazine, but effects a seamless transition from offering
professional (and paid) advice to tending her lover's (and
eventually her husband's) garden (Parv 1988; Hamilton 1987;
Ford 1987; Kirk 1986; Jordan 1986; Hamilton 1986).

The work that heroines in contemporary romance novels
undertake is inevitably of a kind that can easily translate into
caring for men, and their professional status is one in which a
transition from paid work to supportive wife is accomplished
with suspicious ease.

It is the nurturing and 'feminine' aspects of the protagonist's
work that are foregrounded; most heroines continue to be
depicted in the kind of job that is in the service of a man. The

secretary may no longer be a standard position for fictional women workers, but research assistants, public relations officers, even civil servants, accountants and lawyers can come to fulfil the same narrative function, that of serving the domestic, practical and emotional needs of a man. The romantic heroine's attitude towards work in her life is neatly represented in *A Man of Contrasts*, which demonstrates the ways in which romance narratives elide the contradictions of work and personal life. Elaine is a successful estate agent but, significantly, it is a business which she has inherited from her father; the business has status for her as the fulfilment of family and daughterly duty. Despite the assertion of the heroine's pleasure in her work, there are repeated denials that this is her 'natural' bent: 'she was not business orientated. . . . Her own small business did not involve any pressure, any complications, in fact, she didn't even think of it as a business. To her it was just a living, a living earned in a way that gave her enormous pleasure' (Jameson 1987: 14). Similar passages can be found in most contemporary romance novels, in which the demand for romance always represents the heroine's working life as in some way unfulfilling.

Contemporary Mills & Boon romances may have incorporated the increased numbers of women in paid work into their narratives, and a broader range of professional work for women. But they continue, as they have done since the war, to support an ideology of women's paid work as marginal to their 'femininity'. The romance novel continues to negotiate and to support a discourse of the working woman as a temporary phenomenon, in which their heroines can slide between the public and the private workplace, between the professional and the domestic, with no discernable contradiction.

If it is the case, as Alan Sinfield argues, that fiction offers 'constructions of conceivable lives . . . interpretations and evaluations of perceived possibilities in the real world. . . . And these constructions are not just responses, they are interventions: their publication feeds back possible images of the self' (Sinfield 1983: 5), then the constructions offered to women by the contemporary Mills & Boon romance are severely limited. Nevertheless, the writers of popular romances during the war years and in the immediate post-war period did offer new forms of 'images of the self', and new 'perceived possibilities' for women. And they did contribute towards establishing a new discourse for femininity;

their fictional heroines stand as interventions through which a language is established for the working woman.

CONCLUDING COMMENTS: A SERIOUS BUSINESS

We have been arguing for the exploration of a number of paradoxes: the atomization of our social life in a context of densely packed populations; the privatization of the act of consuming, even in apparently public spheres; and the generating and reflecting dimensions of popular culture in contemporary life.

This has involved seeing the consumer as active, never passive – but also as highly constructed and relatively limited in the choices which can be exercised in the act of leisure consumption. And it has certainly meant that the consumer is more individualized in an increasing range of social and cultural spheres. Claims have been made about the inadequacy of 'the idea of "privatization" ' to capture 'the character of contemporary social change': 'the spheres of family, home and leisure still overlap far less frequently than the notion of privatization tends to imply' (Allan and Crow 1991: 20). But this notion of overlapping spheres is a rather simplistic version of the social relation implied in 'privatization'; for a combination of individualized modes of consuming, within privatized contexts, has been a formative contemporary dynamic.

The contemporary leisure industries are keen to encourage such a trend. If an ethos of self-contained individualism can be cultivated then those industries will impact upon hugely expanding markets. This trend is affecting old and young alike, women as well as men. We hope to have shown that two of the most resilient of leisure forms – sport, and popular fiction targeted at women – have been transformed under such influences.

Tony Bennett has suggested four available uses of the term 'popular culture': the popular is what the many like and do; the popular is that which is outside the sphere of 'high culture'; popular equates with 'mass', implying manipulation and passive consumption; and the popular might be that which is done by and for those who do it, rooted in the 'creative impulses of the people' (Bennett 1981: 83–5). Watching sport, reading fiction and other such everyday activities – things which have featured prominently in this chapter – look like majority activities, in the first sense of the popular. And they certainly express lived cultures with a variety of creative and interpretive dimensions – the fourth sense of the term. But they are as much a culture from above as one from below, a construction of the leisure industries and the consumer market. Tony Bennett argues that 'what is needed is a definition that falls somewhere between the third and the fourth options' (1981: 86). And certainly in our two case-studies this rounded definition applies. Paperback romance and media sport can be multilayered in meaning, but they remain highly constructed forms of consumption. They embody the major trend of retreat from public spaces of unpredictability to the safe private spaces of the domestic haven. They might also speak of some continuities too, but the familiar must also now be the novel, the new: 'Everyone has to be up-to-date and recycle himself annually, monthly, seasonally in his clothes, his things, his car. If he doesn't, he is not a true citizen of consumer society'. (Baudrillard, cited in Bowlby 1985: 26). Where's my new Budweiser boots? When's the new Mills & Boon due? When are the next game highlights? I want a body-suit like Linford Christie's! I'm a popular consumer capitalist, I'm part of the universal market.

Much of our subjectivity comes from our most intimate and private acts of consumption, the breaking of routine via fantasy – whether as armchair sports fan or reader of popular romances. The changing context of forms of popular consumption has vital consequences for people's sense of self-identity. Popular culture is not just the reflection of the time: it is its very consciousness. How meanings are made in popular culture, values accepted or challenged, pleasures packaged and cultures commodified – these are the challenging questions which make the study of leisure and popular culture a very serious business indeed.

REFERENCES

Allan, Graham and Crow, Graham (1991) 'Privatization, home-centredness and leisure', *Leisure Studies* 10 (1), January.

Anderson, Rachel (1974) *The Purple Heart Throbs – The Sub Literature of Love*, London: Hodder & Stoughton.

Barnett, Steven (1990) *Games and Sets – The Changing Face of Sport on Television*, London: BFI Publishing.

Bennett, Tony (1981) 'Popular culture: defining our terms', in *Popular Culture: Themes and Issues*, Units 1/2 of U203 Course on 'Popular

Culture', Milton Keynes: Open University Press.

Bishop, Jeff and Hoggett, Paul (1986) *Organizing Around Enthusiasms: Patterns of Mutual Aid in Leisure*, London: Comedia.

Bowlby, Rachel (1985) *Just Looking: Consumer Culture in Dreiser, Gissing and Zola*, London: Methuen.

Braverman, Harry (1974) *Labour and Monopoly Capital*, New York: Monthly Review Press.

Cecil, Mirabel (1974) *Heroines in Love*, London: Michael Joseph.

Clarke, John and Critcher, Chas (1985) *The Devil Makes Work: Leisure in Capitalist Britain*, London: Macmillan.

Corrigan, Philip (1983) 'Film entertainment as ideology and pleasure: a preliminary approach to a history of audiences', in James Curran and Vincent Porter (eds) *British Cinema History*, London: Weidenfeld & Nicolson.

Critcher, Chas (1989) Address to BSc Sports Science Forum, Brighton Polytechnic, Eastbourne.

Dighton, Chris (1989) 'Poll blow for ID card scheme but athletics comes out tops', *Sunday Times*, 17 September: A28.

Dore Boylston, Helen (1942) *Sue Barton: Student Nurse*, London: The Bodley Head.

Ferguson, Marjorie (1983) *Forever Feminine: Women's Magazines and the Cult of Femininity*, London: Heinemann.

Finnegan, Ruth (1989) *The Hidden Musicians – Music Making in an English Town*, Cambridge: Cambridge University Press.

Ford, Rachel (1987) *Bring Back Yesterday*, London: Mills & Boon.

Greenfield, George (1989) *Scribblers for Bread*, London: Hodder & Stoughton.

Hamilton, Diana (1987) *Impulsive Attraction*, London: Mills & Boon.

Hamilton, Rosemary (1986) *Plain Jane*, London: Mills & Boon.

Heal, Jean (ed.) (1955) *Book of Careers for Girls*, London: The Bodley Head.

Henley Centre (1989) *Leisure Futures*, London: Henley Centre for Forecasting Ltd.

HMSO (Her Majesty's Stationery Office) Reports from various years on *Social Trends* and the *General Household Survey*.

Holt, Richard (1990) *Sport and the British: A Modern History*, Oxford: Oxford University Press.

Hughes, Colin (1991) 'Colin Hughes examines the *Social Trends* survey and finds some changes in the British way of life', *The Independent* 17 January: 9.

Jameson, Claudia (1987) *A Man of Contrasts*, London: Mills & Boon.

Jordan, Penny (1986) *Capable of Feeling*, London: Mills & Boon.

Kirk, Muriel (1986) *Prisoner of Shadow Mountain*, London: Mills & Boon.

Leisure Consultants (1990) *Leisure Trends: The Thatcher Years*, a research report, Sudbury: Leisure Consultants: November.

Lewis, Peter (1986) *A People's War*, London: Methuen.

MacLeod, Jean (1947) *The House of Oliver*, London: Mills & Boon (reprinted as one of Mills & Boon's 'Nostalgia Collection', 1985).

Maguire, Joe. A (1988a) 'Race and position assignment in English soccer: a preliminary analysis of ethnicity and sport in Britain', *Sociology of Sport Journal* 5 (3).

Maguire, Joe. A (1988b) 'The commercialization of English elite basketball 1972–1988: a figurational perspective', *International Review of the Sociology of Sport* 23.

Maguire, Joe. A (1990) 'More than a sporting touchdown: the making of American football in England 1982–1990', *Sociology of Sport Journal* 7 (3), September.

Marwick, Arthur (1986) 'A social history of Britain 1945–1983', in David Punter (ed.) *Introduction to Contemporary Cultural Studies*, London: Longman.

Mason, Tony (1989) 'Football', in Tony Mason (ed.) *Sport in Britain: A Social History*, Cambridge: Cambridge University Press.

Parv, Valerie (1988) *Centrefold*, London: Mills & Boon.

Philips, Deborah (1990) 'The marketing of moonshine', in Alan Tomlinson (ed.) (1990) *Consumption, Identity and Style: Marketing, Meanings and the Packaging of Pleasure*, London: Routledge.

Radway, Janice (1987) *Reading the Romance*, London: Verso.

Roberts, Ken (1981) *Leisure*, London: Longman.

Roberts, Ken (1981) 'Great Britain: socio-economic polarization and the implications for leisure', in Anna Olszewska and Ken Roberts (eds) *Leisure and Lifestyle: A Comparative Analysis of Free Time*, Sage Studies in International Sociology 38, London: Sage.

Seale, Sara (1953) *Turn to the West*, London: Mills & Boon (reprinted as one of Mills & Boon's 'Nostalgia Collection', 1985).

Sinfield, Alan (1983) 'Introduction' to *Society and Literature 1945–1970*, London: Methuen.

Tomlinson, Alan (1990) 'Home fixtures: doing-it-yourself in a privatized world', in Alan Tomlinson (ed.) *Consumption, Identity and Style: Marketing, Meanings and the Packaging of Pleasure*, London: Routledge.

Whannel, Garry (1983) 'Narrative and TV sport: the Coe and Ovett story', in Michael Green and Charles Jenkins (eds) *Sporting Fictions*, University of Birmingham: Centre for Contemporary Cultural Studies/Department of Physical Education.

Whannel, Garry (1986) 'The unholy alliance: notes on television and the remaking of British sport', *Leisure Studies* 5 (2), May.

Williams, Raymond (1974) *Television: Technology and Cultural Form*, London: Fontana/Collins.

Williams, Raymond (1983) *Towards 2000*, London: Chatto & Windus.

Williamson, Judith (1986) *Consuming Passions: The Dynamics of Popular Culture*, London: Marion Boyars.

Willis, Paul (1977) *Learning to Labour: How Working-class Kids Get Working-class Jobs*, Farnborough: Saxon House.

Willis, Paul (1990a) *Moving Culture: An Enquiry into the Cultural Activities of Young People*, London: Calouste Gulbenkian Foundation.

Willis, Paul (1990b) *Common Culture: Symbolic Work at Play in the Everyday Cultures of the Young*, Milton Keynes: Open University Press (with Simon Jones, Joyce Canaan and Geoff Hurd).

Worpole, Ken (1984) *Reading by Numbers: Contemporary Publishing and Popular Fiction*, London: Comedia.

Chapter 2

The taste of America
Americanization and popular culture in Britain

Dominic Strinati

IS THIS THE 51st STATE?

America is the only place you can do as you like in.
(Anonymous traveller on the 'tube' or 'subway',
London, 1943)

The Yanks colonized our subconscious.
(Wim Wenders)[1]

Consume any particular item of popular culture and you may well be 'Americanized'. There won't be any warning on the product and few people will be able to give you any information about the symptoms. None the less, if you listen to certain albums, watch certain videos, films and TV programmes, eat your dinner in a fast food chain, follow American football and baseball, read certain examples of mass fiction, or even take in news from abroad, try to complete a crossword, wear a particular type of jeans as well as other items of clothing, then in some people's eyes you will have come under the influence of American culture and the massive commercial industries behind it. The signs are, it is asserted, self-evident. But do you know this is happening to you and should it matter? Has Britain become the 51st state of the USA?

To evoke in this way the spirit and the journeys of Walter Benjamin's *flâneur* may strike an anachronistic and discordant note for travellers in the late twentieth century (Benjamin 1978: 156 and 1979: 12). For many there may well be better and more engrossing ways to cross the countries of modern culture, ways better suited to the terrain and more likely to illuminate it. Yet it remains one of the most positive ways to begin to encounter such a pervasive but elusive phenomenon like Americanization – its productions, its forms and 'texts', and its status as an aspect of cultural tatse. There are many possible routes by which to reach the 'America' or 'Americas' that we have come to know, and this essay will try to explore some of them. In doing so the question of whether Britain is the 51st state of the USA is something which has to be viewed in terms of the complexities associated with the production and consumption of modern forms of popular culture, and the different interpretations of 'America' which have emerged since its popular culture began to be internationalized.

Fears and controversies about Americanization have formed major and long-standing points of contention in the study and interpretation of popular culture. To some degree, Americanization has been almost synonymous with both the substance and the appreciation of modern publicly available forms of culture, making it elusive and difficult to corner as an object of study: it appears to be pervasive and, at the same time, elusive. With the academic interpretation and critical evaluation of popular culture from the middle of the nineteenth century onwards, the benign or malign effects of America have often provided the focus and substance – the image and the proof – of a whole range of political and intellectual arguments and prejudices.[2] And in so far as intellectuals have tried to act as arbiters of cultural taste and have entered, however furtively, into the politics of popular culture, then a whole cluster of themes concerned with the relationships between class and culture have attached themselves to the phenomenon of Americanization in the various guises its reception and evaluation have taken, from the academy to advertising.

MASS CULTURE AND ELITE CULTURE

One of the most important turning points in the developing interest in twentieth-century popular culture – one which signalled at the same time the prominence of the role of intellectuals in trying to police cultural standards – came with the debate about mass culture, which began to take on some of its characteristically modern motifs in the 1930s with the growth of media communicating culture to the masses (Rosenberg and White 1957; Bennett 1982). This debate involved traditional intellectuals on both the left and right trying to come to terms with, and fashion a critical language to evaluate, the emerging forms of commercial mass culture disseminated by the mass media, like Hollywood cinema, 'cheap' pulp crime novels serialized in American magazines, and popular music like catchy, repetitive tunes or advertising jingles which orginated from Tin Pan Alley and Madison Avenue.

The result of this consternation was often the derogatory dismissal of mass culture in terms of what were seen as the supreme artistic virtues of representative figures in either the received and tradition-bound canons of high or elite culture, like Shakespeare, Beethoven and the rest, or in the radically innovative and anti-commercial refusals of the modernist avantgarde, like Schoenberg and Joyce. At stake was a long-standing set of concerns about art and the proper role of culture in the lives of the masses, the people, the working class, those not privy to the cults of aesthetic appreciation; and these became increasingly urgent in an age when mass communications seemed to have the potential not only to manipulate and stupefy the masses, to alienate them even further, but also to commodify art, to drag the artist into the marketplace, and to enlist both in the cause of capitalist exploitation.

What united these interpretations was ultimately more important than what divided them. The cause of the anxiety was then, and has been almost ever since, the erosion of grass-roots, 'organic' communal structures and 'authentic' values associated with the production and enjoyment of truly authentic popular or 'folk' culture, even if it could never aspire to be great art. In these pre-industrial, pre-commercial, pre-capitalist communities, deference on the part of the people to elites and to elite culture could be relied upon. The people got on with making their own cultural pastimes while respecting without having the capacity truly to appreciate 'great' art and 'great' literature. This community represented a purely idealized vision of a pre-industrial or early capitalist past; a rural idyll, a bastion of tradition, one which changed over time to become the traditional, urban working-class community (Hoggart 1958).

Intellectual and elitist anxiety over the emergence of mass culture usually expressed itself as disdain and contempt for contemporary popular culture, and for the mass media, since they were seen as the sources or the signs of decline and the passing of authentic folk culture. The real villain of the piece was a media-produced mass culture, aimed at a mass and passive consuming public, and systematically poisoning and corrupting what had once been a genuine and authentic popular culture emerging more or less spontaneously from the 'people' or the 'folk'. Through the manipulation of taste available to the emerging mass media like cinema, paperback novels, radio and eventually TV, a trivial and mindless culture came to be circulated, or so it was thought, purely and simply for commercial gain, thereby leading to the erosion of artistic and intellectual standards. Americanization, emanating as it did from the home of monopoly capitalism and commercialized culture, was perceived as one of the greatest threats.[3]

It is useful to be more precise about these themes but I first want to pick up one particular strand here which concerns postmodernism. For not only does it relate directly to Americanization, resurrecting some of the themes and fears of earlier debates, but it equally raises some new questions about how this process may be understood.

DEGREE ZERO CULTURE: AMERICANIZATION AND POSTMODERNISM

In a claim which may not reflect everyone's lifestyle, one of the foremost theorists of postmodernism, Jean-François Lyotard, has argued that 'eclecticism is the degree zero of contemporary general culture: one listens to reggae, watches a western, eats McDonald's food for lunch and local cuisine for dinner, wears Paris perfume in Tokyo and "retron" clothes in Hong Kong; knowledge is a matter for TV games' (1984: 76).[4] It was, of course, part of Roland Barthes's argument that 'degree zero' writing could not, and did not, exist, and we might raise the same objection to 'degree zero' culture (Barthes 1967);[5] also, though passages as clear and specific as this are not always to be found in the writings of postmodernists, it does contain an argument about Americanization and the international cultural economy which needs to be clarified. For what it seems to imply, as does the postmodernist notion of the 'decentredness' of subjects, space and texts, is that postmodernity represents (in so far as it can represent anything at all) the decline of a specifically Americanized, and the rise of an internationalized popular culture, to say nothing of the fact that we might be becoming 'Europeanized' as we are being 'Americanized'.

It is stretching the point a bit but another way of making it is to say that postmodernism is a theory of the transnational flow of information and culture which cross-cuts and transcends traditional and fixed centres and boundaries; a real culture *sans frontières*. It could be argued – if this aspect of postmodernism and Americanization were to be pursued – that the 'meta-narrative' of America may have begun to give way to the fragmentation and decentralization associated with the reality of globalization, the idea being that there is no definable cultural and geographic centre in the postmodern world.

In a similar vein Jameson has referrred to 'the even more global and totalizing space of the new world system', and to 'the truth of postmodernism . . . its fundamental object – the world space of multinational capital' (1984: 88, 92). Yet he has also identified this process as still being distinctively American. Insisting that 'aesthetic production today has become integrated into commodity production generally'[6] by means of the example of architecture,[7] Jameson says, 'We must remind the reader of the obvious, namely that this whole global, yet American postmodern culture is the internal and superstructural expression of a whole new wave of American military and economic domination throughout the world' (1984: 56-7).

The difference in emphasis that can be noted here may have something to do with the varying influence of Marxism on the emergence of postmodernist theory. Seeing America as the centre of multinational capitalism may be more consistent with the Marxist stress on material reality – and Jameson's argument is, in a way, very orthodox – while other postmodernists seem to have no difficulty in denying that there is any such thing.[8] But whatever the inflexion, some interesting questions are raised about how Americanization in the modern world may be understood.

Many of those who think we are entering postmodernity are merely echoing the moral and political pessimism, and cultural elitism, which resonated through the mass culture debate (Collins 1989). It is therefore necessary to remark upon the potentially subversive implications of postmodernism for the intellectually policed boundaries between 'high' culture and popular culture, the threats to which have lain at the centre of intellectual and political panics about the incursions of Americanization. Instructive and interesting parallels can thus be drawn

between postmodernism and mass culture theory. I will try to
trace out below the links between Americanization, the dominant
international role of American money and American culture, and
the increasingly transnational character of culture and information in the modern world. But to clarify the relevance of the
postmodernist debate for the moment, it can be suggested that
postmodernism once again rehearses while transforming the
points of contention in the debates over mass culture as popular
culture. Whether it is celebrated or condemned, it clearly poses a
challenge to the elevated claims of high cultural theory.
Postmodernist theory in the work of Baudrillard and Jameson,
for example, represents a continuation of the concerns of critics
like the Leavises and Adorno over the 'decline' of culture, its
standardization and trivialization at the hands of the mass media,
the 'barbaric' culture now having become an 'excremental' one as
well, dominated by signs and surfaces rather than substance and
content, by the tyranny of images and hyper-reality as opposed to
the 'democratic' integrity of 'real' values. In this sense, postmodernism, like Americanization, threatens to collapse the
barriers erected between high and popular culture. So to draw
some conclusions about Americanization in this regard may also
say something about postmodernity.

POPULIST VERSUS ELITIST THEORIES

Intellectual and political responses to Americanization have
tended to take two relatively distinct forms almost irrespective of
whether the arena in which the engagements have taken place
has been academic or more publicly available. I have chosen to
call these respective positions elitism and populism, and a few
words of definition and criticism can be mentioned here. So-
called elitist arguments tend to condemn Americanization as the
source of all that is bad and harmful, trivial and banal,
unintelligent and undemanding, standardized and repetitive,
showy and vulgar, manipulative and mercenary, commercial and
barbaric, in our culture. The blame is not always or totally laid
on America since natives can be seduced into believing they were
born in the mid-Atlantic if not in the USA itself. The major
problem is thus seen to be a decline or erosion of domestic high
and indigenous cultures, and of the communities which sustained them be they elite intellectuals and critics, highly educated

taste-makers, or traditional grass-roots and working-class communities (the 'real folk' and their authentic popular culture), a decline directly attributable to the invading capitalistic cultural and communication industries from America.[9]

The populist case tends by contrast to celebrate or to find common cause with America and its commercial spirit and cultural artefacts. Either Americanization is unthinkingly and cynically celebrated as another way of making money, Americanism representing the true spirit of capitalism, 'real capitalism' or, with more credibility and integrity, the values associated with it by the elite critics are adopted or endorsed precisely because of their clash with domestic elite cultural values. In this latter view, unreflexive populism turns into a spirited democratic impulse, and the egalitarian and modernizing tenor of Americanism becomes a weapon with which to criticize and combat British old worldliness, complacency, hierarchicalism and traditionalism.[10] These are merely bald and abbreviated statements, and it is perhaps wise and fair not to go too far in generalizing these positions. They will, I hope, be easily recognized when they crop up elsewhere in this paper, particularly in the section below on post-war Americanization and the working class.

Before proceeding, however, it might be useful to indicate some problems with both of these arguments since they relate directly to the general problem of how to interpret Americanization. The elitist view can be criticized on a number of grounds. First, it assumes that popular culture can only be 'read' or understood from the vantage point provided by either high elite culture or abstract and 'avant-garde' theory, be it Marxist, structuralist, or an amalgam of the two. It thus fails to consider how other classes and cultural groups, and other theories which do not depend upon such strict lines of demarcation between art and mass culture or between ideology and science, might appropriate and understand American culture. Second, it tends to ignore the diversity and tensions within and between popular cultures, assimilating them instead to either the standardized mass of trash culture, or the fetishistic masks of a dominant ideology; and thereby dismissing them politically and aesthetically in terms of either the revered canons of high culture, or the theoretical rigour of 'real' science. Lastly, it fails to realize that appreciating and appropriating certain facets of America and its culture does not mean that all things American will be slavishly

worshipped. As was once remarked, eating cheeseburgers need
not be taken as a sign of support for Cruise Missiles.

The populist standpoint can equally be criticized for comparable if distinct reasons. Like the elitist position, it tends to
assume that popular culture can only be interpreted from one
viewpoint, even if this is from below rather than from above.
This problem is compounded by the fact that, like elitist theories,
it does not usually tell us how real audiences actually consume,
understand and make use of popular culture (Allen 1990). The
theory is often as likely to infer this from an analysis of the text as
it is to engage with the practices of diverse and stratified
audiences. For example, if a text is read as being subversive by a
theorist, it must therefore also be read as being subversive by the
audience (other people) which reads it; however, it is merely
assumed that the audience reads the text in the subversive manner
defined by the theorist. Finally, while the hegemony of America
might be more open to question and reinterpretation by
audiences in the areas of consumption and the 'texts' of popular
culture themselves, it is difficult to carry this argument over
wholesale and without qualification into the areas of production
and finance where the dominance of American corporate and
global capital seems much less open to opposition, 'appropriation', 'subversion', and resistance.

AMERICANIZATION AND THE CIRCUIT OF POPULAR CULTURE

What I have said so far, in particular the critical points I have
made, suggest that we need to rethink our approach to the study
of Americanization. This is especially significant in view of two
distinct tendencies in the ways Americanization has been defined
and discussed. There is first the tendency for Americanization to
be discussed in terms of its appearances in cultural forms, a trait,
on the whole, characteristic of Webster's recent and illuminating
book on American populism and popular culture (1988). It is
likewise notable that while Hebdige (1988) does discuss the
economic influence of America in consumer goods markets and
over consumption patterns, he does not integrate this effectively
with his reading of how British working-class subcultures have
appropriated American popular culture. It is not, of course,
impossible to gauge how British audiences have consumed

American culture, as Swann has demonstrated in his study of the impact of the Hollywood feature film in Britain (1987). By contrast, there is the tendency for the economic dimensions of American communication industries to be discussed, but for the cultural forms of Americanization, and their possible interpretations by audiences to be neglected. This is arguably the case, for example, with Tunstall's well-known study of American cultural imperialism (1977). There exists therefore a reasonable amount of argument and evidence about Americanization, sufficient to generate ideas and interpretations; but the point is how to use it.

I want now to make use of Thompson's conception of popular culture as a kind of circuit in order to provide a potential focus for the analysis of Americanization.[11] This conception, to my mind, is particularly useful in that it may take us beyond the terms of the elitist – populist debate, and the divide between the undiscriminating celebration of the popular, and the pessimistic condemnation of mass ideological manipulation. Thompson argues that the study of popular culture can be broken down into three distinct objects of enquiry, or stages, which are linked together by the ways they influence each other. They concern the social and historical conditions under which the production of popular culture takes place; the 'formal or discursive analysis' of the discourses of popular culture as texts, as sets of images, words, and representations; and 'interpretation', how these aspects of popular culture have been understood and interpreted by those who consume, produce, and evaluate them. I have simplified and taken some, I hope not diabolical, liberties with Thompson's ideas, and it is important to realize that in practice it may not be so easy to separate these stages out from each other. They are parts of a circuit which can influence and change each other, as well as being subject to the overall constraints of the structure of the circuit itself, and to the consequences of the ways each part can 'over determine' the other. That I shall try to discuss these parts separately should not be viewed as an act of defiance in the face of these problems, to say nothing of the fact that the difficulties entailed in successfully carrying through such a task may be raising some critical points about Thompson's general argument.

However, I think that the formulation I have outlined can be used to make some sense of the relationship between popular culture and Americanization, bearing, as it does, certain similarities to Marx's analyses of the circuits of capital.[12] The first stage, as it involves issues of money, power, and control, could incorporate much of the evidence on America's cultural imperialism, the role of American capital, finance, and companies in mass media industries, and in the production of popular culture. The second stage of the argument would then entail the analysis of the cultural forms that Americanization has taken, and would concern arguments about the formal interpretation of popular culture as a set of discourses about America. The third or last stage could then cover the reception or consumption of American popular culture which would itself help to define the overall process as Americanization. There is, after all, a difference between the former and the latter in that it is possible to consume American popular culture without becoming Americanized – the latter is not an inevitable consequence of the former, but is dependent upon the meanings and interpretations implied by the act of consumption. This last stage would thus involve the variable cultural interpretations of American popular culture and Americanization made by producers, intellectuals, and audiences or publics divided by factors like class, gender, ethnicity, age, region, status, and so on. Just to identify certain examples like this is already to indicate some of the problems associated with maintaining the distinctions outlined. Whatever the drawbacks, however, I think this is a useful basis on which to proceed. Let me turn, first of all, to what may be termed the political economy of Americanization.

WALL STREET SHUFFLES: THE POLITICAL ECONOMY OF AMERICANIZATION

'We have what we call a special relationship. It used to be with America, now it's with American Express' (a British diplomat in Paris providing a Tory Euro MP with a government credit card in the film *Paris by Night*) (Hare 1988: 39).

The size and scale of the American economic invasion of Europe and the rest of the world by its cultural industries has been noted by many commentators. Bigsby, for example, cites Guback's famous study which found that by the early 1970s American films occupied 'more than 50 per cent of world screen time', and that since American companies had 'a virtual monopoly of international distribution networks', and played 'a dominant role in financing European films [in the period 1962–72] two out of three "British" features exhibited on the country's two main circuits were partially or entirely financed by American subsidiaries', they exerted a 'considerable influence on the kinds of films produced'. He therefore concludes that while cultural messages deriving from such an influence may reflect the diversity of the America they come from, and be mediated by the foreign audiences which consume them, it still means that 'American corporations shape the physical and mental environment, influence eating habits, define leisure pursuits, produce television programmes and movies; devise, in other words, the fact and fantasy of the late twentieth century' (Bigsby 1975: 4; Guback 1969, 1974).

The problem with this, of course, concerns the extent to which the manipulation of cultural tastes can be 'read off' from the structure of ownership. To what extent does American economic control of cultural industries give rise to its control of the output of these industries and thus of the tastes and preferences of their audiences? No doubt there are influences at work of the kind that Bigsby and others refer to, but it cannot be directly inferred from evidence about ownership and control. This is precisely why I have tried to distinguish these issues in my discussion, and I shall return to the assessment of the cultural impact of American economic power in the next sections. For the moment we need to consider the latter a bit more fully in its own right.

Probably since the emergence of the global dominance of the Hollywood film industry in the 1920s, if not before, the political economy of Americanization can be viewed as a process in which American-based capital has exerted increasing worldwide control over mass communication industries, and thereby over the financing, production and distribution of popular culture. This process may not have unfolded in an even or uniform manner or followed the same pattern in all societies; nor will it have carried on without being resisted, sometimes successfully: but whatever qualifications need to be made, its historical power as an economic force is undeniable. Even authors who have been sceptical of the 'media imperialism' thesis have provided sufficient evidence to chart its course. Tunstall, for example, provides ample evidence of the increasing worldwide power of American communication industries in the post-war period, even though he disputes what he calls the stronger versions of the thesis because they do not take account of any of the countervailing forces to American hegemony, including the resilience of local cultures, and the competition of other media imperialists like Britain in the exporting of TV programmes. It is necessary, therefore, to look at a number of points in relation to what I have called the political economy of Americanization. These concern the size and scale of this dimension of Americanization, the range of media covered, their interconnectedness and diversity in the changing structure of America's global cultural power, and the varied resistances this power has encountered. This will then open up the question of how to evaluate the new forms of internationalism.

It is not difficult to give some indication of the scale of Americanization. If we refer, for example, to the worldwide influence of the Hollywood film industry, we have to bear in mind the fact that such claims might not be sustainable to the same degree with other media, and that Hollywood itself since its cinematic heyday in Britain, which lasted from about the 1920s to the early 1950s (Tunstall 1977: 39) has since diversified into making films and series for TV. In fact, film-making seems to be the popular cultural area in which the economic power of America has been most notable. As Tunstall, among others, notes, 'By 1972 the majority of films made in Britain were Hollywood financed and distributed' (ibid.: 62). Though Britain remained, then, a major film exporter in terms of worldwide trade, in the same period, 1971–2, over 50 per cent of the feature films it imported came from the Unites States, markedly overshadowing domestic production (ibid.: 282–3).

This was much less than the share Hollywood was able to take in the 1920s and 1930s, when it virtually dominated the production of films overall, but its domination has still been remarkable since then – in 1948 American films accounted for 68 per cent of exhibited films, and domestic films for only 23 per cent, while the UK has remained a highly lucrative market for Hollywood since the 1960s and 1970s in terms of the global profits it makes on the export of its films (ibid.: 289–91, 299). No doubt the fact that Britain and America share a common language must make the UK market more open to imports of American films, but this relative uniqueness must to some degree work both ways. In turn, this is relevant to the content of such imports and exports of films and TV programmes in that Americanization may also take the form of Britain selling to Americans 'Americanized' representations of itself, and buying back American produced and validated versions or constructions of 'Britishness'.[13]

So whether we are talking now about feature films which are made in the UK, or films which are shown in the UK, or both, the importance and influence of American capital and the American film industry is undeniable. It is less easy to be so clear cut and conclusive about TV. Not much research seems to have been devoted to international flows of TV programmes since the mid 1970s, just as little research has been done on what audiences think of foreign media and popular cultures. Tunstall argues that TV is not the best example to demonstrate the global power of the American media (ibid.: 40–2). America is a TV and media saturated society, and more and more advanced capitalist societies are starting to take on similar characteristics; it is equally a world leader in the use of TV, and a key disseminator of TV images. But it is arguably more difficult to turn these features into technical economic dominance than it is with certain other media. For example, TV is a more privatized and domestic medium than cinema, and audiences tend to respond accordingly (Lealand 1984: 94). There are therefore more immediate constraints upon the extent to which British TV can screen direct and unmediated pictures of America, though its more distant shadows may still be casting their patterns over what may be seen.

Having said this, it is equally difficult to dispute the fact that, as a more recent study has put it, 'Research so far has confirmed that the United States does dominate world trade in TV exports' (ibid.: 5). But as it goes on to note, more up to date evidence on trends in the export of American TV programmes is needed to add credibility to the media imperialism thesis, as is more evidence on the question of whether foreign audiences are manipulated and seduced merely by the sheer volume of US TV programmes that may be screened. It notes also, for example, how comparable advanced capitalist societies are important revenue earners for US TV. For American TV exporters, Lealand comments, 'Every hour exported to this country is financially golden', placing the UK 'in the forefront of profitable markets' (8–9), profitability rather than hours being, of course, the main concern of American TV enterprises. From the start, commercial TV in Britain found it profitable to import American TV programmes because they could ensure high audiences (they were usually among the most popular), and their costs were relatively low, although overall they took up a small proportion of total screen time, and their popularity opened up opportunities for comparable British programming.

Interesting here are the questions of why American programmes should have proved to be popular with British audiences, and how far such British programmes betokened Americanization of a more pervasive and subtle kind in that they were often domesticated and anglicized versions of American programmes. Even the BBC made more use of American programmes, supposedly as ready-made time fillers, than its Reithian-inspired rhetoric may have implied, though less than its commercial rival before the more intense and open competition of the late 1970s and the 1980s (Bartlett 1986; Crook 1986). On the basis of what evidence exists, Lealand concludes as follows: 'One can only assume that the two major trends of the past decade will persist: American television producers will continue to see the rest of the world as a market for increased profit margins and will continue to dominate the international flow of television programmes; and this imbalance will be increasingly challenged by rival exporters, especially Brazil and Britain' (10).

What is likewise notable in the present context is the range of media across which the process of Americanization may be assessed. For while the economic power of the American media may be more difficult to define with respect to TV than to the movies, it is still very evident in both instances, and I have yet to take into consideration other media and other popular cultural forms.

I shall not try to provide a detailed list, however, although the example of advertising is particularly interesting, not only in its own right, its distinctive character as an 'all-American' quality and ability, but also for the way it feeds off and links into other economic, media and cultural flows like TV and consumption patterns. By 1972 eight out of the top ten advertising agencies in Britain were American owned, and this reflected a general global situation in which 'only three of the world's top thirty agencies were not US owned (two Japanese and one British)' (Masson and Thorburn 1975: 101). This in turn is manifest in the higher proportion of the USA's GNP going to advertising expenditure (Tunstall 1977: 295–6). Thus, whether we are concerned with ownership or the placement of advertising expenditure, the global power of America can be observed. This is accentuated by the way the assumed superiority of America in this area has fed into, and benefited from, its dominance in other areas like commercial TV and marketing. This dominance has been embedded not only in the direct provision of advertising for particular transnational clients, and thus in the internationalization of advertising under the hegemony of America, but also in the business advantages which accrued to American agencies due to their presumed superior know-how in dealing with commercial TV, and in their more general ability to influence consumption patterns, to sell commodities to the public. As such, American advertising has been at the forefront of the increased market and commercial orientations of the modern media (ibid.: 55).

One last way of charting the dimensions of the global power and importance of American based communications industries in the post-war period is to look at their revenues. This will admittedly add little to what has already been said about the external processes of Americanization, except in quantitative financial terms, but it will give a clear if not conclusive indication of the relative importance of different media in such processes. Tunstall estimates that the major revenue earner among American media in 1975 was probably the Hollywood feature film. Equal second were the record industry and advertising agencies. Then came the money earned by US TV exports, and lastly there were the earnings of US based and owned international news agencies (ibid.: 43). This, however, has to be balanced against the fact that by this time Britain's TV exports 'were probably earning about as much as those of the United States, if feature films on television are excluded' (ibid.).

The qualifications which need to be made about the scope and extent of the economics of Americanization thus must also enter into our considerations. For what this particular point indicates is the more general thesis that 'the countries which are strong regional exporters of media tend themselves to be unusually heavy importers of American media' (ibid.: 62), thereby putting into perspective the Americanization of British culture in that Britain is a media imperialist in its own right, and has had as a consequence some impact upon America and the American market, even if we are talking about an unequal relationship between two media imperialists. While I am concerned for the most part with the Americanization of Britain, these two reservations, that Britain is a media imperialist, and that America itself has succumbed to British influences in its popular culture, for example in its music, form crucial limits to Americanization which any adequate assessment must take into account.

Equally important to any consideration of the limits to Americanization are the conscious efforts which have been made to limit the opportunities for American culture to be consumed in countries like Britain. One example has been the quota system which British governments have tried, with varying degrees of success, to impose upon imports of Hollywood feature films intended for cinema screenings (Swann 1987: 84-5). But given that TV is now a more important mass medium, perhaps it is a better example to look at. It is generally recognized that commercial TV operates under a 14 per cent quota ratio, which means that 86 per cent of its programmes must be domestically produced, with restrictions also being placed upon the scheduling of imported material in peak-time viewing slots, and the number of feature films and repeats shown. For the BBC the level of the restriction seems to be a question of practice and precedent rather than the self-imposed limitation it is with commercial TV, though it appears to be comparable to the quota the latter adheres to (Lealand 1984: 14-25).

This says nothing, of course, about the increasing number of TV programmes produced by companies from different countries in new forms of transnational commercial co-operation, nor about the obvious dominance of American programmes in the space allowed for foreign viewing material which is, as expected, usually very high (ibid.: 120-1). Furthermore, Lealand argues that 'the self-ordained ordinance of an 86:14 ratio still remains unwritten' (1984: 17), while noting important exceptions to the quota like information, news, sport, educational programmes, and 'all silent films and any outstanding films and programmes which date prior to 1945 "provided that any of these are run in a series with a clearly defined theme"' (ibid.: 15). Also, as he points out, American TV programmes are attractive to the production controllers or buyers for British TV because they are comparatively cheap and therefore cost-effective schedule fillers, as well as because they 'give the people what they want', because they have high entertainment value as escapist culture (ibid.: 18–25).

What needs to be considered now is the changing structure of American popular culture's global power, and the new international communications order. I have tried to outline the general contours of America's domination of the mass media in the post-war period while also indicating some of the limitations this power has had to encounter. I have noted how the Americanization of Britain has to be set in the context of Britain's role as a media imperialist, and I now want to assess the extent to which this point may be generalized as a feature of the structure of media and cultural relationships worldwide. That is to say, does America still dominate as the world's leading media imperialist, or has its position come to be challenged by successful competitors, leading to a situation in which there are several and competing foci of power in a more truly internationalized order?

Studies of the international flow of TV programmes have shown how the USA had been the leading producer and distributor in this circuit in the mid-1970s. And this dominance in one of its weaker media areas can be taken as a symbol of its wider cultural power. The available evidence for the 1980s suggests that this situation has not changed that much. If we take some of the examples we have already used we can see that American feature films continue to have a 'dominant share of the international film market, and, combined with French, Italian, British and German (Federal Republic of Germany) films, provide 80 to 90 per cent of all imported films in non-socialist countries' (Mowlana 1986: 82). By 1988, in Britain, 80 per cent of the box office take went on American films (*Sight and Sound* 1990: 250). Furthermore, by 1982, 'The principal American motion picture firms constitute the only integrated, worldwide network for theatrical film distribution'. This network facilitates global dissemination of television material as well, and results in relatively few foreign films being commercially distributed in the United States. In addition, American films abroad have 'cultivated patterns of public taste for decades, and this undoubtedly has facilitated the distribution of American television material' (ibid.). The study cited comes up with similar conclusions regarding the sound recording industry. Yet again, advertising in terms of sources of ownership and expenditure seems to provide evidence of the continuity of American dominance. The study cited concludes as follows: 'As one reviews the existing literature and available data at the beginning of the 1980s, three general conclusions are apparent: (1) the United States is the model within the field of advertising, (2) the obvious sources of the majority of international consumer and industrial advertising are transnational companies and international advertising agencies [most of which at least will have their nominal domestic base in the United States], and (3) the flow of international advertising is mostly vertical, from developed and industrialized nations to the third world . . . [Also] . . . The world's top 50 advertising agencies in terms of gross income and billings include, first, the United States agencies, followed by the Japanese, British, German, French, and Italian agencies' (ibid.: 85; my parentheses).

America therefore seems to have retained its hegemony as the most powerful global cultural and mass media force; it does not appear to be sinking into a decentred, geo-politically ambiguous, and structurally fragmented postmodern world. This conclusion should come as no surprise, even if it partly reflects the lack of more up to date information, for as Mowlana argues, 'The nature, pattern, and direction of the world economy more or less parallel and depict the directionality of world information flow' (ibid.: 198). America is still strategically central to the direction of this flow, from more to less advanced capitalist societies, from north to south, and from west to east. However, as I have noted with some of the examples I have referrred to, and as Mowlana points out in his conclusions, America is now having to compete more seriously with European and Japanese rivals – Japanese companies, after all, are now buying up Hollywood – and is having its position in global cultural and media relations challenged by spatially distinct advanced capitalist societies (ibid.: 198–9).

AMERICAN GRAFFITI: THE DISCOURSES OF AMERICANIZATION

'All right, take it. I'll fix it up when you want to score, man. Let me know the room and what time.'
'Speak so I can understand,' the clerk said.
'I'm practicing my American,' Rafi said.

(Leonard 1988: 94)

I now want to turn to the second stage of the circuit of popular culture and Americanization. This concerns the formal or discursive analysis of the texts or representations of popular culture, the reading of the cultural landscape of Americanization, the images of America to be found in British popular culture and in popular culture in Britain. This is clearly an enormous task in view of the amount of materials which could be covered, and the typical representations which could be detailed. I shall therefore confine myself to one focus of the intellectual debate within the field of cultural studies. In order to initiate a discussion, I shall look at some examples of writings, reflecting differing theoretical positions, which have responded to, and attempted to evaluate, Americanization in terms of its relationship to the post-war formation of the urban working class in Britain.

Living in America . . .

I have already noted how it was from within an elitist framework that the Americanization of popular culture was initially understood. To give more content and history to this brief note I want to consider two very different evaluations which I think illustrate many of the points at stake in the Americanization debate.

In his book, *The Uses of Literacy*,[14] the arguments of which have been central to the study of popular culture in Britain, Richard Hoggart tried to document how the traditional and closely knit working-class community was being taken over by what he called a 'shiny barbarism'. There are no prizes for guessing that this barbarism derived from the ways by which an alien invader from across the Atlantic was colonizing this community, particularly its younger members. This was the America of the Hollywood film, the cheap and brutal crime novel, 'milk bars', and juke-box music. As Webster has pointed out (1988: 187), Hoggart's view of the value and influence of American culture is not a totally dismissive one; he recognizes, for example, the vibrancy and relevance of the more realistic and straightforward style of the 'tough guy' American crime novel in its appeal to a working-class audience. But there is little doubt that, overall, Hoggart lumps together Americanization and youth in an elegantly argued moral warning (panic?) about the debasement of working-class culture. Hoggart saw the 'newer mass arts' like 'sex-and-violence novels', 'the "spicy" magazines',

'commercial popular songs', and the 'juke-box', inviting people
to lose themselves and their culture in a mindless and trivial
'candy-floss world'.

While Hoggart is careful not to conclude that working-class
youth as a whole has fallen prostrate before the star-spangled
invaders, he does reserve some of his most scathing comments for
the 'juke-box boys' who frequented what were known in the
1950s as milk bars. A short quote can perhaps capture some of the
flavour of Hoggart's argument:

> Compared even with the pub around the corner, this is all a
> peculiarly thin and pallid form of dissipation, a sort of
> spiritual dry rot amid the odour of boiled milk. Many of the
> customers – their clothes, their hair-styles, their facial
> expressions all indicate – are living to a large extent in a myth-
> world compounded of a few simple elements which they take
> to be those of American life.
>
> (Hoggart 1958: 204)

The 'aesthetic breakdown' represented by these milk bars is so
complete that 'in comparison with them, the lay-out of the living
rooms in some of the poor homes from which the customers
come seems to speak of a tradition so balanced and civilized as an
eighteenth-century town house', while the 'young men' who go
to these places are so completely taken in by their imaginary
America that they 'waggle one shoulder or stare, as desperately as
Humphrey Bogart, across the tubular chairs' (ibid.: 203–4).

This is not America

In this and other works Americanization is one of the means by
which cultural domination is exercised over the working class
and other subordinate groups in modern capitalist societies.[15]
The extent to which such domination is in fact exercised is what
is questioned by the populist argument. For example, the
adoption of the style, manners and language of the gangster
figure popularized by Hollywood films on the part of young
working-class men in the early 1930s has been interpreted as a
democratic process which gave some 'hero' status to these men,
one which their domestic society and culture could not afford
them (White 1986: 166). It has also been suggested by Worpole
that in the 1930s and 1940s American crime and detective

fiction gave male, urban working-class readers access to a language, a style, and a subject matter that was more 'realistic', more about their own lives and the way they spoke, than could be found in the literature written for and by the English middle and upper classes. As Worpole writes:

It was in American fiction that many British working-class readers . . . found a realism about city life, an acknowledgement of big business corruption, and an unpatronising portrayal of working-class experience and speech which wasn't to be found in British popular fiction of the period [the 1930s and 1940s], least of all in the crime novel obsessed as it was with the corpse in the library, the Colonel's shares on the stock market, and thwarted passion on the Nile.'
(1983: 35; my parentheses. Compare Chandler 1980: 186).

It has been precisely this kind of argument, standing as it does in marked contrast to 'elitist' evaluations like Orwell's assessment of the impact of Americanization on the crime novel and the English murder (1965: 9–13, 63–79), which Hebdige has tried to present in a systematic manner in his assessment of Americanization.

For Hebdige, fears about Americanization in the post-war period were linked to fears about the threat posed to traditional elites and intellectuals by the 'levelling down process'. Thus ideas about America being more populist and democratic fed into concern about increasing working-class affluence and conspicuous consumption, things which, in a way, people like Hoggart wanted them to be protected from. As both Hebdige and Webster have indicated, these fears reflected, to some degree, worries on the part of the establishment over the decline in Britain's world role and her increasing dependence upon the American state, economically, as well as militarily and diplomatically. But what Hebdige is at pains to question is whether the working class, and particularly young working-class males living in large cities and beginning to construct their own subcultures, could be characterized as Hoggart wished to describe them.

Hebdige's argument is that Americanization has not resulted in more cultural uniformity and homogeneity as the mass culture critics feared. On the contrary, he points to the 'sheer plethora of youth cultural options currently available . . . most of which are refracted through a "mythical America" ' (1988: 74). This is because young working-class males do not consume this 'America' passively, automatically and unthinkingly. They consume and construct styles in dress, clothes, and music in an active, meaningful, and imaginative fashion – one which transforms, through its very uses, the meanings of Americanization and converts them to different purposes and statements. What is implied by Hebdige, in line with the kind of interpretation he has offered of subcultures more generally, is that young urban working-class men have used the images, style, and vocabulary of American popular culture in their own distinctive, positive, and constructed fashions as an empowering and 'subversive', if not radical, riposte or 'resistance' to the conventions of middle-class and upper-class elite or high culture, and as a spirited defence against their own subordination.

Moreover, this assimilation and transformation of 'America' went along with, and was sometimes take over by, the appropriation of European styles and fashions; the 'mods' in the 1960s, for example, borrowing as much from Italy – suits and scooters – as they did from black American culture – modern jazz and soul music. This latter point should also warn us against treating American culture as homogenous and uniform. It should equally alert us to the cross-fertilization between American and European culture which influenced, for example, the development of the crime novel (Bigsby 1975).[16] And we should never forget that intellectuals are socially and culturally distinct from, and often have very strange and idiosyncratic attitudes towards, the popular culture of the 'ordinary people' whose tastes they presume to judge.

'GONE TO LOOK AT AMERICA': BRITISH AUDIENCES AND AMERICAN POPULAR CULTURE

The American films are far more superior to the British films. In the former the scenery and effects are more elaborate and natural, whereas in British films the majority seem to be stunted and too artificial. The players themselves in American films have a knack of living the part they are acting, and the players in British pictures mostly seem to be 'acting' the part they are supposed to be living.

(A sixteen-year-old commenting on cinema-going in 1938)

There was a tremendous romance about America. America was the place where we all wanted to be. America was closer than London. . . . The most exciting thing about being alive was looking at Americans.

(Ray Gosling)[17]

The popular cultural consumption of America, the ways in which the process of Americanization has been constructed by audience preferences in Britain, has conformed most closely to the populist conception of taste. The focal point of consumption in the circuit of popular culture, while being bound up with academic evaluations of American culture and its effects in the UK, has to be treated in its own right as well. For any comparisons have to be set against the seemingly strong and positive responses of British audiences to American popular culture.[18] Class differences may be significant here, and though the evidence overall is clearly not strong enough to sustain any firm conclusions, we have already seen how the urban working class has been more likely to favour American popular culture than the 'intellectual' middle class. This has not entailed mere imitation but also active reconstructions in associations with both indigenous and continental European influences. The obvious and direct presence of America is readily apparent in the dominant images and representations circulated by the mass media in Britain, but our concern is now with the meanings and interpretations audiences have placed upon these images and representations. And these, rather than being anything more than a lame and deferential endorsement of American values, have tended to possess their own creative rationales which need to be understood in the context of British society.

I have already indicated some ways by which this might be understood in terms of the relationship between working-class and elite or high culture. It may not be possible to divide easily the views I considered in the last section from those of wider and larger audiences, but it is clearly essential to get some idea of how these audiences look at, listen to, make sense of America. On the face of it, cinema-going audiences in Britain, for example, have appeared to prefer American to domestic films. This was particularly true of the high point in cinema attendance between the 1930s and the early 1950s, as Mass Observation surveys and other evidence of the time demonstrates (Mass Observation 1987: xiii–xx). As a Mass Observation survey of cinema audiences in Bolton in 1938 concluded: 'The greatest majority [of the survey's respondents] chose to write about why they preferred American films to British films. The overwhelming complaint was that there was not enough action in British films. They were dull and lifeless. The settings were restricted and poverty–stricken. The acting was stiff and artificial. By contrast, American films were slick, polished, fast-moving, often spectactular and American actors were natural and lifelike' (1987: 39). These qualitative preferences rested upon the numerical popularity of American films: 'out of the total of 559 respondents, 350 (63 per cent) preferred American films, 100 (18 per cent) preferred British, 104 (19 per cent) thought they were about the same and 5 did not know' (ibid.: 34).

These popular cultural tastes are open to interpretation in the light of certain structural and ideological differences between British and American societies. Miles and Smith in their extensive and detailed coverage of the relationship between elite and mass culture to be found in cinema and literature in Britain in the 1930s suggest that 'The vision of America that was so appealing to the interwar generation of British cinema-goers was of a violent but vibrant society, in which things went wrong but could be changed and were being changed, an apparently classless society which could be contrasted with the patronizing formal hierarchy of the British community' (1987: 175).[19] They note, for example, how Hollywood film stars like Bette Davis, Joan Crawford, and Greta Garbo did at least raise the relevant issues associated with the idea of the 'new woman', even if in the end the films themselves confirmed traditional gender roles, while British films tended to ignore the issues all together (ibid.: 176–7). The same could presumably be said about working-class life as well, as we have seen above with respect to the crime novel and film. This interpretation of audience taste is tied into a wider context of hegemony by Miles and Smith: 'A crisis of hegemony was fought out internationally in the interwar years – not just liberalism against socialism, though certainly that as well – but between two hegemonic styles within Western liberalism: on the one hand, British elite culture, leading from the top; on the other hand, the more actively populist American mass culture which in the view of the British elite vulgarized and thus jeopardized the cultural inheritance' (ibid.: 11).

The populist character of audience tastes has, of course, to be related to the economic power of American media and culture.

The emerging hegemony of American popular cultural representations among British cinema-goers cannot be divorced from the fact that American films were more likely to be seen in Britain due to such practices as the chain-booking system, and were likely to 'look' better than British films as far as things like scenery and technology were concerned because of the greater capital assets and worldwide profitability of the Hollywood film industry. This last point meant, for example, that Hollywood already had a strong financial advantage over the British film industry when sound was introduced in the late 1920s, while the efforts of British governments to impose quota restrictions on the importing of American films were relatively ineffective (ibid.: 167–9).

But this kind of argument can only take us so far. There is only so much about audience preferences which can be 'read off' from the economics of popular culture. While the greater exposure of British audiences to Hollywood films and to the American dream – equality, democracy, populism, social mobility, modernity, openness, the 'frontier spirit', and so on – and to the publicity machines surrounding the films and their stars, may have fostered Americanization, there appear to be so many other things going on in the consciousness and practices of audiences which cannot be reduced to or explained by the economic power of the American culture industry alone.

From at least the 1930s onwards, if not earlier, a significant difference between certain clusterings of class taste and aesthetic appreciation seems to have emerged which has become central to the consumption of American popular culture. Writing about the situation in the 1930s and 1940s in his detailed study of the Hollywood feature film in Britain, Swann argues: 'Some conservative groups found the general preference for American feature films inexplicable and, in a sense, disloyal . . . they could not understand why most Britons expressed a preference for a culture so different from their own. Their position is best interpreted in the light of the very different class outlooks of Britain's working class, who went to the cinema regularly, and Britain's ruling elite, who did not. In fact, throughout the 1930s and 1940s, it was the cinema exhibitors who perhaps knew best what audiences wanted (Swann 1987: 38). Importantly, cinema exhibitors themselves did not only rely upon populist intuition and word of mouth, presuming they knew what audiences wanted, for their assessments of audience preferences, but, like Hollywood itself, used market research and opinion polls to arrange their film programmes, though the former does seem to have been more extensive than the latter in Britain. For what they are worth, the attitude studies which did appear tended to affirm what we have already seen, namely that British audiences, most notably working-class audiences, did prefer to go and watch American films (ibid.: 38–9, Mayer 1948).[20]

This sort of populist taste provoked the fears and anxieties lying at the heart of intellectual and political panics about the corrupting influence of Hollywood's vision of glamorized consumption, thus merging, as Hebdige notes, two identifiable processes in post-war Britain, consumerism and Americanism: 'Where changes in taste and patterns of consumption did occur, they tended to be associated with changes in the composition of the market (i.e. the "intrusion" into the sphere of "conspicuous consumption" of the working class and the young), and these changes in turn were linked to objects and environments either imported from America or styled on American models (e.g. film, popular music, streamlined artefacts, milk bars, hair styles and clothes)' (Hebdige 1988: 73). As Swann argues with respect to Mayer's 1948 study, many of the respondents, 'predominantly women, noted how they lusted after the clothing and the consumer durables they saw in American films. . . . The constant reiteration of visions of "the good life" in American feature films . . . was an important fuel for the emergence of a fully-fledged mass consumer society in Britain in the 1950s' (op.cit. 43). What is crucial about this is that American popular culture showed how consumerism was something which did not have be restricted to the upper or middle classes, but could be made available to the urban working class as well. It therefore became part of what Hebdige (1988: e.g. 47) has called the levelling down process which began to develop in Britain with the rise in mass consumption from the 1950s onwards. This fact is all the more striking if we realize that it was the urban working class which formed the vast majority of cinema-goers until the cinema began to decline as a mass attraction in the mid-1950s, working-class consumerism and privatization playing their part in this decline.

The contrasting sentiments about Americanization identified in this essay continued to be reconstructed and reapplied to different media and different cultural expressions in subsequent contexts of interpretation and conflict over the process of Americanization. The obvious and contemporary example to take is TV, especially since it is supposedly a private and domestic mass medium and can therefore be usefully contrasted with the public and sociable cinema. Clearly long-term familiarity with, and appropriation of, American popular culture, and the emergence, proliferation, and competition between increasing numbers and types of media and cultural forms since the heyday of cinema, radio, sheet music, comics, and 'pulp' literature must have affected the structure of audience tastes since the 1930s and 1940s. It is therefore interesting that strong continuities with this period can still be found, together with changes which have become more apparent as time has gone on. To illustrate some of these points I shall refer to Lealand's 1984 study of the relationship between British audiences and American TV programmes.

The consumption of popular cultural representations of American ways of life by audiences in Britain is something which has not attracted a great deal of research. Instead, commentators have more usually relied upon patronizing dismissals of audience preferences for American culture (or, of course, upon an unthinking celebration), and, as Lealand notes, when the charge of 'rubbisl h is being levelled at TV programmes, it is often accompanied by the adjective 'American'. This is linked to the fact that, according to Lealand, 'a survey across the British press soon reveals an anti-American bias in television reviews' (1984: 69). Indeed it could be argued, although it might be stretching the point a bit, that TV critics can be seen as the intellectual upholders – or perhaps more realistically as the cultural 'gate-keepers' – of a type of cultural elitism which again contrasts with the populist tastes of the wider audience. For irrespective of whether it is expressed in the diverging styles of the quality or popular press, there is a consensus among TV critics which can be said to draw upon the assumptions if not always the exact vocabulary of the elitist approach to popular culture. Thus, 'the majority of newspaper television critics agree, for the most part, on the failings and shortcomings of American television imports . . . one often waits for the following epithets to follow on any mention of American television programmes: "mindless", "glossy", "shallow", "junk", "inane", "pap", "bilge", "bland, brainless and boring" ' (ibid.).

These judgements do not seem to describe the responses of

British audiences to American TV programmes, among whom many are highly popular. People may watch well aware of elitist cultural condemnations but be content to use such programmes for other purposes which they deem harmless like leisure and entertainment.[21] Not enough is yet known to confirm this suspicion, though its very potential does raise questions about the position adopted by TV critics. There is, however no well-defined populist stance to be set against the latter since British audiences appear to be ambiguous about US TV programmes overall even if they are evidently popular, and audiences responses are more populist than anything else (ibid.: 71). Viewers do not always know or care about the national source of particular TV programmes, and American programmes like most tend to lose their audience over time as their increasing predictability reduces audience enjoyment. Indeed, according to Lealand, American programmes seem to be more prone to this tendency than domestic ones, notably 'those American pro-grammes that are rigidly formulaic, and dependent on one or two characters. The success of American television series lies in the tension generated between invention and convention [it could be argued that this is true of all cultural products made to be identified in terms of their distinctive genre] and when the latter dominates over the former the series has usually exhausted itself' (ibid.: 44, my parentheses; see also 72–5).

Bearing these points in mind we can now turn to Lealand's findings on the tastes of British audiences. On the simple question of preferences most people responded positively to American programmes, even though the majority surveyed wanted the number reduced, and few wanted an increase. The reasons given for liking and disliking American TV programmes capture very effectively the populism and ambiguity that mark popular taste regarding the process of Americanization. In any event, they differ significantly from the judgements made by TV critics. 'In the favourable assessments of American material there was a recurrent appreciation of the fantasy–fulfilment strengths of American programmes and the colourful alternatives they offer to the sometimes more dour and "realistic" local product' (ibid.: 80). These included an appreciation of the more varied 'locations and scenery' and the pleasures of being able to view 'different kinds of lifestyles' offered by US TV programmes, their emphasis on glamour and more generous production values, the fantasy and escapism allowed for in their storylines, and their stress on action and adventure. The dissatisfactions expressed by British audiences with American TV programmes appear to be very much the flip side of the reasons given for their preferences and pleasure. As Lealand notes, 'The attractive alternatives, in terms of style, pace and content, that these [US programmes] offer was seen as a positive contribution to British television schedules. The greater stress on fantasy or "escapist" values of many programmes was seen as adding a balance to the more strongly "realistic" bias of many domestic programmes. The ability to entertain – perhaps the greatest strength of American programmes – was acknowledged by a significant number of respondents. This aspect is not always appreciated by the critics and is a major factor in sustaining an appreciation gap between the critics and their reading public' (ibid.: 89; my parentheses). The popular points of criticism made of American programmes on UK TV screens, according to Lealand, cover a larger and more diverse range than the points of appreciation. They include inferior technical quality, an exaggerated sense of glamour and style, absurdly formulaic and predictable plots, a destructive use of language, lack of discrimination regarding humour (hence the much criticized use of canned laughter), moralizing and preaching, e.g. about the virtues of the 'American way of life', clear inferiority compared with British equivalents, and a frequent and seemingly vicarious use of fictionalized violence (ibid.: 84–6).

One possible construction which can be placed upon these findings is that 'American programmes were disliked more for their content than for their style' (ibid.: 89). If this is the case, it has to be interpreted in the light of the much observed fact that the 'The majority of viewers in Western countries prefer locally produced television programmes to imported equivalents' (ibid.: 94), something which clearly contrasts TV and cinema as popular cultural mass media, and as determinants of cultural taste. Also, British audiences do quite obviously discriminate and, despite the conflicting evidence and evaluations outlined, they seem to like American programmes, and certain distinct traits associated with them, in so far as Americanization is raised as a specific focus of cultural consumption and appreciation.

A useful resumé of Americanization in post-war Britain and its relevance to audiences' cultural tastes is provided by Swann: 'As part of the social history of the post-war decade, it is clear that

Britain was a principal beneficiary – or victim – of Americanization. Sometimes this was a consequence of conscious cultural
policy on the part of the culture industries and the American
government. More generally it was linked to the commercial
basis and commercializing nature of American cultural forms as
a whole. This gave these forms a dynamic appeal which made
them very attractive to European audiences, who were especially
vulnerable to outside influences in the post-war years. Also, and
this was very apparent to the European intelligentsia, American
popular culture was often more attractive and appealing to the
working classes of Britain and elsewhere than anything they
themselves could produce' (1987: 150–1; cf. Lealand 1984: 71).

I have dealt in this section with ways of 'looking at America',
with the consumption and appreciation of American popular
culture by popular audiences or 'ordinary people'. In so far as
any definite inferences can be made – and a lot more needs to be
said and done – I would argue that the structure of audience taste
in Britain can be seen as confirming populist rather than elitist
assessments of American popular culture, even if intellectual
evaluations tend to endorse elitism, and can draw comfort for
their position from the importance of American cultural industries in the production and distribution of popular culture in
Britain. This point has to be taken seriously in any attempt to
come to some kind of conclusion about the process of Americanization in Britain.

CONCLUSION

> The problem is rather this: whether America, through the
> implacable weight of its economic production (and therefore
> indirectly), will compel or is already compelling Europe to
> overturn its excessively antiquated economic and social basis.
> . . . The reaction of Europe to Americanism merits, therefore,
> close examination.
>
> (A. Gramsci)

> SR: . . . you are the only French person I know who has
> told me he prefers American food.
> FOUCAULT: Yes. Sure. [Laughter] A good club sandwich
> with a coke. That's my pleasure. It's true.[22]

The difficulties associated with coming to any firm conclusions about whether Britain has become America's '51st state' should by now be apparent. The presence of America is not in question, Americanization is. Economically and politically, American media and popular culture have established positions of power and influence around the world. As we have seen, it is relatively easy to document the historical dimensions of this presence in Britain, one which has its parallels in other parts of the globe. There should be little need to review the political economy of Americanization. What does need to be mentioned in this conclusion is the Americanization of audiences and popular culture.

Locating Americanization in these areas raises problems for a number of reasons which have already been identified. I shall outline these in conclusion below, but before doing so it has to be made clear that I equally wished to locate Americanization in its theoretical and contentious contexts. This is because it seems to me that to take up a position about popular culture is, quite often, to take up a position about Americanization. Hence, by crudely distinguishing between elitist and populist theories I tried to bring out precisely what has been at stake – not just theoretically, but politically and morally as well – in the responses to, and debates about, the process of Americanization. These debates and arguments have taken place in the spaces between 'elitist' fears about American domination and American consumer capitalism on the one hand, and the 'populist' consumption of American popular culture on the other, and suggest that we need to move beyond the lines drawn by these positions. As Webster has argued, the questions ultimately raised concern the 'use-value of cultural products', the politics of pleasure, and the extent to which it is necessary to sustain 'an identification of enjoyment of American cultural products with capitulation to the official ideologies of America' and, we might add, to the political economy of Americanization more generally, a problem that has been central to this paper; and, as he adds, 'are these not better questions, and better answers, than talk of banana republics and cultural imperialism? Perhaps it is to pop art, certainly to popular culture, that we should turn rather than to George Orwell' (Webster 1988: 211 and 247; cf. 245–7).

In the end, it is not easy to treat either American popular culture or British society as monoliths which are uniform in their structures, behaviours, and effects. Class differences in cultural taste appear to have influenced people's responses in the UK to

American popular culture. The latter in turn is not all the same, covering different forms and media, and, very importantly, deriving from different ethnic and racial as well as class sources in the USA. Neither of these features are readily accounted for by theories which assume an all-powerful and monolithic culture industry, and a passive and docile mass consuming public, but an unthinking and celebratory populism won't do either. Moreover, while direct support cannot be found for a postmodernist theory of transnationalism, it is clear that the isolated splendour of America's global hegemony is now coming to be challenged not only by Europe and Japan, but by an admittedly embryonic set of cosmopolitan and cross-national relations (Hebdige 1990). The opening of the world's largest McDonald's restaurant in Moscow in 1990 may seem to be merely the latest and most graphic – to some the most gross and grotesque – phase of Americanization, but the bent yellow M is by now an obvious transnational symbol, a quality merely confirmed when the hammer and sickle became part of its display.

NOTES

I wish to thank Rosalind Gill and Stephen Wagg for their comments on an earlier draft of this paper. Needless to say, all the errors are mine.

1 For the sources of the above quotes see A. Calder and D. Sheridan (1984: 106) and S. Frith (1983: 46).
2 For examples of nineteenth-century opposition to the spread of American values in Britain see M. Arnold (1971: 19) and D. Webster (1988: 180). For an informative and persuasive account of the relationship between intellectuals and popular culture see A. Ross (1989).
3 See F. R. Leavis (1930), Q. D. Leavis (1932), and R. Hoggart (1958). Also M. Jay (1973): chap. 6), D. Kellner (1989: chaps 5 and 6), and M. Horkheimer and T. Adorno (1973: 120–67).
4 On postmodernism, aside from J. F. Lyotard (1984), see D. Hebdige (1989), S. Lash and J. Urry (1987: 285–300), T. Gitlin (1989), F. Jameson (1984), F. Pfeil (1985), J. Collins (1989), S. Connor (1989), M. Featherstone (1988), and L. Hutcheon (1989). By far the best account, in my view, is to be found in D. Harvey (1989), particularly Part 1.
5 Barthes's idea is that all writing is ideological to some degree; it can never be totally neutral, bland, grey, uncommitted, non-ideological – 'degree zero'.
6 It could be argued that aesthetic production has always been integrated with commodity production to some degree because commodities, notably those produced by more complex divisions of

labour, have to be designed; they have to be put together, and aesthetics would usually be expected to play some part in this process. On this see A. Forty (1986).

7 On postmodern architecture see, for example, R. Venturi *et al.* (1977), P. Portoghesi (1982 and 1983), C. Jencks (1984) and D. Harvey (1989).

8 This is not a totally frivolous point. See, for example, J. Baudrillard (1987). The point here is this: if the 'real' has 'imploded', as Baudrillard argues, then what 'real' evidence can we refer to in order to show that it has done so. If we could find this evidence then the point would be disproved, but if we couldn't then we wouldn't know whether it had or it hadn't. For a critical account of Baudrillard see D. Kellner (1989).

9 See the sources cited in note 3 above.

10 For examples of this see D. Hebdige (1988), K. Worpole (1983), P. Miles and M. Smith (1987), D. Webster (1988), and R. Banham (1975 and 1977).

11 See J. Thompson (1988) who tries to bring together a number of differing theoretical developments in the analysis of culture and communication.

12 Namely, Marx's idea that the circuit of capital consists of interdependent links between financial, industrial and commercial capital. I am not suggesting, however, that popular culture can be reduced to, or explained by, this circuit.

13 At the time of writing, fairly recent examples of this could be found in those domestically produced mini-series, aimed at the US as well as the UK market, such as *Jack the Ripper* and *Dr Jekyll and Mr Hyde*, which seem to exploit caricatures of British settings and characters, like rainy, cobbled streets, and well-meaning policemen with mutton-chop whiskers.

14 See R. Hoggart (1958). This was one of the earliest studies in what became a growing sociological preoccupation with the working class in post-war Britain. See the article by K. Dodd and P. Dodd elsewhere in this volume as well as S. Laing (1986), C. Critcher (1979), J. Goldthorpe *et al.* (1969), M. Bulmer (1975), and G. Marshall *et al.* (1988).

15 This is one of the reasons why Americanization is so bound up with the interpretation of popular culture.

16 An equally important example of this cross-fertilization is *film noir* which, while producing a distinctive cinema in its own right in the 1940s and 1950s, is still exerting an important influence today.

17 For the sources of the quotes in order see J. Richards and D. Sheridan (1987: 44), and A. Ross (1989: 148).

18 I do not wish to exaggerate this point: there have obviously been strong anti-American sentiments at work in Britain, not just those emanating from the socialist left or the culturally elitist right, but hostility of a more populist kind such as that directed at American servicemen stationed here during the Second World War. (See N. Longmate (1975).) But these sentiments have clearly to be set alongside the popular cultural tastes I have identified in this paper.

19 Clearly, it is not being claimed that America was or is a classless

society. It is just that it can often appear to be less class bound when compared with Britain.

20 It is perhaps worth pointing out here that middle-class groupings on both the left and right have often provided political and intellectual opposition to Americanization. See, for example, M. Barker (1984).

21 For some accounts of TV viewing and audiences see J. Root (1986), D. Morley (1980 and 1986), and E. Seiter *et al.* (1989).

22 For the sources of the above quotes see A. Gramsci (1971: 317 and 281) and the interview by Stephen Riggins with Foucault in Foucault (1988: 12).

REFERENCES

Allen, R. (1990) 'From exhibition to reception: reflections on the audience in film history', *Screen* 31 (4), Winter.

Arnold, M. (1971) *Culture and Anarchy*, Cambridge: Cambridge University Press.

Banham, R. (1975) 'Mediated environments or: You can't build that here', in C. Bigsby, op. cit.

Banham, R. (1977) 'Representations in protest', in P. Barker (ed.) *Arts in Society*, London: Fontana.

Barker, M. (1984) *A Haunt of Fears*, London: Pluto Press.

Barthes, R. (1967) *Writing Degree Zero*, New York: Hill & Wang.

Bartlett, K. (1986) 'British television in the 1950s: ITV and the cult of personality', paper presented to the 1986 *International Television Studies Conference*, London.

Baudrillard, J. (1987) *The Evil Demon of Images*, Sydney: Power Publications.

Benjamin, W. (1978) *Reflections*, New York: Harcourt Brace Jovanovich.

Benjamin, W. (1979) *One-way Street and Other Writings*, London: New Left Books.

Bennett, T. (1982) 'Theories of the media, theories of society', in M. Gurevitch *et al.*, op. cit.

Bigsby, C. (1975) *Superculture*, Bowling Green, Ohio: Bowling Green University Press.

Bulmer, M. (1975) *Working-class Images of Society*, London: Routledge & Kegan Paul.

Calder, A. and Sheridan, D. (1984) *Speak for Yourself: A Mass Observation Anthology*, London: Jonathan Cape.

Chandler, R. (1980) *Pearls are a Nuisance*, London: Pan Books.

Collins, J. (1989) *Uncommon Cultures*, London: Routledge.

Connor, S. (1989) *Postmodernist Culture*, Oxford: Basil Blackwell.

Critcher, C. (1979) 'Sociology, cultural studies and the post-war working class' in J. Clarke *et al.* (eds) *Working-class Culture*, London: Hutchinson.

Crook, G. (1986) 'Public service or serving the public: the roots of popularism in British television', paper presented to the 1986 *International Television Studies Conference*, London.

Featherstone, M. (1988) 'In pursuit of the postmodern', *Theory, Culture, and Society*, 5 (2-3).

Forty, A. (1986) *Objects of Desire*, London: Thames & Hudson.

Foucault, M. (1988) *Politics, Philosophy, Culture*, London: Routledge.

Frith, S. (1983) *Sound Effects*, London: Constable.

Gitlin, T. (1989) 'Postmodernism: roots and politics', in I. Angus and S. Jhally, *Cultural Politics in Contemporary America*, London: Routledge.

Goldthorpe, J. *et al.* (1969) *The Affluent Worker in the Class Structure*, Cambridge: Cambridge University Press.

Gramsci, A. (1971) *Selections from the Prison Notebooks*, London: Lawrence & Wishart.

Guback, T. (1969) *The International Film Industry*, Bloomington: Indiana University Press.

Guback, T. (1974) 'Film as international business', *Journal of Communication*.

Guback, T. and Varis, T. (1982) *Transnational Communication and Cultural Industries*, Paris: UNESCO.

Gurevitch, M. *et al.* (1982) *Culture, Society, and the Media*, London and New York: Methuen.

Hare, D. (1988) *Paris by Night: Screenplay*, London: Faber & Faber.

Harvey, D. (1989) *The Condition of Postmodernity*, Oxford: Basil Blackwell.

Hebdige, D. (1988) *Hiding in the Light*, London: Routledge.

Hebdige, D. (1989) 'After the masses', *Marxism Today*, January.

Hebdige, D. (1990) 'Fax to the future', *Marxism Today*, January.

Hoggart, R. (1958) *The Uses of Literacy*, Harmondsworth: Penguin.

Horkheimer, M. and Adorno, T. (1973) *Dialectic of Enlightenment*, London: Allen Lane.

Hutcheon, L. (1989) *The Politics of Postmodernism*, London: Routledge.

Jameson, F. (1984) 'Postmodernism, or the cultural logic of late capitalism', *New Left Review* 146, July/August.

Jay, M. (1973) *The Dialectical Imagination*, London: Heinemann.

Jencks, C. (1984) *The Language of Post-modern Architecture*, London: Academy Editions.

Kellner, D. (1989a) *Critical Theory, Marxism and Modernity*, Oxford: Basil Blackwell.

Kellner, D. (1989b) *Jean Baudrillard*, Cambridge: Polity Press.

Laing, S. (1986) *Representations of Working-class Life*, Basingstoke: Macmillan.

Lash, S. and Urry, J. *The End of Organized Capitalism*, Cambridge: Polity Press.

Lealand, G. (1984) *American Television Programmes on British Screens*, Broadcasting Research Unit Working Paper, London.

Leavis, F. R. (1930) *Mass Civilization and Minority Culture*, London: Minority Press.

Leavis, Q. D. (1932) *Fiction and the Reading Public*, London: Chatto & Windus.

Leonard, E. (1988) *Cat Chaser*, Harmondsworth: Penguin.
Longmate, N. (1975) *The G. I.s*, London: Hutchinson.
Lyotard, J.-F. (1984) *The Postmodern Condition*, Manchester: Manchester University Press.
Marshall, G. *et al.* (1988) *Social Class in Modern Britain*, London: Hutchinson.
Mass Observation (1987), *The Pub and the People*, London: Century Hutchinson.
Masson, P. and Thorburn, A. (1975) 'Advertising: the American influence in Europe', in C. Bigsby, op. cit.
Mattelart, A. *et al.* (1984) *International Image Markets*, London: Comedia.
Mayer, J. (1948) *British Cinemas and their Audiences*, London: Dennis Dobson.
Miles, P. and Smith, M. (1987) *Cinema, Literature and Society*, London: Croom Helm.
Morley, D. (1980) *The Nationwide Audience*, London: British Film Institute.
Morley, D. (1986) *Family Television*, London: Comedia.
Mowlana, H. (1986) *Global Information and World Communications*, London: Longman.
Orwell, G. (1965) *The Decline of the English Murder and Other Essays*, Harmondsworth: Penguin.
Pfeil, F. (1985) 'Makin' flippy-floppy: postmodernism and the baby-boom PMC', in M. Davis *et al.* (eds) *The Year Left*, London: Verso.
Portoghesi, P. (1982) *After Modern Architecture*, New York: Rizzoli.
Portoghesi, P. (1983) *Postmodern Architecture*, New York: Rizzoli.
Richards, J. and Sheridan, D. (1987) *Mass Observation at the Movies*, London: Routledge & Kegan Paul.
Root, J. (1986) *Open the Box*, London: Comedia.
Rosenberg, B. and White, D. (1957) *Mass Culture*, New York: Free Press.
Ross, A. (1989) *No Respect: Intellectuals and Popular Culture*, London: Routledge.
Seiter, E. *et al.* (eds) (1989) *Remote Control*, London: Routledge.
Sight and Sound 59 (4) Autumn 1990.
Swann, P. (1987) *The Hollywood Feature Film in Postwar Britain*, London: Croom Helm.
Thompson, J. (1988) 'Mass communication and modern culture', *Sociology*, 22 (3).
Tunstall, J. (1977) *The Media are American*, London: Constable.
Venturi, R. *et al.* (1977) *Learning from Las Vegas*, Cambridge, Mass.: MIT Press.
Webster, D. (1988) *Looka Yonder!: The Imaginary America of Populist Culture*, London: Routledge.
White, J. (1986) *The Worst Street in North London*, London: Routledge & Kegan Paul.
Worpole, K. (1983) *Dockers and Detectives: Popular Reading, Popular Writing*, London: Verso.

Chapter 3

The impossibility of *Best*
Enterprise meets domesticity in the practical women's magazines of the 1980s

Janice Winship

'SELLING KINDER AND KÜCHE?'

If one were looking for signs of postfeminism[1] in the 1980s, the new practical and domestic magazines for women would not seem the most fruitful cultural texts to scrutinize. Indeed it is indicative of the cultural hierarchies and priorities in play for intellectual commentators that while the so-called style and youth magazines (for example, *The Face, i-D, Just Seventeen*) and the slicker women's magazines (*Cosmopolitan, Elle* and *Marie Claire*) feature in critical discussion of postfeminism (usually yoked to postmodernism)[2] there has been a veritable silence on the subject of the boom which has, in fact, most shaken the magazine market. In this article it is this slighted culture in its unlikely relation to postfeminist developments, and this boom, that I wish to investigate.

In the old camp, *People's Friend, My Weekly, Woman's Weekly, Woman's Own*, and *Woman's Realm*; in the new camp, *Chat, Best, Bella, Hello!* and the latest recruits, *Me* and *Take A Break*.[3] Since the 1950s a large number of women's magazines have been launched[4] but until 1985, just two of them, enjoying only brief lifespans, were weeklies.[5] For many in the industry the demise of the *mass* weeklies was inevitable. To survive they would have to target editorial at a focused band of readers, in the way of the monthlies' narrow casting (*Advertising Age's Focus*, May 1984). After all, circulation figures indicated that while total sales of all women's magazines had declined, the weeklies had been worst hit, with sales falling by almost half (from approximately 9.3 million in 1958 to 5.6 million in 1985).[6]

First the tabloid magazine *Chat* from the publishers of *TV*

Times and then, more dramatically, the 'European invasion' of magazines (*Best* and *Bella* are owned by two arch-rival German giants in publishing, Gruner & Jahr, and Bauer, respectively, *Hello!* by the Spanish company Hola, SA) challenged the insular British view. The new weeklies, *Best* and *Bella* especially, have been remarkably successful. The latter, admittedly with the aid of a massive advertising campaign ('an unprecedented £1 million a month' during 1988, *Observer*, 21 May 1989), has achieved a circulation of 1.3 million and *Best* 950,000. These launches, together with the spate of new monthlies[7] has meant that by 1988 women's magazines were reaching more than 60 per cent of all women as compared to 42 per cent in 1986 (*Observer*, 30 October 1988). This is well down on the 1950s when it was reckoned that '5 out of 6 women saw at least one women's magazine every week' (cited in White 1970: 216), but the increase is still worth comment.

The expanding number of titles and increased readership have several explanations. One view is that by the 1980s women's magazines had lost sight of where women were at, and what they wanted from a magazine. New magazines with different editorial formulae were therefore attractive to women who had stopped buying, or never had bought, a magazine. (Research on *Prima* suggests that over half of its readers are in that category: White 1987.)

Another view highlights a favourable economic climate and availability of advertising, encouraging expansion on the part of producers and increased consumption on the part of readers. Yet what has been innovative about the German launches has been their determination to go ahead without first securing advertising, a strategy anathema to UK publishers. Gruner & Jahr's conviction that spend hard enough to get editorial right and advertising will soon flow in has rubbed off on to an ever-cautious IPC, whose ill-fated upmarket weekly, *Riva* (1988), closed after just seven weeks. They are currently allowing *Me* four or five years before its 'red ink turns black' (*Observer*, 21 May 1989).

More cynically, it can be argued that regardless of women's objective requirements for their light reading matter, large conglomerates have their own insatiable economic needs. No less in publishing than in other industries, companies need to be strengthened to maintain steady profit margins. Diversification of products and a move into international markets are part of the process.

The form of the latter by European publishers is interesting. Until *Chat* appeared *Cosmopolitan* was the only women's magazine in the UK which had its roots elsewhere – in the USA. Owned by the Hearst Corporation, *Cosmo* is published under a franchise system allowing the *Cosmo* recipe to be modified for local tastes under local control. *Prima, Best* and *Bella,* however, are editorally organized and run in Britain but owned and managed by German publishers who also direct operations in other Eurpean countries. There is a German and French *Prima,* while *Best* is based on a French magazine *Femme Actuelle,* which also has a Spanish version, *Mia.* More than that, all three of these magazines are printed in Germany and then sent back to the UK. In a similar way *Hello!* (a cloning of the Spanish *¡Hola!*) is printed in Spain. Spreading the net wider, Rupert Murdoch's News International has gone into partnership with Hachette to deliver *Elle,* and brought the US title *New Woman* to the UK. Not to be outdone IPC have joined forces with Groupe Marie Claire (as European Magazines) to offer *Marie Claire* to British readers.

Until recently, language and custom as well as government regulations have tended to keep the various national media markets apart. Hamish McRae suggests that in contrast cars, for example, are manufactured within a more integrated industry, 'in that you cannot tell in which country the car you are buying is made. . . . Buy a Peugeot and it may be made in Coventry', but 'up to now, it simply has not been worth trying to build a cross-European media group ·because it has not been possible to add value by passing experience across borders' (*Guardian,* 24 June 1988). One exception to that, Rupert Murdoch's News International has worked not because of cross-border fertilization of ideas but 'because of the personality of its chief executive'. If amid noisy publicity, but as yet with little cultural impact, satellite television is in the throes of undermining national sovereignty over our TV screens, the new women's magazines represent a comparable trend. For the first time in the magazine industry, 'Continental magazine skills [are] being let loose on the British marketplace' (*Guardian,* 24 June 1988). Publishing concepts have become transnational, though like many a current commodity exchange, the movement was initally one way – into the depressed UK market only. As Maggie Brown asked, only half facetiously: 'Where . . . is the [British owned] magazine . . . which will have German *Hausfrau* knitting their own fish fingers?' (*The Independent*, 12 August 1987). Late off the starting blocks, IPC has been playing European publishers at their own game in France, Spain and Italy, where IPC claim *Essentials* is already the top selling monthly (*The Independent*, 19 June 1989).[8]

The transferability of publishing concepts rests on the premise that 'women have common areas of interest across national frontiers' (*Campaign*, 1 July 1988). But therein lies the issue on which I primarily want to focus. Whereas *Hello!* is a photo-news and *paparazzi* magazine, *Best* shares with *Chat*, *Bella* and *Me*, as well as with the monthlies *Prima* and *Essentials*, a practical emphasis in its editorial approach. Journalist critics have tended to regard this return to recipes, patterns and household tips (or as Deirdre McSharry describes *Prima*: 'It tells you all the things you can do with dead mince', *Sunday Times*, 5 February 1989) as, necessarily, a return to old fashioned femininity. 'Selling Kinder and Küche' proclaimed one headline: '*Bella* is a soft-centred, soggy traditional read' (*The Independent*, 30 September 1987). These are 'wholesome, housewife-and-mother' magazines, insists the *Sunday Times* article. They 'bring homecraft out of the closet' maintains a *New Society* piece (White 1987: 15). And in a stinging review, 'Why the total woman is a real turn-off', Michele Hanson inveighs:

> A new woman has emerged: she who brandishes her knitting patterns and makes her jam shamelessly. She is not so much Superwoman as Mrs Totality, unashamed of any aspect of herself, even the ordinary-homey-embroidering-a-cushion part. . . . Naturally, enraged feminists have accused these magazines of setting women back 50 years. Is this the way to treat grown-up ladies?
>
> (*Guardian*, 22 January 1987)

Such comment does not allow that the 'grown-up ladies' might just *like* these magazines.[9] The question then is why? What is their appeal? It is too glib to equate a magazine content that foregrounds doing things in and around the home with any necessary ideological backwardness on the part of either magazine or reader.

One simple, but not to be underestimated, attraction of these magazines is their value for money. But we also have to move beyond the obvious. Research by Valerie Walkerdine on girls' comics (*Bunty* and *Tracy*) provides some useful pointers in thinking about a more complex appeal. The views expressed by Hanson and other commentators about what women's magazines *should* be doing echo what Walkerdine calls a 'politics of rationalism' (Walkerdine 1984: 167): do away with the biased, bad, unreal ideas about women (Kinder and Küche) and put in their place an undistorted reality (women juggling and struggling with home and work, maybe?). But Walkerdine warns:

> If new content in whatever form does not map on to the crucial issues around desire, then we should not be surprised if it fails as an intervention.
>
> (Walkerdine 1984: 182)

The success of these new magazines suggests that their content does indeed 'map on to the crucial issues around desire'. Notwithstanding their allegedly Germanic, no-nonsense editorial mix do 'they engage with the very themes, issues, problems, fantasies (of escape, of difference) which the realist "telling it like it is" ' (ibid.: 168) magazines, that Hanson and others implicitly seem to be advocating, do not?

In the remainder of this article I shall argue that the 'Kinder and Küche' label attached to these magazines is misplaced. Clearly magazines of a 1980s enterprise culture, yet they are more than the sum of their obsessively practical and rational parts. They tell of women's uneasy desires and their still prevalent feelings about the impossibilities of womanhood.[10]

But first the mass weeklies in the 1950s, the period to which critics suggest that the new magazines are trying to return women.

BEYOND A TRADE PRESS

Writing about the weeklies of the 1950s Mary Grieve, long time editor of *Woman*, was in no doubt that 'Because woman has this preoccupation with, and responsibility for, material living, she feels the need for what is virtually a trade press' (Grieve 1964: 138). Over twenty-five years later Iris Burton, editorial director of

Prima and *Best*, suggests that her magazines are 'centre of interest'. By the latter she means:

> Shared by you and me, by your mother, my sister, the lady down the road, the girl in the office next door. It doesn't matter what you are doing by way of a career or lifestyle, there are certain elements that you still like to maintain and they tend to be the practical elements. . . . But the other thing is that there are very few women, whether they are living on their own or have huge families or working or not, who don't maintain a home and who don't have the interest in it to want it to be lovely, who want to be creative with their homes.
>
> (Personal Interview, 1988)

Despite a similarity in these two statements there is a difference between the idea of a 'trade press' and that of 'centre of interest' magazines. 'Trade press' and the perpetration of what Marjorie Ferguson has critically referred to as 'the cult of femininity' (Ferguson 1983: 5) go hand in hand, whereas there is no *inevitable* yoking of 'centre of interest' magazines and femininity. This argument rests on a further one: that 'trade press' depends on the operation of a dominant ideology of femininity, 'centre of interest' presupposes its dissolution. The dissolution involves a change in the magazine text and in readers' relation to that text.

The term 'trade press' is sign of how women's housewife role was 'professionalized' in the 1950s as her trade, or career. The language of paid work transferred to unpaid work upheld the prevailing belief that women were equal but different from men.[11] In weekly magazines it was skills around consumption that were paramount to women's success in trade or career (Winship 1981; Partington 1989). Mary Grieve believed that:

> The professional man's wife struggling to manage her money so that her children could get a better education was just as glad of the practical recipes, the well-designed clothes, the hints on value-for-money, as was the welder's wife who found that she too could benefit from that kind of service and information in her weekly magazine. Furnishing schemes and attitudes of mind which were hopelessly out of her reach and experience before the war were within her ken now.
>
> (Grieve 1964: 135)

As printing restrictions were lifted (1951) and supplies of goods filtered onto the domestic market (all rationing finally ended in 1954), the number of pages in the weeklies expanded and advertising blossomed into full page colour. More dispersed throughout an issue rather than clustering at front and back, advertising's design and aesthetic seemed to lead the way for editorial spreads, with which it also shared a similar ideological framework. White is critical of such advertising copy:

> It was calculated to focus attention on their domestic role, reinforce home values, and perpetuate the belief that success as a woman, wife and mother, could be purchased for the price of a jar of cold cream, a bottle of cough syrup or a packet of instant cake-mix.
>
> (White 1970: 158)

But like successful advertising at any historical moment it encapsulated values that were appealing to potential female consumers. After the drabness of war and austerity the possibility of once again buying, and in plenty, promised the selfish pleasures so long denied in the cause of nationhood (Winship 1984). For women the assumption was that 'normal' housekeeping could be resumed after years of disruption and the availability of goods contributed towards making that an attractive proposition.

The weeklies educated working-class women to choose and spend wisely, 'to help people towards their best use of rising standards', as Mary Grieve put it (1964: 139). Proper engagement in consumption work, on the person and on the domestic front, was held out as a source of pleasure and of success, and feminine desire and identity were bound by those parameters, what elsewhere I have described as 'that oppressive nexus of femininity-desire-consumption' (Winship 1987: 161).

In a 'Spring Wedding Number – Everything here for happiness' (*Woman*, 2 March 1957) one bride, on her 'trousseau hunt', is reported as saying, 'I'll be coping with a full-time job as well as housework so I plumped for nylon: no trouble at all and such pretty things to choose from. My nightie's a dream. . .' But femininity could also be undone by inappropriate consumption, as the magazine warns: 'With so many lovely things in the shops, trousseau-hunting can be a dangerous pastime.' And in the same issue of *Woman*: 'Elegant women the world over know the importance of the *Underneath* Look. They know that the prettiest dress, the loveliest gowns are made or marred by what is worn beneath' (advertisement for Bear Brand 'loveliest of nylons'). An editorial item in another issue – 'Edith Blair Tests and Tells' – featured the 'Bra Apron':

> Frilled plastic apron that does an excellent 'cover-up' job, is boned so that its bib top stays up without the need for a tie. This means that party cooks stay unspattered and tidy in an apron that's whipped off in seconds as the guests arrive.
>
> (*Woman*, 5 January 1957)

Retrospectively it is doubtful there were takers for this one: the bra apron is risible, too close a relation to the kinkier merchandise in (later) sex shops. This item is useful nevertheless in raising the issue of readers' relation to the magazine text. For it is one thing to describe the construction of femininity in magazines, another to suggest that readers identified with or behaved in the ways advocated.

In 'The designer housewife in the 1950s' Angela Partington argues that women withstood the ideological messages beamed in their direction by magazines and – her particular interest – by design professionals:

> Women's consumption of designed objects in the fifties was profoundly equivocal. 'New ideas' in design, which usually embodied Functionalist principles, were well represented in women's magazines. . . . But very often the deployment of these ideas ran contrary to the ideals and principles they were supposed to represent.
>
> (Partington 1989: 211)

Highlighting women's autonomy with respect to domestic design concurs with wider theoretical attention focusing on readers' active appropriations of media texts (e.g. Morley 1980, Radway 1984, Ang 1985, Fiske 1987, Gray 1987). Such studies reject the concept of ideology where it might be inferring that subjects are its passive dupes. Along these lines Elizabeth Frazer, writing about 'Teenage girls reading *Jackie*' proposes, first, that we dispute there is

> one valid and unitary meaning of a text. Second, we may care to check whether, even if we grant there is one meaning it does have . . . an ideological effect on the reader.
>
> (Frazer 1987: 411)

Her own study suggests that

> the kinds of meanings which are encoded in texts and which
> we might want to call ideological, fail to get a grip on readers
> in the way the notion of ideology generally suggests. Ideology
> is undercut, that is, by these readers' reflexivity and reflective-
> ness.
>
> (Frazer 1987: 419)

Frazer introduces the concept of 'discourse register' to help
conceptualize the means by which readers may be reflexive in
their relation to a text. She defines discourse register 'as an
institutionalized, situationally specific, culturally familiar, public way of talking' (Frazer 1987: 420). Thus a reader commenting
on a text may, so to speak, switch hats in terms of the discourse
register she is deploying: from 'literary criticism' to 'feminism' to
'tabloid press' in the case of the teenage girls reading *Jackie*. Such
switches, which are dependent on the topic and forum of
discussion, most significantly involve a change of ideological
premises and hence on what can and cannot be said. ('Discourse
registers both *constrain* what is sayable in any context and *enable*
saying': Frazer 1987: 421.) Frazer illustrates that within a 'feminist' register a group discussion around the double standard of
sexuality between girls and boys is initiated:

Jane   I dislike the way boys treat girls in the sense that
            they've got the front to call them slags

Stella   when they're sleepin' around more than you are

Jane   yeah and they think that they're hard if they go out
            and do something, like . . . but if a girl does it she's
            stupid and things like that

Janine   if a girl wants to do the same job as a boy it's too
            hard.

But this 'feminism' is followed up by a 'tabloid press' style tirade
against mothers who abuse their babies:

Janine   that's what gets me they beat up their kids and get
            about six months, especially the mothers right, cos
            you know in the [local newspaper] there was this
            woman she picks up her baby and hit his head on the
            banister and it was just born it was most probably

three months and she was most probably still giving
it milk still and it was hungry still so she picked it up
right and she goes it was after feeding and she hit it
across the banister and it died . . .

(Frazer 1987: 422–3)

What I want to draw attention to here is the possibility that in
the 1950s, although the reader of women's magazines can be
regarded as active in her meaning-making, available discourse
registers did not offer alternative ideologies to allow the reflex-
ivity Frazer points to. There *was* a dominant ideology of femininity, and the women's weeklies were contributors to the cultural
processes by which hegemonic consent around women's position
was strived for, if never finally won. As Elizabeth Wilson has
described,

the orchestration of consensus on the position of women . . .
was the achievement of a deceptive harmony out of a variety of
noisy voices . . . [but] in the end the attempt failed, and
something broke through that was called women's liberation.

(Wilson 1980: 3)

The dominance of the ideology was reflected in the paucity and
weakness of alternative and oppositional views on women's
position. Betty Friedan's attribution of 'the problem that has no
name' to their situation (Friedan 1965: 13) gives credence to how
difficult any formulation of dissatisfaction with the housewife
role was for women. Within the prevailing terms of the debate,
despite their difference from men, women were regarded as equal:
within marriage the roles of husband and wife were complemen-
tary. It was thus virtually impossible to articulate the view that
difference was less sign of equality than manifestation of
subordination. As Wilson indicates, many middle-class women
writers at that time

chose to locate their novels in the past, or wrote of obviously
abnormal marriage relationships, or of madness as a female
response to life . . . because in the modern world it was not
possible to suggest that a woman's *normal* lot was captivity,
sexual frustration, and the battle with patriarchal authority.

(Wilson 1980: 151)

Readers of women's magazines may not have been committed to
their domestic text but where else was there to go except into

madness and 'failure'? Like one of Barbara Pym's single women characters, Dulcie Mainwaring: 'Once again Dulcie felt . . . that she was somehow a *woman manquée*' (Pym 1961: 250; my emphasis).

The material effects of twenty years of feminism sometimes seem negligible when hard evidence shows that 'in almost 90 per cent of households, women do the washing and ironing, in 75 per cent they do the cleaning and in 70 per cent they make supper' (Neustatter 1989: 223). Nevertheless, as radical barrister Helena Kennedy comments: 'The great advance has been in women's perceptions of themselves' (ibid.: 225). 'Trade press' to 'centre of interest' magazines perhaps less presupposes changes in the magazine text than these changes in readers. Suzanne Moore insists of contemporary magazines that:

> Although the content of women's magazines may be exactly that of marriages and mortgages, we need to separate pleasure from the text and commitment to the text. We can enjoy browsing without necessarily buying everything on offer.
>
> (Moore 1986: 10)

Or as Mica Nava puts this argument, 'Women can read glossy magazines critically and selectively and yet not disavow more traditional feminine identities and pleasures' (Nava 1987: 207). This seems to me to be a right we have won. It rests on the dominant ideology of femininity having been disrupted and on the availability of discourse registers, including feminist ones, that allow criticism and reflectiveness on the themes for which 'Kinder and Küche' is shorthand. In yoking 'centre of interest' magazines necessarily to femininity, Hanson and other commentators entrap readers in a 1950s time warp.

I shall return to the issue of reading these 'centre of interest' magazines later. For the moment I want to contemplate their text whose similarity to a 1950s content is, in fact, skin deep.

THE DOMESTIC FACE OF ENTERPRISE

From peak sales in the late 1950s for *Woman* and *Woman's Own* to the depressed mid-1980s the route was troubled. Cynthia White blames an editorial conservatism in the 1960s on dependence on advertising revenue. Yet, as she also notes, there were attempts to update the weeklies. In 1964 Ernest Dichter, an American 'motivational researcher' brought in by IPC advised four kinds of change for *Woman's Own* (White 1970: 220): 'a more realistic' editorial approach reflecting 'the broadening horizons of women's lives'; 'improvements in format, type, and art-work to bring them into line with modern tastes' (one could read graphic design taste as created by advertisers); 'the acquisition of a special character and stated purpose with which groups of readers could identify' (an early fomulation of niche marketing/narrow casting); and a fostering of ' "reader-involvement" and a "dialogue" between magazine staff and their readers'. Implementation of these changes in the weeklies, however, was 'too drastic and too abrupt, and had an adverse effect on sales' (White 1970: 228) with the result that, with the exception of a bolder presentation, transformation was gradual until the mid-1970s when the impact of feminism achieved some public legitimation (for example, in 1975, the operation of the Equal Pay and Sex Discrimination legislation)[12] and its ideas produced the kind of shifts Dichter had recommended, first in *Woman's Own*, under the editorship of Jane Reed and then Iris Burton, later in *Woman*.

By the time of the 'Euro-invasion', however, a combination of Thatcherite policies – engendering unemployment, cutbacks in local authority control and a shift in ideological focus from group and social needs to those of the private individual – and a fractured and softer feminism had virtually eliminated the campaigning element around the position of women which had characterized *Woman's Own* and *Woman* for almost a decade (Winship 1987). When Burton left an uncertain *Woman's Own* in 1985, Bridget Rowe began to wield a tabloid brush (she had worked on the *Sun* and the *News of the World* magazine) in an attempt to invigorate the magazine.[13] Richard Barber (who went on to edit *TV Times*) did likewise for *Woman*. This was partly a matter of journalistic style – profuse use of exclamation marks, and a vocabulary of excess emphasizing fun, entertainment, pleasure on the one hand, melodrama and tragedy on the other – partly a matter of a similar reliance on scoop stories and on royalty and television as the shared reference points for readers and the subject matter around which an extraordinarily large number of features revolve. The contrast between the forced hedonism of a tabloid style (even conceding that *Woman's Own* and *Woman* do not adopt either the viciousness or the intemperance of *The Sun*) and the busyness promoted by the Euro-magazines could not have been greater. Meanwhile other weeklies, most notably *Woman's Weekly* as the unlikely leading weekly, held to a more traditional mix of 'practicals' and a heavy dose of (romantic) fiction.

The new magazines eliminated the tabloid-style journalism and considerably increased practical coverage. The latter, in the form of knitting, had always been a steady earner for *Woman's Weekly* but had been drastically pruned in *Woman's Own* and *Woman* as a more 'progressive' edge had informed their editorial.[14]

The titles and uncluttered typefaces of the logos of *Prima, Best, Essentials* and *Me* made clear where they stood: no reference to women and femininity, giving support perhaps to them not endorsing a conventional femininity[15] and a self-promotional thrust. The titles have echoes of the sales pitch for the *Sunday Telegraph*: 'Cut through the waffle' (Iris Burton claims she tells her writers: 'Pack it with facts. No waffle'), combined with that of the Department of Trade and Industry's enterprise initiative scheme (that advertisement where all the paper 'whooshes' out of the office in a blue streak).

On inside pages *Woman's Own* often adopts a help-line approach to cookery, fashion and beauty. A way of involving readers, this also means that women are invoked as wives, partners, mothers. Thus: 'Help! How do I feed a little fusspot!' is accompanied by a photo of mother and toddler. The copy begins: 'For all mums with youngsters it's a worrying problem. . .' (*Woman's Own*, 14 March 1989). But *Best*'s pages confirm that domesticity does not have to imply femininity and it does not involve readers in a participatory way. When 'ordinary women' are included (in 'Woman of the week', 'Career of the week', 'Talking point') there is no indication they are readers and they are more likely to be recounting paid working lives or discussing ways of reconciling domestic responsibilities with a career. As far as cookery is concerned only rarely are assumptions made about who is going to produce or consume the cooked items as in: 'Delight friends with these tempting cocktail canapés. . .' (6 January 1989). Interestingly in 'Kids' kitchen' the warning that children should be supervised is addressed to 'Mum and Dad'. In addition *Best* sometimes widens the domestic sphere: mopeds and motor cycles in a 'Home equipment' slot, for example. Singly none of these points amounts to a shift but cumulatively their effect is significant in contributing to an ideological framework which binds women less to traditional femininity than that of *Woman's Own* where marriage, motherhood and heterosexuality provide the consistent reference grid. Femininity is further tempered in *Best* by its forceful 1980s-style work ethic, imbued through design and content.[16]

More a formula magazine than *Woman's Own*, in that slots regularly appear in the same position and with the same layout, *Best* adheres tightly to a five-column (sometimes four-column) ruled grid. Short items are boxed off, photos – many small ones – are framed and placed in orderly layout on the page. Abhorring white space the overall effect is busy, dense and newsy, having none of the hallmarks of the advertising-led design, which I mentioned in the last section. Rather then merging, advertising and editorial in *Best* are counterpointed, enhancing each other.

Whether it is tackling the several word puzzles, dress-making from the free pattern or following instructions for building a garden pond, as one IPC executive described *Essentials*, these are magazines for 'active doers'. There is also a firm strand of utilitarianism, the notion of a useful and practical knowledge, with much informative reporting, little discursive writing. Asides about reducing time spent – ' "One pan meals" save on washing up' (*Best*, 7 April 1989) – signal time as a commodity in short supply. Even time saved should be dutifully filled while leisure is to be worked at or hastily taken. Thus travel is more a guide of things to do than alluring holiday brochure hyping that which can be consumed. And 'Games' are to be played: no passive enjoyment in tackling 'Crosswords', 'Arrow-words' and 'Fig-jigs'. Light relief takes the form of quirky, and brief, news items or cartoons and 'Laughter lines'. Fiction is no lengthy and self-indulgent read but '5-minute fiction'.

The language that *Best* uses to describe slots also cultivates a brisk efficiency. Where *Woman's Own* has 'Extra' in each issue, *Best* has a 'Six-page dossier' (from hair problems to 'Know your biorhythms . . . and plan success and happiness'). *Woman's Own* carries several interview-based features with television and film celebrities; *Best* offers a 'Profile' on the likes of Stephen King, Patty Hearst or Robin Day. 'Cookery' in *Best* is labelled 'In the kitchen', carefully subdivided into 'Kitchen notes', 'Step by step', 'Recipe cards'. Such headings stress food production. Likewise,

'Knitting' in *Woman's Own* becomes in *Best* '*To* knit, *to* sew, *to* make' (my emphases).

Women have always torn pages from magazines and stored up useful tips, recipes and advice, but this process has been formalized. *Prima* offers sturdy red boxes to file away relevant items. *Essentials* gave a ring binder, complete with topic dividers, free with its first issue and every month the (practical) sections that editors believe suitable for reference are perforated to make removal easier.[17]

A report on the launch of *Essentials* ('Woman in View', Channel 4, January 1988) suggested that it had some of the characteristics of a part work: each month readers were buying one magazine but adding to several 'works' – cookery, dressmaking, etc. Maybe. But as the domestic face of 1980s enterprise a stronger idiom for these magazines is fact sheet cum personal organizer.[18] Whether it is the pages of Oracle or a company's databank, the fact sheet presupposes a glut of information in relation to which the user must fittingly choose for her own ends. The ethic of the personal organizer also demands that individuals select and order information appropriately. For people with demanding jobs and too-full lives who need the right information, in the right place, at the right time, the well-devised personal organizer requires methodical devotion; without it the striver is flailing.[19]

The possiblity of so *much* information at the touch of a few keys and the infinite capacity for its rational organization belies an underside: human life's messiness. Classifying and filing electronic information or bits of paper can persuade us that all is under control in situations where our capacity for control is on a knife edge. It is the latter, it seems to me, that the overbusy and ordered *Best* points to.[20]

However, before I properly explore *Best*'s underside I want to return to the issue of reading and readers' relation to their magazine. To follow through with the analogy of fact sheet and personal organizer, they suppose a different mode of reading and a different relation to the text.

READING STRATEGIES: 'KEPT STRICTLY FOR THE POTATO-WATCH'?

Suzanne Moore suggests that:

Unlike books, magazines can be read in a whole number of ways – there is no correct order we have to follow in order to obtain meaning.

(Moore 1986: 10)

One implication of the multiple narrative form of a magazine as opposed to the single linear narrative of (some) novels is that the text has a less compulsive pull and the reading process is more under the reader's control.[21] Yet magazines are not alike in the reading strategies they encourage. Burton maintains that *Best*'s bitty approach supports the busy 'dip in and dip out reader' whereas the long features in *Woman's Own* invite a relaxing and absorbing read:

In the *Woman/Woman's Own* area women will curl up with a cup of coffee and their magazine, maybe in the afternoon or the morning. With *Best* they will dip into it. You'll find that they'll read it last thing at night just as they go to bed, something quick and fast. Maybe in the bath even, or on the tube. It's a very useful magazine to have when you're travelling to the office. It's a useful magazine when you're sitting on a bus. It's the dip in and dip out reader: 'I haven't got much time to read, but I want to read something that is not trivial.'

(Personal interview, 1988)

If the dip in and dip out reader suggests a fairly disinterested reader, curling up with a magazine carries a stronger association of reader-involvement. For Jill Churchill the absence of the latter in the new magazines – 'There is no answering back, apart from the letters' page' (*The Independent*, 12 August 1987) – as well as their lack of attention to campaigning over issues is cause for concern. But this overlooks that *Best* predisposes readers to relate to their magazine in other ways.

My own characterization of women's magazines has been that they stand as paternalistic friend to readers but encourage a reader-involvement in which the magazine occupies the authoritative position. In *Best* the paternalistic friendship role is overlaid by a more detached relation to readers and the balance of power between editorial text and reader has shifted towards the latter.

Best operates with a marketplace definition of individuals with different consumer needs. The two-page 'Your rights' slot including housing, money, legal and consumer issues gives some sense of the ground on which *Best* operates and its mode of attracting different constituencies (*Best*, 2 June 1989). An item on the implications for tenants of opting out of council control takes a *married* couple as its case-study. The consumer piece tackles the raw deal meted out to *single* people when they book hotel rooms or obtain mortgages. Money matters, on 'the new Capital Bond', discusses investing £1000, while another item addresses itself to the question asked by a woman bringing up a large family on a *low* income: who still qualifies for a free eye test? Whether it is 'Your rights' or health (a substantial element in *Best*),[22] or more obvious consumer areas like fashion and home, readers, like consumers going to the shops, are likely to dip in and dip out of different items, as well as use them in their own way, depending on individual interests and social position.

The mass media's popular appeal is sometimes critically attributed to its offering a 'lowest common denominator' content. White, for instance, maintains that:

> In the past publishers fastened upon this 'lowest common denominator' [a domestic focus] in writing for women as the surest way of building and maintaining multi-million readerships. In the 'forties and 'fifties it was possible to be 'all things to all women' – the deprivations of war and the restrictions of peace were great levellers.
>
> (White 1970: 287)

This view assumes that diverse readers are responding to the same textual elements, in the same way. More recent theoretical approaches that I mentioned earlier (see p. 89) hold that the popular text is characterized by its 'potential of meanings' whose realization depends on the activity of readers. In *Television Culture* John Fiske suggests that

> these groups actively read television in order to produce from it meanings that connect with their social experience . . . the television text is a potential of meanings capable of being viewed with a variety of modes of attention by a variety of viewers. To be popular, then, television must be both polysemic and flexible.
>
> (Fiske 1987: 84)

Further:

Its popularity among its diversity of audiences depends upon its ability to be easily and differently incorporated into a variety of subcultures: popularity, audience activity, and polysemy are mutually entailed and interdependent concepts.

(ibid.: 107)

Yet if there is variability in the relation between text and reader Fiske also warns that 'this variety is not anarchic, but is delimited by the structure of the text' (ibid.: 117).

What I have already suggested is that the position of women and the available ideological fields have changed so that they may be the uncommitted reader Moore and Nava refer to (see p. 92). Now I want to indicate how 'the structure of the text', specifically in *Best*, facilitates that uncommittedness but also allows for a diversity of readings. In this respect *Best* is, I think, potentially more flexible than *Woman's Own*.[23]

There are two formats in *Best* – fashion and the problem page – that I want to examine to substantiate this argument further. Both adopt multinarratives (offering a necessary 'consumer choice') and in both, though through different mechanisms, the reader is placed so as to appraise the text.

Fashion is one editorial area relying on large images. But its rhetoric is not that of much advertising, nor indeed of much other fashion coverage. Juliet Askew (fashion editor of rival *Woman's Own*) implied that its imagery was bland and boring; it was 'cataloguey' (Personal interview, 1989). From *Best*'s point of view this catalogue look is deeply intentioned. Partly, in order to provide what Mary Weaver (*Best*'s fashion editor) described as a 'visual relief' to otherwise hectic editorial pages (Personal interview, 1989). But there is another aspect to it.

Writing about *Picture Post* in the 1940s Stuart Hall contrasts the magazine's visual exposition with that of the Sunday colour supplements. *Best* is hardly a photo-news magazine and yet, to some extent, the rhetoric of its fashion pages can be similarly counterpointed to that of advertising (and of other fashion photography). Hall suggests that 'No one in the Colour Supplements is interested in looking hard or straight: everything is angled, posed, framed, prettied up, cocooned' (Hall 1972: 84) such that readers are caught up in the glossy images of the 'good life'. Whereas in *Picture Post*:

The layout is straightforward, the pictures disposed on the

page within an uncomplicated aesthetic. They are square-on to the reader, speaking straight *at* or *to* him . . . photograph size is not dictated by exaggerated blow-up, fancy blocking or cutting. The photographs are large but remain life size . . . We are not invited *into* the picture . . . Margins, for the most part remain, and frame the photographs, distancing them.

(Hall 1972: 79)

Best's three fashion spreads, having working titles of 'Every-woman', 'Young' and 'Classic', the latter regularly alternating with 'Outsize' and 'His and hers', or at times children's and older women's fashion – something for everyone – are also character-ized by a straightforward visual presentation. They less seduce or catch us in connotations of the 'good life' than present. With a camera angle slightly tilting upwards, models are lifesize and lifelike and the high quality printing provides a clarity of detail augmented by more verbal information than in most magazines: price, range of sizes, colours, materials, stockists.

The catalogue look thus enables and positions us as readers to contemplate and adjudicate as seasoned consumers. Are these fashion looks for us? What are the merits of a garment worn this way, or that way?

The problem page is a very different slot, yet it too positions readers to make assessments. Borrowed from *Femme Actuelle*, *Best*'s problem page departs from the usual format where reader writes in, agony aunt responds. In 'A problem shared, You reply' the agony aunt has been done away with and instead reader writes in, other readers respond. Some weeks later a resumé of the problem letter appears together with a selection of edited replies (the original letter writer is sent all the mail *Best* receives).[24]

Discussing the more usual problem page, Rosalind Coward has pointed out how the letters

always offer a narrative in certain distinctive ways. . . . Certain information is vital in problem page stories which is not vital in other advice. . . . They [problem pages] incite women to reveal and read about how an individual reached a certain point in her life. . . . The ideology behind this is clear. Speak out. It will make you feel better. Organize your crisis into a narrative, be honest and perhaps then you will see the causes, the reason why you feel like this.

(Coward 1984: 137–8)

Erica Carter points to the autobiographical aspect to the narratives:

> The conventions of problem-page writing demand an encapsulation of complex thoughts and emotions in minuscule autobiographies, hopelessly compacted. Each letter briefly details age, sex, marital status; then a handful of intimate confidences, tersely formulated.

But the narrator in these 'minuscule autobiographies' is not that of 'the full blown autobiography':

> While in the latter, the writer is free to imprint a retrospective coherence on collected images of her past selves, the 'I' of the problem-page correspondent necessarily remains fragmented. There must remain a residue of fear, anxiety, resentment – 'I can't forget', 'I live in fear'. Each letter is edited to end on a question: 'What use is it?' 'Where will it all end?' Through this opening in the narrative, the agony aunt is called upon to enter; the writer looks to her for the solution that allows narrative closure.
>
> (Carter 1989: 71–2)

The narrative closure offered by the agony aunt's solution lays the basis for the re-establishment of a coherent sense of self for the correspondent, as well as providing a satisfactory resolution for readers.

In *Best*, however, several answers mean several narratives which rub against each other in the advice they offer and in the ideological assumptions they make. Rather than agony aunt stepping in with her authoritative words of wisdom to effect ideological and narrative closure and put the 'I' together again, the reader must plunge in to assess for herself the merits of conflicting advice and divergent ideologies. If narrative closure does occur and the fragmented 'I' is made coherent it is the reader who achieves that in the way she sees fit.

More generally the 'structure of the text' in *Best* is, then, sufficiently flexible to *encourage* different appropriations of it. Michele Hanson suggests, mockingly, of *Prima* readers that they

> want to be dibble-dabbling into the bits and pieces of *Prima*. This is reality. To read about cherry stencils while your potatoes boil.

That's what my neighbour does. 'When you don't want to tax your brain,' she says, 'but you don't want to be doing nothing, then you read *Prima, Bella* and *Best*. . . . But they're a waste of time if you've got anything else to do. I don't keep them in the living room any more.' They're kept strictly for the potato-watch in a corner of the kitchen. Not in an embarrassed or shifty way, you understand. Just for convenience. That's where they're read.

(*Guardian*, 1 January 1987)

Whether Hanson's neighbour exists or is a figment of journalistic licence, she illustrates the critical distance a reader *may* adopt. But while the magazine may be kept for the potato-watch and have little significance beyond that, it should not be forgotten that *Best*'s, as well as *Prima*'s contents may also be incorporated into a traditional femininity or be read and used in more serious vein.

But assuming for the moment a potato-watch reading mode which does not tax the conscious brain, can *Best* still speak to and nurture the unconscious mind?

SOME DAY . . .

Taken at face value the new practical magazines are exhausting to contemplate. Their readers, it appears, hold down a job, look after children, run a household *and* find time to do all this domestic craft activity: a driven lifestyle unrelieved by real time off. But does such an emphasis in these magazines mean readers *are* into practical home-making in a big way? Doubtless some are. Yet Iris Burton commented that:

For the most part, even with *Prima* readers, the magazine is a kind of wish fulfilment thing. It's, 'I think I'm capable of doing this. I want to because I'm a loving wife, mother.' Etc. etc. And, 'I'm sure I'd be very, very good at it.' But you know, finally, 'I'm not going to have any time to do it so I'll look at the pictures, put it away, save the magazine.' In the case of *Prima*, there are probably people with two years' worth of *Prima* and they're still saying, 'One of these days I'll do that pattern for the trousers and I'll stipple that vase.'

(Personal interview, 1988)

Burton may not be correct in imputing to women the association between engagement in these activities and a successful femininity ('I'm a loving wife, mother') but what is raised is the idea of magazine as wish fulfilment – that these magazines have found a response from women because, as Walkerdine puts it, their content maps 'onto the crucial issues around desire' (1984: 182). If the latter is the case then:

> What we have to examine is the materiality of the fantasies created in these [magazines], in terms of what is spoken, what is understood, and how it is resolved.
>
> (Walkerdine 1984: 167)

In examining fantasy in the areas of craft/practical home-making and fiction I shall not adopt wholesale Walkerdine's psychoanalytic framework but I do want to borrow the notion that our feminine identities are constantly being struggled over. According to Jacqueline Rose, 'the unconscious constantly reveals the "failure" of identity'. She argues that:

> 'Failure' is not a moment to be regretted in a process of adaptation, or development into normality, which ideally takes its course. . . . Instead 'failure' is something endlessly repeated and relived moment by moment throughout our individual histories. It appears not only in the symptoms, but also in dreams. . . . Feminism's affinity with psychoanalysis rests above all . . . with this recognition that there is a resistance to identity which lies at the very heart of psychic life.
>
> (cited in Walkerdine 1984: 181)

The 'failure' of identity is most evident in *Best*'s fiction which clearly speaks of women's unease about an identity defined in relation to men's demands on them, yet narratively has trouble in delivering the longed-for, but vaguely specified, alternative.

As far as craft and practical home-making are concerned there is an irony in the situation whereby a domestic craft revival occurs at the juncture where there is no longer either a practical or ideological need for women to do it. The amounts of money saved are negligible and anyway the woman doing it is not likely to be someone who needs to be a prudent housekeeper; similar products could be purchased and it is no slur on her femininity simply to go to the shops. But then craft and practical home-making cannot be the nub of a certain kind of fantasy until those practices are no longer part of the daily grind. If, as Burton outlines, women are not largely engaged in these tasks, only wish that they were, what is it that the doing and the made objects represent?

To try to answer that I want to make a slight detour to consider the meaning of artefacts in our lives. In *Material Culture and Mass Consumption* Daniel Miller discusses how artefacts provide fine discriminations – more easily perceived than verbally expressed – about our values and interests. He suggests that:

> Divisions which may appear important in language and ideology may be absent from object differentiations while distinctions within the domain of artefacts may constitute important divisions which would elsewhere be ignored or denied.
>
> (Miller 1987: 106)

In their assembly on our person or in our homes artefacts are proof of who we are; they carry our histories. (Such that sitting among packed-up tea chests, no longer buttressed by carefully arranged belongings, our sense of self may crack. Moving house is often one of life's crises.) But the expressive environment we have created can also silently signify tension, differences and the fragmentation of self.

In an article concerned with taste and aesthetics in western thought and culture, Dick Hebdige also deals with the meaning of artefacts. He illustrates his complex and theoretical arguments by reference to an American Thunderbird car, owned and lovingly cared for by a Turkish Cypriot, Mr H., who lives in a terraced street in Hackney and for twenty years has worked on the night shift in a bakery. Drawing on the work of Jean-François Lyotard, Hebdige describes Mr H.'s car as an 'impossible object' and 'sublime', where 'sublime' is

> the socio-political aspiration to 'present the unpresentable', to embody in the here and now the that-which-is-to-be, is deemed untenable: 'paranoid'. The sublime by definition is *das Unform* – that which is without form, hence that which is monstrous and unthinkable.
>
> (Hebdige 1987: 65)

Lyotard himself emphasizes that the term 'sublime' points to

contradictory feelings: 'a feeling of both pleasure and dis-
pleasure, together' (Lyotard 1989: 22). Thus Mr H.'s car is an
'impossible object',

> not because it encapsulates an unattainable dream of opulence
> – I don't really think that Mr H. craves to join the interna-
> tional jet set or to live inside an episode of *Dallas*. It is
> impossible because it serves so many different (symbolic)
> functions, supplies so many diverse needs – the need for
> recognition and respect, yes, but also the need for something
> to care for and care about, to bring up, cultivate, stand in awe
> of. It is impossible because it is a screen on to which so much
> inchoate yearnings and desire are projected that putting them
> into words is impossible.
>
> (Hebdige 1987: 72)

Mr H. appears as a humble man and yet his choice of 'impossible
object' is the grandiose gesture men, but less often women, can
indulge in. Women too have recourse to impossible objects but
they are less spectacular, less visible (unless it is the fashion item:
stiletto, red lipstick) and 'the impossible' is spread, I suspect,
across a diversity of small artefacts.

Arguably magazines are one. As a mix of the prosaic and the
utopian and as small treats women buy themselves are not they 'a
screen on to which so much inchoate yearning and desire are
projected'? Iris Burton was surprised at the 'love affair' *Prima*
readers had with their magazine:

> Once they have the magazine they can't stop handling it,
> talking about it and one *Prima* reader will try and convert the
> rest. It's an extraordinary phenomenon.
>
> (Personal interview, 1988)

Craft and practical home-making is 'the impossible' because it
too 'serves so many different (symbolic) functions, supplies so
many diverse needs'. Bringing it out of the closet in the late 1980s
is neither an actual return to, nor a symbolic hankering for, the
good/bad old days of the 1950s. But it does mark tensions around
femininity and women's relation to mass consumption. At one
and the same time there is a desire for a more leisured life with
time and space to allow pursuit of these activities, *and* a defiance
about 'independence', which currently means doing it all: child
and husband care, and paid work.[25] At one and the same time

there is a desire to personalize and 'undo' mass consumption (even if it is only a soft toy made from a kit, courtesy of a magazine, the object becomes more emotionally loaded, made with love, than one bought over the counter) *and* an increasing dependency on the tastes shopping provides: mix 'n match from Laura Ashley or BHS.

Meanwhile, in the absence of spare time, looking at pics, reading instructions, is sublime (pleasurable and unpleasurable) surrogacy for practices that might construct another self; another place for women?

The fantasy of *Best*'s fiction is striking: an unconscionable number of men are literally bumped off in what Burton aptly calls 'odd ball' fiction.[26] Feminine narratives in that they deal with relationships between women and men, they diverge from an earlier genre in which, as one *Woman's Own* fiction editor put it, they would not leave readers 'at the gas oven door'. In this respect short stories had much in common with problem page letters. The positive narrative closure associated with the agony aunt's resolution of problems also characterized their denouement. In story as on problem page, in the terms Carter suggests, the fragmented 'I' is coherently reassembled. Evidently made of sterner stuff, readers of *Best*'s fiction as well as its problem page are left more troubled. Story endings defy optimism and the final narrative equilibrium tends to throw up, not resolve, ideological problems: the 'I' remains disturbed.

There are, however, certain devices that distance readers from events: an element of being over-the-top; the advanced age of protagonists given that 81 per cent of *Best*'s readership is under fifty-five. Nevertheless, the lives of the elderly do also link back to those of the young.

In 'The Waiting Game' (John Mount, *Best*, 26 August 1988) there are three women: a middle-aged woman who quietly observes life in her coffee shop; Penny, a visitor that morning; and an old and sad woman, a regular frequenter. Most of the story is about Penny who, young and hopeful, awaits the one-time and no-good boyfriend. When he does not turn up Penny leaves but seeks reassurance from the woman behind the counter: 'I'm sure that it's next week he meant us to meet. Don't you think so?' The woman, at this late point in the story, now named, replies, 'Oh, I certainly hope so'. And it is her observations on the old lady that resolve the narrative:

Kathy Stevens closed the door of the Copper Kettle behind the old lady and watched as she shuffled away, clutching her two crumpled carrier bags. In the twelve years that she had been running the coffee shop she had watched the old lady go through this ritual every Friday without fail, and every week Kathy found herself wondering just who it was that had caused the old lady so much pain all those years ago. Where was he now? Had he any idea what he had done? She wiped a glass with her tea towel and watched as she crossed over the road and disappeared among the throng of shoppers. Kathy shook her head sadly and went back to her work.

(*Best*, 26 August 1988)

The splitting of the female subject in this story hardly offers readers security. Penny may come to her senses or she may continue to be fooled. Kathy is wise – has she already been in Penny's shoes? – yet is represented alone and outside the action. And the old bag lady is in a world of her own. Does she come to the coffee shop to daydream about what might have been? Or is she still trying to come to terms with the pain? Either way it is not a cheering thought.

Longevity of marriage is also common, facilitating a more convincing portrayal of women's weariness. Marcia in 'A House with Potential' (Anne Goring, *Best*, 7 April 1989) reflects on her life with a selfish husband and daydreams about their retirement home:

Home. She'd stared that morning around the dark kitchen with its battered furniture and the damp flagged floor that tortured her chilblained feet in the winter. She'd felt hope rise like a fledgling bird in her breast at the prospect of leaving. . . . A warm house with a kitchen full of gadgets that would be so easy to use that she would never be tired again.

Emma in 'The Legacy' (Valerie Edwards, *Best*, 17 March 1989) muses on how, now that Bert, with his 'smelly pipe', 'the eyes . . . brilliant with spite and malice' and 'that peculiarly penetrating voice', is dead 'she could have an after-lunch snooze every day if she chose'.

Both Marcia and Emma contrast their youthful romantic dreams, when their menfolk were heroes, with the later harsh realities of their shared daily lives. Both look on as their men lie

dying, actively choosing not to call the alarm or lift the finger
that would prevent death. These self-conscious moments differ
from the acts of fate pushing the narrative to its resolution in
more conventional short stories. In the latter the protagonist is
victim of the outside chance; in the former she takes destiny,
though in a passive mode of deciding *not* to do something, into
her own hands. From the window of the property she is being
shown around, Marcia watches her husband drown. She reflects
that as he had not helped her (when she was losing her baby),
why should she help him. Turning to the estate agent who has
not noticed the drama, she comments thoughtfully: 'D'you
know, Mr Dale, I do believe you're right about one thing. This is
a property with a great deal of potential.' Now she can spread *her*
wings.

Domestic imagery is recurrent. In 'The Perfect Wife' (Monica
Porter, *Best*, 22 May 1988), Veronica's dreams of being an actress
are 'buried somewhere beneath all the years, beneath the pink
mounds of smoked salmon' on the dinner table she has so
perfectly prepared. Celia puts the finishing touches to a sampler,
'Behind every man . . . there is a woman' (Buzz Rodwell, *Bella*, 11
March 1989). As her boss hangs it on the wall and stands back
admiringly, she stabs him to death with her scissors. It then
transpires that she is in a psychiatric institution for murdering
an earlier boss-cum-lover who had risen to fame on the back of
her unacknowledged efforts – just as she feels her *doctor* has now
done. (Did the 'Needlecraft Book Society', whose adjacent advertisement, 'Picture it in Cross Stich', shows a sampler of smiling
family, appreciate quite what it was rubbing shoulders with?)
Emma's dreams of what she will do with 'The Legacy' lovingly
revolve around home:

> She'd be able to afford the rethatching now, and a decent
> bathroom. Pink, she thought. She'd always favoured a pale
> pink suite, a good-sized bath and washbasin; maybe she could
> even have Bert's room turned into a nice cloakroom, with a
> proper modern loo and everything. And she'd make a special-
> occasion trip into Tiverton to order one of the Dralon velvet
> suites she'd always coveted. If she moved the china cabinet to
> the right-hand side of the fireplace . . . the settee could be
> squeezed against the wall with an inch or two spare . . .
> Perhaps she'd treat herself to some new curtains too. It had

been years since she'd treated herself. Surely she deserved it.
'Yes,' she thought to herself. 'It's about time I considered my
needs.'

(*Best*, 17 March 1989)

As a loaded terrain for women, the domestic provides an evoca-
tive vocabulary that most readers will recognize.

Emma's dreams are, in fact, foreshortened. As she enters her
cottage after the funeral Bert (her brother, though he may as well
have been her husband) returns to haunt her. His Parrot Pegleg
has finally learnt to mimic the penetrating voice which pierces
her eardrums:

> 'Oh no,' Emma breathed, covering her ears. 'I could put up
> with any revenge except for this!'
>
> But even as she said it, she knew that Bert wouldn't be
> listening to her. After all, he never had.'

Emma, like other protagonists has not won; she and the readers
are left troubled. The 'I' remains with 'a residue of . . . anxiety,
resentment – "I can't forget" ' (Carter 1989: 72). Whereas a
conventional happy ending tends to leave the reader complacent
and with problems temporarily massaged away, the sad ending
tends to provoke self-reflection. Happiness does not require
explanations, misfortunes do. Why have events turned out like
this? Does it have to be this way? Without a closure of the
conventional sort, feminine behaviour is less easily kept in place.
The final word *is* Emma's and her reflections are an indictment
of Bert and maybe of men more generally: 'Bert wouldn't be
listening . . . he never had.'

What readers actually make of these stories will depend on
their situation. But the themes of romantic hopes dashed; of
women having little space or time to cultivate their own lives
when bending themselves all ways to fit in with family interests;
of being at others' emotional and domestic beck and call, but
themselves able to demand little; and over the years getting very
weary of it all, can appeal to a much wider constituency than the
domestic emphasis in these stories might first suggest.

That these stories so often centre on women killing or allowing death is a sign of desperation, especially since they are also
characterized by a degree of fatalism and pessimism about
women's position and men's behaviour ever being different. The

resistance to patriarchal relations is, in the end, a 'passive dissent' (Clarke cited in Roman and Christian-Smith 1988: 13).

A TERSE CODA

At the time I was beginning to think about *Best* and *Prima* and bought the first issue of *Essentials* the annual statistics from *Social Trends* were published. One item, reported in the press, but not commented upon, caught my eye:

> The Samaritans received 2.5 million calls for help in 1986, with the largest number of callers being women aged between 25 and 39.
>
> (*The Independent*, 14 January 1988)

In real life women to not bump off husbands (even if they do divorce them in large numbers).[27] But is the reality and underside of what is representationally dealt with in *Best* these pleas from women for someone to listen to *them*?

NOTES

1 By postfeminism I am not referring to the notion that feminism has been and gone, like some passing fad, but to political and cultural shifts whereby:

   (a) Some of the presuppositions of a feminist practice and its aims are less oppositional than taken for granted, and

   (b) Feminism has burgeoned into a rich if sometimes contradictory mix of femin*isms* such that the boundaries between feminist and non-feminist have become fuzzy. Furthermore,

   (c) A postfeminist cultural practice seems to allow the possibility of a *play* around modes of femininity not simply antagonism towards, or an evacuation of, this oppressive territory.

2 See, for example, Evans and Thornton 1989, especially chap. 4, 'Women, fashion and postmodernism', Hebdige 1988, 'The bottom line on Planet One: squaring up to *The Face*', McRobbie 1989, 'Introduction' and chap. 2, 'Second-hand dresses and the role of the ragmarket', Mort 1988, Winship 1985.

3 Launch dates are: *My Weekly* 1910, *People's Friend* 1869, *Woman* 1937, *Woman's Own* 1932 and *Woman's Realm* 1958, *Chat* 1985 (*Chat* began life as a tabloid but by 1990, after it had been bought by IPC, was looking much like *Bella* and *Take A Break*), *Best* 1987, *Bella* 1987, *Hello!* 1988, *Me* 1989 and *Take A Break* 1990. There is also *More!* 1988, a fortnightly, for the graduates from *Just Seventeen*.

4 Pre-1985, and omitting publications intended largely for the under sixteens, there have been at least twenty births.
5 The two exceptions were *Candida* brought out by IPC in 1972 and *Eve* launched the following year by Morgan Grampian. Neither magazine survived a year.
6 Figures are an estimate based on the Audit Bureaux of Circulation figures. The estimate is rough because in 1958 a circulation was not available for *People's Friend*.
7 New monthly magazines' launch dates are: *Chic* 1984, *Elle* 1985, *Prima* 1986, *Essentials* 1988, *Marie Claire* 1988, *New Woman* 1988.
8 *Essentials* is published under the title of *Avantage* in France (which edition it is worth noting is printed in Italy), *Práctica Mujer* in Spain and *Pratica* in Italy (*The Independent*, 19 June 1989).
9 Table refers to women readers only. Taken from the National Readership Survey, January to June 1988 (JICNARS, Joint Industry Committee for National Readership Surveys).

Table 3.1 Readership profiles

| | Age | | | | | | Social grade | | | | | |
	15–24 %	25–34 %	35–44 %	45–54 %	55–64 %	65+ %	A %	B %	C₁ %	C₂ %	D %	E %
Estimated % of population 15+	18	17	16	13	13	22	3	15	23	25	17	17
Woman's Own	20	21	17	15	11	15	2	13	25	29	18	13
Woman	18	23	18	15	11	14	3	14	27	28	17	12
Best	29	23	17	12	10	8	2	11	27	31	20	8
Bella	27	22	18	11	10	11	1	12	22	31	22	11
Family Circle	13	24	22	17	12	12	5	18	28	28	12	8
Good Housekeeping	12	20	19	15	17	17	8	26	29	19	9	8
Woman & Home	8	12	16	18	20	26	5	22	29	21	12	11
Prima	26	29	20	12	7	5	3	16	29	29	16	7
Essentials	32	25	17	13	10	4	3	17	28	29	17	7

This table shows well both the younger and more downmarket profiles of the new launches compared with those of the longer-established competitors. For example, 52 per cent of *Best*'s readers are under thirty-four as compared to 41 per cent of *Woman's Own*'s and *Woman*'s; 53 per cent of *Bella*'s readers are in social grades C₂D as compared to 45 per cent of *Woman*'s. Likewise 55 per cent of *Prima*'s readers are under thirty-four as compared to 32 per cent of *Good Housekeeping*'s and 46 per cent of *Essentials*' readers are in social grades C₂ D compared to 33 per cent of *Woman and Home*'s.
10 Although I draw examples from, and refer to, the range of new practical magazines the arguments I am making apply best to *Best*, which I have researched more closely than the others.
11 As Elizabeth Wilson points out, for middle-class women the process

was more one of 'proletarianization': having lost her servants, like her working-class counterpart, she too now had to perform domestic drudgery (Wilson 1980: 12–13). Somehow, though, the hoover and refrigerator improved the status of housework and of the housewife (from manual, i.e. dirty and heavy work, to mental, i.e. clean and supervisory work).

12 The Equal Pay Act was passed in 1970 but not enforced until 1975.

13 Bridget Rowe has kept up a campaign around rape but the emphasis is on increasing sentences for rapists. A suitably Thatcherite, and tabloid, aim?

14 Since the launch of the Euromagazines, *Woman* and *Woman's Own* have begun to increase their practical coverage and tried to offer greater value for money. At the same time, by summer 1989 *Best* seemed to have edged its way just slightly towards its older rivals, so that by the time this is in print it is likely that the differences I am suggesting between the two sorts of magazine will have blurred.

15 IPC apparently has copyright for most of the titles denoting or connoting femininity. That might explain why European publishers have adopted new-style titles, but not why IPC itself has chosen similar ones.

16 For a more detailed comparison of *Best* and *Woman's Own* than I can engage in here, see Winship 1990.

17 IPC has again adopted this plan with *Me*. It has 'tip strips' to be used in the kitchen with a hanging clipboard (also a launch-issue freebie) which can also be used as an ordinary writing clipboard, as I regularly do.

18 Young magazines like *Smash Hits* and *Just Seventeen* also adopt something of a facts approach (20 facts about favourite pop stars) and they too are certainly busy magazines. But they do not combine that with the personal organizer work ethic. Rather, there is a humour running throughout the magazines; nothing is to be taken too seriously (McRobbie 1988).

19 I have purposely not wanted to suggest the stylish filofax which has yuppie associations (Campbell and Wheeler 1988), though Braithwaite and Barrell refer to *Essentials* and its give-away ring binder as a 'sort of magazine Filofax' (1988: 113). The personal organizer, by contrast, is the more mainstream copy. A clumsier artefact, it is owned by provincial businessmen not London trendies.

20 *Best* and the other practical magazines were launched before the explosion of concern about green issues. What seems like the escalating scale of environmental damage and ecological imbalance would suggest that at the macro level as well as at the micro and personal level I am talking about we are in serious danger of flipping out of control. Since in my view the two are connected it will be interesting to see in which direction these magazines shift as green issues dominate the social and political agendas.

21 It should be noted, though, that sometimes even the most compulsive of texts, for example, romantic fiction, which the non-enthusiast might consider to be spoilt by reading the end first, is not read as its

linear narrative dictates. Janice Radway details how women readers check out the last pages to make sure it is going to provide the resolution and satisfaction they want (Radway 1984: 70).

It is also worth noting that it is only relatively recently and partly because production processes now make this easier, that women's magazines recognize that the reader can as well flick backwards as forwards, and therefore keep as much interest going in their back pages as in their front.

22 Rosalind Coward has noted that 'health has stepped into the fading arena of sexuality'. That would certainly seem to be the case in *Best*, where sexuality is notable by its relative absence. Coward argues that 'previously it was through sexuality that individuals were required to make decisions about how to use their bodies and exercise the greatest degree of self-determiniation . . . [now] it is health which has picked up the discourse of traditional religious morality' (Coward 1989: 31).

23 In Iris Burton's view, one sign of *Best*'s flexibility was its appeal, judging from letters she had received, to older women. They did not feel that the magazine concentrated on those topics of interest only to young upwardly mobile women. Yet you would be hard put to find one photo of a woman over fifty, let alone of retiring age. And the readership figures do not suggest that *Best is* read by a large proportion of older women. See note 9.

24 By spring 1990 *Best* had in fact installed an agony aunt, Elizabeth John, but without getting rid of the 'You reply' format.

25 Between 1971 and 1987 the proportion of married women in employment grew from 47 per cent to 60 per cent. There was a large rise in the economic activity rate of the 25 – 44 age group: in 1971 it was 52.4 per cent; in 1987 68.6 per cent and the projection for 1991 is 72.5 per cent. Between June 1983 and June 1988 the number of employees in employment rose by over 1 million, with virtually all the rise accounted for by females, both full time and part time (*Social Trends* 1989).

26 When *Best* opted for this kind of oddball story they were few and far between. But once authors, mainly female, realized this was what the magazine and its readers relished they began writing them in large numbers.

27 Seven out of ten divorce petitions are filed by wives (*Social Trends* 1989).

REFERENCES

Ang, Ien (1985) *Watching Dallas*, London: Methuen.
Braithwaite, Brian and Barrell, Joan (1979) *The Business of Women's Magazines*, London: Associated Business Press.
Braithwaite, Brian and Barrell, Joan (second edn 1988) *The Business of Women's Magazines*, London: Kogan Press.
Campbell, Beatrix, and Wheeler, Wendy (1988) 'Filofaxions', *Marxism Today*, December.

Carter, Erica (1989) 'Intimate outscapes: problem-page letters and the remaking of the 1950s German family', in Leslie G. Roman and Linda K. Christian-Smith with Elizabeth Ellsworth (eds) *Becoming Feminine: The Politics of Popular Culture*, London: Falmer Press.

Coward, Rosalind (1984) *Female Desire*, London: Paladin.

Coward, Rosalind (1989) 'A whole lot of health', *Marxism Today*, June.

Evans, Caroline and Thornton, Minna (1989) *Women and Fashion: A New Look*, London: Quartet.

Ferguson, Marjorie (1983) *Forever Feminine*, London: Heinemann.

Fiske, John (1987) *Television Culture*, London: Methuen.

Frazer, Elizabeth (1987) 'Teenage girls reading *Jackie*', *Media, Culture and Society* 9 (4), October.

Friedan, Betty (1965) *The Feminine Mystique*, Harmondsworth: Penguin.

Gray, Ann (1987) 'Reading the audience', *Screen* 28 (3).

Grieve, Mary (1964) *Millions Made My Story*, London: Gollancz.

Hall, Stuart (1972) 'The social eye of *Picture Post*', in *Working Papers in Cultural Studies* 2.

Hebdige, Dick (1987) 'The impossible object: towards a sociology of the sublime', *New Formations* 1 (Spring).

Hebdige, Dick (1988) 'The bottom line on Planet One: squaring up to *The Face*', in *Hiding in the Light*, London: Routledge.

Lee, Janet (1988) 'Care to join me in an upwardly mobile tango?', in Lorraine Gammon and Margaret Marshment (eds) *The Female Gaze: Women as Viewers of Popular Culture*, London: Women's Press.

Lyotard, Jean-François (1989) 'Complexity and the sublime', in L. Appignanesi (ed.) *Postmodernism: ICA Documents*, London: Institute of Contemporary Arts.

McRobbie, Angela (1988) 'You should be so lucky', *New Statesman and Society*, 9 September.

McRobbie, Angela (ed.) (1989) *Zoot Suits and Second-hand Dresses*, Basingstoke: Macmillan.

Morley, Dave (1980) *The Nationwide Audience: Structure and Decoding*, London: British Film Institute.

Mort, Frank (1988) 'Boys Own? Masculinity, style and popular culture', in Rowena Chapman and Jonathan Rutherford (eds) *Male Order: Unwrapping Masculinity*, London: Lawrence & Wishart.

Moore, Suzanne (1986) 'Permitted pleasures', *Women's Review* 10 (August).

Nava, Mica (1987) 'Consumerism and its contradictions', *Cultural Studies* 1 (2).

Miller, Daniel (1987) *Material Culture and Mass Consumption*, Oxford: Basil Blackwell.

Neustatter, Angela (1989) *Hyenas in Petticoats. A Look at Twenty Years of Feminism*, London: Harrap.

Partington, Angela (1989) 'The designer housewife in the 1950s', in Judy Attfield and Pat Kirkham (eds) *A View from the Interior*, London: Virago.

Pym, Barbara (1961) *No Fond Return of Love*, London: Jonathan Cape.

Radway, Janice (1984) *Reading the Romance*, London: Verso.
Roman, Leslie G. and Christian-Smith, Linda K. with Ellsworth, Elizabeth (1988) *Becoming Feminine: The Politics of Popular Culture*, London: Falmer Press.
Walkerdine, Valerie (1984) 'Some day my prince will come: young girls and the preparation for adolescent sexuality', in Angela McRobbie and Mica Nava (eds) *Gender and Generation*, Basingstoke: Macmillan.
White, Cynthia (1970) *Women's Magazines 1693-1968*, London: Michael Joseph.
White, David (1987) 'The women's market', *New Society*, 12 June.
Wilson, Elizabeth (1980) *Only Halfway to Paradise: Women in Postwar Britain: 1945-1968*, London: Tavistock.
Winship, Janice (1981) 'Woman becomes an "individual" - femininity and consumption in women's magazines 1954-69', Stencilled Paper no. 65, Centre for Contemporary Cultural Studies, University of Birmingham.
Winship, Janice (1984) 'Nation before family: *Woman*, the national home weekly, 1945-53', in *Formations of Nation and People*, London: Routledge & Kegan Paul.
Winship, Janice (1985) ' "A girl needs to get street-wise": magazines for the 1980s', *Feminist Review* 21 (Winter).
Winship, Janice (1987) *Inside Women's Magazines*, London: Pandora.
Winship, Janice (1990) 'Book 2 Women's magazines', PU712, *Women, Writing and Culture*, Milton Keynes: Open University Press.

Chapter 4

From the East End to *EastEnders*
Representations of the working class, 1890–1990

Kathryn Dodd and Philip Dodd

What kind of thing do you imagine when you are promised a film, TV drama or a book which deals with 'traditional' working-class experience? Have you been schooled to expect the world of the Hovis advert with unemployment thrown in: cobbled streets, hunched figures, northern accents, children in oversize cloth caps and a brass band playing somewhere in the distance? Perhaps you carry around gendered images, either of male working-class labourers, coal miners, ship builders, steel workers – or of the working-class housewife, beloved of northern comics, with or without teeth, on the doorstep in her pinafore, having a laugh with her neighbour. Or coming south, it may be the world of *Minder* or *EastEnders* that comes more immediately into focus: the labyrinthine street-world of east London, small-time crooks, cockney wit or 'er indoors.

What is the power of this repertoire of representations? Why is the working class so relentlessly discovered in the same places – up north and in the East End? Are there no working-class people worth representing in Suffolk or Somerset, in Leicestershire or Cornwall? One response to these questions is to show that the working class of, say, Orwell's *The Road to Wigan Pier*, or of the BBC's *EastEnders*, to take two classic representations, bear scant relationship to the actual working class of, respectively, Wigan in the 1930s or the East End in the 1990s. This demonstration 'proves' that the works do not reflect the 'real' working class, and are therefore to be condemned. The assumption hidden in this position is that works reflect the world beyond them, and ought to provide untroubled access to it.[1]

A related and more sophisticated response to this one relates the varying cultural representations of the working class to wider historical shifts when the working class was remade. Such an argument might note, for example, three historical moments in which the working class and the north became synonymous: the late nineteenth century, during which the north was associated with industry and the 'southlands' came to be associated with finance; the 1930s, when middle-class 'anthropological' writers and artists – such as Humphrey Spender, George Orwell, L. S. Lowry, as well as Mass Observation, identified the working class as unemployed and northern, flat capped and mufflered; and the 1950s, when a generation of northern writers, such as Richard Hoggart, David Storey and Stan Barstow, seemed in their own person to confirm the 'commonsense' that the working class belonged in the north.[2]

Clearly, there is profit to be had from this more sophisticated attempt to contextualize representations of the working class. But what the sophisticated shares with the crude sociological position is an extraordinary indifference to the writings, art, drama or films themselves. So eager is this argument to relate the works to a wider history that it pays no serious attention to the nature of the works themselves, how, in formal terms, they produce meaning. In his book, *Culture,* the late Raymond Williams compared the sociological and formal, acknowledging that the strength of the formalist position was precisely that it attended to what was specific about particular works – their forms and conventions – rather than reducing them, as is the tendency of the sociological position, to their conditions of production (Williams 1981: 138–9).

What is particularly disabling about this sociological position is that it assumes history is somehow outside the works by insisting that the works be brought into relationship with it, rather than recognizing, as we shall argue, that history is inscribed in the forms and conventions of the works themselves, and that forms and conventions of writing are primary evidence of larger social and historical relationships.[3] The stance of this essay, then, is to try to answer the question about the social meaning of representations of the working class, not by simply contextualizing the works, but by examining the conventions of the works themselves – describing the social meaning of these conventions, and how contemporary works make their meaning not by ignoring or transcending forms and conventions but by inflecting them in new directions.

In the following pages we draw on quite a wide range of
works, contemporary and historical, but pay substantial attention to two contemporary works: the BBC serial, *EastEnders* and
Pat Barker's award-winning novel, *Union Street*. The choice of a
television series and an acclaimed novel from a progressive
publisher, Virago, enables us in the short space available, to
discuss a work made *about* the class (*EastEnders*) and one, it is
claimed, made from *within* the class (*Union Street*).

In order to understand the representations of the 1980s, we
need to return to the crucial period when the working class was
made and remade in cultural terms: the late nineteenth century.
The nature and condition of the 'labouring classes', and particularly the poor, was a middle-class obsession throughout the
nineteenth century. Novelists such as Dickens spring to mind,
but there were also Royal Commissioners, Poor Law Inspectors,
Factory Inspectors and wealthy philanthropists who poured out
hundreds of reports and pamphlets which simultaneously made
the urban working class (by defining it) and then proceeded to
contain it within a middle-class politics.[4] It is crucial to remember that such representations are made by one dominant class of
another less powerful class, not only in fictional writings but in
this kind of 'documentary' writing too. Thus, across a large
range of mid-Victorian writing, we get a dominant cultural
representation of the working class taking shape: the working
class is seen as the 'other', and the middle-class observers rarely
disguise their horror at the way the lower classes lived and
worked. But towards the turn of the century there was a change in
the stance and in the representation, the reasons for which are
beyond our concern here. It was during this period, as Stedman
Jones has described, 'in London at least – that middle-class
observers began to realize that the working class was not simply
without culture or morality, but in fact possessed a culture of its
own' (Stedman Jones 1983: 183).

The study of the working class now took on epidemic propor-
tions as a new breed of investigators took to the streets. William
Booth of the Salvation Army, with his volume *In Darkest
England and the Way Out* (1890), and Charles Booth with his
seventeen-volume study of poverty in the East End, *Life and
Labour of the People in London* (1903), set the tone for what was
to follow. A whole band of reformers, sociologists, journalists
and writers began to construct a new, endlessly fascinating and

varied working class in texts that could vary from the statistical survey to sensational journalism, for a middle-class readership whom it was hoped would be receptive to the 'real' facts of a newly discovered working class. As Peter Keating has shown, the overriding metaphor was one of anthropological exploration into 'Darkest England', with intrepid adventurers reporting back on their voyages into unknown and alien cultures. Here is George R. Sims from *How the Poor Live and Horrible London* (1889):

> In these pages I promise to record the result of a journey into a region which lies at our own doors – into a dark continent that is within easy walking distance of the General Post Office . . . the wild races who inhabit it will, I trust, gain public sympathy as easily as those savage tribes for whose benefit the Missionary Society never cease to appeal for funds.
>
> (Quoted in Keating 1976: 65–6)

The aim of Sims and other explorers was sympathetically to expose the hidden lives of the labouring classes and so advertise their conditions to their unknowing and blind middle-class readership. But what this anthropological representation of the working class also succeeded in doing was to produce a sense of rigid class separation and difference. 'They' could never be 'us'. 'They' suffer, 'we' act to mitigate that suffering. Others were not so sympathetic. 'They' could also be a race apart, living in 'the abyss' and slowly degenerating.[5]

But from this moment, the working class would never be represented as merely an undifferentiated mass, characterized by the complete absence of middle-class values and standards of behaviour. The class was observed to have a 'lived' culture of its own, which in some ways exposed an over-sophisticated middle-class way of life. Charles Booth thought the 'simple natural lives' of the labouring classes 'tend to their own and their children's happiness more than the artificial complicated existence of the rich' (*Life and Labour of the People in London*, quoted in Keating 1976: 127).

Generally, however, the accounts were much more likely to be concerned with the laborious and exhausting lives of the working class. 'Labour here is laborious' as one observer, George Haws, noted (quoted in Keating 1973: 600). Working class comes to equal hard, physical labour and so, from this period, we get the elaboration of the distinction between the 'mental' and the 'manual' in terms of class distinction. (The *Oxford English Dictionary* notes a shift in the meanings of these words during the 1890s.) The strengths of the working class were inseparable from what they were constitutionally unsuited for: their skills were practical (not intellectual or rational), their nature decent and simple (not sophisticated or artificial), their proper sphere local (not metropolitan or national). What this did was to humanize, but also to fix and circumscribe working-class concerns and competence.

Subsequent representations have had to wrestle with this dominant version forged in the late nineteenth century. One example is perhaps the most famous commentary on the working class, or rather the one which continues to excite most controversy – George Orwell's *The Road to Wigan Pier* (1937).[6] In this work, styled as a 'documentary', Orwell casts himself as the middle-class outsider (15) who visits the industrial working class to report back to members of his own class what his explorations have revealed. Just like his earlier counterparts, Orwell mediates between the two classes, trying to impress on his own class that the work of the labouring class is equal to theirs. It will come as no surprise that the terms in which Orwell speaks are those from the earlier moment:

> They may be any age up to sixty or sixty-five, but when they are black and naked they all look alike. No one could do their work who had not a young man's body, and a figure fit for a guardsman at that; just a few pound of extra flesh on the waist-line, and the constant bending would be impossible. You can never forget that spectacle once you have seen it – the line of bowed, kneeling figures, sooty black all over, driving their huge shovels under the coal with stupendous force and speed.
>
> (21)

The working class in *The Road* is respected, but in terms which identify it as an essentially male community and keep it fixed at the level of the physical.

Now of course there may be those who say what else can one expect from a middle-class author? Just turn to writers from the working class and all will be transformed. Unfortunately, that is not always the case. Take the 1950s, when a whole generation of male working-class writers were hailed as authentic recorders of their class. Their contribution was to identify both an old, settled working-class community and its young rebels. Hoggart's *The Uses of Literacy* (1957) classically sets up this split. He invoked such a settled community in Hunslett, Leeds, that he remembered from his childhood in the 1930s and used it for his political purposes in the present: the denunciation of the 'shiny barbarism' of mass popular culture – TV, radio, popular music, coffee bars – which he felt corrupted working-class youth of the 1950s. The settled culture was seen by Hoggart as predominantly domestic, a domain presided over by 'our mam', the beacon in the kitchen, to whose warm presence the men and boys return. The general 'structure of feeling' that pervades the representation of class in *The Uses of Literacy* is one of warm directness, together with a fierce sense of the local and concrete, sustained at the expense of intellectual and 'bookish' pursuits (Hoggart 1958: 104–5).

The transition from Orwell to Hoggart may well signal a shift from a concern with the working class through the observation of men's paid work, to one constructed through domesticity and, more particularly, leisure.[7] But there is a more important continuity: the conviction that working-class life is, to use the words of Charles Booth quoted earlier, bounded by the local, and is 'free' from the 'artificial complicated existence of the rich'.

If for male middle-class writers (and documentary film-makers of the 1930s), this simple working class offered to them an image of 'physical' splendour to complement but not challenge their own 'mental' prowess, for the 'scholarship' working-class boys of the 1950s, the working class represented the community and fierce physical pleasures that were now denied to them as 'cissy'[8] writers who did not do 'real' men's work. In Alan Sillitoe's *Saturday Night and Sunday Morning* (1958), the protagonist is Arthur Seaton, the restless and unattached young man who rejects what he sees as the conforming values of his class (the daily grind of manual work, the narrowness of experience) and who aspires to a sense of personal, individual style. There are real differences between Sillitoe and Hoggart and Orwell: in Sillitoe, there is no bestowal of dignity on working-class manual labour, as there was in Orwell and the working-class family and community of Hoggart is seen with the jaundiced eye of a male rebel. But there is still the siting of working-class distinctiveness in physicality – in getting drunk, hooliganism, fighting and sexuality – even if, in the end, the rebel is led back into the community by Brenda, his bride-to-be.

The most obvious continuity between writing about working-class rebels in the 1950s and the representations of the 1980s is the Frank Clark/Chris Bernard film, *Letter to Brezhnev*: the only difference being that the protagonists, Eileen and Teresa, are young working-class *women* from Liverpool who swear more. Like *Saturday Night*, the film begins with the night exploits of the heroines, which include going out on the razzle, one dressed like Marilyn Monroe, pick-pocketing a punter, picking up two Russian sailors and spending the night with them in an hotel room. Sunday morning, as the earlier film makes explicit, brings the reawakening. Teresa's disgusting work at the 'Kirby Spring Chickens' factory is constantly alluded to – and seen as stifling her real potentialities, which find expression in her out-of-work pleasures. Only Eileen escapes by falling in love with one of the sailors and getting the Russian President Brezhnev, no less, to arrange her emigration in order to marry him. She is seen by the friend she leaves (and implicitly by the whole film), as lucky to escape the dead-end of working-class Liverpool. So what we get is gutsy working-class women having a good laugh and getting a bit of what they want – sex and/or love – if they are lucky. This film, like *Saturday Night and Sunday Morning*, cancels hope that working-class life as a whole can change, from the inside, for the better. Only exceptional individuals can struggle, and usually fail, to escape.

But can we look to any other contemporary work for a new representation of the working class? Certainly Pat Barker's novel *Union Street* (1982) has been acclaimed as a 'new' departure in the depiction of working-class characters. A 'long-overdue working-class masterpiece' is how one critic in the *New Statesman* reviewed it, and it has since won the Fawcett prize for fiction and been reprinted four times. But Barker's novel is still very much *about* the working class, not of it. The title, *Union Street*, geographically places the kind of working class that is about to be invoked: one that lives in terraced streets, which *ipso facto* means 'up north'. In case we are really slow, we are also given the name of the street – 'Union': simultaneously connecting community and manual work. So before we've even got to page one, we've got the picture. But have we? The novel is set 'at the heart of a northern English city' as the blurb tells us (incidentally, as we shall see, it is set not at its heart but in the genitals), and is about 'the grit, the humour, the reality of working-class life'. So far, so predictable.

But the protagonists of the novel, each given a separate chapter, are unexpectedly seven women, aged between eleven and seventy-odd, chronologically representing each 'age' of woman. Here in the range of individual, but interconnecting voices of working-class women, we are surely to find a challenge to previous, available, male-centred representations of working-class life? From the sexual attack on Kelly, the eleven-year-old, to the death of Alice on the park bench we are presented with a number of crises in these women's lives: unmarried and married motherhood, sorting out a teenage daughter's illegal abortion (and then burying the remains), making a living as an aged prostitute, and widowhood. Remarkably, Virago, the publishers, claim that the appeal of Barker's story is that it is a 'universal' one. It is instructive to imagine some of Virago's readers, with their nannies, cleaners and well-paid professional jobs, popping out to make a few bob on the side as streetwalkers, or contemplating their child's aborted foetus on the lavatory floor, and thus appreciating the universality of their night-time reading. Not only is the novel *not* humanistically universal (which only means in publisher-speak that it will appeal to you – the middle-class reader), it is highly specific in its traditional form of representing a working class of the imagination.

First, let's be clear about what representation Barker is rejecting. *Union Street* does not draw its female working-class iconography from the 1950s. Her heroines are neither rebellious nor part of Hoggart's community of hearth-loving, plump-armed matrons always ready with the tea. The range in the ages of her protagonists ensures that women in the novel are not frozen at some imagined 'homely' stage of evolution. Even when Barker does feature motherhood, it is the costs that are recorded as much as the pleasure. By giving a female point of view of working-class life (though the novel is narrated in the more objective third person, rather than the more subjective first person), Barker ensures, at least, that women are not mere onlookers, static unchanging features in a landscape in which only the male protagonist is on the move.

To find the proper antecedent of Barker's iconography it is necessary to reach back to our starting point. For what is striking about Barker's women is that they are fixed at the level of the physical and the manual in exactly the same way as the men were placed by the middle-class observers at the turn of the century. Her women are essentially people who exist through and suffer because of their biological, physical functions – sex, pregnancy, abortion, motherhood, ageing and death are the leitmotifs of female experience in the novel.

These working-class lives are seen at a sympathetic distance; Barker's stance, like the nineteenth-century sociologists, is that of the observer. We see 'Blonde Dinah' the prostitute, now in her sixties (appropriately named by her appearance, not her surname), through the eyes of her equally aged customer, George. What he experiences is a mouth and a 'cunt' which are apparently interchangeable:

> her voice came out warm and splutterly between badly fitting teeth . . . her hand went down between her legs and came up again. She smeared cunt juice all over his nose and mouth . . . 'Here, give us a lick'. She took him into her mouth . . . Almost against his will he knelt down until it [her cunt] was on a level with his face. The lips gaped, still dribbling a little milky fluid. And there it was. A gash? A wound? Red fruit bitten to the core? It was impossible to say what it was like.
>
> (Barker 1982: 226, 229, 230–1)

This is no new feminist breakthrough in the representation of working-class women, as the marketing by Virago would have us believe. Rather, the whole form of *Union Street* is drawn from extreme versions of nineteenth-century naturalism (the literary sibling of positivist sociology) which exposed in appalling detail the dirt, the squalor and the nauseous bodily functions of the deprived and the depraved. Not only do we have the same detached stance of the zoologist–observer examining her biological specimens, trapped in their environment, even as they heroically struggle to escape, we also get the concomitant obsession with animal analogies. Barker's obsession with women's mouths (Maureen Sullivan's 'teeth were missing so that the flesh was pleated over bare gums') is not new. 'One recurring symptom of middle-class anxiety', writes Gill Davies in an essay on the representation of working-class women in nineteenth-century naturalist fiction is 'a preoccupation with the mouth, both as a form of appetite and locus of speech' (Davies 1988: 69).

Barker is as sympathetic and as grimly fascinated by the working class as any nineteenth-century traveller into darkest England.

Let's take some of the many examples of Barker's zoological narrative stance. Kelly's mother sees her own 'ox-jawed and brutal' reflection (34). Joanne Wilson's workmate at the bakery factory is (black!) Bertha, who 'bull-like' attacks another woman by hitting her in the mouth (here it is again), her eyes 'bloodshot, giving her a look of bridled ferocity' (83). Kelly Brown looked as 'wild and unkempt as an ape, as savage as a wolf' (54). Iris King, the most resilient character in the novel, who, if male would have been a rebel/leader, instead is stoical and has 'the dull eyes and permanently grey skin of somebody who keeps going on cups of tea, cigarettes and adrenalin' (180). The description of the worst street in Barker's imaginative world, Wharfe Street, sums it all up. Its inhabitants, we are told, 'inhaled' their problems with the air as they breathed like passive dumb beasts (74). Not even suicide, crime and incest, we are led to believe, are due to the active initiative of these grey, downtrodden people. All they had to do was breathe in the virus of their environment to catch their disease of deprivation.

If *Union Street* is depressingly similar to nineteenth-century representations of working-class life, one of the most popular contemporary British soaps, the BBC's *EastEnders*, avoids being so reductive of working-class experience. Instead, it gathers up many of the constituent elements of the tradition described so far, but develops and inflects them in interesting directions. Certainly its current audience of twenty million viewers means that this dramatic representation of working-class life is familiar to a large proportion of the population, a process reinforced by the popular press. For example, Den Watts, the first publican of the *Queen Vic* pub who was murdered in 1989 by an East End criminal gang, became 'Dirty Den', to quote the *Sun* byline,[9] entered popular vocabulary as a synonym for a working-class jack-the-lad, both semi-criminal and lecherous, and so sustained the 1950s representation of a cynical but contained male rebelliousness.

If 'Dirty Den' is no more than a grown-up, and southern, Arthur Seaton, perhaps other elements of the serial might suggest something new in the way of representing working-class life. Both *EastEnders* and *Brookside* (another soap devised in the 1980s which has since become Channel 4's most popular

programme), while drawing on the format of the longest running television series, Granada's *Coronation Street,* have tried to
break from some of its characteristics, most notably its lack of
ethnic minority households, its preponderance of middle-aged
characters and its lack of discussion of 'social problems'
(Buckingham 1987: 15–16). Like the literary tradition we have
excavated, the writers and producers of *Coronation Street* have
constructed a closely bonded, intimate, working-class northern
community, anthropologically distinct and cut off from the
wider world. The anachronism of the series is caught in both the
word 'Coronation' in the title of the show (which suggests the
habitation of a class that is old, and rooted, and traditionally
loyal) and in the opening shot of the smoking chimneys over the
terraced rooftops.

Yet *EastEnders* appears to be equally anachronistic. The East
End that is featured on the map which opens and closes each
episode is no longer – if it ever was – a homogenous working-
class area, thanks to Docklands City Development and gentrifica-
tion. Yet a description written by Charles Booth about an East
End pub at the turn of the century could so easily call to mind
Angie Watts and the *Queen Vic*:

> perhaps half-a-dozen people, men and women chatting
> together over their beer. . . . Behind the bar will be a decent
> middle-aged woman, something above her customers in class,
> very neatly dressed, respecting herself and respected by them.
> The whole scene comfortable, quite and orderly.
>
> (Booth, quoted in Keating 1976: 129)

So, once more, working-class life is represented as communal,
close knit, locally based.

If community is one of the necessary ingredients for the
representation of working-class life, then the contribution of the
long-running television series to the tradition we have described
is the forging of strong, female working-class characters as a
counterweight to the more usual celebration of masculine
physicality and identification of the working class with that
masculinity. Again, if we take *Coronation Street* as the early
1960s model, it appears that strong, sexualized middle-aged
working-class women characters are one of the major reasons for
its abiding popularity. Elsie Tanner, one of the central characters
in the early years of the series, epitomized the kind of working-

class woman, a divorcee, that Terry Lovell isolates as a new kind of representation in post-war popular culture, a woman with 'experience and a degree of financial independence' who was as likely to 'work outside the home as well as within it'.[10] There are thus multiple representations of older working-class women, not only the desexualized 'shapeless lump' in a pinafore, but also those who are attractive and sexually aware. If Tanner was not quite the Sillitoe/Storey working-class rebel, she certainly had more in common with the pleasure-loving non-conformers than with Hoggart's 'mam at home' – and is hardly found at earlier moments in the tradition.

Both *EastEnders* and *Brookside* have confirmed and developed this new representation of women by presenting a number of such independent working women as central characters. Hardly a woman in *EastEnders* is a full-time housewife: their generally low-skilled jobs have included: barmaid, shop assistant, market stall and café owner, launderette attendant, hairdresser, doctor's receptionist, cleaner, primary school teacher and health visitor. Some of the women are single, others have young children, another group are in late middle age. All work, inside and outside the home.

The tradition of the glamorous working-class woman has also been sustained with characters such as Angie Watts, Kathy Beale (now a divorcee) and, most recently, Sharon Watts, Angie's adopted daughter and new licensee of the *Queen Vic*. None of the women in *EastEnders*, not even the oldest, Ethel, who at one point in the series was trying to attract an elderly boyfriend, is uninterested in her sexuality and none resembles the broken, or animal-like representations found in *Union Street*. Only one character, Pauline Fowler, whose function in the series is to represent the Hoggart-like remnants of the matriarchal, extended Beale family is presented as homely and domestic. But she is the exception, not the rule.

What we want to stress, however, in this discussion of *EastEnders* is the different ways in which the series has *extended* the scope of the popular soap and not merely aped tried formulae. As one recent critic has stated, some episodes, had they been presented as social-realist plays on BBC 2 in, say, the mid-1970s, would have received a BAFTA award. This is an accurate assessment of the quality of the writing and acting; when the character Arthur Fowler had a nervous breakdown spread over many weeks, general practitioners commented at the time that they had never seen the trauma and distress so brilliantly depicted. In terms of contemporary 'social problems' the series is every bit as hard-hitting as *Brookside* (which was supposed to be the brand leader in 'realism'). The series has explored such issues as unemployment, imprisonment, rape, drugs, alcoholism, attempted suicide, crime, murder, homosexuality, infidelity, divorce, AIDS, abortion, ageing and death. That these traumas can be absorbed in a format that foregrounds an integrated, self-contained community of relatives and neighbours is a credit to both the writers and the actors. Certainly *Coronation Street* rarely allowed such issues to intrude on its peace and quiet.

But perhaps the most important development that *EastEnders* has effected within the tradition, and it cannot be overestimated, is the depiction of the English working class as multi-ethnic. For the first time, Afro-Caribbean, Asian and Turkish-Cypriot households have been represented, not as transient visitors but as part of the community: an Asian Muslim household at one stage owned the local grocery, the Cypriots ran the café (at least to 1989) and, at the time of writing (October 1991), a middle-class Afro-Caribbean household has become the focus of a major plot-line, as the son, Clyde Tavernier, has been accused of murder by the only overt racist in the series, Nick Cotton.

What is striking about the representation of non-white characters is that they appear to be part of Albert Square's communal life. To take some examples: there have been two inter-ethnic marriages (though neither has survived); the Afro-Caribbean health visitor regularly visited and advised local people; the Asian household organized a neighbourhood wake after the death of two local people; and black Hatty Tavernier is working in a local catering business. However, this attempt at inclusion is the single clue to an understanding of why *EastEnders* is a development of an old form of representation of working-class life, rather than a creation of something new. The ethnic minority households are accepted as present in a working-class community but the black, white and Asian families remain culturally distinct. There is none of the hybridity between black – white cultures that recent films such as Isaac Julien's *Young Soul Rebels* have been trying to explore and identify through politics and music.[11]

So the working class of *EastEnders* is no longer a little white club, but a multi-ethnic club, whose boundary can never be as secure as that in *Coronation Street*. Hostile 'outsiders' in the form of criminal organizations, drug pushers, squatters, loan sharks, middle-class rapists, the police – constantly disrupt the fragile integration of the *EastEnders* which has then to be painfully re-established. What is being said in this process of representation is that camaraderie is still the means of keeping the working-class club going, but that its black and white members have to fight against the forces which constantly threaten it. This is why racism has to exist outside the club, not in it: the racist Nick Cotton, though sporadically *in* the community, is not *of* it and is routinely shunned or abused. The representation of the working class as community-oriented, but defensive, explains the semi-comic character of Nick's mother, Dot Cotton, the middle-aged evangelist-cum-launderette supervisor. Eagle-eyed, she patrols the Square, confronting evil and despair and asking those stricken by doubt to trust God, while simultaneously organizing the local Neighbourhood Watch scheme. Vigilance is all when outside forces of darkness threaten, which perhaps provides a reason for the enormous viewing figures for the programme over the Christmas and the New Year; *EastEnders* is the last representation of an English community which carries any contemporary conviction. The middle class has been looking for an authentic community for a hundred years; the working class for around the last thirty. *EastEnders* provides the last bastion of community in a fictional 'Walford' square.

From the 1890s to the 1990s is a long way, but it should be clear that history is not simply of the past, but a particular discourse to be struggled over in the present. The theoretical last word can be given to Raymond Williams. The truth of what he say is, we hope, confirmed in our argument above:

> It is necessary and wholly intellectually defensible to analyse serials and soap operas. Yet I do wonder about the courses where at least the teachers . . . have not themselves encountered the problems of the whole development of naturalist and realist drama, of social-problem drama, or of certain kinds of serial form in the nineteenth century; which are elements in the constitution of these precise contemporary forms, so that the tension between that social history of forms

and these forms in a contemporary situation, with their partly new and partly old content, partly new and partly old techniques, can be explored with weight on both sides.

(Williams 1989: 159)

The implications of Williams's argument, if taken seriously, would take us far beyond the scope of our essay – and would certainly go against the grain of one kind of orthodoxy in 'popular culture' work. That, to put it crudely, tries to establish, say, the legitimacy of work on television by separating it out from film and literature. Historically, an analogous example would be the way film slowly established its legitimacy by sliding out from under the shadow of the literary and claiming autonomy as a discrete area of study. As a strategy, this is perfectly understandable, but if both Williams's argument and our own historical connections are persuasive, it must be misguided. Perhaps Marx was wrong when he claimed that the dead generations weigh like a nightmare on the brains of the living, but what we have tried to suggest is that pretending they don't weigh at all is the surest way of being held and oppressed by them.

NOTES

1 Accounts of the limits of what is known as 'reflectionism' are legion: see, for example, Raymond Williams (1977: chap. 4).
2 See Alun Howkins (1986); Stephen Edwards (1986: 34–5); Stuart Laing (1986).
3 The theoretical underpinnings of this position can be found in Williams (1977), *passim*, where he develops his arguments about the materiality of writing.
4 Relevant works can be counted in the hundreds. Contributions include Gareth Stedman Jones (1983); Philip Corrigan and Derek Sayer (1985); F. S. Schwarzbach (1982: 61–84); Peter Keating (ed.) (1976).
5 The 'abyss' is one of the seminal metaphors of the 'Unknown England' tradition: see extracts from William Booth 'On the verge from the abyss' in *Darkest England and the Way Out* (1890), Jack London, *The People of the Abyss* (1903), C.F.G. Masterman, *From the Abyss* (1902), in Keating's anthology (1976: 167–73, 223–39, 240–56).
6 All subsequent references are to George Orwell, *The Road to Wigan Pier* (Penguin edition, Harmondsworth, 1962); first published by Victor Gollancz, London, 1937.
7 In the 1950s the sociologists' fascination with working-class work

did not disappear; see John Clarke *et al.* (1979: 13–40). The argument in this essay is less concerned with 1950s sociologists as with what we call, after a phrase in Hoggart's work, the point of view of 'the scholarship boy', someone born into the working class, but separated from it, either as a consequence of education or because of the occupation of writer.

8 The reference to 'cissy' is taken from Tony Harrison's poem, 'Me Tarzan', which is itself indebted to Hoggart's structure of feeling: see Hoggart (1991: 40). For a critical discussion of Harrison's poetry see Philip Dodd (1990: 17–28).

9 See David Buckingham (1987: 118). For a discussion of the unprecedented mediation of *EastEnders* by the press, see chap. 3.

10 Terry Lovell (1981: 52). See also the essays in the same volume (Richard Dyer *et al.*) by Marion Jordan: 'Realism and convention' (32) and 'Character types and the individual' (68–74).

11 For a discussion of Julien's film see Stuart Hall, Paul Gilroy and Homi Bhabha (1991: 17–20).

REFERENCES

Barker, Pat (1982) *Union Street*, London: Virago.

Buckingham, David (1987) *Public Secrets: EastEnders and Its Audience*, London: British Film Institute.

Clarke, John (1979) 'Sociology, cultural studies and the post-war working class', in John Clarke *et al.* (eds) *Working Class Culture: Studies in History and Theory*, London: Hutchinson.

Corrigan, Philip and Sayer, Derek (1985) *The Great Arch. English State Formation as Cultural Revolution*, Oxford: Basil Blackwell.

Davies, Gill (1988) 'Foreign bodies: images of the London working class at the end of the 19th century', *Literature and History* 14.

Dodd, Philip (1990) 'Lowryscapes: recent writing about the north', *Critical Quarterly* 32.

Dyer, Richard *et al.* (1981) *Coronation Street*, London: British Film Institute.

Edwards, Stephen (1986) 'Disastrous documents', *Exposure* 24.

Hall, Stuart, Gilroy, Paul and Bhabha, Homi (1991) 'Threatening pleasures', *Sight and Sound*, August.

Hoggart, Richard (1958) *The Uses of Literacy*, Harmondsworth: Penguin (first published in London by Chatto & Windus in 1957).

Hoggart, Richard (1991) 'In conversation with Tony Harrison', in Neil Astley (ed.) *Bloodaxe Critical Anthologies: Tony Harrison*, Newcastle upon Tyne: Bloodaxe Books.

Howkins, Alun (1986) 'The discovery of rural England', in Robert Colls and Philip Dodd (eds) *Englishness: Politics and Culture 1880–1920*, London: Croom Helm.

Keating, Peter (1973) 'Fact and fiction in the East End', in H. J. Dyos and Michael Wolff (eds) *The Victorian City: Images and Realities*, II, London: Routledge & Kegan Paul.

Keating, Peter (ed.) (1976) *Into Unknown England 1866-1913. Selections from the Social Explorers*, London: Fontana/Collins.

Laing, Stuart (1986) *Representations of the Working Class Life 1957-1964*, Basingstoke: Macmillan.

Lovell, Terry (1981) 'Ideology and *Coronation Street*', in Richard Dyer *et al.*, op. cit.

Orwell, George (1937) *The Road to Wigan Pier*, London: Gollancz.

Schwarzbach, F. S. (1982) ' "Terra incognita" - an image of the city in English literature, 1820-1855', in Philip Dodd (ed.) *The Art of Travel: Essays in Travel Writing*, London: Frank Cass.

Sillitoe, Alan (1958) *Saturday Night and Sunday Morning*, London: W. H. Allen.

Stedman Jones, Gareth (1983) 'Working-class culture and working-class politics in London, 1870-1900: notes on the remaking of a working class', in his *Languages of Class: Studies in English Working-Class History 1832-1982*, Cambridge: Cambridge University Press.

Williams, Raymond (1977) *Marxism and Literature*, Oxford: Oxford University Press.

Williams, Raymond (1981) *Culture*, London: Fontana.

Williams, Raymond (1989) *The Politics of Modernism*, ed. Tony Pinkey, London: Verso.

Chapter 5

British soaps in the 1980s

Christine Geraghty

Finally, a word of advice for *Coronation Street*. Forget the social action garbage with councillors and social services. Your research is totally up the spout. Besides, if we want to be depressed, we'll watch *EastEnders*.

(TV critic, *Evening Standard*[1])

Soap operas have always dealt with social issues although media critics have not always recognized it. Soaps have traditionally dealt with the fabric of personal relationships, setting up a network of gossip and support, conducted by women who were both the strongest characters in the programmes and their most faithful viewers. It was the drama of personal relationships within a homogenous community which was the hallmark of *Coronation Street*, establishing a sense of geographical place so strongly that it over-rode the boundaries of the family. *Coronation Street*, and *Crossroads* after it, placed a strong value on friendship between women as the bedrock for plots of romantic encounters, marital quarrels and everyday happenings. Routine such stories may have been, but they posed the question of how one's personal life was to be lived and gave endless opportunities to examine issues of fidelity, consistency, disappointment and personal choice which inevitably arise when love and friendship are put under such close examination.[2]

British soap operas in the 1980s, however, took up social issues in a more overt way and publicized their concern for social problems which represented more than the plight of individual characters and dealt with the public sphere rather than the personal. Elsie Tanner's love life was not an issue in this sense but gay relationships in *EastEnders* and *Brookside* were; Ena

Sharples's bad back was an opportunity for the Street community to rally round to help but Gordon's cold in *Brookside* was woven into the programme's long-term approach to the subject of HIV/ Aids. As the quotation from the *Evening Standard* illustrates, the new soaps were understood to be different from the old in their subjects ('social action garbage') and their effect on audiences ('if we want to be depressed'). Never had soap operas been so scrutinized, so subject to comment by pressure groups, experts and 'ordinary' viewers, concerned about how certain subjects are handled. Mary Whitehouse was not the only commentator to be worried about the effects of *EastEnders*.[3]

In the 1980s, then, British soaps became a matter of public debate and judgements about how they handled sensitive issues were continually being made, sometimes as a central point, sometimes as a casual remark in an interview dealing with something entirely different. In particular, the soaps were felt to have responsibility for how they dealt with the new issues. On *Right to Reply*, Channel 4's programme for viewers' comments, gay and lesbian viewers questioned the representation of gay men and lesbians in soaps, arguing that 'Many gay people find it hard to identify with any of the three gay characters currently seen in British soaps and since there is no such thing as a typical heterosexual or homosexual person, why are the gays in these series shown as bland and two-dimensional characters?'[4] The call here is for greater plausibility and a less precious acceptance of the reality of gay and lesbian sexuality. In *Nursing Times*, the magazine's 'Media Watch' page featured Carmel, then the health visitor in *EastEnders*, and remarked that she 'has come in for quite a bit of stick from HVA (Health Visitors Association) members who haven't felt that the character gives a good impression of their role'. Disappointment was expressed that the character 'has not developed in a way which promotes the role of the health visitor more positively' and Roma Iskander, who discussed the role with *EastEnders* scriptwriters on behalf of the HVA, remarked: 'Carmel isn't a positive image of a black woman or a health visitor,' (*Nursing Times* 84 (26):25). *Midweek*, a giveaway London magazine, interviewed a black London Labour local councillor, Merle Amory, about her political career; the interviewer reported that 'Merle loosens up more while speaking of her life away from politics. She is a fan of *EastEnders* ("I'm not ashamed to admit it!"), although she feels the rebellious side of

Kelvin's character has been played down: "In politics, when black people are seen to be achieving something that's received positively then people get a little scared." She also doesn't like the way Naima's character has become "the stereotypical hardened Asian businesswoman with a scheming cousin".' [5]

One doesn't have to be a soap opera scriptwriter to reel a little at the range of the comment and the scope of the demands. *EastEnders* was accused of raising the suicide rate when Angie attempted to overdose, *Brookside* of increasing anxiety about AIDS when Paul Collins, speaking as an anxious father and not an expert, gave wrong information about the HIV virus. But both *EastEnders* and *Brookside* have been quite overt about their commitment to social issues and the publicity aroused by their handling of some of these issues is presumably not unwelcome. Cynics might indeed describe the whole phenomenon of the socially realist soap as an exercise in increasing the audience and feeding the need of the tabloids for scandal. But in reflecting on popular culture in this period it is important to look more closely at the conflicting demands made of soaps as they set about their self-appointed task of reflecting the reality of Britain in the 1980s.

Much of the tension exemplified in the quotations above arises from a conflict between a desire to be positive about a particular issue and a commitment to credibility in terms of characters and setting. The HVA, it would appear, wanted Carmel to be a model health visitor, demonstrating a wide range of skills in a professional manner. The magazine article even suggested, tongue in cheek, that Carmel's various personal problems with family and clients served her right 'for moving into Albert Square in the first place. Health visitors be warned – don't live on your work patch.' But the credibility of Carmel's character in the soap depended on her being part of the life of the Square, regularly and unproblematically available as a source of advice and support in her professional capacity as well as the focus of interest in terms of her personal life. Quite clearly, the demands for a positive image for health visitors as a profession were less pressing than the necessity for the programme to be able to deploy Carmel as a soap opera character. Those making the programmes are quite clear that this is the way it must be. *EastEnders* and *Brookside* are besieged by a plethora of groups wanting space for their particular cause but not all can be accommodated. Julia Smith and Tony Holland, the originators of *EastEnders*, are clear that 'issues, like everything else in a realistic soap, must come naturally out of the characters and community' (Smith and Holland 1987: 204), and the writer John McCready argues that *Brookside* has to resist the 'constant pressure from social and political agencies who want this or that issue to be brought into the programme. If they had their way, *Brookside* would become nothing more than a documentary with a scouse accent' (Redmond 1987:11). The emphasis in both cases is on raising the issues naturally rather than adopting a heavily didactic or documentary approach.

But the dilemma is not always resolved so readily in favour of British soap opera's traditional mode of working through credible and engaging characters. Both *Brookside* and *EastEnders* have a commitment to dealing seriously with social problems and indeed to appealing to viewers who watch these soaps and not *Coronation Street* or *Neighbours* precisely because they attempt to deal with social issues in a positive way. This phenomenon is recognized by the programme-makers. Phil Redmond, *Brookside*'s creator and executive producer, argues that the appeal and impact of *Brookside* and *Grange Hill*, its school-based predecessor, 'are due to their relevancy – allowing most people to identify with the situations or characters – and their willingness to tackle so-called difficult subjects or social issues' (Redmond 1987:5). Tony Pearson suggests that *Brookside* appears to have a special appeal for viewers who 'appreciate a blend of serialized entertainment with the responsible handling of hard topical issues (ibid.: 111). And certainly, those working on the programmes themselves retain an avowed commitment to working on such terrain. Redmond goes on to say:

> As we look forward from 1987 towards the next five years, we must also reflect the changing view and in particular, the geographical and social shift in population and resources which has become categorized by the North–South divide. Similarly it must cover in a realistic and responsible way issues such as AIDS – something that was not even heard about when the programme started five years ago. The programme will have to explore these issues and reflect their development if it is to retain its reality and its relevance.
>
> (Redmond 1987:7)

Similarly, Julia Smith, *EastEnders*'s first producer, told David Buckingham, 'We decided to go for a realistic, fairly outspoken type of drama which could encompasss stories about homosexuals, rape, unemployment, racial prejudice, etc. in a believable context' (Buckingham 1987:16). Clearly, social issues are integral to the dramas and to the appeal they make to their audiences. It is hardly surprising, then, given the nature of these issues and the conflicting conventions of soap opera and realism that the handling of such material can become a somewhat fraught exercise.

Realism is a key concept for these new British soaps and is called on as a justification or a rationale for the world which they depict. The claim to reflect reality helps the producers to combat those who claim the 1980s soaps are too outspoken and brutal in what they show.[6] Lying behind the claim is an assumption of the nature of reality which has underpinned much TV drama. Conventions established through the history of British film-making as well as television demand a realism based on the representation of working-class life which speaks for and about a specific region. *Coronation Street*, first appearing at the same time as the new British films of the early 1960s such as *Saturday Night and Sunday Morning* and *A Kind of Loving*, spoke for the north in a new way on television and claimed an authenticity based on an unprecedented attention to the detail of working-class mores. *Brookside* and *EastEnders* picked up this task, the former speaking for Liverpool and Merseyside, the latter for the fast disappearing East End. But the British 1980s soaps promised more than *Coronation Street*. They were concerned not so much with what holds a community together but with what threatens to splinter or disrupt it. They were appealing not predominantly to women but to men and young people as well and they had to demonstrate that they were breaking new boundaries, moving away from the traditional soap territory of women's problems. The soaps of the 1980s claimed to appeal to a diverse audience and to deal realistically with difference and conflict; therein lay their appeal and their dilemma.

Before moving on to discuss how particular examples of issues of conflict and difference are dealt with in *EastEnders* and *Brookside*, it is worth noting that both soaps take the family as the basis of their structure. This may be a surprising assertion in the light of their apparent emphasis on family break-up and tensions. At face value, it would seem that the more traditional soaps, *Coronation Street, Crossroads* and *Emmerdale Farm*, are more reliant on family groupings for the organization of narrative and the creation of a coherent fictional world. In their different ways, however, the older soaps blurred family boundaries by emphasizing other sets of relationships. In *Crossroads*, the motel was deemed to create a family out of those who worked there, bringing them together at moments of crisis or celebration; Meg Mortimer wielded her matriarchal control well beyond the limits of her own small family. In *Coronation Street* the community, while modelled on the family, contained within it a surprising number of individuals who had no family of their own; in the 1970s and early 1980s, there were very few children or even married couples in the Street and the cast was dominated by middle-aged women who lived on their own. It was the community which sustained these individuals and ensured that despite the lack of family relationships no one was without support.[7]

Brookside and *EastEnders* specifically turned their back on what were seen to be nostalgic notions of neighbours turning to each other for help. In *Brookside*, the Close was divided on class lines and it was rare for the boundaries to be breached. When Jonathan held a party for his yuppie friends, the young Corkhills, far from joining in, held their mocking parody of the event in the garden next door, the garden fence marking a symbolic as well as a literal boundary. In *EastEnders*, the notion of community was certainly invoked but it was not always seen to be effective; it belonged to the 'good old days' about which the older women reminisce but whose very existence is questioned by the younger characters. The notion of the community was thus rendered problematic and a vacuum left in *Brookside* and *EastEnders* which had to be filled; somewhat ironically, it was the family which emerged as the model.

The loss of the community as a practical force and a sustaining ideal drove characters back into family relationships at key moments in the narrative. Certain ideals were set up in both *EastEnders* and *Brookside* which centred on a white, working-class family offering each other support and reassurance in the face of the harsh reality of unemployment and financial crisis. In *Brookside*, this model was initially represented by the Grant family and subsequently by the Rogers family; in *EastEnders*, this role was undertaken by the Beale/Fowler extended family. In each case, there were clearly tensions within the family, struggles over male and female roles, arguments over the adolescents' attempts to escape the overclose family embrace, disagreements over priorities and loyalties. Despite this, in both programmes, characters aspired to a notion of family unity and harmony even if it was rarely achieved and support from members of the family was looked for although not always found. Moments of happiness or sorrow were marked by the coming together of the family, the return of those who had strayed and the momentary suspension of rivalry and tension. Even when such moments do not actually occur they are consciously sought. Christmas in these soaps offers a good example of this. Christmas was nearly always marked in the programmes by a series of disagreements over how the celebrations should be organized, who should spend time with whom and what was appropriate behaviour on the Day. But it was always quite clear what ideal lay behind the pressures to have a proper family Christmas and the arguments tended to be about how that could be achieved rather than the desirability of the ideal itself. The audience was thus invited to identify with these families and to see their struggles towards family unity as a realistic reflection of the difficulties which face families in the audience.

This model of an imperfect family working towards an harmonious ideal has important consequences for the way in which the 1980s issues identified by the programme-makers have been dealt with. The notion of model families at the heart of the soaps implied the existence of deviants from that model. These deviants divided into two groups – those who could be part of the family but have chosen not to be and those who never can be. Into the first group fall those whose behaviour has pushed them out of the family structure or who have rebelled against some of its restrictions. In *Brookside*, Bobby Grant, for a long time central to the Grant family, in the end broke it up by his refusal to accept the changes that were occuring in it – the growing independence of his wife, Sheila, and the death of his son, Damon. On a less momentous level, Sam Rogers' interest in green politics caused her parents concern when it took her out into the public world of demonstrations and action. In *EastEnders*, both Mark and Michelle Fowler have had to fight for their independence against their mother's demands in the same way that Arthur Fowler had to assert himself, somewhat fruitlessly, in the face of his mother-in-law's inperious assumption of control. In these cases, conflict could be expressed within the family and resolution of differences could be achieved, however tenuously, within the family model.

The other group raised problems for the programmes because they were much more difficult to accommodate within the family. The white working-class family, however extended and open, does not readily or realistically (in the programmes' terms) accommodate black people or lesbians and gay men, for instance, and yet their presence was essential to the programmes' claims to deal with current social issues. These characters thus hovered on the fringes of the central families, sometimes allowed in to observe the drama, but never quite part of the action. Their treatment tended to be exemplary rather than passionate and they represented problems to the audience rather than demanding identification. This can be seen in the handling of gay men and black characters in *EastEnders*. Colin, the main gay character in *EastEnders*, was warmly treated by the Fowler/Beale family who offered him sympathy but not a sense of belonging. Neither Colin nor his erstwhile lover Barry were seen in the context of their own families and they thus lacked a crucial dimension in the programme's own terms. Queenie, the gay man Den met in prison, was completely outside the family and specifically presented as bizarre and deviant. The treatment of black characters in *EastEnders* also proved problematic in the 1980s; none of the black families rivalled the Fowler/Beale position at the heart of the programme's structure and black characters have been pushed to the margins of the story-lines. Carmel and Darren clearly had an extended family along the lines of the Beale/Fowler nexus but its other members were rarely seen. Kelvin Carpenter hung around with Ian, Michelle and Sharon but his personal life, outside his relations with his father, received little attention compared with the others. Darren operated on the fringes of the criminal world to which Den was central and the treatment of Naima was sketchy compared with that given to the white female characters. It seems indicative that *EastEnders*, during this period, should get rid of certain black characters, including Naima and Tony Carpenter, by sending them 'home' to Bangladesh and Trinidad, as if they had never been at home in the square.

In *Brookside*, similar problems have been experienced in the representation of gay and black characters. Gay characters were represented through Gordon Collins and his lover Chris but the programme made no attempt to place them in the context of the gay community and they moved somewhat uneasily in and out of the Collins's family home. *Brookside* did attempt a lesbian character but only in the context of the break-up of a family, since she was the former wife of Heather Haversham's second husband, Nick. *Brookside* did not, during this period, have a black family and its black characters appeared on the margins of the programme. Isolated black characters like Jonah, Kate and latterly Nisha therefore had to represent the issues of race which the programme aspired to accommodate.

This emphasis on the family as a supportive structure and the difference betwen deviant or troublesome characters within the family and those outside it helps to explain why certain issues are taken up in the way in which they are. In soaps, problems are attached to or worked through with particular characters and the handling of a specific issue depends very much on the way in which that character has already been established. Some social issues can be taken up through a character in one of the established families and derive much of their impact from that setting. In 1986/7, for instance, Arthur Fowler went through a traumatic period of redundancy, unemployment and debt which led to a mental breakdown and a prison sentence for stealing. Clearly Arthur was being used by the programme to exemplify the pressures and problems which were facing the four million people then unemployed and to draw drama out of a national issue. One trade union newspaper commented that, through Arthur's plight, '*EastEnders* has brought the evils of unemployment to people's attention'.[8] Sympathy was demanded for Arthur himself, particularly in the moving scenes when he could no longer cope mentally with his situation, but the strains on his family were also carefully drawn out. Arthur's character was already known to the audience before this particular series of events and the story developed gradually out of Arthur's position in the programme (he was unemployed when the serial began). In other words, this was a classic example of Julia Smith and Tony Holland's dictum that issues must arise naturally from character and the story fitted well into the soaps' ethos of the family pulling through.

Brookside too dealt with unemployment in the 1980s through an emphasis on its consequences for the family. In the main, unemployment was seen to be a male problem. Women like Sheila Grant, Doreen Corkhill and Chris Rogers had part-time work outside the home, but it very rarely impinged on their stories. The shattering and debilitating effects of unemployment were presented through male characters such as Damon Grant, Billy Corkhill and Terry Sullivan. For Billy, like Arthur Fowler, unemployment threatened his standing in the home, eating away at his pride and sense of usefulness so that his energy turned into violence which was painfully and searingly redirected against his wife and children. For Damon and Terry, unemployment condemned them to be 'one of the lads' with an eye out for a quick buck; it trapped them into dead-end jobs with no hope and prevented them from establishing their own families. Bobby Grant blamed unemployment for his son's demise and his assessment had a symbolic aptness since it was Damon's move out of the protection of the family to look for work which led him to his death.

But other issues fitted more problematically into the structure provided by the family model. The stories about Gordon Collins in *Brookside* provided an interesting example of the soaps' drive to solve problems if at all possible within rather than outside the family. Gordon had been in *Brookside* from the start and had, as it were, a pre-gay existence and a role in the Collins's family. His coming out as gay caused his parents, and particularly his right-wing father, much anguish and his lover Chris was not a popular figure within the home. Indeed, Paul Collins's intolerance provided Gordon and Chris with the opportunity to lecture him (and the audience) about their right to lead their own lives as a gay couple without interference or condemnation. The programme addressed some of the difficulties faced by gay men such as 'queer bashing' and put Gordon through an HIV test. It is striking, however, not only that Gordon consistently returned home (a move demanded by the soap convention that the programme is organized around the houses in the Close) but in times of crisis was able to turn to his parents and particularly his father for support. Thus, when Chris and Gordon were beaten up and arrested outside a gay club, it was Paul Collins who got up in the middle of the night to get them out. He stood by them in the subsequent feud when the attack by the gang was significantly made not merely on Chris and Gordon but on the family home. It was Paul, also, to whom Gordon turned when he decided to have the HIV test; during the tense period of wating Paul tried to reassure him about the outcome and anxiously watched over his health. There was no indication that Gordon had other gay friends to turn to for reassurance and there was little reference to more organized gay support systems such as Gay Switchboard or the Terence Higgins Trust. During this story, *Brookside* realistically represented the panicky and uncertain attitudes of many parents faced with a gay son and it could be argued that Paul Collins's defence of Gordon was a positive and exemplary approach within a family setting. But the representation was unlikely to satisfy those in its audience who were looking for a positive representation of the gay community or for a hint that gay politics could challenge the ideology of the family rather than be incorporated within it.

Given this framework, it is hardly surprising that both *EastEnders* and *Brookside* found HIV/AIDS a very difficult issue to deal with as information on the syndrome developed in the 1980s. It was, of course, a subject which they were expected to take on precisely because of their self-proclaimed stance of dealing with social issues. But positive images were difficult to develop given the prevailing metaphors of plague and punishment and the soaps' approach has been a cautious one. Both *EastEnders* and *Brookside* were careful to avoid AIDS being automatically linked to gay characters. *Brookside*, for instance, had a relatively self-contained story in which Bobby Grant had to deal with a union member with AIDS who was being ostracized by his own workmates as well as being discriminated against by his employers. Again, the issue was directly brought into the family and was presented through the reactions of Sheila, who was fearful for her child's safety but was seen to work through her own prejudices and come to terms with her irrational fears. Like Paul Collins, in his dealings with Gordon, Sheila's position was offered to the audience as representative of the way in which ignorance and fear can be overcome. *EastEnders* also ran a story in which one of Den's fellow-prisoners was identified as being HIV positive, and had to cope not only with his own fears but those of his wife. As with the *Brookside* example, however, this was a relatively self-contained story and the prisoner was not one of the serial's long-running characters. In both cases, AIDS as an issue for heterosexuals was dealt with through characters who appeared to have been brought into the programmes specifically for that purpose.

So far as the gay characters were concerned AIDS during this period was an issue which could not be ignored but was never confronted. Colin in *EastEnders* talked of the death of friends but they were in the United States. Chris in *Brookside* lent his flat to a friend who was dying of an AIDS-related illness but this was something of a plot device, forcing Gordon and Chris back into the family home, and the opportunity to show the experience of care and bereavement was not picked up. Instead, AIDS tended to be used as a suspense element when any one of the gay characters was ill. Thus, Barry, Colin, Chris and Gordon were all suspected of 'having' AIDS and the audience was invited to share a period of anxious waiting with them while they went through the test. During this period, the 'all clear' verdicts relieved the programmes of having to pick the issue up more seriously.[9]

If it is difficult to fit gay issues into the model of the white, working-class family which underpins the soap structure, it is impossible for it to accommodate issues around race. Black characters cannot fit into the model and all too often during the 1980s their differences were presented as deviances. One clear example of how this occurred, despite the programmes' good intentions, was offered by the stories in which both *Brookside* and *EastEnders* featured the problems of Asian schoolgirls. In many ways, this was an ideal social problem for the 1980s soaps. It combined issues of race with stories about the relationships between parents and children, an element which has featured strongly in both *EastEnders* and *Brookside*, with sympathetic emphasis on the adolescents' point of view. In *Brookside*, Nisha was introduced into the programme through her schoolgirl friendship with Sammy, the elder daughter of the Rogers family. She and Sammy both had part-time jobs in the local supermarket and Nisha gradually let slip the difficulties she faced in dealing with her parents, the restrictions they placed on her social life and the work they demanded of her in contributing to the family business. The pattern which emerged was one of the normal, white girl getting ready to enter the world with the loving if anxious support of her parents and of the deprived Asian girl whose unseen parents were behaving unreasonably and whose life deviated unsatisfactorily from the British norm. Nisha thus followed the *Brookside* tradition during this period of using a single black character as a focus for a particular set of problems without making them central to the programme as a whole, and it set up the black family in this story as being different from and less supportive than its white counterpart.

EastEnders fell into corresponding difficulties in its handling of a similar story. As is usual in *EastEnders*, the narrative was much more highly compressed than in *Brookside* and the melodramatic speed with which the plot moved forced the issues into the open very quickly. The Indian family in the Square took over the running of the corner shop but did not feature as a family in any of the stories – and so the audience had no sense of their characters before the issue of the Asian daughter began to emerge. Shireen, the teenage daughter, began a relationship with a white boy, Rick, and as in *Brookside* the restrictions placed on her were emphasized so that while the programme was careful to show that Shireen loved her parents and did not want to hurt them the impression given was of an unusual and undesirable way of life. Any sympathy that might be felt for the Asian parents' view that white teenagers were too wild and free was undermined by the father's commitment to the concept of an arranged marriage and his determination to arrange one for the schoolgirl Shireen as soon as possible. An arranged marriage was thus presented in the worst possible light, as alien to the values of the white families and as a punishment for Shireen for her relationship with Rick. The representation of Mr Kamir's genuine concern for his daughter was finally destroyed for the audience by his outrageous demands that Dr Legge test his daughter to establish that she was still a virgin and the doctor's response that no doctor in the country could do such a test underlined the deviancy of the father's request. The audience was thus drawn to Shireen's distress and to her demand that she be treated as a person in her own right, not as an object to be manipulated at her father's will. As with Nisha in *Brookside*, the parents were presented as abusing their daughter by refusing to adopt an approach more in tune with British mores.

The *EastEnders* example is a particularly interesting one because of the programme's genuine efforts to include a much wider range of black characters than is usual on British television. Shireen's story provides an example of how the conventions of 1980s soap opera, a particular use of social problems for realistic purposes and a demand that black characters be treated positively, can clash in a way that undermines the black family. The Kamir family were not well established in soap opera terms; unlike the Beales, they had not been known to viewers over a number of years and the audience was given little access to the internal discussions within the family. Mr Kamir could claim little credibility with the audience before the story started and what he had was lost almost immediately through his extreme attitudes. The mother was seen to be subservient to her husband in a way that was in line with the programme's 'realistic' attempt to present traditional attitudes within the Kamir family but out of tune with the normal emphasis in soaps on a strong matriarchal presence in the family, thereby once again calling attention to the Kamir family's difference from the norm. Intellectually, the programme went to considerable lengths to present positively Mr Kamir's determination to maintain his own culture. He pointed out forcibly to Dr Legge that the isolation of the immigrant community was not a matter of choice but a means of protection in the face of the hostility of the white community; even Frank Butcher, Rick's father, was given a speech in which he pointed out that arranged marriages might have a better chance of success than western marriages based on romance. Emotionally, though, we were asked to identify with Shireen's rejection of her father's values and her desire to be more integrated into the life of her friends. In presenting Shireen positively, the programme did scant justice to the Kamir family as a whole and invited the audience to make its judgements from the point of view of a white family.

The structural deviancy of gay and black characters, illustrated by these examples, is a particular problem for the 1980s soaps given their proclaimed intention of treating social issues positively. Indeed, lying behind the dilemma which gay and black characters pose for soaps is the demand that they be at the same time realistic, representative and positive. By their very isolation, Colin and Gordon 'stood for' homosexuality in Britain in a way that was never demanded of the heterosexual characters. A bad, boring or bland gay character is dissatisfying to gay people precisely because they find it difficult to identify with them, but no-one is concerned if they cannot identify with Pete Beale or Paul Collins. Heterosexual problems are presented across a whole range of characters; those of gays through only one or two per soap.[10] Similarly, black characters, because of their limited

numbers on British TV, run the risk of being read as representative, as standing for the black community as a whole, in a way in
which white characters do not. The likelihood of this happening
is increased because in the soaps 'ethnic minorities' are
represented by one or two characters and are presented in
isolation; we did not see the Turkish Ali's mother and father in
the way in which we know generations of the Beale/Fowler
family; we did not know the Kamir family home in the intimate
way we know Pauline's. The representative nature of the black
characters causes particular tensions when the realism on which
the programme-makers pride themselves comes up against
notions of a positive image. Realism may demand a recognition
that 'bad' black characters exist and thus black Darren was set up
as a counterpoint to the white Dirty Den, but it is all too easy for
a character like Darren to be read as representing all young black
males as skiving, irresponsible and up to no good. Realism may
also demand that black characters are represented in recognizable
and familiar situations but such a strategy again runs the risk of
reinforcing rather than challenging stereotypes. Thus, Naima
and the Kamir family ran the corner shop, inviting criticism that
EastEnders has fallen into the trap of automatically associating
the Asian community with shopkeeping and acquisitiveness.
David Buckingham argues that 'The crucial question is not
whether *EastEnders*'s black characters are "realistic" but how the
serial invites its viewers to make sense of questions of ethnicity –
and in particular, how it defines ethnic difference and inequality
or racism' (Buckingham 1987:102), and he is right to try and
move the argument away from questions of accuracy. Nevertheless, it is important to recognize that it is precisely because of the
contradictory claims of realism and representativeness that problems arose over the way in which the 1980s British soaps
presented their black characters.

Soaps have traditionally been explained through gender; the
implied audience has been a female one and the position from
which the programmes were best enjoyed and understood was
that of the female viewer. As we have seen, *Brookside* and
EastEnders have sought a more diverse audience that includes
other members of the family and the strategy for doing so has
been to use the family itself as model. Traditionally, also, soaps
defined their communities narrowly, concentrating on women,
and presenting them as the principal source of support and

understanding. The newer soaps introduced a wider range of characters and with them new sets of problems but at their heart, as a structure for dealing with these problems, was the white working-class family. The handling of these new problems depended on how far they could be accommodated within the family and those characters placed outside it by sexuality or race in particular were, however sympathetically or positively treated, likely to be understood by the audience as being troublesome and deviant. The movement of such characters during this period tended to be centrifugal, moving always towards the margins until, like Tony, Naima or Chris, they are finally 'expelled' or, like the Kamirs, they are hauled back into focus by a spotlight which serves only to emphasize their differences.

In some ways, the new soaps got into a double bind over the representation of the social issues which became their hallmark. On the one hand, if their gay or black characters were integrated into the soap community, treated positively and became familiar and well loved, the soaps were likely to be accused of presenting a utopia of positive images in which the implications of sexual and racial difference were ignored; on the other hand, if gay and black characters were treated as different, the soaps stood to be accused of marginalizing them, of making them exceptional and placing them outside the norm. These problems were not only or even primarily caused by the intentions of the programme-makers and in many ways 1980s soaps deserve credit for attempting to address dramatically contemporary issues to huge audiences. But the conflicting pressures of soap opera conventions, social realism and the representative nature of key characters need to be better acknowledged by both the programme-makers and their critics if the implications of the claim to represent the cultural diversity of contemporary Britain are to be understood.

NOTES

1 Jaci Stephen in her TV column, 'Review', *Evening Standard*, London, 29 December 1988.
2 For influential accounts of the relationship between women viewers and soap operas see Charlotte Brunsdon (1981) and Tania Modleski (1982). For comments on the change in the intended audience for 1980s soaps and its effects for the woman viewer see Christine Geraghty (1991).
3 Peter Dawson of the Professional Association of Teachers, for

instance, spoke of *EastEnders* as 'evil' and warned that 'the whole nation is drugged by *EastEnders*' (*Guardian*, 2 August 1989).

4 These dissatisfactions were voiced by viewer Tony Gregory on *Right to Reply*, Channel 4, 4 June 1988. Andy Medhurst's views, also expressed on that programme, gave considerable impetus to this article and I acknowledge my debt to him.

5 Quoted in an interview with Pete May in *Midweek*, 23 April 1987:10.

6 David Buckingham offers an interesting account of the kind of criticism made of *EastEnders*, in particular by one such critic, Mary Whitehouse (Buckingham 1987:146–52).

7 For an analysis of *Coronation Street*'s invocation of community see the essays in Richard Dyer (ed.) (1981).

8 Mary Maguire in an interview with the actor Bill Treacher (who plays Arthur Fowler) in *Public Service*, NALGO, May 1987:5.

9 It was not until 1991 that a regular character, Mark Fowler in *EastEnders*, appeared with HIV contracted through heterosexual sex. Many of Mark's subsequent problems have been generated by his family's response to this news.

10 It is perhaps worth noting the disappearance of the regular gay characters from these programmes. However flawed, the attempt now looks a brave one.

REFERENCES

Brunsdon, Charlotte (1981) '*Crossroads*: notes on soap opera', *Screen* 22(4).

Buckingham, David (1987) *Public Secrets*, London: British Film Institute.

Dyer, Richard (ed.) (1981) *Coronation Street*, TV Monograph 13, London: British Film Institute.

Geraghty, Christine (1991) *Women and Soap Opera*, Oxford: Polity Press/Basil Blackwell.

Modleski, Tania (1982) *Loving with a Vengeance*, London: Methuen.

Nursing Times 84(26), 29 June.

Redmond, Phil (1987) *Phil Redmond's Brookside: The Official Companion*, London: Weidenfeld & Nicolson.

Smith, Julia and Holland, Tony (1987) *EastEnders: The Inside Story*, London: BBC Books.

Chapter 6

'One I made earlier'
Media, popular culture and the politics of childhood

Stephen Wagg

He had an aristocratic way with a commonplace. A long and fractious discussion concerning child development theory had been brought to a useful standstill by his weighty intervention – 'Boys will be boys'. That children were averse to soap and water, quick to learn and grew up all too fast were offered up similarly as difficult axioms. Parmenter's banality was disdainful, fearless in proclaiming a man too important, too intact, to care how stupid he sounded.

(Ian McEwan, *The Child in Time*)

Childhood often seemed a pain to me
So hard, waiting to be grown
Childhood climbed up in a wide oak tree
I blinked once and it was gone.

(Steve Forbert 'I Blinked Once')

Look, I know this sounds a bit *Blue Peter*-ish, but it's actually quite sensible. Don't take risks with fireworks. OK?

(Radio 1 disc jockey)

A few moments on a recent Saturday morning, 15 June 1991, encapsulate much of what I want to discuss in this essay. It's around ten o'clock. BBC 1 is showing *The 8.15 From Manchester,* a magazine programme aimed primarily at children and the young and, in terms of its format and content, not unlike a dozen others on various television channels. The presenter of the programme, Ross King, is doing what presenters of such programmes quite often do: he is talking to someone from another TV programme about what it's like to be in that TV programme, and others. In this case it is Jonathan Morris, an actor in the TV comedy series *Bread*. And, muses King, hasn't Jonathan also, like himself, been a children's TV presenter? Yes, replies Morris:

> It was something I always wanted to do – presenting. But it was always adult programmes. I wanted to work with children. With them, not against them. Only I don't call them children. I call them adults. I loathe the word 'children'.

This comment, however unknowingly, poses the important question of how British television addresses children. What assumptions do British programme-makers have about the nature of children, how have these assumptions changed, and how are they expressed in the content of children's television? Morris's remark, and indeed the whole context of it, would have been unthinkable thirty years ago, so apparently stable and well defined were the working notions of childhood and the child that broadcasters had then. Today these notions, while less stable and less well defined, are observably different, as Morris implies. So I want to examine this change historically and, in doing this, I will concentrate on the *magazine* programme, typified in many or most people's minds by the BBC's *Blue Peter*. This in turn will be related to the politics of childhood – that is, to ideas of what children *are* and of what they *should be*. Central to this, and clearly interlinked, are arguments about the impressionability, vulnerability, activeness and passivity of children.

I want to stress two things at the outset. First, the fact that I am concentrating here on the *production* of children's television does not mean that I regard questions of how this television is *consumed* as unimportant. I do not: it's simply a matter of focusing, in this instance, on what is prescribed for children. Second, following on from this, I recognize – and research since the 1950s has shown – that children often prefer to watch 'adult' programmes than programmes specifically designated for them. Indeed, this recognition forms part of my argument.

THINKING OF THE CHILDREN: SOME PREFATORY REMARKS ABOUT CHILDHOOD

It is now over thirty years since the publication of Philippe Aries's hugely influential *Centuries of Childhood* (Aries 1962/1973). This book established that childhood was a social construction, relative to particular cultures and historical epochs.

Few informed observers now doubt that 'children' in any given society are what that society has helped to make them.

In the western context, the fundaments of modern childhood were devised and propagated by Jesuit theologians in the Catholic church between the fifteenth and seventeenth centuries. Central to this development was a transition from 'immodesty to innocence' (Aries 1973: chap.5). Immodesty had meant, among other things, a close acquaintance on the part of the very young with matters of sex and violence. That's to say, the dealings, both verbal and physical, that very young people had had with adults had invariably been sexually explicit and that children, particularly male ones, participated in the bearing and use of arms. The 'innocence' that replaced this 'immodesty' in western societies has always been associated with *vulnerability* to dark forces – the nature of which (sin, crime, communism . . .) has varied according to time, place and political formulation. In recent times, and most especially this century, these dark forces have been thought by many to emanate from popular entertainment and the mass media (Murdock and McCron 1978). The argument is a familiar one, re-run in innumerable different contexts, and it rests on broadly the same assumptions as behaviourist psychology: through witnessing, via the mass media, the portrayal of some malign activity (related invariably to sex and/or violence) the child will assuredly be moved to imitate it. The conceptualization of the child as a passive receptacle, and the accompanying clamour for standards, decency, censorship and so on, are usually associated with the political right, but historically these assumptions and arguments have been embraced by important sections of the left: Martin Barker, for example, has documented the role of the British Communist Party in the campaign to ban American horror comics in Britain in the 1950s, on the ground that they were a pernicious influence on the nation's children (Barker 1984).

There was also wide political consensus around the prescribed antidote to these dangers: passive and vulnerable creatures should be exhorted to *activity*, because the devil made work for idle hands. Again, in this context, one thinks primarily of the political right: the imperialist Robert Baden-Powell, for example, in founding the Boy Scout movement, defined a scout as one who 'looks down upon a silly youth who talks dirt, and he does not let himself give way to temptation either to talk it or to think, or do anything dirty' (Baden-Powell 1908: xiii) and instead dedicates himself to the acquisition of a range of outdoor skills: stalking animals, lighting camp fires and so on. But the left developed parallel organizations, such as the Woodcraft Folk, which, while dissenting in particular from the royalist and religious values of the Boy Scout movement, nevertheless expressed the same belief in the improving nature of *activity* for the children involved. Likewise, it has always been a central axiom of anarchist educational philosophy that the only effective way that children can learn is through *doing*.

I'd like now to consider this paradigm of the improving nature of activity in relation to the development of broadcasting, which, in the British case, means looking at assumptions made at the BBC in the 1920s and 1930s about the child.

HULLO CHILDREN, THIS IS AUNTIE

From its inception, BBC culture was, according to Tom Burns, 'not peculiar to itself but to an intellectual ambience composed out of the values, standards and beliefs of the professional middle-class, especially that part educated at Oxford and Cambridge' (Burns 1977: 42). This culture was personified by the BBC's first Director-General, Sir John Reith. Reith and the early British broadcasters were aware that, in a culture stressing the improving nature of activity, broadcasting – radio, in the first instance – carried the potential for a dangerous passivity:

> The central Reithian principle was that the wireless listener should be treated as active rather than passive, and the recurring BBC distinction between 'serious' and 'tap' listening was applied in particularly pressing terms to entertainment programmes precisely because their staple content, light music, was so obviously liable to 'passive consumption'.
>
> (Frith 1988: 28)

Reith's BBC strove to create the ambience of the middle-class home – what Frith calls the 'radio hearth' – within which children were accorded a place of their own: a programme called *Children's Hour* (Frith 1988: 32).

'For the children', wrote Derek McCulloch, Head of Children's Broadcasting at the BBC between 1933 and 1951, 'nothing is too good' (quoted in Briggs 1981: 92). This helps to illustrate the prevailing notions of childhood at the pre-war BBC. Children were conceived of as a separate species, and one that should be protected. In 1937, for example, the editor of *Radio Times* wrote of the corporation's resolve 'that everything broadcast . . . shall be fit to appeal to the keen, fresh unspoiled mind of the child' (ibid.: 93). Thus idealized, they could not be treated as equals but should nevertheless be given their dignity, and a certain amount of debate took place among children's broadcasters in the 1920s and 1930s as to how this dignity might be protected. Considerable soul-searching, for instance, surrounded the practice of giving the broadcasters nicknames: usually Uncle or Auntie ('Uncle Caractacus', 'Auntie Cyclone'. . .), but occasionally, as with the BBC's Aberdeen station, animal names such as 'Squirrel' or 'Giraffe'. These names were adopted in pursuance of the 'radio hearth' atmosphere and in an attempt to distance *Children's Hour* from the formality of the schoolroom. However, a proposal to drop the titles of Uncle and Auntie was made as early as 1926 (they were retained) and argument rumbled on over the use of words such as 'kiddiwinkies' and over what Hilda Matheson, the BBC's first Head of Talks, described as 'studied facetiousness . . . [and] condescending heartiness' (ibid.: 95).

In general, *Children's Hour* 'often sounded as if it were run by prep school masters' (ibid.: 93) who wished their young listener 'pleasant dreams and a hot bath' and exhorted them to: 'Be good. But not so frightfully good' (Hartley 1983: 29, 38).

The Reithian paradigm for children's radio was not unlike that of the Boy Scout movement, leavened by elite cultural assumptions. The BBC sought, like Baden-Powell, to promote a national family of children, bonded across the social classes. 'Beryl in Blackpool may like stories' suggested the *Children's Hour Annual* of 1936, 'while Brian of Bournemouth has a marked preference for plays.' The Beryls and Brians were to be united in pursuit of 'the arts of discrimination' and in them was to be developed 'the divine faculty of imagination' (Briggs 1981: 92). This faculty was important to Reith, first because, without it, he feared children would lose interest in radio after a few weeks but, second, because of the likely status of radio in relation to the ideals of activity and improvement that surrounded childhood. Radio was, on the face of it, a medium that invited passivity: it involved listening, merely – in constrast to the apparently imaginative and self-enhancing act of reading a book. *Children's Hour* therefore drew as closely as it could on the themes and approaches of approved children's literature. Writers such as L. du Garde Peach produced 'a torrent of potted histories under the series titles of *Arthurian Legends, Fables of Aesop, Nordic Sagas, Tower of London, Roads of England, Waterways of England* and *Castles of England*' (Hartley 1983: 47). There were regular adaptations of British literary classics – by Dickens, Defoe, Scott, Stevenson etc. – and talks on the countryside, like the popular *Out With Romany* series of the 1930s, given by the Revd G. Bramwell Evans.

So, when the Uncles and Aunties of the early BBC affirmed that 'nothing' was 'too good' for the nation's ten year olds, this meant 'good' in the cultural sense. Improving material would be delivered with an adjustable degree of informality, to remove the connotation of school. But, as with radio for adults (see chap.10 in this volume), the content and mode of children's broadcasting was severely circumscribed – a minor furore, for example, attended the decision in 1942 to commission a play about Christ for *Children's Hour* from the writer Dorothy L. Sayers: there was much concern about her use of 'updated language' and her ascription to Christ of a 'full character' (Hartley 1983: 56). The children of *Children's Hour* read books, pleaded with nurse for just one more game before bedtime and slept soundly after a hot bath. They were active and unthreatened by insidious influences. They lived in suburban families. They were energetic, but decorous. They had imagination, but no sensuality.

SCREENS AND SCREAMS: THE 1950s

Developments in British popular media culture in the two decades which followed the Second World War posed grave threats to these cherished ideals of childhood by the radio hearth. The popularization of television ownership, the establishment of ITV in 1954 and the growth of pop music confronted the adult protectors of childhood dignity and innocence with their three greatest fears: sex, violence and commerce.

For social conservatives, television was a close relative of the cinema but, unlike the cinema, which could be visited voluntarily, it intruded upon the home, where it could be seen by children. In the cause of entertainment, films would often portray people behaving badly. According to the behaviourist assumptions of the time (by no means extinct today) children would see this and want to imitate it. For instance, Enid Blyton, the most important and popular children's author of the period and creator of young suburban heroes *The Famous Five* and *The Secret Seven*, wrote in 1950:

> It cannot be said too often that the cinema is one of the most formidable powers for good or evil in this world, and most especially for children. Its great danger lies in the fact that it can make evil so attractive, so tempting and irresistible. Adults are mature, they can resist the attraction portrayed if they wish to. But children are not mature, they are credulous.
>
> *(Church of England Newspaper*, quoted in Stoney 1986: 148)

These anxieties were held in check while television broadcasts were monopolized by the BBC, whose programmes showed suitable restraint and, in any event, only reached a comparatively small number of (largely middle-class) homes. But feeling ran high in the early 1950s with the campaign, conducted from the Conservative backbenches in parliament (Wilson 1961), to bring in commercial television. The Archbishop of Canterbury attempted to block the move 'for the sake of our children' (Hartley 1983: 99) and Christopher Mayhew, a leading member of the lobby against commercial television, warned of a serious undermining of British childhood. In a pamphlet that sold 40,000 copies at the time Mayhew, a Labour MP on the right of the party, argued that British TV would be Americanized (see chap. 2 in this book). In the United States, he suggested, TV programmes for children gave the impression 'that life is cheap, death, suffering and brutality are subjects of callous indifference': parents in the US had protested against violence and crime on television, he observed, but to no avail; meanwhile, such programmes 'have a hypnotic fascination for the average child'. 'The apparent aim of commercialized television', wrote Mayhew, was 'to give pleasure: the real aim is to sell toothpaste.' He called for the banning of commercial TV for children (Mayhew 1953: 13–16).

This foreboding was fuelled by trends in popular music (see chap. 12 in this volume) where, again, the fearsome spectre of Americanization was raised.

Broadcasters, whether in the 'public service' tradition of the

BBC or on the commercial stations such as Radio Luxembourg, had always played music to children from within the 'radio hearth' tradition. In the commercial sector Luxembourg, most notably, broadcast *The Ovaltiney Concert Party* between 1937 and 1957, which usually featured children singing. Apart from the bedtime drink of Ovaltine these programmes celebrated the carefree innocence of 'happy girls and boys' and their snug, fireside imagery is still familiar in TV advertising.

An important feature of BBC radio output, from 1953 onwards, was *Children's Favourites*, a request programme broadcast on Saturday mornings. The records were introduced by Derek McCulloch, readopting his pre-war title of 'Uncle Mac', and were drawn, in the 1950s and early 1960s, from a semi-official pool of 'children's songs': Michael Holliday's 'The Runaway Train', Charles Penrose's 'The Laughing Policeman', 'Nellie the Elephant' by child star Mandy Miller, and so on. Later in his tenure, however, McCulloch was, as his secretary later recalled, 'not always approving of the songs he was asked to play' (BBC Radio 4, 23 May 1991).

The spread of pop music, so disquieting to Uncle Mac, was invariably associated with the United States, but has, perhaps more accurately, been seen as part of the 'Africanization' of western societies (Vermorel and Vermorel 1989: 11). Dancing that was physically expressive and sensual began to be imported into white culture in the 1920s, via the American black. This ran against the grain of temperate Protestant conventions and, by the late 1920s, medical experts in Britain were claiming already to have discerned the harmful effects of dancing upon children: 'Children of all ages seem unable to keep their feet still whether standing in the street, looking in shop windows, or waiting for tram-way cars,' reported the chief medical officer of Walsall in 1927 (quoted in Vermorel and Vermorel 1989: 10). Along with dangerous dancing had come a more emotional and obliquely sexual response to popular cultural figures, particularly on the part of young females. The early objects of this adulation were the silent-film actor Rudolph Valentino in the 1920s and the crooners Frank Sinatra, in the 1930s, and Johnny Ray, in the 1950s. Sinatra had been one of the first to elicit screams from his young female admirers – known as 'bobby soxers' – and young women at Ray's concerts wet their seats in excitement (ibid.: 24). A year or two later, Elvis Presley was driving predominantly female and progressively younger audiences to hysteria, 'hips grinding and shaking, legs jerking and snapping, arms flailing the guitar to a fast drum beat' (quoted in Goldman 1982: 196). For Presley's third appearance on coast-to-coast TV in the United States, on the *Ed Sullivan Show*, cameramen had orders to film him only from the waist up – either to protect, or to tease, young members of the audience.

In Britain, lower middle-class entrepreneurs were anxious to promote a British dimension to this phenomenon. One such was Larry Parnes:

> Although Larry was ignorant of rock 'n' roll, he had seen hundreds of kids screaming at Johnny Ray and frequently wondered why Britain could not produce a similarly sensational home-grown star.
>
> (Rogan 1989: 23)

In May 1958, one of Parnes's protégés, a young singer from London's East End whom he had given the name 'Tommy Steele' – 'a neat amalgam of the homely and sensual' – was dragged from the stage of Dundee's Caird Hall by excited members of his young audience and knocked unconscious (ibid.: 24, 26). By the mid-1960s, this kind of fervent response had become widespread among the nation's teenage females, several hundred of whom were observed at a concert by the Beatles

> hunched into a foetal position, alternately punching their sides, covering their eyes and stuffing handkerchieves and fists into their mouths . . . Hundreds of the cinema seats were wringing wet. Many had puddles of urine beneath them.
>
> (Norman 1982: 202)

The British popular press, known throughout the post-war era for its eager participation in moral panics about the nation's young, in this instance, in the face of overwhelming popularity of bands like the Beatles, offered reassurance. The *News of the World* carried an article by a psychiatrist who suggested that, for girls, 'Beatlemania' was

> one way of flinging off childhood restraints and letting themselves go . . . the fact that thousands of others are screaming along with her makes the girl feel she is living life to the full with people of her own age . . . this emotional outlook is very necessary at her age. It is also innocent and

harmless. The girls are subconsciously preparing for motherhood. Their frenzied screams are a rehearsal for that moment.

In this latter regard, he concluded, the many jelly babies found lying in the puddles of urine were greatly symbolic (quoted in Norman 1982: 212).

In the 1970s this kind of latently sexual reaction to pop stars became legitimated for a younger age group. The 'Teenybopper' phenomenon provided an even earlier subconscious preparation for womanhood (Frith 1983: 226–8): in 1974 eleven and twelve year olds bombarded the Bay City Rollers with panties and teddy bears (Allen 1975: 22). 'Why', asked one of them ten years later, 'do adolescent girls go loopy over gawky, sometimes talentless young men?' She concludes that it's in part because they aren't girls at all: the scream 'is the sound of young women, not "hysterical schoolgirls" as one reporter would have it – a scream of defiance, celebration and excitement' (Steward and Garratt 1984: 142).

This steady trend toward greater sensuality in children's popular culture will have made for heightened embarrassment and friction in millions of homes: Bob Geldof provides a perfect evocation of this when he describes how, one day in the early 1960s, his father insisted that his sister Lynn put on her new party dress and demonstrate the twist for him and his friends:

> There was no music but she softly hummed a Chubby Checker song to herself and began to twist. Everyone clapped, she was bright red. 'Show us again, how does it go?' my father said, and joined in in a grotesque shamble of arms and legs.
> (Geldof 1986: 55–6)

Equally, from a number of socio-political standpoints, there was concern about the perceived erosion of conventional childhood. Where social conservatives, typified by the National Viewers' and Listeners' Association, saw the break-up of order and discipline and the decline of moral standards, others, not all of them on the right, were concerned about commercial exploitation of the young and the transmutation of increasing numbers of children into gullible and emotionally distracted consumers. In this regard, the fears of people such as Mayhew and the Campaign

Against Commercial Television were strengthened by the publication of books such as Vance Packard's *The Hidden Persuaders* (1957, 1961) about modern advertising strategies and techniques (see chap. 8 in this volume). Here, apparently, were the bitter fruits of passivity: children, no longer active and vigorous on their own account but eaten up with passive hero worship and prey to all the attendant merchandising.

TELEVISION AND THE CHILD

Because it was a visual medium, television was thought by many people – parents, teachers and numerous broadcasters themselves – to be inherently less suited to maintaining the nation's children in active and stimulated mode. Indeed, in 1957, David Davis of BBC Radio, wrote in a memo of

> those who believe in, and want their children to enjoy, the things that sound alone can give: the freeing and setting to work of the child's imagination; active as opposed to passive participation; such parents will continue to make up [*Children's Hour's*] audience.
>
> (Hartley 1983: 64)

For their part, BBC television programme-makers strove hard to reaffirm the ideal of activeness – an early example being *It's All Yours* (later *All Your Own*), a late afternoon programme, often repeated in the evening for adults, in which children demonstrated their skills to presenter Huw Wheldon. During the programme, first broadcast in 1954, Wheldon 'stood, forever questioning, finger spread over cheek, the little finger bent to the corner of his mouth, nodding his obvious interest as small boys explained how they made a boat out of matchsticks' (ibid.: 143). Wheldon, wishing to avoid a 'procession of precocity' insisted 'that every programme include a failure, a disaster or a confession of some kind: the girl who ruined a trumpet solo, the boy who made a model boat but had to admit it sank' (Ferris 1990: 88).

But other broadcasters, in their dealings with children, found an effervescence which could not be contained within this paradigm of diligent and worthwhile activity. Eamonn Andrews, for example, helping to devise *Crackerjack*, the children's variety show, for BBC television in the mid-1950s was already convinced of the need to 'treat children as adults. To treat them as equals. To cut out the itsy bitsy boos and aren't-we-all-good-little-girls-and-boys' (Andrews 1963: 165). Nevertheless, he and others were quite surprised by the expressiveness of their young audience. One such was the entertainer, Max Bygraves:

> As I remember it, everything was going fine until Max started to ask questions. Rhetorical questions, no doubt. But to a children's audience, a question is a question and Max started getting answers. I can tell you it was a hectic five minutes or so that followed.
>
> (Andrews 1963: 166)

Similarly, when pop singer Cliff Richard appeared on the show, 'I thought somebody had let half a dozen mice loose in the theatre. In fact I sat there petrified, watching the gallery, as the girls jumped and shrieked' (ibid.: 167). On *Crackerjack*, this exuberance was harnessed and structured so that, whenever a member of the cast uttered the name of the show, the audience had to scream it back.

Crackerjack was, none the less, firmly within the Reithian scheme of things, having been conceived as 'a pleasant time between school and homework' (Hartley 1983: 144). Moreover, early evening 'family' viewing was often overtly didactic, with the predominantly middle-class television audience in mind. An example was the first TV 'soap' (ongoing family drama), *The Grove Family* (1954–7), wherein the children were the model of rectitude and the scripts contained homilies on such matters as looking after your elderly neighbours and making sure you had a TV licence (see the retrospective *The Grove Family*, BBC2 TV, 26 August 1991).

This sort of programme-making was born, as I've argued, out of certain assumptions: that doing was better than watching or listening, that television was potentially passivity-making and should not exceed the terms of its guarded welcome by tempting children from their homework and hobbies.

But a steady retreat from this ethos is observable from the late 1950s, in the wake of powerful legitimations for the new medium. In 1958 a report commissioned by the new Independent Television Authority on parents, children and television was published (Research Services, HMSO 1958). A majority of parents, it argued, were in favour of television. There must be moderation and guidance, of course, but in general they felt it improved their children's minds and enhanced family life. Many preferred their children to watch TV than to pursue 'any other single activity'; nor were they unduly concerned about the effect on their offspring of 'scenes of fighting' (ibid.: 8). Sceptics might have been unconvinced by findings so apparently favourable to the commissioners of the research, but academic research published the same year by Himmelweit and her colleagues, while more sophisticated in its arguments, was similarly approving television.

Himmelweit recognized the increased pervasiveness of television, which was reflected in the difficulty she and others were having in finding children who hadn't any experience of TV, to compare them to some who had (Himmelweit *et al.* 1958:1). But, although most children watched television, the ones who watched it most were found to be the less intelligent and the working class, who appeared to have later bedtimes (ibid.: 11). Himmelweit's team rejected the simplistic 'effects' perspective on TV, arguing instead for an interplay between the 'characteristics of the viewer and the characteristics and content of the media' (ibid.: 4), but they had moderately bad news for the pedagogic tendency among children's broadcasters. Competition (from ITV), they had found, was likely to diminish interest in educationally oriented programmes like *Science Review, Animal, Vegetable and Mineral, Meet the Commonwealth* and *From Tropical Forests*. A number of children with access only to one channel (BBC) stayed with such programmes rather than switch off 'and in fact enjoyed them'. But those with the option changed channels, rather than watch programmes 'with educational value or those which have been especially produced for children' (ibid.: 14–15).

Some acknowledgement of this is reflected in the children's television schedules of the late 1950s and the 1960s. At the BBC, the Reithian balance between edification and 'light entertainment' was steadily tilted in favour of the latter: both channels now offered roughly the same permutation of cowboys, adventure serials, cartoons and animal, puppet and magazine programmes. A considerable number of the adventure serials, both on BBC and on ITV, were imported from the United States, along with many of the puppet shows (Hartley 1983: 97–117).

ONE I MADE EARLIER

All this, of course, entailed a recognition of children as *consumers*: they were now *viewers*, with preferences, and they (or their parents, on their behalf) were *purchasers* – of toys, comics, books, memorabilia. In the – for many families – increasingly affluent, hedonistic 1950s children were a *market*. This recognition was not confined to ITV; indeed, it had been acted upon by children's broadcasters before ITV had been established. For instance, Annette Mills, who presented *Muffin the Mule*, a BBC TV programme featuring the popular string puppet of the same name, in the late 1940s and early 1950s, had a company called Muffin Syndicate Ltd which licensed Muffin products. Similarly, Harry Corbett, inventor of the glove puppets, Sooty and Sweep, formed Sooty Ltd which by 1956 was the centre of a merchandising operation which encompassed forty companies (Tibballs 1990: 28, 45). Sooty Ltd grossed £50,000 in 1956, a considerable amount of money in those days.

But *Blue Peter*, first broadcast by the BBC in 1958, remained, in the face of these new trends and possibilities, firmly wedded to the values of the radio hearth. Children, once again, were encouraged to be *active*: to make, to mend, to collect, to care for animals and to help other people. This was allied to an explicitly anti-commercial ideology, as recalled by Biddy Baxter and Edward Barnes, both of whom worked on the programme in its formative years:

> The Christmas display of toys had been a regular feature on *Blue Peter* . . . and had enormous co-operation from the toy trade. . . . Biddy was worried about the families who could not possibly afford these expensive toys but Edward was more concerned that because children have no real buying power, the commercials were encouraging their desire to receive presents.
>
> (Baxter and Barnes 1989: 49)

(This led to the first *Blue Peter* appeal – for toys for deprived children – in 1962.)

But this anti-commercialism was not based solely on deference to 'those less fortunate than ourselves' or a snobbish disdain for profit; it was also born of a belief that children should resist the blandishments of the market and create their own world. For example, the *Blue Peter* cliché 'Here's one I made earlier' originated with Margaret Parnell, who appeared on the programme between 1963 and 1987, telling children what they could make, and who felt her work to be subversive of commercial culture for children:

> Like us she delighted in creating anti-commercials, making the accessories for *Action Man* and *Sindy* and *My Little Pony* for a fraction of the retail cost. . . . One survey undertaken by *Blue Peter* showed it would cost nearly a thousand pounds to buy all the accessories for one heavily advertised doll. Margaret's ideas like a Quartermaster's Stores or Ski Bob for *Action Man* or a caravan for *My Little Pony* cost mere pence and included hours of play value as well as the joy of making them.
>
> (Baxter and Barnes 1989: 39)

Moreover, despite growing financial stringency at the BBC in the early 1960s, which was brought on by the increased keenness of competition from ITV and which caused the virtual closing down of the corporation's children's department in 1963, *Blue Peter* badges continued to be dispensed free of charge to any children entitled to them (ibid.: 32–5). This matter was handled by a special correspondence unit atached to the programme, which the BBC agreed to fund, and this unit also dealt with the famed *Blue Peter* appeals from 1962 on. These appeals – for the homeless, for guide dogs for the blind, for the victims of war in Cambodia – were, once again, placed by the programme's makers within the traditional paradigm of childhood *activity*: 'further evidence that the *Blue Peter* audience was not passive' (ibid.: 49). Likewise the anti-commercialism persisted: in the late 1970s, for instance, when *Blue Peter* presenter John Noakes left the BBC he refused to give an undertaking that the programme's dog, Shep, would not be used for advertising, if the animal were allowed to remain with him. So the *Blue Peter* producers withheld the dog. (Noakes subsequently made a commercial for Pedigree Chum dog food, featuring a dog called Skip; ibid.: 42–3.)

GOING LIVE: THE BATTLE FOR SATURDAY MORNING

The pattern of BBC programming for children in the 1970s and 1980s has to be seen in its political and cultural context.

Politically, ever since the campaign for commercial television in the early 1950s, the tradition of 'public service broadcasting', and the institution which upheld it, the BBC, had been on the defensive. From the 1960s onwards, with the established popularity of ITV programmes, the BBC was likely to be told by government, whether Conservative or Labour, that continued financial support would be conditional upon winning a greater share of the national audience. At the BBC, in many areas, this led over time to a more full-hearted pursuit of the popular.

Children's programming was particularly important, in this context, for two reasons. First, the BBC was felt to produce better programmes for children, so this was a sphere of operations where ITV might still be shown a clean pair of heels. Second, more credence was being given to the argument that children were a means to capturing a whole household of viewers for the evening: if the children could be persuaded to watch BBC TV at teatime, maybe the family would stay with BBC until bedtime. By the mid-1970s this consideration had been extended to morning time at the weekend. In 1978, Brian Cowgill, Controller of BBC 1 informed the Head of Children's Programmes: 'You're doing alright in the week, but you're not doing much on Saturday mornings' (Baxter and Barnes 1989: 141). This admonition led to the Saturday morning magazine programme *Multi-Coloured Swap Shop*, and its subsequent mutations, *Saturday Superstore* and the current *Going Live* and the *The 8.15 From Manchester*. These shows, and their kindred programmes around the networks (notably ITV's *Disney Club* and *Motormouth*), illustrate a number of important and decisive departures from the traditional childhood of the broadcasting 'hearth', which I'd like briefly to discuss.

First, the traditional paradigm of autonomous *activity* is largely abandoned in these shows. Children are now assumed to be active principally in relation to *consumption* (equated with passivity in the 'hearth' paradigm). This consumption is principally of media products; pre-eminently, therefore, it involves buying, listening and watching rather than the previously valued pursuits that entailed making or doing. Thus much of the show features pop stars with a new album or video to promote, people who appear in other TV programmes, and so on. Doing-things-for-oneself is, as a theme, very much subordinate to these matters and, if it is pursued at all, this may be in the context of a media promotion: the golfer Nick Faldo, for instance, dropped into the *Going Live* studio one morning (21 September 1991) and helped a handful of young golfers with their technique, but his appearance was principally in connection with TV coverage of the Ryder Cup golf competition, forthcoming on BBC.

Similarly, these programmes often include cartoons such as the *Teenage Mutant Hero Turtles* and *Masters of the Universe*, whose characters are available in toy form. The BBC will not normally buy cartoons which have actually been financed by toy companies (Taylor 1990) but, given the promotional value of broadcasting the cartoon in any event, the distinction seems arbitrary. This centrality of commercial discourse (see chap. 8 in this book) in *Going Live* was acknowledged in 1990 by the Office of Fair Trading who published a magazine called *VFM* (Value for Money), which was aimed at the 'Young Consumer'. The stars of *Going Live* were used to promote it: '*VFM*' they informed readers, 'tells you all you need to know about money and shopping' (Office of Fair Trading 1990: 2).

Second, as I've said, these programmes borrow heavily from, and mesh into, pop culture. The presenters of *Swap Shop* and *Superstore*, Noel Edmonds and Mike Read respectively, were both, initially, disc jockeys. Timmy Mallett, presenter of *Wacaday*, TVam's programme for the school holidays, released a record in 1990 which entered the top ten. In this sense, the programmes presuppose children as *fans* and, especially in the case of girls, the spontaneous squeals of the 1950s and 1960s have become routinized: they're expected. When the pop duo Bros come out to be interviewed by presenter Ross King on an edition of *8.15 From Manchester* in 1991, the screams had a prescribed ring about them. The boys looked suitably humble and sheepish. Having some star or other as an object of ado-ration was normal for a pre-teenage girl in the 1980s and 1990s as having a pet rabbit was in the 1950s: on *Going Live* in 1990 presenter Philip Schofield suggested to a young woman who had just put a question to TV/pop star Jason Donovan that she might care to spend the remaining time 'gazing into his eyes'.

A third element is satirical humour. This was imported into children's television by ITV in the late 1960s, notably with *Do Not Adjust Your Set* (1968), a programme written and performed by Oxbridge comedians later to form the *Monty Python* team. In

the 1970s ATV developed *Tiswas*, a children's magazine programme based on pop, irony and self-conscious mayhem. More
recently, such magazine programmes, most of which are approx-
imations of *Tiswas*, have often featured Oxbridge or 'alternative'
comedians and the discourse of the presenters has become
reflexively ironic. *Going Live*, for example, has resident comedians who, for several series up to 1991, were Trev and Simon, a
double act recruited from the alternative cabaret circuit. Much of
Trev and Simon's comedy plays off the idea of the young, media-
wise consumer-fan: their routines invariably include references to
the stars in this week's show, whose names and sources of
celebrity they are Always Getting Wrong: no, no, silly, it's *Kylie*
Minogue, not Kelly, and so on.

This resident skittishness can be taken together with a fourth
element – a mock cruelty – which, again, seems to have originated with ATV's *Tiswas*. In *Tiswas* there were seldom more
than a few minutes before the next custard pie or bucket of
whitewash. In the 1980s and early 1990s children's magazine
programmes usually ran competitions wherein the losers (or even
the winners) were variously slid into tanks of brightly coloured
gunge, dropped into swimming pools, hit over the head with soft
mallets or required to pay some such forfeit. On BBC 1's *The 8.15
From Manchester* (a summer show) teachers, wearing the archaic
garb of gown and mortar board, are tipped, ceremonially, into
swimming pools. All this illustrates how contemporary TV
programmes for the young *take the part of the child*, attempting
to appropriate elements of his/her culture. Previously, broadcasters, when they addressed children, took the part of the parent/
teacher/adult. Away from adults, children had, as they still have,
a social world of their own – out playing, in school corridors, in
their bedrooms, up town – and this world always had a harder
edge to it than the sentimental childhood-of-the-hearth notion
suggested. The duckings and the tubs of gunge represent an
attempt to capture this edge, with its constituent sense of
opposition and subversion. The forfeits are determinedly
unsentimental; they say, just as the paternalists said, 'We don't
talk down to children'.

This process is also reflected in the changing face of the
children's broadcaster. In the 1920s and 1930s such people were
men and women of early middle age who styled themselves
'Uncle' and 'Auntie'. By the late 1950s, this age group was

beginning to be considered unviable for the task: the first presenters of *Blue Peter*, in 1958, were a male of twenty-five (Christopher Trace) and female of twenty-one (Leila Williams). By the 1980s, this age, or the appearance of it, was the norm for children's magazine programmes: when Yvette Fielding was recruited to present *Blue Peter* in 1987 she was only eighteen. 'Right now', said Andy Crane, twenty-seven-year-old (but looking younger) presenter of *Children's BBC* and *Motormouth* recently, 'I think that me and Philip Schofield are like older brothers to the viewers' (*Guardian*, 27 September 1991: 38). Comparative youth is, moreover, allied to a radically changed presentation of self, as noted with some acerbity by Georgia Campbell: Jean Morton, of ITV's *Tinga and Tucker Club* (1950s and 1960s), is remembered as 'wearing clothes that are creaking with starch and propriety, and her hair has been freshly pin-curled, rococo style. She is not, please note, trying to pretend she is five years old.' Similarly

> On bygone *Blue Peter*, Val is wearing a polite blouse and sensible flats, while Pete 'n' John look crestfallen because they were forced to leave their club ties in the dressing room.

Today's presenters, by contrast, 'look like a gang of inner city crack dealers . . . hyper-groovers filling in time before the next acid party' (Campbell 1991).

Lastly, as I've already observed, these programmes are substantially about the media themselves. The subject matter (the latest records, CDs, videos, films and TV programmes) and the discourse – the phrase 'going live', for example – are drawn from the media. Indeed, a regular feature of *Going Live* involves one of the presenters telephoning a viewer so that they can talk 'live on television'. There are regular trips 'behind the scenes' to see producers and control panels, technicians are frequently hauled on screen, cameras whirl round to reveal other cameras and their crew. On *The 8.15 From Manchester* (14 September 1991) presenter Ross King talks to other 'children's presenters' Andi Peters and Simon Parkin (both of *Children's BBC*) and then interviews his fellow *8.15* presenter, singer Sonia, about her new record, asking her ultimately: 'What was your most wonderful moment – apart from working with me?' Sonia is then complimented by *her* fellow presenter, Diane Oxberry, on her 'brilliant new image'. Similarly, on *Going Live*, presenters and children-fans have a 'Press Conference' where they interview celebrities: in the progamme of 21 September 1991 presenter Philip Schofield asks both Bros and Kylie Minogue if they think they sell more newspapers (through being famous) than records. Likewise, the show's resident furry animal, Gordon the Gopher, is asked how did he 'get into presenting'?

This self-referential media culture reflects what might be called a postmodern childhood, wherein children's TV troubles less and less to mediate the world to the child, or to impart knowledge or skills. Instead, TV (along with other mass media) *is* the world, and it happily discusses itself.

I want to close by looking at the ramification of these changes for the contemporary politics of childhood, chiefly in the British context.

TALKING DOWN? TELEVISION, POLITICS AND CHILDHOOD

Most of the people who sought to address children through the British mass media from the 1920s onwards professed the same guiding principle: it was important not to 'talk down' to children. But, of course, this crucial avoidance was seen to be achieved by different people in different ways. Until the 1950s it was most likely to be sought through promoting creative *activity* within the separate and secure social world of the child. But steadily, since the 1950s, this paradigm of childhood has been eroded within British children's media and popular culture. Children, as I've argued, are now invariably recognized as *consumers*, as important figures in the market place, discriminating between this programme/style/good, and that. Within this recognition is an acknowledgement that children didn't necessarily want what was prescribed for them in previous social climates – as, for example, the report of Himmelweit *et al.* make clear for TV in the late 1950s. So, progressively, other areas have been legitimated for the young – notably in the field of popular music, where their sensuality and sexuality have to some extent been accommodated: through dancing, screaming and being otherwise expressively devoted as a *fan*. The *media* themselves are now recognized as a key element in the modern child's social world, and this recognition is supported by the latest evidence: 98 per cent of homes in the UK now have TV and children, although they are not the heaviest viewers, increased their average TV watching time from two-and-a-half to three hours a day between 1982 and 1987 (Gunter and McAleer 1990: 5). But the traditional paradigm of childhood has not been replaced by any perceptible new framing of the young and this, I suggest, has sharpened the political and social contradictions with which children live.

Take, first of all, the important notion of the *vulnerability* of the child. Principal stewardship of this idea seems to have passed from the political right to a section of the liberal left. For example, one of the most convincing reassessments, recently, of the links between TV , violence and the young has come from the left feminist writer Ros Coward:

> *Transformers, Gobots, Masters of the Universe* are all children's programmes which are barely concealed promos for boys' toys. Watching the adverts between children's TV programmes is like entering a feminist nightmare where boys build up grotesque arsenals and girls endlessly comb the pastel mane of *My Little Pony*. . . . In September American children had their first chance to shoot back with 'interactive toys' when *Captain Power and His Soldiers of Fortune* quite literally hit the screen. In this form of 'entertainment', the TV programmes are linked to sales of guns and weaponry with which the child is encouraged to participate in the programme . . . we are now in an altogether more gendered and imperialistic phase, where violence and owning weapons is seen as a vital part of masculine identity.
>
> (Coward 1987: 26)

Coward deals explicitly with cultural *meanings*, and not 'effects'. But the behaviourist supposition that if violence on TV is witnessed by children it will cause them to be violent in real life is, of course, still around. In the political sphere it has been evangelised principally by Mary Whitehouse and the National Viewers' and Listeners' Association and it underpinned their successful sponsorship of the Video Recordings Act of 1985. There have also been ritual allusions to an alleged 'copycat effect' in the urban riots of 1982, 1985 and 1991, whereby young people are said to have been provoked to disorder by seeing other young people engaging in it on TV. These arguments have always been given short shrift by the majority of sociologists (see, for example, Murdock and McCron 1978) and many psychologists

acknowledge slow progress in the search for a causal link here
(Hodge and Tripp 1986: chap. 7). But these notions now have
fewer and fewer vocal adherents on the political right. This is
partly because of the declining influence within the British
Conservative Party of social conservative and paternalist positions generally, and the ascendancy of free market and libertarian
groups. This ascendancy was reflected in the passing of the
Broadcasting Act of 1990 which was characterized by a 'lighter
touch' in the regulation of TV programming: commercial TV
companies would no longer be bound by the terms of their
franchise to broadcast programmes of particular kinds. Instead,
they would be subject only to a vague 'quality threshhold' and
viewers would have access to a 'Broadcasting Standards Council'
which would 'reinforce standards on taste and decency and the
portrayal of sex and violence' (Home Office 1988).

Three points should be made here. First, the question of
children's access to sensitive material is effectively *privatized*.
Parents who wish to allow their children to see such material
will do so; those who don't will either control family viewing
accordingly, or seek the (minimal) redress of having their complaint upheld by the Broadcasting Standards Council. Second,
there are no guarantees of 'children's programming'. 'It is hard
. . . to suppress one's incredulity', wrote TV executive David
Elstein, 'that the Broadcasting Minister (then Timothy Renton)
should confidently inform Parliament in the summer of 1989
that "we see no reason why high quality children's programmes, sustained by viewer demand, should not continue to
flourish on British television after 1992"' (Elstein 1990: 97).
Third, to go on subscribing to the idea of a simplistic vulnerability of children to TV influence, while politically advant-
ageous perhaps in the case of *violence*, would create intractable
difficulties for the contemporary right if applied to *advertising*.
In this context, children are now a major market for the
transnational corporations, whom much Conservative legislation in the Thatcher years – notably the Broadcasting Act – was
designed to accommodate. There are some restrictions on
advertising to children (see, for instance, Committee of Advertising Practice 1988), but they are milder than in many other
countries (Harty 1985: 6–7). The only significant political
intervention in this area by a Conservative in recent times –
when Schools Minister Michael Fallon called the BBC 'wicked,

brazen and sinister' for showing programmes such as *SuperTed* and the *Teenage Mutant Hero Turtles*, proving that 'the non-profit-making BBC is heavily into merchandising' (*Today*, 30 May 1991) – may safely be interpreted as an attack on the BBC rather than an attack on merchandising.

Merchandising in children's broadcasting is furthest advanced in the United States, following the effective deregulation of the American mass media under the Reagan administration (Tunstall 1986). This legislation brought a virtual end to public service broadcasting for children in the States (including the much-praised *Sesame Street*): most children's TV programmes in the US now are cartoons financed by the toy companies and featuring their products (Engelhardt 1986). By the time of these changes Vance Packard's *The Hidden Persuaders* had emerged in a second edition (1981) with further thoughts on 'the psycho-seduction of children'. Selling to children, he pointed out, had reached the level of intensity whereat 'children's reactions to commercials, programmes and products' were laboratory tested 'by pupil-dilation machines, finger sensors, and so on' (Packard 1981: 238). Similarly, the influential work of Neil Postman, whose book *The Disappearance of Childhood* came out in the US in 1982 (Postman 1985), and Marie Winn (Winn 1984, Winn 1985) argued that TV had eroded childhood and brought the very young into a cognisance of things, such as sex, that they could not yet handle.

In Britain, on the liberal left, there is more unambiguous support for television as a medium – typified by Maire Messenger Davies's *Television is Good for your Kids* (1989) – and some commentators (e.g. Buckingham 1990) have gone so far as to claim that children show a 'lucid understanding of the codes and conventions' of TV genres, know exactly what they want, watch many 'adult' programmes and are not taken in by advertisements. Notwithstanding this view, the group British Action for Children's Television was formed in 1989 as a response to the British government's proposals for broadcasting, and the neglect in those proposals of children's programming. Again, BACT grows out of the liberal left and, more specifically, out of the ranks of media professionals – writers, teachers, researchers, producers, etc. – and from such bodies as the British Film Institute.

BACT calls for quality and diversity in children's television and it seeks to sustain the public service tradition in some form. Whether BACT members are unanimously for the retention of *Blue Peter*, however, is doubtful, if the fierce denunciation of the programme by Bob Fergusson, Head of Media Studies at London University's Institute of Education, is any guide. Fergusson watched an edition of *Blue Peter* in June 1984 which featured a choir of young black Christians; presenter Janet Ellis learning to skate; a barbecue with several simple recipes; and a story about the East India Company and a prince from a Pacific island who ended up in Rotherhithe in East London. He then set about the programme with a New Left bludgeon (Fergusson 1984). The presenters, he said, were patronizing to the black choir; the young woman learning to skate was reminiscent of heroines of girls' annuals in the 1940s; the barbecue represented 'conspicuous middle-class consumption', insensitive to the fact that many children have no garden; and the story about the prince omitted to mention the cruelties inflicted by imperialists such as the East India Company. *Blue Peter*, he concluded, was racist, sexist and reactionary – a veritable 'vector of true bourgeois ideology' (Fergusson 1984: 40).

This prompts several comments. First, it's difficult to quarrel with much of it. *Blue Peter* does contain these elements – but then so do most other magazine and information programmes, be they for adults or children. A similar case could be made, for example, against *News at Ten*. TV programmes are, after all, constructed within a framework of power relations where various ideological assumptions prevail. *Blue Peter* looks more vulnerable in the political/cultural climate of the 1990s *not* because it is uniquely 'bourgeois' – the post-*Tiswas*, *Going Live* genre of shows is scarcely Marxist, or even more socially aware – but because it is *old* bourgeois. *Blue Peter* is essentially the children's television of the romantic right: it's fuddy-duddy. Second, and related to this, Fergusson does not acknowledge the usefulness of *activity* or *social concern*, as earlier left commentators might have done. Such notions are washed away in a torrent of scorn for 'charity, caring and the removal of history' (Fergusson 1984: 34). Certainly, *Blue Peter* depoliticizes issues such as poverty and ecology but concern for, say, the Third World doesn't *have* to be racist or imperialist. Likewise, skating can be fun, even if the person who encourages you to learn how to is a bit patronizing. Access to ideas and information is what counts here, and children may perhaps take care of the rest themselves. As Ken Worpole said in 1987

> Thanks to television our two children know immeasurably more about the world than either their mother or I ever knew at their age. Through [TV] . . . they have travelled to more countries, seen more cities, learned how other people live and die . . . seen the urgency of natural conservation (we may deplore *Blue Peter*, but it may have produced the generation that follows Greenpeace and the animal liberation movement).
>
> *(New Socialist*, February 1987: 37)

(It's worth adding, in this connection, that although serials such as *Neighbours* and *EastEnders* are the most watched TV programmes among pre-teenagers, *Blue Peter* is nevertheless the most popular *children's* programme. See Gunter and McAleer 1990:8.)

Third, and here I'd like to broaden the political context – Fergusson's implied call for a left children's television seems less likely than ever to be answered. Developments during the 1980s in the social world of children produced a contradiction which, to a greater or lesser extent, all British children face. The media, as I've argued, increasingly address and define children as *consumers*. Today, in a growing volume of writing across the political spectrum, consumption means choice, fulfilment and the finding of the self. So an area of behaviour – consumption – previously thought *passive* is increasingly seen as *active*. But in other, parallel and equally vital areas – notably *education*, wherein the greater part of a child's waking life is spent – the opportunity for self-determination is more firmly closed off than ever. This is the result of recent legislation, and the politicking around it, which I'd like briefly to discuss.

The third Thatcher administration, which came to power in 1987, swiftly passed the Local Government Act and the Education Reform Act. Under the former it became illegal for a public employee (such as a teacher in a state school) to advocate homosexuality as a way of life; the latter imposed a National Curriculum on all children in public sector schools. These enactments were presaged in a speech by Margaret Thatcher to the Conservative Party Conference of 1987 in which she claimed the nation's children had fallen under the spell of left-wing teachers, who had taught them 'anti-racist mathematics, political slogans, that they had an inalienable right to be gay and that our society offered them no future' (quoted in Simon 1988: 18). This rhetoric, and the attendant clamour by the popular press for action against such perversions, once again invokes the *vulnerability* of the child and the Education Reform Act of 1988 purports to provide the remedy: by giving priority to the 'wishes of parents'.

In the New Right ideological formulations of the 1980s, children were more than ever the responsibility of their parents with, generally speaking, no rights as individuals. But there has been a degree of collusion here from the left. There was, for example, Labour Party leader Neil Kinnock's famed reassurance to the nation, via *Everywoman* magazine, that he was a 'reactionary' father, concerned about the impact on his son and daughter of 'the permissive society' (reported in *The Times*, 29 August 1986). Likewise, Angela McRobbie attempted in 1987 to present a left defence of 'parent power', accusing teachers of 'condescension' and reminding readers of *Marxism Today* that many parents were working class, female, immigrant, black or some combination of these (McRobbie 1987). But so, the supporters of children's rights would undoubtedly argue, are many children – and, in stressing this, I'd like to offer some brief concluding comments on where the notion of the vulnerability of the child stands now.

CONCLUSION: WHITHER CHILDHOOD?

The logic of the evidence presented here is that less credence is now given by adult society than in former times to the notion of the child's vulnerability, via media or other discourses, to material touching on sex, violence or commerce. On the first two counts, Buckingham's research (1990) confirms what many of us already suspected from our own experience: that many children have access, using the family video or simply watching TV after the 9 o'clock watershed, to sexually explicit or violent material. On the third count, opposition to the commercialization of childhood through TV is stronger in the United States than it is in the UK. Indeed there are some piquant ironies here – not least the fact that the same government that enforced the National Curriculum placed no obstacle to the use of prescribed school knowledge for advertising purposes. For example, the cereal manufacturers, Weetabix, in exchange for so many packet tops, offer schools their own, company-produced history books and atlases: in *The Weetabix Illustrated British History Book* the arrival of Weetabix on British breakfast tables for the first time (in 1936) is equated with the rise of Hitler and the discovery of penicillin in historical importance (Wright 1989: 56). So children, as consumers, should no longer be protected from the blandishments of commerce.

The real vulnerability, inherent in the current political consensus, is to *politics*. Talking politically to children is to indoctrinate them, thus deflecting them from their legitimate studies and pleasures, and undermining the authority of their parents.

I want to oppose this consensus. The notion of the vulnerability of children is, in large part, a red herring. The erosion of traditional childhood to the point where the expressiveness of the young, their sensuality and their access to consumption have been acknowledged, has, it seems to me, been socially beneficial. But this erosion should be extended into other areas such as politics and education (Franklin 1986). And the arguments about media, popular culture and consumption should be applied to people and society in general, and not just to children. These arguments must, ultimately, be about access to consumption (the national and international distribution of wealth) and about cultural priorities: for example, whether having the right tops and trainers is more important than, say, a sense of community and social justice. We have, in other words, to determine as a society the degree of commercial discourse we want, for people of any age, in our media (again, see chap. 8 in this book). We must oppose any perspective in which merely to suggest this is indoctrination, pomposity or, simply, no fun.

NOTE

I want to thank Dominic Strinati for his helpful comments on the earlier draft of this essay, and Lord (formerly Christopher) Mayhew for sending me a copy of his pamphlet of 1953.

REFERENCES

Allen, Ellis (1975) *The Bay City Rollers*, London: Panther.
Andrews, Eamonn (1963) *This is My Life*, London: Macdonald.

Aries, Philippe (1962) *Centuries of Childhood*, London: Jonathan Cape.
Baden-Powell, Robert (1908) *Scouting for Boys*, London: C. Arthur Pearson.
Barker, Martin (1984) *A Haunt of Fears*, London: Pluto Press.
Baxter, Biddy and Barnes, Edward (1989) *Blue Peter: The Inside Story*, Letchworth: Ringpress Books.
Briggs, Susan (1981) *Those Radio Times*, London: Weidenfeld & Nicolson.
Buckingham, David (1990) 'Seeing through TV: children talking about television', in Janet Willis and Tana Wollen (eds) *The Neglected Audience*, London: British Film Institute.
Burns, Tom (1977) *The BBC: Public Institution and Private World*, London: Macmillan.
Campbell, Georgia (1991) 'Watch with horror', *Guardian*, 18 February.
Committee of Advertising Practice (1988) *The British Code of Advertising Practice*, London: CAP.
Coward, Rosalind (1987) 'Violent screen play', *Marxism Today*, December: 24–7.
Elstein, David (1990) 'Children's television after 1992', in Janet Willis and Tana Wollen (eds) *The Neglected Audience*, London: British Film Institute.
Engelhardt, Tom (1986) 'The shortcake strategy', in Todd Gitlin (ed.) *Watching Television*, New York: Pantheon.
Fergusson, Bob (1984) 'Black Blue Peter', in Len Masterman (ed.) *Television Mythologies: Stars, Shows and Signs*, London: Comedia/ MK Media Press.
Ferris, Paul (1990) *Sir Huge: The Life of Huw Wheldon*, London: Michael Joseph.
Franklin, Bob (ed.) (1986) *The Rights of Children*, Oxford: Basil Blackwell.
Frith, Simon (1983) *Sound Effects: Youth, Leisure and the Politics of Rock 'n' Roll*, London: Constable.
Frith, Simon (1988) *Music For Pleasure: Essays in the Sociology of Pop*, Cambridge: Polity.
Geldof, Bob, with Paul Vallely (1986) *Is That It?*, Harmondsworth: Penguin.
Goldman, Albert (1982) *Elvis*, Harmondsworth: Penguin.
Gunter, Barrie and McAleer, Jill (1990) *Children and Television: The One Eyed Monster?*, London: Routledge.
Himmelweit, Hilde *et al.* (1958) *Television and the Child*, London: Nuffield Foundation/Oxford University Press.
Hartley, Ian (1983) *Goodnight Children . . . Everywhere*, Southborough: Midas Books.
Harty, Sheila (1985) *The Corporate Pied Piper*, Penang: International Organisation of Consumer Unions.
Hodge, Bob and Tripp, David (1986) *Children and Television: A Semiotic Approach*, Cambridge: Polity.
Home Office (1988) *Broadcasting in the 1990s: Competition, Choice and Quality*, London: HMSO, Cmnd 517.

McRobbie, Angela (1987) 'Parent power at the chalkface', *Marxism Today*, May: 24–7.

Mayhew, Christopher (1953) *Dear Viewer . . .* , London: Lincolns Prager.

Messenger Davies, Maire (1989) *Television is Good for your Kids*, London: Hilary Shipman.

Murdock, Graham and McCron, Robin (1978) 'Television and teenage violence', *New Society*, 14 December.

Norman, Philip (1982) *Shout! The True Story of the Beatles*, London: Corgi.

Office of Fair Trading (1990) *VFM*, London: OFT.

Packard, Vince (1981) *The Hidden Persuaders*, Harmondsworth: Penguin (first published in the United States in 1957, UK 1961).

Postman, Neil (1985) *The Disappearance of Childhood: How TV Is Changing Children's Lives*, London: Comet.

Research Services Ltd (1958) *Parents, Children and Television* (Report for the Independent Television Authority), London: HMSO.

Rogan, Johnny (1989) *Starmakers and Svengalis*, London: Futura.

Simon, Brian (1988) *Bending the Rules: The Baker 'Reform' of Education*, London: Lawrence & Wishart.

Steward, Sue and Garratt, Sheryl (1984) *Signed, Sealed and Delivered: True Life Stories of Women in Pop*, London: Pluto.

Stoney, Barbara (1986) *Enid Blyton: A Biography*, London: Hodder & Stoughton.

Taylor, Peter (1990) 'Beeb in soup over Turtles', *Guardian*, 10 December.

Tibballs, Geoff (1990) *The Secret Life of Sooty*, Letchworth: Ringpress Books.

Tunstall, Jeremy (1986) *Communications Deregulation: The Unleashing of America's Communications Industry*, Oxford: Basil Blackwell.

Vermorel, Judy and Fred (1989) *Fandemonium! The Book of Fans, Cults and Dance Crazes*, London: Omnibus.

Wilson, H. H. (1961) *Pressure Group: The Campaign for Commercial Television*, London: Secker & Warburg.

Winn, Marie (1984) *Children Without Childhood*, Harmondsworth: Penguin.

Winn, Marie (1985) *The Plug-In Drug*, Harmondsworth: Viking Penguin.

Wright, Christopher (1989) *The Weetabix Illustrated British History Book*, Burton Latimer: Weetabix Ltd.

Chapter 7

The price is right but the moments are sticky
Television, quiz and game shows, and popular culture

Garry Whannel

Competition, in various forms, has always been part of the popular repertoire of British television. Game shows, quiz games, panel games and sport itself have been prominent in the schedules since the 1940s. Before this, of course, they were also a significant part of radio programming.

The appeal of quiz and game shows is rooted in a range of pleasures – the narrative structure of competition, the process of identification with competitors, surrogate sharing in the joy of winning, spectacle, excitement and humour, and the opportunity to play along by attempting to get answers before the contestants (Fiske and Hartley 1978: chap.10).

But such shows have always had a very low cultural status. The IBA have periodically intervened to restrict the number of game shows and the amount of prizes. The Pilkington Report was disdainful about the quality of many quiz shows, singling them out as an instance of triviality, and arguing that they involved the exploitation of artificial situations and personalities, while having no real subject matter. The issue would appear to hinge partly on one's attitude to triviality. A great deal of popular entertainment could fairly be called trivial, and indeed makes no claims to be anything else. There seems no necessary reason to insist that all cultural production be serious, worthy or weighty, and Pilkington's notion that triviality is a natural vice of television, more dangerous to the soul than wickedness, has more than an echo of senior common room pomposity (Pilkington 1962).

However, these criticisms clearly also had some resonance in the corridors of power. When the highly successful company Associated Rediffusion lost their ITV franchise in 1967, it is possible that their unabashed pride in their high prize game shows *Double Your Money* and *Take Your Pick* had an adverse effect on the Independent Television Authority.

If the intelligentsia have characteristically shown a lofty contempt for the quiz show, radical critical analysis has been equally hostile. Quiz and game shows are derided as a celebration of consumerism, a part of the society of spectacle and a form of commodity fetishism. Yet like all judgements of taste, class values underlie the critiques of both right and left. No programme currently can incite more disdain from the middle-class intelligentsia than *The Price Is Right*, which has the brash vulgarity not merely to discuss the price of objects, but to make the price the main feature of the show.

At work here is also a hidden structure of values rooted in gender difference. It is a perfectly respected and valued social skill to be able to distinguish the value of different stock market shares or different cars or even different footballers, but *The Price Is Right* features a different level of skill, based upon domestic luxury goods, window shopping and bargain hunting. As an ascribed female domain this skill, although central to the core working of the economy, has low social status.

In order to understand how competition in its various forms works it is necessary to suspend temporarily these questions of taste and social judgement. It must be established that quiz and game shows are not simply about prizes, but are also rooted in implicit statements about the nature of knowledge. They are one of the few areas of television in which ordinary people appear as a matter of course, and compared to 'doggedly serious' television have a high level of humour.

It is also important to examine changes in these forms. Knowledge became less crucial with the rise of the new 1980s game shows (*Play Your Cards Right, Blankety Blank, Family Fortunes*), which depended not on factual information but on offering answers as close to the typical or average as possible. In place of factual knowledge, these programmes valued an ability to produce the 'typical' or 'average' answer.

The role of celebrities has grown. On *Blankety Blank* it is not so much the prize that is the reward of victory, but the rite of passage into the world of the glitterati. While losers are wheeled off set mechanically, winners are given the gift of movement, being allowed to walk across the set to meet the stars. From game show to sport contest this celebration of winners and magical disappearance of losers is a characteristic feature of competition on television.

PRE-HISTORY

It has been argued that quiz shows are one of the few forms that broadcasting has invented for itself. Largely a hybrid medium, much of broadcasting's content is an adaptation from earlier media – films, plays, music-hall variety, and so on. Quiz and panel games may, by contrast, appear as relative innovations, but even these have their antecedents.

The games during the 1950s of *Beat the Clock* on *Sunday Night at the London Palladium* echoed those of fairground sideshows. The tradition of parlour games in Victorian and Edwardian times spawned a whole subgenre from *Animal, Vegetable and Mineral*, in the 1950s to *Call My Bluff* in the 1970s.

Ever since the emergence of a mass circulation popular press at the start of this century, newspapers have made use of the quiz as a means of forging reader involvement. Games like 'Spot the Ball' grew alongside the football pools in the 1930s. *Opportunity Knocks* and other talent shows merely echo a cultural practice that can be traced back via holiday camps to the heyday of the nineteenth century music hall. The huge popularity of bingo is proof enough that broadcasting must be regarded as appropriating, rather than inventing, a national penchant for games that combine skill and chance.

Radio preceded television in pioneering broadcast quiz and game shows; indeed, panel games were incubated in the economics of radio. Such programmes had the merit of being cheap, needing no script, often involving the public but giving scope for celebrity involvement, and offering an opportunity for dramatic tension within the panel. Witness, for example, the huge wartime popularity of *The Brains Trust*, based in part on the interplay between Huxley and Joad, or the part played by Gilbert Harding's notorious testiness on *What's My Line*.

The greatest of all was *Have a Go*, with Wilfred Pickles. In the late 1940s this show had the largest ever regular audience for any British radio or TV programme: 54 per cent of the population tuned in regularly (Tunstall 1983). Other long running formats included *Top of the Form, Round Britain Quiz, My Word* and

My Music, and even the early ITV shows, *Double Your Money* and *Take Your Pick*, were originally radio shows, broadcast by Radio Luxembourg.

In the early 1950s television was still the poor relation of radio. Regarded by many in the BBC as rather trivial and something of a novelty, the television service was nevertheless still formed in the same mould – the Reithian legacy of cultural paternalism, overlaid with a more middle-class suburban layer of English gentility. So it is not surprising that the early panel games on BBC reflected this, in their lack of brashness, relative erudition and absence of prizes.

Ironically, it was precisely by periodically breaching the codes of English gentility that the notoriously testy Gilbert Harding became one of the first TV stars, making the show on which he appeared, *What's My Line*, such a success. It began in 1951, was for a while the most popular programme on television, and has been revived periodically ever since, most recently on ITV.

FROM THE BIRTH OF ITV TO THE PILKINGTON REPORT

So in the context of British television the arrival of ITV ushered in a major shift in the public manifestation of popular taste. Until ITV arrived the British public had, as Peter Black put it, 'never seen anyone earn a pound note for correctly distinguishing his left foot from his right, or a wife win a refrigerator for whitewashing her husband in 30 seconds starting from now' (Black 1972).

Black suggests that quiz shows were central to the building of a big ITV audience. *Double Your Money* and *Take Your Pick*, featured from the very start, were the first television quiz games to have cash prizes. By 1957 there were eight quiz shows a week.

The arrival of this new cultural form was greeted with considerable critical distaste:

> Frivolity and triviality were the order of the day. The commercial channel was the place where couples in boiler suits could win refrigerators if they smashed enough balloons with needles pinned to their noses. It was the channel where silly quiz games like *Double Your Money* and *Take Your Pick* (in which you might win a bedroom suite if you happened to

know that Shakespeare wrote *Hamlet*) were kept running
regularly for twelve years.

(Shulman 1973)

The distaste, echoing from both right and left, has persisted to the
present. Milton Shulman speaks with a traditionally elitist
cultural paternalism, but his tone is characteristically echoed by
forms of media criticism more influenced by the left-wing cultural
paternalism of the Frankfurt School. For instance, Stephen Dark
recently described *The Price Is Right* as 'a new blatantly commercial, aggressively self-centred form of spectacle' (Dark 1985).

Equally striking is the way so many books on television ignore
quiz and game shows entirely. *Inside BBC Television*, by Rosalie
Horner (1983), an otherwise fairly comprehensive account, con-
tains no section on *A Question of Sport* or *Blankety Blank*, which
in 1983 were two of the BBC's most popular programmes.

However, from the start the form met with considerable popular
success. Light entertainment producers have rarely needed or
attained critical acclaim, instead relying on the ratings as proof
that they are giving people what they want. Typically they rest on
a conviction that they are closer to the audience and more in tune
with what it wants than the producers and executives of informative programmes (Bakewell and Garnham 1970), or for that matter
the critics. William G. Stewart, producer of *The Price Is Right*, is
typically confident that, unlike the critics, he understands his
audience.[1]

The principle was etched deeply into professional practice from
the early days of ITV. The initial aim at the popular nerve did not
always hit the target, and in its first year ITV went through a crisis
of confidence, but the technique of winning and holding large
popular audiences was soon refined, as Associated Rediffusions's
Roland Gillette made clear:

> Let's face it once and for all. The public like girls, wrestling,
> bright musicals, quiz shows, and real-life drama. We gave them
> the Hallé Orchestra, Foreign Press Club, floodlit football, and
> visits to the local fire station. Well, we've learned. From now
> on, what the public wants, it's going to get.[2]

The intelligentsia experienced the shock of being confronted with
the realities of the working-class audience, the shock of mass taste.
This is not to suggest that the audience for ITV was exclusively
working class. Television has from the mid-1950s been

seen by large heterogeneous audiences, which, by virtue of the class composition of the country as a whole, are inevitably largely working class. More significant was the new way in which broadcasting, from the earliest days of ITV, began to address the cultural tastes of this audience in a new way. Radio during the Second World War had had to restructure itself to successfully hold and mobilize the mass audience. In the process the narrow class address of the BBC in the 1930s was revealed.[3] In 1955 television was commencing a similar shift, that made the BBC of the early 1950s seem cosily middle class and irrelevant.

Right from the start middle-class, elitist and highbrow concerns were echoed within institutions. The actions of the Independent Television Authority, and the comments of the Pilkington Committee Report on Broadcasting (Pilkington 1962) provide an interesting example both of the ways in which state institutions attempt to structure culture, and an instance of the limitations of that power.

In February 1956 the ITA Director-General Sir Robert Fraser wrote to Richard Meyer of ATV saying that there were too many give-away shows and that the reputation of the programme companies was suffering. But this letter came in the midst of the post-launch financial crisis, with audiences growing very slowly and advertising revenue falling way below forecasts, and Meyer's reply that they needed to use every possible endeavour to obtain maximum audiences was seemingly greeted with sympathy. (Sendall 1982).

The authority did not press the issue at this point but in January 1957, when there were ten give-away quiz shows per week, they suggested that this was too many and should be reduced to seven, and the one-a-day average became the norm. (Sendall 1982).

As always, the ITA was operating within the contradictions of a set of ill-defined roles – bearing a responsibility for making sure that the system was successful, a need to act in the interests of public service broadcasting, and a requirement to ensure good taste. Taste is not only notoriously difficult to define in any absolute or objective terms, it is also almost inevitably structured by class, by gender and indeed by ethnicity. Different cultural traditions have generated different sensibilities, but there is little evidence of a self-consciousness about the process of defining taste in the actions of either the ITA or the Pilkington Committtee.

FROM PILKINGTON TO FRANCHISE RENEWAL

The Pilkington Committee was established in 1960 and reported in 1962. It made a range of criticisms, not least that programmes were trivial and of low quality. In particular it charged that quizzes had potentially harmful social and moral effects. It recommended a reduction in the value of maximum prizes from the existing £1,000 and said that prize winning should be more closely linked to skill and knowledge (Pilkington 1962).

Interesting here is the manifestation of a respectable middle-class disdain for gambling and for the image of people apparently gaining something for nothing. It was clearly felt that reward should only be obtained in exchange for the hard-earned cultural capital of 'skill' or 'knowledge'.

ITA had in fact been limiting the value of prizes since 1957. In his history of the authority, however, Sendall acknowledges a 'retreat from balance' before the looming menace of financial collapse in early 1956 that was, however reluctantly, condoned by the authority. This had meant multiplication in the main viewing hours of relatively cheap programmes of wide mass appeal, such as quiz programmes, party games and audience participation shows (Sendall 1983).

The number of quiz shows had dropped slightly by the start of the 1960s and in 1962 ITV had an average of 120 minutes per week devoted to quiz and panel shows, compared to 80 minutes for the BBC. But the publication of the Pilkington Report served to sensitize the public and the media to the issue and when the autumn schedules in 1962 showed no significant changes, the *Daily Express* greeted the announcement with the headline 'Quiz shows return as ITV defies Pilkington' (Sendall 1983).

The authority continued to exert subtle and gentle pressures in an attempt to steer the quiz form away from the spectacular direction it took in the USA, where huge prizes and dramatic win all/lose all moments had become generic hallmarks. In October 1964 the companies were told by the ITA that they should experiment with more intelligent and more genuine forms of quiz programme. In May 1965 a company was told that an excess of 'give-away' quiz programmes was not good for the image of ITV (Hill 1974).

The pressure was not all in the direciton of restriction. Where a programme seemed to fit middle-class notions about the value of learning and knowledge, the ITA were prepared to push for more air time. When Granada launched *University Challenge* the authority required one company to transmit and another to put it on at an earlier hour (Hill 1974).

However, in 1966 there were still plenty of quiz and game shows on the air. The *ITA Handbook* (1967) listed fifteen different titles including Southern's 'Happy marriage contest', *Seven Year Flitch*, in which married couples competed to prove publicly the strength and quality of their relationship. The programme was loosely derived from a folk tradition, the Great Dunmow Flitch, in which the most happily married couple in the village were rewarded with a gift of a flitch of beef. When *Double Your Money* and *Take Your Pick* were finally taken off, Hughie Green and Michael Miles were soon back on the screen with new formats.

In 1967, Associated Rediffusion found themselves losing their franchise, and were forced into a merger with ABC, in which they became the minority partner in the resultant new company, Thames. There was much speculation about why the ITA had so penalized a company that had not only had great commercial success but had also helped to prop up the ITV system as a whole during its shaky start.

The AR board had always been dominated by businessmen with little direct television experience, and never contained programme-makers. Unlike Granada, they failed to understand the importance of public relations, and of cultivating a well-rounded image. They believed that they should be judged solely on their financial success and programme popularity and failed to realize that they needed to establish their cultural respectability to balance programmes like the critically derided quiz shows. It would be an exaggeration to say that *Double Your Money* and *Take Your Pick* lost them their franchise, but they certainly didn't give them many brownie points with the ITA.

The ITA, in this sense, provides the articulating point of a set of rather confused and ill-defined notions of culture, class and taste. It fulfils the function of imposing a degree of cultural paternalism upon the ITV system without ever really, unlike the BBC in the Reithian era, understanding or articulating what it is doing, or why.

The forms of checks and balances, urges and encouragements that all take place, in fine English fashion, behind closed doors, leave more room for speculation than clarity. However it seems notably to be the case that British television rejected the provision of major spectacular prizes, and the focus of quiz and game shows turned away from that fetishization of commodities characteristic of the American shows of this period. Instead ordinary people, celebrities, and fun and games provided the triple foci of the 1970s generation of shows.

THE COMPONENTS OF GAME SHOWS

While one can fairly identify aspects of the critique of quizzes as pompously patrician and elitist, it would of course be a mistake simply to celebrate the form. But the way to work towards a more informed critique is by first attempting to understand the elements (knowledge, prizes, games, ordinary people, celebrities) and the ways in which they work together in different types of shows.

Knowledge

General knowledge questions of one kind or another have been a quiz show staple from *Double Your Money* and *Take Your Pick* to *The Krypton Factor* and that Victorian schoolroom of the 1980s, *Fifteen to One*. The intellectual quizzes, *Mastermind* and *University Challenge*, that on the face of it may seem radically different, merely depend on a more esoteric and specialized variant of knowledge.

But the form in which these programmes construct knowledge is a very particular one. Specifically, knowledge consists of an accumulation of facts, and these facts exist, severed from any context, as individual and discrete units. Even on *Mastermind*, where in the first round questions all relate to specific narrowly defined specialisms, the facts are disconnected.

John Tulloch points out that quizzes directly penalize any attempt at careful thought, giving no room for interpretation and celebrating knowledge as denoted by possession of facts. Such a view of knowledge abolishes explanation. The presentation of isolated individuals under pressure, needing to produce answers at speed, is at the core of the traditional quiz (Tulloch 1977).

It is worth noting that the set design and staging of *Mastermind* had its origins in the classic film image of interrogation, with lights directed at the victim, while the interrogator (Magnus Magnusson) sits in partial darkness. The original plan was for the contestant to be dragged on by two guards.

It is necessary not only to be in possession of as many facts as possible, but to be able to produce them instantly. In effect the skill most required and celebrated by this type of quiz is the ability to recall, at high speed, single discrete units of factual knowledge. This is, of course, the one function of the brain more efficiently performed by computers. It is ironic that we should, in a cultural form, choose to celebrate this rather than the ability to reason or analyse.

On the importance of a quick, instinctive response, Carl Gardner commented 'Deep thought, hesitation, double-checking, tentativeness, correction, all important features of intellectual processes in social life – are penalised' (Gardner 1980). In addition, of course, the contestant is not permitted to cross-question, or enter into debate with, the interrogator. On television quizzes it is definitely a case of 'we ask the questions'.

If there is a residual presence of the imagery of interrogation, the more dominant referent in the intellectual quizzes is the education system. *Top of the Form* and *University Challenge* draw specifically on different educational levels, while *Mastermind* is always filmed in educational establishments, and *Fifteen to One* adopts a stylized form of traditional learning by rote teaching in which the pupils are interrogated in rotation.

The representation of an isolated individual reached its most alienating form in *Double Your Money* which, starting with absurdly easy questions, gradually works its way towards the climax in which the contestant was placed (locked?) in a sound-proof booth. The image is of education as an individualized trial by ordeal, in which the contestant is publicly examined, with a clear divide between success and failure.

Of course not all quiz shows draw upon an academic form of knowledge. The knowledge required in *The Price Is Right* is, by contrast, a knowledge of the prices of relatively ordinary domestic luxury goods.

It could be argued that the show validates a social skill, not generally given a cultural value, and largely possessed by women rather than men – the skill of bargain hunting. This is acquired by window shopping, catalogue reading and judicious purchasing, but only over time. It is a hard-won form of social knowledge generally given a low social status, precisely because of its having been socially constructed as largely a female domain. *The Price Is Right* brings the skill and its competitive performance into the public domain. It seems to me that this, rather than the acquisition of what are for the most part relatively mundane items, is at the core of the show.

At the same time the show clearly does provide an example of the celebration of consumer culture, produced with all the brashness of an advert for the *Sun*. Indeed, it is the high energy intensity of the programme that most marks it out from some of its predecessors. Slightly frenetic music punctuates the show; contestants, chosen for their vivacity, are encouraged to be demonstrative; the audience are schooled in advance in their participatory role; and even the shimmering backdrop gives an impression of constant movement. The conjunction of everyday domestic goods and glossy showbusiness brings together public glamour and private domesticity. Whereas on *Blankety Blank* the real prize is getting to meet the celebrities, on *The Price Is Right*, more than any other British show, the contestants are the stars, famous for fifteen minutes.

During the last twenty years an increasing number of game shows have drawn upon skills other than that of fact-retrieval. *The Generation Game* required an ability to perform and to memorize items on the conveyor belt, *3-2-1* and *Treasure Hunt* require skills of deduction, and *The Krypton Factor* required a range of physical and manipulative skills. What they have in common is that the skill or knowledge can be traded in for prizes. In Tulloch's terms, what you know can be directly translated into 'things', or what you can do, how you can perform, can be cashed for prizes.

Prizes

Points make prizes, as Bruce Forsyth constantly said in *Play Your Cards Right* – emphasizing the direct link between delivering correct answers and gaining material reward. But the cultural regulation of the Independent Television Authority (later the Independent Broadcasting Authority) has ensured that these prizes in themselves have not become the hugely fetishized lavish rewards typical of the American game show.

As a result it is not so much the prizes themselves but what they represent that is the significant feature. In *Take Your Pick* and *3-2-1* the prize you won had an element of chance – winning is seen as a lottery.

The tendency of the early quizzes to celebrate the prizes reached its height during the 1970s in *Sale of the Century*. The prizes, showcased, lit to emphasize their glitzy properties and surrounded by glamorous models, were presented in the form of vulgar display – winning was portrayed as conspicuous consumption.

By contrast in *The Price Is Right* the rather more everyday presentation of the prizes gives them the appearance of the products of luxury shopping – winning is represented as a free spending spree. The prizes clearly echo patterns of class taste; in a sense, the range of prizes are messages about class taste and it would be possible to chart broader cultural shifts by examining the transitions from the innocent joy of winning fridges in the 1950s, through the vulgar celebration of conspicuous consumption in *Sale of the Century*, to the more complex reactions to commodities in, say, *Blankety Blank*. The audience reaction to the prizes in *Sale of the Century* seems to signify approval and envy. The *Blankety Blank* prizes are deliberately chosen to have low desirability, a reading heavily signalled by the expression and voice tone of the presenter, and underlined by the audience who play along with the gentle parody of the show, by themselves parodying the appropriate audience reaction.

Other game shows have abandoned material goods altogether, by turning people and relationships into objects, to be won and evaluated. *Blind Date*, a show born out of the pre-AIDS 1980s, offers sexuality as a lottery – you win a partner, but one chosen 'blind', while the older and more traditional *Mr and Mrs* rewards winners with public confirmation of their compatibility. Prizes are also de-emphasized in the intellectual quizzes, *Mastermind*, *University Challenge* and *The Krypton Factor*, where the real prize is status.

Some of the new game shows, most notably *Blankety Blank* are self-reflexive jokes about the excesses of the form, and so the prizes are deliberately a bit naff, are presented as such, and the audience, who are in on the joke, respond appropriately, either by groaning or producing on cue, suitably satirical 'oohs' of mock amazement.

While most of these new game shows have prizes, in a sense they are actually not about winning prizes, but are about ordinary people being on television – the real prize is your fifteen minutes of fame (Root 1986: chap. 5).

A similar set of differences can be seen to underlie the role of the audience. In the intellectual quizzes the audiences are there primarily as reverent witnesses – the superior skill of the contestants doesn't really admit any active participation. By contrast, the more populist quizzes have always actively mobilized audience participation. *Take Your Pick* with its frenzied cries of 'take the money/open the box' was the first real audience participation show, and the same device is used to great effect on *Play Your Cards Right* with its shouts of 'higher/lower' and on *The Price Is Right* with its general free-style yelling. And on some of the new game shows the audience are actually the source of knowledge in that they have provided the answers. Members of the audience answer questionnaires to provide the mock-statistical data that then becomes the substance for the 'we asked 100 people. . .' variety.

The process of identification with someone winning and losing is clearly a major element in the way such programmes address their audience and in the way game shows produce pleasures. Just as the prizes seem more important for what they signify than for what they are, the focus of the shows is not the objects that are won, but the process of winning them. In this sense the suggestion that quiz and game shows stimulate greed and acquisitiveness is questionable – as a critique it is not grounded in an understanding of how this cultural form actually operates.

Games

A long tradition of knock-about fun within public entertainment clearly pre-dates television game shows, as anyone who has been to a Butlin's holiday camp or witnessed a knobbly knees contest will testify.

The games in game shows have always featured a combination of slapstick, humour, public humiliation and practical joke, but here too the cultural paternalism of the ITA has occasionally been in evidence doing some subtle behind-the-scenes steering. Derek Roy's 1950s show *People Are Funny* featured practical jokes, such as a woman invited to smash crockery wrapped in cloth, only to find it was her own (Black 1972). The series ended after the ITA asked for it to be toned down, and it was replaced by the funnier but more restrained *Candid Camera* – the current variant on this theme is *Game for a Laugh*. It must be assumed that a combination of self-censorship and discreet IBA guidance continues to police the bounds of good taste.

One of the first shows resolutely to switch the balance decisively away from the prizes and towards the fun and games was Bruce Forsyth's hugely popular *The Generation Game*, which had a regular audience of more than 20 million in the 1970s. Along with *It's a Knockout* and *Jeux sans frontières* (Whannel 1982) that centred upon the willingness of ordinary people to participate in games involving costumes, embarrassments, plunges into cold water and sundry humiliations, it brought the greasy pole principle to a fine television art, our fascination with the greasy pole being in the voyeuristic pleasure of seeing someone fall off.

It is important not to underestimate the role of humour in game shows generally – it marks them off as distinctly different, not just from the doggedly serious world of news and current affairs, but also from crime series and soaps like *EastEnders* and *Brookside*, which may have their moments of humour, but are not primarily about 'fun'. Fiske argues that one of the contradicitons of the game show form, that opens it up to a range of audience readings, is the way it blends a showbusiness sense of fun, glitter and excitement with the knowledge and discipline of the schoolroom (Fiske 1987: chap. 14).

Richard Dyer suggests that entertainment characteristically offers abundance, energy and community, in contrast to the scarcity, exhaustion and isolation more common to lived reality (Dyer 1977). He argues that entertainment is in this sense often rooted in a utopian sensibility, offering an idealized world from which scarcity, tiredness and loneliness have been eliminated.

While it is in no sense utopian, a show like *The Price Is Right* could be seen in these terms, for it is nothing if not exuberant. Everything about the staging of the show is designed to produce the impression of energy and the audience are galvanized into a temporary frenetic community. It cannot be denied that, in the last analysis, the experience is structured around the competition to win commodities; but, to a large extent, it is the process rather than the end result around which identification is constructed.

ORDINARY PEOPLE

Quizzes and game shows are one of the few areas of television in which 'ordinary people' play a central role and as the form has developed they have increasingly been required to perform. Contestants now are often chosen for their personalities, which they are encouraged to display, being required to act as straight men and women for the compère.

Burton Paulu cites an unnamed BBC executive as telling him in the 1950s that the British were naturally shy and would not like to compete – and if they did would make poor performers (Paulu 1981). While the IBA in its role as cultural prefect has steered such shows away from the more bizarre spectacles of American, Japanese and Italian game shows, the success of *Blind Date, Game for a Laugh* and the like suggests that British 'ordinary people' can internalize and reproduce the conventions of public display in a satisfactory manner. Indeed, it is essential for the success of a show like *Blind Date* that the contestants understand and can perform the role successfully – a contestant who wished to challenge the conventions would produce great unease and would risk appearing as a bad sport.

The conventions of game shows, which appear to celebrate a shared culture, act in fact as a rather constricting set of structures in which gender roles are demarcated. Women are expected to respond cheerfully to the flirtatious approach of the compère and play along with the risqué asides and double entendres. The contestants and the brief biographical details they are asked to furnish become no more than the raw material with which the 'spontaneous' comedy is created. Not only must this be experienced by contestants as objectification, but in having to occupy the position of 'good sport' they have to perform social roles, and especially gender roles, they may not necessarily wish to inhabit.

While *Blind Date* offers a small degree of negotiation over gender roles, it is only the start of the road to *Mr and Mrs*, by which time the genders are well and truly straitjacketed. *Blind Date* allows for small variations in the degree of dominance-subordination, extroversion–introversion, around which relationships unfold, but to a very large degree contestants have to perform a public and stagey version of the ritual of chatting-up. A premium is placed on the ability to be wacky, witty and, above all, sexually suggestive. In reporting back on the

course the 'blind date' took, the programme sets up a sexual
tease, but can deliver no revelation on the question that engages
the audience so much: did they or didn't they? The delicate
sensibilities of the TV Act and the IBA in its role as guardian of
public morality allow no such indelicacy, and the 'blind date' is
in any case heavily chaperoned. The programme has at last been
able to celebrate a marriage resulting directly from its match-
making for this is, after all, the ultimate social destiny for the
route that starts with chatting-up and blind-dating. It celebrates
then, not merely a social ritual, but a social career structure. *Mr
and Mrs* sits at the other end of the lifecycle, placing final
validation upon those couples who can demonstrate the
longevity and closeness of their bonding. Couples are judged, not
on how happy they are, but on how well they know each other –
and, not surprisingly, the questions are laden with normative
assumptions as to the nature of married lives and the respective
roles of men and women within marriage.

In the world of blind dates and fortunate families there is little
space for openly gay contestants and, until the rather extraordinary *Sticky Moments*, it was hard to imagine any British
game show being able to handle or even acknowledge gayness.
The show, fronted by alternative comedian, Julian Clary, grew
out of the short-lived and self-consciously tacky *Trick or Treat*.

Where shows like *Blankety Blank* offer gentle and affectionate
parody of the game show form, *Sticky Moments* presents a
surreal satire in which bizarre costume and set design, amateur
dramatic performance by the contestants and wickedly targeted
camp humour by the compère burst through the rather cosy
suburban boundaries of the form in its more conventional
manifestations. The programme's appeal is complex and cannot
be fully disentangled here. In establishing a set of differences and
uneasiness around sexuality, it manages to establish a rather
louche and risqué ambience, sustained by the sense of difference
between the elegant campness of Julian Clary and the more
conventional (and apparently straight) contestants. The questions, answers and prizes are here completely decentred, to be
replaced by camp humour, and the voyeuristic spectacle of other
people in discomfort. It is a combination of some potential force,
not least because it precisely constructs a space for the middle-
class intellectual audience that would not admit to pleasure in a
more straight game show. Similarly, *Style Trial* addresses and

implicates its audience with a sort of covert knowing wink, offering satire of the form, while structurally and formally offering pleasures very similar to those central to more conventional game shows.

There is a relative absence of black and Asian contestants on British game shows, and an unarticulated unease over race. The 'shared culture' that these programmes draw on is in many ways an exclusive and excluding white culture. From the range of subjects on *Mastermind* to the clues on *Treasure Hunt*, the cultural referents are to a distinctly white past, white cultural tradition and even, in the pastoralism of *Treasure Hunt*, to a white geography. Even the lists of *Family Fortunes* and word choices of *Blankety Blank* seem to grow out of a white sensibility. Game show prizes may reflect a working-class taste, but in some ways it is also a distinctly white taste. In the game show world some people are more 'ordinary' than others.

Celebrities

Television as a medium is structured around familiar faces; personalities and celebrities. The very identity of programmes is closely tied to their presenters and compères.

So a change of compère constitutes a problem for the producers as programme image and audience expectation are disrupted. *Blankety Blank* managed the transition from Wogan to Les Dawson successfully, whereas *Family Fortunes* encountered greater problems when Bob Monkhouse was replaced by the rather less quick-fire Max Bygraves.

But it is not just the presenter who provides celebrity appeal. From the 1970's onwards game show formats increasingly incorporated celebrities. *Celebrity Squares* led the way by finding a way of including nine such figures, *3-2-1* brought showbusiness personalities on with clues to aid the contestants, and in shows like *Blankety Blank*, and *Punchlines* the celebrities began to assume centre stage with contestants marginalized. Other quizzes, such as *A Question of Sport* and *Give us a Clue*, reverting to the original panel format of *What's My Line*, eliminate ordinary people as contestants entirely.

The roles of such celebrities are heavily conventionalized, especially in *Blankety Blank*, where there is a seat for the cheeky wise-cracking comedian, invariably male, a back row for those who play second fiddle to the main wit, and a seat, nearest to Dawson, usually occupied by a variant of the dumb blonde.

Blankety Blank commences with contestants on one side of the set, and celebrities on the other. Contestants do not walk on; the elaborate machinery of the set wheels them on and, if they lose, it wheels them off again. To win through the early stages is to win the right of movement – you get to stand up and be pushed into position by Les Dawson. In achieving final victory, you win, as well as the self-consciously 'cheap' prizes, entry into the world of celebrities: the winner is taken over to meet the panel. This, then, is the real 'prize', a brief opportunity to mingle with the glitterati of the world of showbusiness.

And the world of showbusiness is increasingly co-terminous with the world of television. Television as a medium is increasingly self-reflexive. Game shows like *Telly Addicts,* which uses television as its subject matter, *Blankety Blank* which offers a gentle parody of game shows, or the radio programme *I'm Sorry I Haven't a Clue,* which offers a more full-blooded parody, are all instances of the growing tendency for broadcast entertainment to become a closed self-referential system.

Game shows are based on very carefully designed and re-searched formats, many of those we see having been devised by the American duo, Goodson and Todman. They hold rights to formats, titles, set designs and prop designs. Talbot TV, based in New York, has European rights to Goodson Todman games. The package bought by a broadcaster includes script advice, question research advice and sometimes even an American producer as adviser. Rights payments for formats can vary widely but between £1,000 and £5,000 per show would not be untypical (Jeremy Fox, quoted in *Broadcast,* 4 April 1983).

But games cannot always be imported intact. Many of the original US shows have a tougher competitive and acquisitive tone and have been watered down for the British market, a process echoed in title changes. So *Family Feuds* became *Family Fortunes* and *Card Sharks* became *Play Your Cards Right.* Such changes are revealing – not that they reflect directly differences in American and British culture, but that they signify differences in the process of cultural production. Television production is rooted in different institutional arrangements – the IBA imposes a regulatory framework upon competition, and both channels agree to restrict prize value. Producers make different assumptions about audiences, and these assumptions become embedded into programme form. So the contestants in America are characteristically placed within rituals through which they perform a rather atavistic and competitive acquisitiveness. The reconstruction of these rituals in the British context de-emphasizes competitiveness and foregrounds the byplay between contestant and presenter. British audiences and presenters do not appear to respond well to a clever-dick (except within the confines of academe in *Mastermind* or *University Challenge*) and also become distinctly unhappy if a contestant seems likely to lose everything. It would be too simple to relate all this to the much more unabashed competitive individualism of life in the USA, compared to the rather more modest communality of British culture, but it does suggest that cultural images are being constructed with this imaginary contrast in mind.

POPULISM AND THE NEW AUTHORITY

The most significant feature of the new breed of game shows that were dominating the ratings at the start of the 1980s was that they marked a break with the traditional knowledge-as-fact model.

In shows like *Play Your Cards Right, Family Fortunes*, and *Blankety Blank* the type of knowledge used as currency is not 'objective fact' but 'public opinion', or knowledge of social discourse. The questions are based on the answers to various forms of poll. In *Blankety Blank* the audience has been polled as to the most suitable word to fill the blank, and the word chosen most often constitutes the 'correct' answer. In *Family Fortunes*, people have been asked to list objects or activities in various categories (e.g. 'What items might you find on a beach?') and in *Play Your Cards Right* a typical question might be 'We asked one hundred nurses if most doctors have cold hands. How many said yes?' In all cases the correct answer is not determined by absolute fact but by the popular vote, by the weight of public opinion. Mills and Rice argue that it is an understanding of the rules of everyday commonsense discourse rather than the world of objective and authenticated 'facts' that enables success (Mills and Rice 1982).

This indicates a marked shift in the ideological basis from knowledge as absolute to knowledge as attitude. The knowledge is constructed out of public opinion, albeit of a particular kind, so it is not learning or information, but a grasp of popular commonsense that becomes the prerequisite skill. Winners are those who can produce consensual answers, losers produce aberrant answers, so the programmes reward normality and penalize deviance.

Without wanting to force too direct a connection, it is worth noting that the rise of this type of show came during the same period that Thatcherism, by appealing to the 'commonsense' of 'ordinary people', was seeking to overthrow the dominant orthodoxy of the old Butskellite welfare state consensualist politics, which still provided the overarching structure for the increasingly crisis-ridden attempts of the Heath and Wilson governments of the 1970s to control the British economy.

One part of the Thatcherite project was to sweep away old outmoded notions, and to challenge the conventional wisdom, but to do so by addressing ordinary people through the terms of commonsense – 'every housewife knows you can't spend more money than you have', as Mrs Thatcher continually pointed out. The shift involved a populist challenge to the experts, the professionals and the possessors of facts. In similar fashion the new game shows rejected the academy and the authority of the fact in favour of the populism of what ordinary people believe.

But this was only one part of the Thatcher project, and the other was rooted in a return to Victorian values; the imposition of a new social authority rooted in self-reliance, self-discipline, heightened competitiveness and, within the shrunken and faded velvet glove of the old welfare state, a freshly armoured iron fist of repression and authoritarianism.

The old conventional wisdom has been well and truly demolished by the first populist advance of Thatcher's rise to power, and for the last few years the work has been to construct a new orthodoxy. In education this project meant attacking, not knowledge as such, but the liberal pedagogy of the 1960s – mixed ability teaching, child-centred learning, egalitarian strategies and so on. In the place of this ethos, the intention is to reintroduce ability hierarchies, invigorate the private sector and reassert that traditional model in which the teacher as possessor of knowledge transmits this to the student according to a rigid syllabus.

Is it entirely without significance that at least one new game show, *Fifteen to One*, seems to be implicitly rooted in that most competitive of models for education, the Victorian classroom? The presenter (or teacher), William G. Stewart, fires a series of questions at his pupils until one by one they are eliminated by failure, leaving one victor. The show is doggedly serious and those who fail are fairly cursorily dismissed. Contestants stand silent in a disciplined line and speak only when spoken to. The irony is that Stewart was also responsible for producing *The Price Is Right*, in which the cheerfully unruly audience are much more like children let out of school.

It would be absurd to argue that a programme like *Fifteen to One* is planned to buttress a return to Victorian values in education. But popular culture is a part of the climate of the times, and indeed does not just reflect it but helps to produce it. *Fifteen to One* is not alone – there has been a general return of game shows based upon a more traditional performance of intellectual skill – as witnessed in programmes like *Countdown* and *Blockbusters*.   The Thatcher era also seems to haunt Bruce Forsyth's show, *Takeover Bid*, in which contestants start with lots of commodities and have to make shrewd bets and answer questions in order to hold onto them. In an era when the featherbed of the welfare state is being withdrawn, unemployment is endemic and high interest rates are producing record numbers of mortgage foreclosures and business bankruptcies, it is just possible to see the shadow of the bailiff lurking behind this particular show, dubbed by the *Guardian*, the 'Me Generation Game'. Popular culture always has to address, handle and defuse such tensions and anxieties and it does not always do it in overt and explicit ways.

All game shows are clearly also offering particular images of the world and such images have successfully to articulate themes within the structure of lived cultures if the shows are to succeed. In this sense a programme like *Fifteen to One* can be seen as both an oblique response to a reassertion of competition in education, but also part of the process by which a model of competitive acquisition of knowledge gains valid social currency.

The Thatcherite project does not struggle to become hegemonic only by working within the realm of organized political discourse, but also by operating within that area of cultural life in which the confused and chaotic ground of popular commonsense is constantly trod and retrod by more organized public representations. Popular cultural forms like game shows offer fun, pleasure, entertainment and a break from the dogged and grim 'real' world of news and current affairs. But they are also rooted in the process of meaning production and, through them, albeit in confused and contradictory form, elements of common-sense become articulated together in clusters that in turn become available for articulation within more organized and coherent ideological themes. Game shows carry no polemic for a particular form of education, but they do offer a set of messages about the relation between ordinary people, knowledge and material reward.

If the role of knowledge is changing, so is the role of prizes. Pressure is being applied on the IBA to lift the restrictions on the value of prizes, allowing prizes as high as £100,000. Thames producer Bob Louis said: 'I can't see anything wrong with someone winning a house or a Porsche. People have got bored with fridges or small family cars as prizes' (*Daily Mirror*, 21 May 1988). Others have even more grandiose ambitions. Jon Schofield of Central says: 'If someone was going to win a million, it would clear the streets. People would be glued to their sets' (ibid.).

The White Paper on Broadcasting (HMSO 1988) proposes abolishing the IBA and replacing it with a new body which will guide the companies with a lighter touch. Given the heightened competitiveness of the new broadcasting environment which will force the average cost per hour of programmes down, a cheap and yet popular form like the game show is likely to be prominent in the schedules. With deregulation, lavish prizes may well offer a new spectacularization with which to defeat competitors in the race for prime time audiences. It may be that quizzes and game shows are soon to become rather closer to being the celebration of conspicuous consumption that their critics have always alleged them to be.

NOTES

This piece had its genesis in the work of the Media Group at the Centre for Contemporary Cultural Studies, Birmingham University on popular television, between 1978 and 1982. My thanks to Michael O'Shaughnessy, Dorothy Hobson, Hazel Carby and Adam Mills.

1 See comments by Stewart in the television series *Open The Box* (Beat/ BFI for Channel 4, 1986), and also see the accompanying book by Jane Root (1986).

2 Roland Gillette, of Associatied Rediffusion, December 1955, quoted in Peter Black (1972).
3 'Radio in World War Two' in *Popular Culture*, Open University Course U203, Milton Keynes, 1981.

REFERENCES

Bakewell, Joan and Garnham, Nicholas (1970) *The New Priesthood*, London: Allen Lane.
Black, Peter (1972) *The Mirror in the Corner*, London: Hutchinson.
Dark, Stephen (1985) in Dick Fiddy (ed.) *The Television Yearbook*, London: Virgin.
Dyer, Richard (1977) 'Entertainment and Utopia', *Movie* 24.
Fiske, John (1987) 'Quizzical pleasures', *Television Culture*, London: Methuen
Fiske, John and Hartley, John (1978) *Reading Television*, London: Methuen.
Gardner, Carl *Time Out*, 11 April 1980.
Hill, Lord (1974) *Behind the Screen*, London: Sidgwick & Jackson.
HMSO (1988) *Broadcasting in the 1990s: Competition, Choice and Quality*, Cmnd 517, London: HMSO.
Horner, Rosalie (1983) *Inside BBC Television*, London: Webb & Bower.
Mills, Adam and Rice, Phil (1982) 'Quizzing the popular', *Screen Education* 41 (Winter/Spring).
Paulu, Burton (1981) *Television and Radio in the United Kingdom*, London: Macmillan.
Pilkington, Sir Harry (1962) *Report of the Committee on Broadcasting*, Cmnd 17543, London: HMSO.
Root, Jane (1986) *Open The Box*, London: Comedia.
Sendall, Bernard (1982) *Independent Television in Britain: Volume 1 Origin and Foundation 1946–62*, London: Macmillan.
Sendall, Bernard (1983) *Independent Television in Britain: Volume 2 Expansion and Change*, London: Macmillan.
Shulman, Milton (1973) *The Least Worst Television in the World*, London: Barrie & Jenkins.
Tulloch, John (1977) 'Gradgrind's heirs: the quiz and presentation of "knowledge" by British television', in Geoff Whitty and Michael F. D. Young (eds) *Explorations in the Politics of School Knowledge*, Studies in Education, London: Driffield.
Tunstall, Jeremy (1983) *The Media in Britain*, London: Constable.
Whannel, Garry (1982) ' "It's a Knock-Out": constructing communities', *Block* 6.

Chapter 8

Embedded persuasions
The fall and rise of integrated advertising

Graham Murdock

NOW YOU DON'T SEE IT, NOW YOU DO

In 1957 the American journalist Vance Packard published *The Hidden Persuaders*, a trenchant critique of US advertising aimed at the motivation researchers who were designing campaigns that spoke directly to the subconscious fears and desires revealed by depth psychology. For Packard the issues raised were primarily moral. Was it ethically acceptable to play 'upon the hidden weaknesses and frailties to sell products' or to exploit 'our deepest sexual sensitivities and yearnings for commercial purposes' or to seek to manipulate children? (Packard 1963: 209). These worries struck a responsive chord and helped to sell over a hundred thousand copies in the first year of publication. The book also resonated with wider political concerns.

As the Cold War against the Soviet Union intensified it became more important than ever for the United States to present itself as a democracy based on rational argument and open choice. The techniques Packard described smacked of the thought control and brainwashing associated with communist regimes. Suspicion that the activities of depth psychologists might be unAmerican were underscored by a widely publicized marketing experiment in a New Jersey cinema early in 1957, in which the applied psychologist, James Vicary, flashed messages exhorting the patrons to 'Drink Coca Cola' and 'Eat popcorn' during a feature film. These 'subliminal' advertisements as he called them, were projected every five seconds for one three-thousandth of a second, well below the threshold of conscious perception (M.C. Miller 1990). Vicary's claim that sales increased was disputed, but whether the technique actually worked was less important than what it symbolized. Early in 1958, he demonstrated it in Washington, before an audience of congressmen, regulators and journalists. None of them noticed anything untoward and Vicary seemed to have proved his point. As the advertising journal *Printers' Ink* noted, somewhat dryly, 'Having gone to see something that is not supposed to be seen, and having not seen it, as forecast, they seemed satisfied' (quoted in Fox 1985: 186). Soon afterwards, the New York State Senate made subliminal advertisements illegal and the National Association of Broadcasters banned them from the airwaves.

Although Vicary's experiment had been conducted in a movie theatre, many of the deepest fears centred around commercial television. Not only had this new medium overtaken the cinema as the major leisure activity, but unlike the movies it penetrated into the heart of the home and exposed children to visual advertising in its most sophisticated forms. In response to public concern, the three major American television networks were quick to ban subliminal ads from their stations as an illegitimate form of promotion. By this time, the debate had reached the United Kingdom.

When the first English edition of *The Hidden Persuaders* appeared in 1957 Packard's analysis was widely taken as an outline of things to come, and more specifically as a warning against allowing British culture to become too Americanized. The synopsis on the back cover of the Penguin paperback edition was quite explicit:

> Whether we like it or not, most American habits, tastes, and institutions are eventually imported into Britain: American pop-songs and hair styles – and American advertising techniques. Thus the frightening processes evolved and applied by American super-advertising-scientists are having an increasing effect upon the potential victims in Britain.

This concern drew on deep-seated fears of being 'invaded' by American culture that stretched back to the moral panics about the importation of jazz and Hollywood movies in the early part of the century. These fears surfaced again in discussions around the introduction of commercial television. As Lord Reith, the BBC's first Director-General, put it in a famous speech during the House of Lords debate on the subject in May 1952: 'somebody introduced smallpox, bubonic plague and the Black Death [into

England]. Somebody is minded now to introduce sponsored broadcasting' (quoted in Wilson 1961: 107). Few other commentators were prepared to go quite this far, but there was a widespread feeling within the Establishment that a television service funded by advertising was thoroughly alien and unBritish and would undermine public broadcasting's mission to build a common national culture.

They were particularly incensed by the fact that the American networks had broken their gentleman's agreement with the BBC not to interrupt their US coverage of the Queen's coronation ceremony in Westminster Abbey with ads. This hostility was given campaigning form by the National Television Council, founded in 1953 on the initiative of Lady Violet Bonham-Carter, to resist the introduction of commercial television and press for the 'development of public-service television in the national interest' (quoted in Wilson 1961: 157). Despite the support of prominent parliamentarians and churchmen, however, the opponents of television advertising lost the argument, and the Television Act authorizing the new Independent Television service (ITV) became law in July 1954.

That same year, food rationing was finally abolished and restrictions on hire purchase agreements were lifted, giving a major boost to the sales of durable goods, including television sets (Nevett 1982: 178). By the end of the following year, 1955, the four major ITV companies had all begun regular services and were reaching 60 per cent of the population. By 1958 the number of licences issued had risen to 8 million, up from 3 million in 1954, making advertising on the new medium an attractive proposition. It was against this background of rapid expansion, and persistent worries about the abuse of advertising power, that Packard launched his polemic.

Even before his book appeared, *The Times* had carried a piece reporting that American advertisers were beginning to explore subliminal techniques, and the BBC had made two programmes about the issue, and included its own experiments. The professional consensus was that the practice was not well suited to television, with its slower moving image. Even so, concern about its possible use for advertising and political propaganda rumbled on through the early days of ITV. Although there were no recorded cases of subliminal advertising actually being used, the Pilkington Committee which reported on the state of television in 1962 urged that it should be banned. Their recommendation was duly incorporated into the revised Television Act of 1964. That same year, Tony Benn, the Postmaster General in the newly elected Labour government of Harold Wilson which was actively hostile to the BBC (see Cockerell 1988: chap. 9) used his powers under the licence and agreement to issue a directive prohibiting the corporation from transmitting any material:

> which using images of very brief duration or by any other means, exploits the possibility of conveying a message to, or otherwise influencing the minds of, members of an audience without their being aware, or fully aware of what has been done.

> (D. Miller 1990: 35)

This was only the fifth time that these powers had been used since the foundation of the BBC.

These curbs have insulated British public broadcasting from 'hidden' persuasions. But there are other kinds of promotion, midway between the clearly signalled advertisement and the surreptitious plug, that have proved far more resilient and much more extensive in their impact. These are the 'embedded' persuasions that are integrated into the programmes themselves. This paper traces their development on British television and looks at the new forms that are emerging now.

CORPORATE VISIONS: VARIETIES OF INTEGRATED ADVERTISING

There are five main ways in which companies can promote their products and corporate images, over and above 'spot' advertising in clearly designated advertisements.

First, they can supply goods and services to a programme-maker free or at considerably less than the wholesale cost, in return for oral and written acknowledgements on screen. This is common with game shows, where the featured prizes, such as cars or foreign holidays, are frequently provided by companies.

Second, again in return for on-screen credits, a corporation may put up all or part of the money that enables a television station to buy or produce a series of programmes. This practice, known as underwriting, is a simple exchange of cash for publicity. It is a major feature of the Public Broadcasting System in the United States, where companies like Mobil subsidize the purchase of 'high quality' programmes from Britain and elsewhere as a way of improving and softening their corporate image. Although underwriting does not give a corporate sponsor any direct say in editorial decisions, the fact that they are more interested in being associated with some kinds of programmes than others can affect what gets made in the longer term (see Murdock 1989).

Third, there is sponsorship proper. This takes two main forms: sponsorship of a sporting or arts event that is then broadcast with due credit to the sponsor during the programme and in the publicity promoting it, and direct sponsorship of programme-making, either through a co-production agreement with a production organization, or through a commercial company making programmes on its own account. As we shall see, event sponsorship has a long history in British broadcasting, stretching back to the earliest days of BBC radio, but direct programme sponsorship has always been prohibited, apart from a brief flirtation with advertising features and industrial films in the early years of ITV.

The fourth form of embedded persuasion, product placement, involves paying to have a product, or an advertisement for it, appear as a logical part of the action in a drama. It ranges from having a billboard advertising a company brand prominently displayed in a street scene to having the hero or heroine actually use the product. The trick is to incorporate the promotional message into the action in such a way that it appears entirely 'natural'. As one enthusiast has explained: 'The appearance of a product or brand name may *seem* incidental; in reality product placements are deliberately and strategically made' (Zazza 1986: 35). Although it is strictly prohibited in British television programmes at the present time, there are various ways it can enter through the back door.

The final form of embedded persuasion consists of programmes that are made up of advertisements for products or which constitute an extended promotion for a particular product range. The first type is exemplified by rock programmes built around video clips promoting new record releases (and music videos) and by the home shopping shows where viewers are invited to telephone orders for goods they have just seen displayed or demonstrated on the screen. The best examples of the second type, often known as 'long form' advertising or 'programme-length commercials' (to distinguish them from conventional spot ads), are the cartoon series based around ranges of toys. Because they are aimed at young children, who are felt to be particularly suggestible, these shows have been the focus of continual concern. Certainly the figures for toy sales show a strong correlation with cartoon promotion, with the years 1984–7 being dominated by Masters of the Universe and Transformers (see Croft 1989). In the United States, the walls protecting diversity have already come down. The policy of encouraging children's educational programmes has been discontinued and the limits on the allowable amount of spot advertising abolished, shifting the 'authorship' of children's programmes decisively 'from television studios to the toy industry' and a range of other commercial interests, from greetings card manufacturers to cereal-makers and home video distributors (see Engelhardt 1986).

Historically, the British regulatory system has erected a series of Chinese walls to limit the scope of commercial influence and protect the editorial independence of programme-makers. Not surprisingly, advertisers have made continual attempts to scale them or tunnel underneath. Occasionally they have succeeded, as with the advertising magazines in the early days of ITV. More often they have been turned back, only to regroup, returning to chip away at the walls' weakest points. Now, with a more liberal regulatory regime in place for commercial television and a new production system emerging, the walls may finally be coming down, giving advertisers much greater scope to influence the content and mix of programming. This is the latest move in a long war of attrition between public broadcasting and corporate promotion that began with the birth of radio.

RADIO DAYS : EARLY EXPERIMENTS WITH SPONSORSHIP

In the summer of 1922, the American telephone company AT & T opened its first 'phone booth of the air' offering advertisers studio time to make a broadcast on payment of a fee. Some of the early users, like the cosmetics company Mineralava, promoted their products directly, persuading the silent film star, Marion Davies to talk about 'How I make up for the movies' and inviting listeners to write in for a signed photograph. Other companies settled for 'trade name publicity' by associating themselves with a programme. This indirect approach was pioneered by the Browning King clothing company who supported a weekly one-hour series of concerts featuring the Browning King Orchestra. Others soon followed, including the Kodak Chorus and the Goodrich Silvertown Orchestra (Barnouw 1978: 14–20).

According to the conventional wisdom, the BBC resolutely refused to dirty its hands with sponsorship. In fact, the relevant clause in the original agreement with the government which dealt with advertising was somewhat ambiguous. According to at least one senior executive, it only prohibited the BBC from accepting 'money in return for advertising facilities', it did not forbid advertising as such (Smith 1974: 46). During its brief private life as the British Broadcasting Company (before it became a public institution – the British Broadcasting Corporation) this loophole was used to transmit a number of sponsored concerts, beginning with one supported by the Harrods department store in 1923. A number of commentators objected and even queried whether this was legal. Others were more sympathetic, arguing that it was 'rather a tall order' to expect the financially hard-pressed BBC to refuse 'a concert of a character markedly superior to that which they could provide out of their present comparatively limited resources, merely because the giver announced in the newspapers beforehand that he was giving this concert' (quoted in Briggs 1961: 189). This argument carried the day and the relevant clause in the agreement was redrafted, giving the BBC explicit permission to broadcast sponsored events and commercial information, while forbidding spot advertising. During 1925, eight sponsored concerts were broadcast, mostly supported by newspapers, including the *Daily Herald*, the *Evening Standard* and the *News of the World*. Having successfully won the battle to preserve their lucrative monopoly over display advertising, they were happy to use this new promotional opportunity. After this initial flurry, however, the practice was discontinued. There was one sponsored concert in 1926, and then no more. The reasons for this were economic and organizational. As the sale of radio sets boomed, the BBC's income from the licence fee was sufficient to cover its costs without looking for supplementary sources of finance. In addition, as it established itself and became more self-confident, the corporation emerged as a significant patron of music performance in its own right, taking over responsibility for the popular 'Promenade Concerts' at the Queen's Hall in 1927.

Manufacturers looking for sponsorship opportunities transferred their interest to the new commercial radio operations which were beaming signals at Britain from continental Europe. They included stations in Normandy, Toulouse, Lyons, Paris and, most famously of all, Luxembourg, which began broadcasting in 1933 using the American model of brand name publicity with sponsors attaching their name to a regular show. Although the Ovaltinies children's programme is probably the best remembered, Radio Luxembourg's list of sponsors included a number of other leading household brands such as Beecham's Pills, Kraft Cheese, Lifebuoy Soap, Rowntrees Fruit Gums and Crosse & Blackwell foods, as well as a host of now forgotten products such as Bile Beans. Audiences peaked on Sundays when listeners defected from the BBC's religious and uplifting fare in search of light entertainment. On a typical Sunday in January 1935, for example, Luxembourg offered record shows sponsored by Jiffy Washing Machines and Vernons Pools, a variety show sponsored by the English and Scottish Co-op, band shows sponsored by Horlicks and Palmolive, and the Pompeian Beauty Preparations half-hour, in which selections played by the Pompeian Orchestra were interspersed with talk about the products and how to use them. Almost all these programmes were made by 'independent' companies; Luxembourg simply transmitted them. The leading producer was the American-owned advertising agency, J. Walter Thompson, which was turning out forty-four different shows a week in their London studios by the eve of World War Two. Broadcasting on Luxembourg was by no means cheap. On top of the costs of producing programmes and dispatching them to the Luxembourg studios, the station itself charged £400 per hour for air time between 1 pm and 11 pm. In return, sponsors were allowed to attach their company or brand names to the programme title and to have up to two hundred words of direct promotion in each half-hour.

This thoroughly American style of programming was anathema to the leadership of the BBC, but when the possibility of launching a television service began to be discussed, the idea of allowing limited sponsorship was revived. The report prepared by the corporation's Television Policy Committee envisaged that a range of companies, from suppliers of 'ladies' hats, dresses and jewellery' to motor car manufacturers, might be interested in 'providing' programmes with credits at the beginning and end but without 'selling time on the USA or Luxembourg model' (Briggs 1965: 600). This proposal met with stiff internal opposition, and when the report's author argued that sponsoring would provide useful additional money for production and hence raise the standard of programming, he was told that 'considerations of economy' were not a sufficient reason 'for accepting a principle which has never been accepted by the BBC in the past' (ibid.), a position that conveniently forgot the forays into sponsored programming in the early radio days.

This basic antagonism to sponsorship received general backing when the committee on broadcasting, under Lord Beveridge, appointed by the Labour government, reported in 1951. Although they recommended that the new licence should continue to allow for the possibility of sponsored programmes if the Postmaster General gave his written consent, they emphasized that 'the majority of us hope and assume that [this] will mean continuance of the practice under which consent has neither been sought nor given'. At a more general level, however, there was some support for the idea that sponsored programmes had a place in the British television system. Only seven of the committee's eleven members rejected all forms of advertising and sponsorship; the others were prepared to leave it to the government to 'explore the practical conditions under which . . . would-be sellers and would-be buyers' might be brought together. One member, the Conservative MP Selwyn Lloyd, felt strongly enough to issue a minority report calling for the introduction of commercial radio and television services alongside the BBC. It was the first significant broadside in the battle to establish ITV.

His general views received official support when the Conservative government, elected in 1951, published its White Paper setting out their plans for the future of television. They proposed a new public authority which would own and operate a purpose-built network of transmitting stations, and rent these facilities to private television companies who would finance themselves by selling spot advertising. There was to be no sponsorship. It was a typically British compromise designed to avoid the excesses of the American system and ensure that responsibility for what was broadcast remained firmly in the hands of the television companies and the new regulatory authority. Spot advertising was seen as the least worst option because it allowed programmes to be clearly separated from advertising, and confined ads to specified slots. At least, this was the theory. In practice, things turned out not to be quite as clear cut.

THE RISE AND FALL OF ADVERTISING MAGAZINES

The body charged with overseeing the development of the ITV system, the Independent Television Authority (ITA), finalized the rules governing spot advertising relatively quickly, allowing up to six minutes in any hour, confined to slots at the beginning and end of programmes and in so-called 'natural breaks' in the middle (a notion borrowed from the intervals between acts in a theatre or between the main and 'B' features in the cinema). But this was not the only kind of advertising on ITV. Almost as soon as they came on stream, stations began broadcasting whole programmes promoting products, known at the time as 'shoppers' guides'.

There were two basic types. Advertising features, such as the 15 minute programme sponsored by Marks and Spencer, promoted the products or services of a single company, while the more common advertising magazines contained plugs for a variety of different brands. In typical examples, such as *Shop in the South* (hosted by well-known BBC personalities, Sylvia Peters and Macdonald Hobley) or *On View*, a range of goods would be displayed and talked about in a simple studio set of a shop or a domestic interior, usually a kitchen. But some were more adventurous, borrowing widely from established film genres, or creating entirely new televisual forms. In *For Pete's Sake*, for example, the husband and wife comedy duo Janet Brown and Peter Butterworth, helped by a regular team of supporting actors, would integrate the product promotions into sketches parodying popular films. The following scene, based on *The Count of Monte Cristo*, was typical of their approach. Two prisoners have been in their cell so long they have grown long beards. They are discussing the possibility of escape. The first gloomily points out that their beards make them easy to recognize. This allows the second to say: 'Don't worry, I've got something that will get rid of them. Look what I've smuggled in, it's a Telefunken cordless electric razor' (quoted in Gable 1980: Part 8).

But the most successful 'admag' was probably *Jim's Inn* in which the landlord, played by comedian Jimmy Hanley, presided over a pub bar peopled by a variety of stock characters– the local spiv, the brassy beauty salon owner, the pensioner – who talked about and used a variety of products from Player's cigarettes to coats bought in a local department store. Unlike the more static shop and home sets, the bar which in many ways was the forerunner of the *Rover's Return* in *Coronation Street* – allowed a wide range of social types to mix and to talk conversationally. It was such a success with viewers that the cast released an LP record entitled *Singalong at Jim's Inn*.

Since the time allowed for advertising magazines was additional to the hourly quota for spot ads, they significantly increased advertisers' access to the television audience. Enthusiasts supported them on the grounds that, unlike spot ads which were dominated by major manufacturers promoting national brands, they offered promotional opportunities to local firms. Not that advertisers were always pleased with the results. Because the programmes were broadcast live there was the constant threat that things would go wrong in full public view, as they did when the first non-drip paint was introduced on Southern Television. As the Managing Director of the time recalled, the character demonstrating the paint

> got so carried away with what he was saying, he rammed a huge paint brush into a great pot of paint. . . . Rammed it up to the hilt while he spoke into camera, enthusing about the wonders of this paint that never dripped. As he picked up this huge brush it was going to flop . . . flop – all over the studio floor. Nobody could stop him. Flop . . . flop . . . non-drip paint.

> (Quoted in Norden 1985: 184)

If the advertising magazines caused occasional problems for the advertisers, they presented far bigger dilemmas for the regulators. Section 4(6) of the 1954 Television Act clearly prohibited programmes from including any material which stated or implied that it had been supplied or suggested by an advertiser, or which gave that impression. The ITA argued that since 'shoppers' guides' had been envisaged in the 1953 White Paper on which the act was based, they were entirely in keeping with the spirit in which commercial television had been introduced, and that provided the programmes were clearly labelled as advertising magazines in the on-screen titles and in the programme guides, there was no breach of the rule separating programming from advertising (Independent Television Authority 1957: 11–12). Critics, however, continued their attacks, pointing out that advertising features were produced by the firms whose products they promoted and not by the ITV companies, and that even where editiorial control was nominally in the hands of broadcasters, advertisers and their agencies had a considerable influence on the scripts. Indeed, in an effort to draw a firmer line between the admags and conventional programmes, the ITA had originally insisted that advertisers pay for linking material as well as for the descriptions of the products themselves. This requirement was later relaxed, but it did nothing to placate critics (Sendell 1983: 108).

The ITA eventually accepted that advertising features broke the terms of the act and put pressure on the companies to discontinue them (Independent Television Authority 1958: 15). Advertising magazines, however, were still permitted providing that 'the amount of time given to advertising of all kinds is not such as to detract from [their] value as a medium of entertainment, instruction and information' (Independent Televison Authority 1957: 11–12). This position was clearly contradictory since the more successfully the admags presented themselves as entertainment, with resident teams of performers and regular characters, the more indistinct became the dividing line between advertising and programming. The 1960 Pilkington Committee on Broadcasting, which had been set up to evaluate the performance of ITV and the BBC, was quick to pick up on this inconsistency. As was pointed out in their final report:

> The more interesting the magazines become – and . . . it is on their intrinsic interest that their place in programming is justified – the greater the likelihood that the viewer will, on another level of his (sic) mind, cease to realize that he (sic) is being sold something. We consider that . . . the distinction insisted on by the act – between the programme and the advertisement – is blurred.
>
> (Pilkington Committee on Broadcasting 1962: 81)

In their view, advertising magazines clearly violated the spirit of the Television Act and they urged their abolition. They were strongly supported by the ITA's chairman of the time, the patrician art historian, Sir Kenneth Clark, who regarded them with undisguised distaste. Some ITV executives, led by Captain Tom Brownrigg, the General Manager of Rediffusion, fought a rearguard action to persuade the government not to adopt this recommendation. They failed, and by the end of 1962 the Postmaster-General had announced an official ban.

With the demise of the admags, companies had to find another way on to the small screen, and the route they increasingly chose was to sponsor sports and arts events that could command television coverage. This strategy didn't raise any awkward regulatory questions since the programmes were produced by the broadcasting organizations themselves, and it had the extra advantage of giving advertisers access to the BBC as well as to ITV. Tobacco companies had an additional incentive after spot ads for cigarettes were banned in 1965.

BROUGHT TO YOU BY . . . SPONSORSHIP TAKES OFF

> Four minutes to go – and it looks to be a night of disappointment we have brought to you in association with National Power.
>
> (Brian Moore commentating during ITV's *World Cup 90*)

Companies have been sponsoring sporting events since the beginning of the modern corporate system. The very first Tour de France road race was sponsored by a bicycle manufacturer. But it is only in the last two decades that it has become significant in Britain. In 1970 companies spent only £2.5 million on sports sponsorship. By 1977, this figure had climbed to £30 million, and by 1986 it stood at £128 million. Although corporate sponsorship of the arts is on a much more modest scale, its recent growth, from £0.5 million in 1976 to £25 million in 1986 is still substantial. Not all of this activity is linked to television coverage. A good deal is aimed at improving employee relations, generating goodwill in communities where companies have a major presence, entertaining clients and investors, and generally massaging the company's public profile. In 1986, for example, only 11 per cent of the 1,650 major sports sponsors received television exposure. But, for this elite, the publicity pay-offs are considerable, especially if their company name is linked to major events like the Grand National or the London Marathon or to sports with high viewing figures like snooker, cricket, soccer or athletics. In addition to direct mentions during broadcast commentaries and shots featuring their banners and billboards around the ground, they gain prominent mentions in the *Radio Times* or *TV Times* (both of which are among the best-selling weekly magazines in the country) and extensive general press coverage.

These attractive promotional returns coupled with the relative scarcity of television sponsorship opportunities have prompted companies left out of the official deals to look for back-door routes to screen exposure. One favoured tactic is 'ambush marketing', whereby companies seek to associate themselves with a televised event without incurring the costs of full sponsorship. During the 1990 World Cup, for example, Pepsi sought to outflank their great rival Coca Cola, who were the competition's official soft drinks sponsor, by sponsoring the Brazilian team, gambling on their chances of reaching the later stages (Hogg 1990). Even companies who have failed to get any kind of screen exposure can turn their lack of success to advantage, as the London Rubber Company demonstrated in 1976.

In an effort to improve the image of their major product, Durex condoms, LRC agreed to sponsor the Surtees Formula One racing team. The middle man arranging the deal, Terry Reagan, realized that the BBC, who were due to cover the Race of Champions from Brands Hatch, would not allow the Surtees entry to carry the Durex brand name, but successfully argued that this could be capitalized on. He was right. The BBC asked for the name to be removed or covered up. LRC refused and the BBC cancelled the transmision, prompting a mass of press coverage and free publicity for Durex (Ball *et al.* 1980).

Since these relatively early days, corporate interest in television sponsorship has increased substantially. At the same time, developments within broadcasting have forced the television organizations to revise their original rules. Not surprisingly, advertisers have been quick to exploit this more relaxed regulatory climate and to push for more and more concessions. They have met with resistance, but overall there is little doubt that the last decade has seen a significant enlargement in the space allowed to commercial speech within British broadcasting.

Corporate enthusiasm for sponsorship has been fuelled by increasing disenchantment with television spot advertising. Both the costs of producing ads and the prices of prime-time slots have increased substantially since the early 1980s, prompting constant complaints from advertisers. At the same time, discontent with television's effectiveness as an advertising medium has been growing. The audience for ITV programmes is widely felt to be poorer and older than many advertisers would wish. The spread of remote control consoles is seen as making it much easier for viewers to avoid ads altogether by 'zapping' across channels during the breaks. In an attempt to keep peoples' attention, ads have increasingly sought to present themselves as short programmes in their own right, mobilizing the conventions of video clips, soap opera and other popular genres to provide intrinsic aesthetic pleasures. But there are growing suspicions that this may be counterproductive since it increases the chances that viewers will enjoy the ads in and of themselves, without allegiance to the brands they promote. This is particularly likely with the younger, more media-literate viewers, who are one of the advertisers' main target groups (Willis 1990: 48–53).

In contrast, sponsorship has the attraction of being relatively cheap, of being incorporated in the actual programmes and of benefiting from their popularity. Commentators are divided on the question of whether it actually sells products, but most agree that it can play a valuable role in raising public awareness, as the case of Cornhill Insurance shows. When Cornhill first began to sponsor cricket in 1977 only 2 per cent of the general population recognized their name or what they did. By 1981, backed by 166 hours of television time, the figure had jumped to 17 per cent.

The second major drawback of conventional spot ads is their limited reach. Advertisers have been lobbying for the right to advertise on the main BBC channels since the first stirrings of discontent with ITV in the late 1950s and early 1960s (Beadle 1963: 87). So far they have been unsuccessful. Sponsorship is a convenient trojan horse. It gives major advertisers, including the tobacco companies, cost-effective access to BBC audiences. According to one estimate, the BBC carried over 350 hours of tobacco-sponsored sport in 1986 (Roberts 1987), enabling the companies partially to circumvent the ban on direct cigarette advertising on ITV. Sponsorship also increases the geographical reach of promotion. Unlike spot ads, which are only shown on a regional or national basis, major televised sporting events are widely distributed internationally. In 1988, for example, Barclay's sponsorship of the Football League gave them television exposure in fifty countries in addition to 35.30 hours of British screen time (Olins 1989).

Growing corporate awareness of the benefits of sponsorship has been matched by the broadcasters' increased need to strike a new accommodation with potential sources of supplementary funding. In the case of the BBC, the reasons are primarily financial. By the beginning of the 1980s, the corporations's income from the compulsory licence fee had fallen well below the level needed to cover the rapidly rising costs of programme production and equipment replacement. They estimated that the licence for a colour set would need to be raised from £34 to £54. They bid for £50 and got £46. This shortfall prompted a concerted search for ways to boost income and cut costs and a range of options that had previously been ignored or seen as marginal began to be considered more seriously. This new spirit of realism dislodged the traditional distaste for sponsorship, which had led the BBC to refuse credits to sponsors either on screen or in the programme listings in the *Radio Times*, and opened the way for an enlarged arena for commercial speech. When the coroporation televised Sir William Walton's eightieth birthday concert from the Royal Festival Hall in the spring of 1982, the words 'concert and exhibition sponsored by the *Observer*' appeared as a full-screen credit, prompting one senior broadcaster to comment that sponsorship finally 'became legitimate at the BBC that night' (Thomas 1982: 7).

At the same time, attitudes to sponsorship were also changing within the ITV system, though for different reasons. The catalyst here was the launch of Channel 4 in the autumn of 1982, and the need to give the independent production companies who supplied the programmes a reasonable degree of freedom in raising outside money for projects. To clear the way, the Independent Broadcasting Authority (IBA) (which had succeeded the ITA as the regulatory body for television and taken on responsibility for commercial radio) issued a new set of guidelines for 'Programmes Funded by Non-Broadcasters' at the beginning of 1982. This allowed sponsors of programmes consisting of 'a factual portrayal of doings, happenings, places or things' (except news programmes) to have credits at the beginning and end of programmes, subject to the following stipulations. Any events covered had to exist independently of their screen coverage. So-called 'hybrid events' created especially for television did not count. Sponsors could not place spot ads in or around the programmes they were associated with, and the broadcasters had the right to impose restrictions on any publicity they might design for other media (Independent Broadcasting Authority 1982).

Not surprisingly, many potential sponsors regarded these rules as less than generous and began to look for ways of increasing their visibility on the screen. In 1984, for example, the auto parts firm A.C. Delco, who had contributed £100,000 to Channel 4's first magazine programme, *The Motor Show*, boosted their presence in the programme by having their name prominently displayed on the side of the motorhome which served as the show's on-screen base. The resulting row was followed a few months later by complaints that Marks and Spencer had bent the rules with its Celebration of British Fashion show. By featuring only M & S clothes with their prices and by presenting 'historical' costumes made up from items in their household linen collection the programme was in effect an advertising feature. In an effort to avoid a rash of these kinds of surreptitious visual plugs, the IBA granted two important concessions in 1984 and 1985. Sponsors were allowed to place spot ads in shows they had supported, and on-screen credits were permitted to mention specific brand names as well as general company names.

A similar battle over sponsors' visibility was being fought out within the BBC. In 1983 the corporation was forced to accept that players in televised Football League games would have advertising on their shirts. As a leading executive put it: 'We have to face the reality of sport as it is now. We have been trying to find a way of reflecting the sponsors in football. But I don't think we would like to see sportsmen walking about as advertising billboards' (Armstrong 1983). The question of 'walking billboards' was a particularly sensitive one for the BBC at the time. The previous year, British American Tobacco was widely seen as having broken the tobacco companies' voluntary code on advertising and sports by having Martina Navratilova play at Wimbledon in an outfit sporting the characteristic colour scheme of their new Kim brand and bearing the Kim logo. They apologized to the

Sports Minister for this lapse, but in 1983 she was back in the same basic outfit, minus the logo, prompting the Labour MP George Foulkes to complain that she still looked like 'a dancing cigarette packet'.

The BBC's problems with sponsorship were compounded in the mid-1980s when they decided to commission more programmes from independent producers. They rapidly found themselves facing similar problems to Channel 4. In 1986, the scheduled screening of a documentary on truck drivers, 'Night Moves', had to be cancelled when it was discovered that it was partly funded by motor industry interests in the expectation of favourable publicity. The executive who took the decision, Michael Grade, was adamant that the corporation 'is not in business to make programmes advertising people's products' (Fiddick 1986). At the same time, the BBC recognized that it had to offer better opportunities for legitimate promotion if it was going to attract more sponsorship money. Accordingly, new guidelines were issued in 1988. They reaffirmed that under the terms of the BBC's current licence, sponsorship with acknowledgements was restricted to events that have 'an existence independent of television coverage' to which the sponsor has contributed all or part of the costs. In return they could incorporate their name into the title of the event, have two verbal credits within the programme and an end caption acknowledging their role, plus appropriate billing in the *Radio Times* and a mention in any associated article. In addition they are permitted two banners carrying their name within range of the main camera. Direct funding of programmes, however, is only permitted if the sponsor receives no credits and the 'source of funding would stand up to public scrutiny' (BBC 1989).

Although the new guidelines did not go as far as some potential sponsors would have liked, they were widely seen as marking a more positive accommodation. As the Controller of BBC 2 put it: 'We're not opening the doors wide, but we are looking more sympathetically at the situation' (Carter 1990). The first sign of what this new stance might mean in practice came early in 1990, when BBC 2 announced a £1.3 million deal linking Lloyd's Bank to the *Young Musician of the Year* competition. Critics were quick to point out that since the contest had been running for fourteen years, and was created by the BBC, it was not an independent event and fell outside the scope of the new guidelines. Their objections were given an additional edge by the fact that the IBA had banned 'hybrid events' on ITV and Channel 4 the previous November, after a row over the Mitsubishi-sponsored show, *Run The Gauntlet*. The BBC responded by arguing that the programme still qualified as a sponsored event since the Lloyds Bank money went into running it. But since the BBC was responsible for the organization, this was debatable to say the least. Suspicions that the corporation was attempting to steal an unfair advantage in the competition for sponsorship money were revived by the later announcement that they were seeking a sponsor for their long-running programme, *Come Dancing*.

Meanwhile the battle for enlarged sponsorship opportunities and increased on-screen visibility was intensifying within the ITV system. Late in 1989, a dispute broke out over the Kellogg's-funded children's cartoon show, *Magic Mirror*, sparked off by complaints that the large oval mirror which introduced the segments displayed the distinctive Kellogg's 'K' logo too prominently and appeared too many times. Around the same time, the IBA was extensively criticized for allowing Pedigree Petfoods to sponsor the pet care item in Granada Television's regional programme, *This Morning*, although there was no evidence that they had intervened at an editorial level. However much critics disliked such deals, supporters argued that they were inevitable given the new economics of programme-making. As Granada's Head of Factual Programmes explained at the time:

> The programme, as the independents we have commissioned for it will testify, is made on a shoe-string. Conventional advertising revenue is being spread more thinly, a situation which will only get worse, and we have no choice but to look for other sources of income.
>
> (Caird 1990)

The IBA's *Guide to Television Sponsorship*, issued in March 1990, went some way towards recognizing this new economic reality by adding three new categories of programme to the list of those eligible for sponsorship: arts review programmes; instructional programmes; and weather reports. At the same time, they reaffirmed the principle that a sponsor must not have a material interest in the content of a programme, or appear to do so, so as to avoid 'any possibility that editorial choices may be made whose effect may actively promote the sponsor's interests' whether or not the sponsor intervenes directly (IBA 1990: 6). This explicitly precluded links along the lines of Granada's deal with Pedigree Petfoods, such as a package tour operator sponsoring a travel advice programme or a video distributor sponsoring a film review programme.

One of the first companies to take advantage of the new rules was the electricity utility, Powergen, which signed a deal to sponsor the national evening weather bulletins on ITV, though they soon ran into a row when it was revealed that they were under the impression that their contribution gave them some rights over the choice of presenters and their outfits. Such interventions were normal practice on the new satellite channels, which were operating within a much more relaxed regulatory regime. In the words of Roy Dukes, the man responsible for handling the Goodyear tyre company's sponsorship of the weather forecasts on Super Channel, 'Goodyear doesn't have editorial control over the weather, but what's wrong with them asking presenters to wear jackets?' (Burnett 1989: 20).

This may seem like a trivial example, but from the point of view of open public discourse it is the thin end of a very fat wedge which is prising open the regulatory system and moving commercial speech towards the centre of the television system. Charles Dawson, the Director of Horizon Media International, for example, is in no doubt that advertisers can and should become 'an intrinsic part of the TV production machine' and that 'used properly' sponsorship and other forms of 'embedded' persuasion 'can weld your message firmly to the programme which carries it, so that the two become inseparable in the viewer's mind. If you like the show, you get the message' (Dawson 1987).

This process had already advanced substantially within the cable television system during the 1980s, where the Cable Authority's lighter, less directive policy had given sponsors far more scope than on the terrestrial channels. They could pay for the purchase of programming in return for credits along the lines of the underwriting system operating on American Public Television. They could also fund original production, providing that their products were not on the list of items that cannot be advertised under the authority's code, and that their commercial interest in the programme's subject matter was made clear to the viewer. The only categories of programmes not eligible for sponsorship were news and current affairs, though even this rule could be waived with the specific approval of the authority. This dual regulatory regime ended when the provisions of the new Broadcasting Act came into force in 1990, ushering in a qualitatively new environment for sponsorship.

AFTER THE ACT : SPONSORSHIP IN THE 1990s

The act abolished the IBA and the Cable Authority and created a new composite body, the Independent Television Commission (ITC), to oversee all commercial television services. It was expected to operate with a 'light touch', moving away from the paternalism of the IBA towards the more permissive regime pioneered by the Cable Authority. One of its first major acts was to publish revised guidelines on programme sponsorship.

For the first time, sponsors were allowed access to all programmes except for news and current affairs and those dealing with political or industrial controversies or current public policies (ITC 1990: 5). In return for their contribution to production budgets, sponsors on Channel 4 and ITV (now renamed Channel 3) are permitted a 10-second aural and visual credit at the beginning of the programme, a 7-second credit at the end, a 7-second 'bumper credit' before commercial breaks, plus one 5-second mention in any trailer for the programme. However, in an effort to avoid the more blatant plugging common elsewhere in Europe, the ITC has insisted that neither the sponsor nor their products can be mentioned within the programme. The French game show *Intervilles* (shown on the major commercial channel, TFI) illustrates what can happen without such a rule. As contestants 'struggle up a slippery slope, each clutching a giant plastic Kellogg's Cornflakes packet, the compère gushes: 'This is a game of reflexes, and for that you have to eat Kellogg's . . . *Merci*, Dr Kellogg, for inventing cornflakes' (Dawson 1991: 21).

The ITC has also ruled that sponsors' names cannot be used in the title of the programme (except in the case of sponsored events such as the Rumbelows Cup Final) and that sponsors cannot have 'any influence on either the content or the scheduling' (ITC 1990: 4). This is in marked contrast to much more liberal rules issued by the new Radio Authority (which took over responsibility for radio services from the IBA), which allow sponsors to 'contribute to the editorial content of all sponsored programmes' by offering 'advice in or on, or ideas for, a programme's content or presentation' (Radio Authority 1990: 38). The only exceptions are news, current affairs and documentaries dealing with current controversies.

Despite their continued insistence on the absolute separation between programme funding and editorial decisions, the ITC's liberalization of the television sponsorship rules was widely seen as heralding 'a fundamental change in television culture' (Carter 1991: 20). Nevertheless, the Channel 3 companies' initial response was cautious, with the ITV sponsorship committee nominating only eight network programmes for sponsorship in March 1991. Given that all the companies were bidding to retain their franchises in the new competitive auction system introduced by the Broadcasting Act, this hesitancy was scarcely surprising. Potential sponsors were also holding fire, partly because there was no agreement on appropriate rates and no firm evidence on likely returns, and partly because the future shape of the Channel 3 system was not yet clear. The major exception was Croft Port's sponsorship of the courtroom drama series, *Rumpole of the Bailey*. The price, £300,000, was approximately a third of the cost of the equivalent exposure using conventional spot advertising. The transmission of the first episode, on 28 October, marked the long-delayed arrival of domestically sponsored drama on British terrestrial television.

Twelve days earlier, the ITC had announced the winning franchise bids, removing one major source of uncertainty and opening the way for an expansion of sponsorship activity. Within a month the Channel 3 companies had published a revised list of thirty-seven programmes available for sponsorship, while privately admitting that they were prepared to look seriously at more or less any offers that fell within the scope of the ITC's rules. One of the first programmes on the extended list to attract a sponsor (Beamish Stout) was the highly successful detective series, *Inspector Morse*, followed soon after by a deal between Granada Television and the premium French beer brand, Kronenberg 1664, for the new series featuring the Parisian detective, *Maigret*. Because they centre on a sympathetic major character with a clearly defined life-style, popular drama series offer an ideal vehicle for sponsorship. For this technique of promotion through association to work, the main character doesn't even have to use the sponsor's product on screen, s/he simply has to be the kind of person for whom its consumption would be natural and pleasurable. As a publicity briefing from Courage, announcing the *Inspector Morse* deal put it: the series is a 'perfect vehicle for Beamish Stout' because 'Morse is an intelligent, sensitive and reflective character who appreciates a quality product and enjoys drinking in a traditional local' (*Marketing Week* 1991: 10).

Because the plot lines are dispersed across a much wider group of core characters, soap operas are less versatile as a space for sponsorship. As a result, only products in general use are suitable. One obvious candidate is tea, which is why Brooke Bond signed a 12-month deal with Scottish TV's twice-weekly soap, *Take the High Road*, at the beginning of 1992, as a way of promoting the 'Scottishness' of their Scottish blend. This association is cemented by having an opening scene featuring a kettle carrying the brand name which then opens into the programme like a set of window blinds. Single plays offer an even more restricted 'window of opportunity' for sponsors. They are very likely to be shown only once, unlike films there is no guarantee of video release, and because they often deal with the underside of contemporary life, they work with situations and life-styles with which sponsors may not wish to be associated.

Given this differential attractiveness of various forms of fiction, increased reliance on sponsorship funding for prime-time drama may well put additional pressures on one-off productions and accelerate the move towards series and serials. If this were to happen it would further reduce one of the major opportunities that television offers for critical social commentary, stylistic experiment and open exploration of controversial themes. It is not a matter of 'quality' defined in terms of production values, it is a question of diversity of expression, of keeping open public spaces in which questions and puzzles can be articulated, 'uncomfortable contradictions explored . . . invisible experiences brought into the light (and) marginalized groups allowed a voice' (Mepham 1990: 65).

Against this, supporters of sponsorship argue that it is one way of financing programmes that might otherwise be squeezed out of the schedules in the harsher economic climate of the 1990s. As

David Boulton, Granada Television's Commissioning Executive for Arts has argued: 'I don't want to sweep away necessary safeguards. But we have to find new ways of funding artistic and cultural programmes which otherwise won't get made at all because their cost is rising and competitive multi-channel television can't afford them' (Boulton 1988; see also Bragg 1989). For their part, potential sponsors have been quick to assure sceptics that interfering with editiorial decisions is the last thing on their mind, and that programme sponsorship is simply 'a further opportunity to raise the awareness of a company or product's name, very much along the lines of other sponsorship activity' (Capper 1988).

This is disingenous. A sponsor may refrain from intervening in day-to-day production decisions once a project has been agreed on, but she is still in a postition to exercise considerable influence on the overall mix and style of programming by choosing to back some projects rather than others, favouring works and performers who are already well established and shunning controversy and experiment. Moreover, it is by no means clear how many advertisers are prepared to adopt a hands-off approach. When the sponsorship consultancy, Granard Rowland, questioned marketing directors in the top 150 UK companies, half said that they believed that sponsors should have some influence on programme content (Lee 1989).

But a company doesn't have to sponsor a production to influence its contents. It can achieve considerable visibility for its brands by paying to have them featured in film or television programmes – the process known as product placement.

BRANDED IMAGES : PRODUCT PLACEMENT

There are two basic kinds of placement opportunity: 'creative' placements, where a product (or an advertisement for it) is featured in the background of a shot, and 'on-set' placements, where the product is displayed more prominently or is used or mentioned by one of the central characters. Both forms are currently prohibited in all BBC productions and in all programmes that fall within the ITC's terms of reference. Although real products do feature in television dramas and brand names are clearly visible, since no money has changed hands these instances are not counted as product placement. This flexible attitude to product display is relatively recent, however. Previously, programme-makers went to considerable lengths to conceal brand names or to substitute fictitious ones. Brands are now accepted in the interests of dramatic realism, providing that no one product is given undue prominence. In an effort to ensure equality of visibility, most programmes have house rules on product display, though not all are as stringent as those operating on the set of the BBC's highly successful soap opera, *EastEnders*. These require that even the soap powders used by the main characters entering the laundrette [one of the major locations] rotate between the major brands (Mills 1990: 30).

There will always be individual breaches of any set of rules, as when Rusty Lee was accused, at the end of 1991, of accepting money from food manufacturers in return for promoting their products during her cookery demonstrations on TVam's breakfast show. Pesonal payola of this kind can never be completely controlled but it is far less significant than the increased scope for placement produced by changes in the organization of television production.

As British television comes to rely more and more on programming supplied by independent producers, so the lines of communication linking commissioning editors and production teams become more attenuated and checks on procedure more difficult to conduct. Set dressing is a particularly difficult process to monitor, especially where props are being supplied by an outside agency. As Sarah Fiddian, head of the property placement company, Prop Place, explains: 'We deal with props buyers who need to fill their sets as cheaply as possible. There are going to be branded products on show. We just try to make sure they are ours.' As she points out: 'What we do is not illegal, underhand or unprofessional' (Goldston 1991:32), but by promoting some brands rather than others, it clearly breaches existing broadcast conventions on equality of visibility. Bought-in feature films present an even greater problem, since they regularly contain clear instances of product placement proper.

This is not in itself new. From its inception the cinema has enjoyed an intimate relationship with mass consumption. Filming the modern world meant filming a world saturated with branded goods and advertising displays. This symbolic relation was put on a secure commercial footing well before the First World War, with Hollywood studios regularly accepting fees for featuring particular goods on the screen. This practice intensified in the early 1930s, as producers looked for ways of supplementing falling income from box office receipts. Not only did the business of supplying props become more professionalized, as broking agencies emerged offering to place products for a fee, the studios themselves became more active in soliciting placement, often sending out shot-by-shot breakdowns of scripts with likely placement opportunities clearly marked. (Eckert 1991: 111–17).

The present intensification of placement activity dates from 1982, when the alien in *ET* was enticed from his hiding place by a trail of Reese's Pieces sweets, producing a 300 per cent increase in the brand's sales. Since then, placement has become an integral part of Hollywood film-making, with Associated Film Promotions and similar agencies continually scanning new scripts for placement opportunities for their clients. Sums for on-set promotions regularly range from the $100,000 Kimberly-Clark paid to have Huggies nappies used in *Baby Boom* and to use its infant star in publicity, to Philip Morris's $350,000 outlay on *Licence to Kill* to have James Bond use their Lark cigarette brand. Most major films now have multiple placements.

The main value to the client lies in 'product positioning'. As Nick Farley of the Dorlands advertising agency points out:

> With ordinary advertising you can only say so much. With placement you can hint at what kind of product it is far more effectively. For example, you can always see cars, but placement says this is the kind of car driven by this kind of man.
>
> (Appleyard 1986)

The other major advantage is that, unlike spot ads, placements have an extended life in space and time as the film moves from the cinema, to video release, to showing on a cable or satellite channel, and finally to broadcast television. And because placement opportunities are expressly designed to be integrated into the action, they are almost impossible to excise. It is difficult to imagine any broadcasting organization cutting the crucial sweets scene in *ET* even though it involved a substantial placement deal.

The problem is even more intractable where programmes are actually made up of promotions for products, as with rock shows built around video clips. It is not simply that the programmes contain publicity for products. The plugs *are* the programme. As Linda Argus of MTV, the most successful of the rock video channels, has explained, clients are attracted to the service precisely because the high production ads merge seamlessly into the high production videos to sell a total 'rock 'n' roll youth lifestyle' in which all desires and wants can be satisfied by buying commodities (Burnett 1989: 22). Similarly, the cartoon shows built around particular toy ranges are designed to colonize the imagination of childhood and link fantasy and play securely to purchases through which animals are transformed into Care Bears and My Little Pony, and dolls become Sindy or Barbie.

This is a particular instance of a more general problem: 'Who now controls our major cultural spaces and determines which visions of ourselves and the world around us will dominate?'

COMMERCIAL SPEECH AND PUBLIC DISCOURSE

The rise of integrated advertising raises serious questions for the ideal of public service broadcasting as an open imaginative space in which the widest possible range of voices can speak and argue, providing a diversity of perspectives on contemporary experience and the forces shaping it. To ensure that this space remains as open as possible, public broadcasting needs to keep the main sources of institutional discourse at arm's length and provide room for alternative and oppositional points of view. To this end, it must remain independent of the major centres of political power – state agencies, the government of the day and the major political parties. But, equally importantly, it must keep its distance from the core institutions of corporate capital and the avalanche of advertising, promotion and public relations they generate every day. These communications constitute a particular kind of speech – commercial speech – produced by and for the major corporations and designed to promote both their products and their perspective on the world. It speaks to viewers as consumers and not as citizens. For every problem they face it offers a commodity. Social action becomes a matter of making the right purchase.

Faced with the rapid expansion of advertising-supported services and the crisis of public funding, many people now working in British broadcasting see the struggle to contain commercial speech as the key to the survival of the public broadcasting ideal.

As Michael Grade, the Chief Executive of Channel 4, has put it:
'People strive for a definition of public service broadcasting, but I
always think it's very simple. Public service broadcasting is
creating programmes totally free of any commercial consideration' (Campbell 1990: 5). Sponsorship, product placement and
other forms of embedded persuasion are key battlegrounds. As
Grade told his colleagues, in an impassioned speech at the 1989
Edinburgh International Television Festival, 'We must keep
broadcasting out of the hands of advertisers' (quoted in Brown
1989: 4).

As I have tried to show, embedded persuasions can limit the
overall diversity of broadcasting at several levels. First, and most
obviously, the fact that a company has sunk money into a
particular production opens the way for it to influence the content
and style in line with its corporate interests. Beyond this, they can
substantially affect the general mix of programming by deciding
to back certain kinds of projects and not others. The result is a
programme system in which commercial speech is increasingly
privileged over other voices by virtue of its financial leverage and
where corporate interests regulate which other voices may be
heard. This may be good for business, but whether it is good for
democracy is a question in urgent need of exploration.

REFERENCES

Appleyard, Bryan (1986) 'Salesmen of the big screen', *The Times*, 4
    March : 10.
Armstrong, Robert (1983) 'TV driving a hard bargain', *Guardian*, 30
    April: 13.
Ball, Peter *et al.* (1990) 'And now a word from our sponsors', *Time Out*,
    30 May: 10–13.
Barnouw, Erik (1978) *The Sponsor: Notes on a Modern Potentate*, New
    York: Oxford University Press.
BBC (1989) *BBC Producers' Guidelines*, Section 18, London: BBC
    Information.
Beadle, Gerald (1963) *Television: A Critical Review*, London: George
    Allen & Unwin.
Boulton, David (1988) 'And now a song from our sponsors. . .',
    Guardian, 18 January: 13.
Bragg, Melvyn (1989) 'The art of sponsorship', *Listener*, 12 October: 13–
    14.
Briggs, Asa (1961) *The History of Broadcasting in the United Kingdom
    Volume I: The Birth of Broadcasting*, London: Oxford University
    Press.

Briggs, Asa (1965) *The History of Broadcasting in the United Kingdom Volume II: The Golden Age of Wireless*, London: Oxford University Press.

Brown, Maggie (1989) 'Advertisers "set to exert greater influence on TV"', *The Independent*, 29 August: 4.

Burnett, Claire (1989) 'TV's hidden spots', *Cable and Satellite Europe*, December: 18–22.

Caird, Rod (1990) 'Brand news', *Listener*, 5 April: 13.

Campbell, Beatrix (1990) 'Making the Grade', *Marxism Today*, June: 4–5.

Capper, Alan (1988) 'Fair dos for sponsors', *Marketing Week*, 26 February: 27.

Carter, Meg (1990) 'BBC moots head of sponsorship', *Marketing Week*, 16 February: 15.

Carter, Meg (1991) 'Television limbers up for a sponsored run', *Marketing Week*, 11 March: 20–1.

Cockerell, Michael (1988) *Live From Number 10: The Inside Story of Prime Ministers and Television*, London: Faber & Faber.

Croft, Martin (1989) 'Ghostbusters of Christmas present', *Marketing Week*, 15 December: 32–7.

Dawson, Charles (1987) 'TV ads: time to break the mould', *Marketing Week*, 24 April: 21.

Dawson, Charles (1991) 'Sponsors eager to cash in on TV's change of heart', *Independent Business on Sunday*, 10 March: 21.

Eckert, Charles (1991) 'Carole Lombard in Macy's window' in Charlotte Herzog and Jane M. Gaines (eds) *Fabrications: Costume and the Female Body*, London: Routledge: 100–21.

Engelhardt, Tom (1986) 'Children's television: the shortcake strategy', in Todd Gitlin (ed.) *Watching Television*, New York: Pantheon Books: 68–110.

Fiddick, Peter (1986) 'Grade defends dropping of product-linked film', *Guardian*, 23 December: 3.

Fox, Stephen (1985) *The Mirror Makers: A History of American Advertising and its Creators*, New York: Vintage Books.

Gable, Jo (1980) *The Tuppenny Punch and Judy Show: 25 Years of TV Commercials*, London: Michael Joseph.

Goldston, James (1991) 'Deals on reels', *Observer*, 5 May: 32.

Hogg, James (1990) 'Pop goes the market', *Listener*, 21 June: 14–15.

IBA (1982) *Programmes Funded by Non-Broadcasters*, London: Independent Broadcasting Authority, News release 15 January.

IBA (1990) *A User's Guide to Television Sponsorship for Programmes on ITV, Channel 4, and BSB: Some Notes on IBA Practice*, London: Independent Broadcasting Authority, March.

Independent Television Authority (1957) *Annual Report and Accounts for the Year Ended 31 March 1957*, London: HMSO.

Independent Television Authority (1958) *Annual Report and Accounts 1957–58*, London: HMSO.

Independent Television Commission (1990) *Draft ITC Code of Pro-*

gramme Sponsorship, London: Independent Television Commission, 25 October.

Lee, Harvey (1989) 'A new brand of screen sponsorship', *The Independent*, 11 October: 21.

Marketing Week (1991) 'Beamish stout to toast Morse's good health', *Marketing Week*, 20 December: 10.

Mepham, John (1990) 'The ethics of quality in television', in G. Mulgan (ed.) *The Question of Quality*, London: British Film Institute: 56–72.

Miller, David (1990) 'The history behind a mistake', *British Journalism Review* 1 (1), Winter: 34–43.

Miller, Mark Crispin (1990) 'Meddling with the movies', *Review Guardian*, 7 June: 21–2.

Mills, Deborah (1990) 'Which powders do soaps use?', *Daily Telegraph*, 15 August: 30.

Murdock, Graham (1989) 'Televisual tourism: national image-making and international markets' in Christian Thomsen (ed.) *Cultural Transfer or Electronic Imperialism?*, Heidelberg: Carl Winter-Universitätsverlag: 171–83.

Nevett, T.R. (1982) *Advertising in Britain : A History*, London: Heinemann.

Norden, Denis (1985) *Coming to You Live: Behind-the-screen Memories of Forties and Fifties Television*, London: Methuen.

Olins, Rufus (1989) 'In this sporting life, the race is for sponsorship money', *Sunday Times*, 20 August: D5.

Packard, Vance (1963) *The Hidden Persuaders*, Harmondsworth: Pelican Books.

Pilkington Committee on Broadcasting (1962) *The Committee on Broadcasting 1960: Report*, Cmnd 32262, London: HMSO.

Radio Authority (1990) *Code of Advertising Standards and Practice and Programme Sponsorship*, London: Radio Authority, 25 October.

Roberts, John (1987) *The Name of the Game: Selling Cigarettes on BBC TV*, Manchester: North-west Regional Health Authority, Prevention Department.

Sendall, Bernard (1983) *Independent Television in Britain. Volume 2: Expansion and Change, 1958–68*, London: Macmillan.

Smith, Anthony (1974) *British Broadcasting*, Newton Abbot: David & Charles.

Thomas, Howard (1982) 'The financier takes a little credit', *Financial Times*, 29 June: 27.

Willis, Paul (1990) *Common Culture*, Milton Keynes: Open University Press.

Wilson, H.H. (1961) *Pressure Group: The Campaign for Commercial Television*, London: Secker & Warburg.

Zazza, Frank (1986) 'Product placement in motion pictures', *Time and Space* 68: 34–8.

Chapter 9

'You're nicked!'
Television police series and the fictional representation of law and order

Alan Clarke

There has long been a resistance to taking popular culture seriously, first as an object of study and second as a way of spending one's leisure time. There are still people who will not admit to the secret fetish of watching television soap operas and even more who will watch and analyse one-off television dramas but not watch a series format. In studying the development of the television crime series in Britain it was startling to find just how many of those amazing dramatists had learned their craft writing for George Dixon, Barlow and Regan in the humble series. However, I do not want to argue for taking the series seriously simply because of the quality of the production, although I think I could, but because of the world they create on the small screen for the mass audience. For many people their only contact with a speaking policeman is on the television and this reinforces the aura of reality which police series strive so hard to construct. I also want to focus on the fictional representations rather than the documentary and the news images because historically these have often been overlooked when the influence of the media is being debated.

My interest in the police series began in the 1970's when their dramatic significance was brought home to me when, in discussion with law students, they could only understand the changes in the police force when I contrasted the avuncular George Dixon's style of community policing with the then current hero, Jack Regan, in *The Sweeney*. The discussion of change suddenly came alive and ranged across different types of specialist police squads – Regional Crime Squads (*Softly Softly*, *Task Force*), the Bomb Squad, Fraud Squad – and their television referents. In this article I want to try to recreate my process of analysis by presenting an account of the major changes in the police series since *Dixon* and including the more recent examples of the genre, *The Bill, Juliet Bravo,* and *The Gentle Touch,* with these changes located within a concern to unpack the ideological construction and reconstruction of genres within popular television:

> He's not the sort of copper you'd ask for directions, not Jack Regan. Not as his super-charged Ford slews to a halt spraying gravel and burning tyre rubber like he owns shares in Pirelli. He's not the sort of copper you'd ask to find your dog. Not as the car door bursts open and he leans over it pointing a police .38, so big it needs two hands to hold it. He's not the sort of copper you'd even ask for a warrant. Not as he grinds his knee into the pit of the villain's back as an added refinement to a half nelson, spitting out 'The Sweeney! you're nicked!' But isn't he lovely?
>
> (Walker 1977: p 26)

This cameo captures the essential character of Jack Regan and of the series which gave him life, *The Sweeney,* and of the police series as a genre which can be reduced to a very simple story line consisting of the basic components of crime, chase and arrest. As I have argued elsewhere (Clarke 1986), *The Sweeney* worked this formula into a popular art form and changed the direction of the police series in the mid-1970s. It was a particular inflection and reconstruction of the genre which owed much to the work of American film and television staff who had produced a brand of films and television police series known as 'action series'. By making use of the full potential of film, police procedurals had been shaken out of the 'drama-documentary' format of slow-moving narrative and static camerawork. They had been transformed into a fast-moving entertainment for the 1970s. This entertainment can only be understood within a discussion of the institutional changes which were taking place in the media during this period as these created the conditions of production surrounding any one series.

AN AMERICAN POLICEMAN IN LONDON

American film and television are an integral part of the television schedules in this country and they also form part of the culture of the production of television series in studios in this country. The late 1960s saw three new elements introduced into the series which produced a profound change in the presentation of crime in American television programmes (Kerr 1981). These were violence, action sequences and the increasingly prominent role accorded to music in the development of the narrative. Action sequences covered everything from the variants on the car chase to the choreography of the stunts in series like *Kojak* and *Starsky and Hutch*. Indeed, the title sequence of *Starsky and Hutch* was an excellent example of what 'action' meant in this context. The two heroes are introduced squealing round cars and corners in a rapid car chase. Even when the two are on foot, they run, and in one memorable, bone-jarring leap jump off walls onto the roof of a car. There is no time to walk, no time to use the stairs. All of this helped to create a sense of urgency which was consistently underpinned by a musical score which pushed the action on at a relentless pace. This twinning of music and action was a distinctive feature of television shows during this period and is one demonstration of the relationship which exists between the film and television industries (Wicking and Vahimagi 1979).

The introduction of violence dramatically changed the nature of police series on television. This stemmed from the breakthrough made in the so-called 'spaghetti westerns' which demonstrated the inadequacy of the bloodless bullet holes and the bruiseless punches of conventional westerns. By dwelling on the painful and bloody consequences of violence, the spaghetti western showed in gruesome detail that even the good get hurt. With slow motion action revealing the progress of the bullet through the exploding flesh of the victim, it became difficult to accept the authenticity of massacres without any blood. The contrast can be sharply drawn between the 1930s gangster movies and Arthur Penn's 1967 film of *Bonnie and Clyde* (Cameron 1985). The standard depiction of a shooting had been to show the shooter while he is firing and to cut to the victim, if at all, only after he has been hit and is clutching the wound. After the spaghetti westerns, and the less well known samurai films of the early 1960s, these conventions were changed to allow graphic portrayals of murder and mayhem. The flood of police movies which came out of America in the late 1960s and early 1970s used this new convention to construct a view of policing in which violence was represented as a way of life for the police in modern cities. This more explicit portrayal of the violence could be seen as completely gratuitous unless it had gained a symbolic value as the necessary background to the war against crime which the police were fighting.

At the forefront of the transformation of the values of the police programme was a set of films made by Don Siegal and starring Clint Eastwood. In *Coogan's Bluff* (1968), Eastwood plays a cop from Arizona flown into New York to bring home a villain who has been arrested in the big city. He makes his appearance fully kitted out in his 'cowboy' outfit much to the amusement of the locals. The only thing missing from his character in the spaghetti westerns is the poncho; he retains the hat, boots and inscrutable expression. He loses his prisoner and tracks him using physical confrontaions as the quickest way of gaining co-operation. By the time *Dirty Harry* (1971) appeared the character had become more refined and the Arizonan edges had been polished. The character (dedicated to hunting villains) was often at odds with the legal system which set strict parameters on the methods he could use in the chase. He did not operate outside or above the law, merely bending it on occasion where a minor technical infringement would hasten the course of the villains' arrest. *Magnum Force* (1973) clearly demonstrated the difference between these values and those of a group of rogue cops who had set themselves up as executioners of the local villains. The hero refuses to take part in the death squad as this enterprise invalidates the rule of law and the entire legal system. This step towards anarchy is not and cannot be what the character stands for. A redrawing of the boundaries of acceptable behaviour in favour of the hard-pressed policeman is permissible, but at the cost of the whole value system. It is this tradition which Regan steps into, a British Eastwood without the hats.

'WHEN DO YOU EVER HAVE A SMALL CASE, JACK?'

Jack Regan was a Detective Inspector in the 'Sweeney' which became one of the best known pieces of cockney rhyming slang: Sweeney Todd – Flying Squad. This was portrayed as an elite squad of detectives operating throughout the Metropolitan police area. The purpose of the squad is to track down major criminals and prevent, wherever possible, such crimes taking place. This made the 'Sweeney' ideal material for a fictional treatment, particularly within the action series format. The remit of serious crime across London gave the production team ample scope for different locations and fast-moving sequences between scenes, and it is important to note that the series was shot on film. Equally, by concentrating solely on serious crime, *The Sweeney* again fell neatly within the requisites of the action series. It was also a logical development in terms of the internal history of the police series, for the 'Sweeney' was not the first squad to be featured in such series. Indeed, the television archives are littered with attempts to dramatize the action of the specialized sections of the police force. Constant attempts to move the genre on had seen *Special Branch, Fraud Squad* and the BBC's chronicling of the move from divisional to regional criminal investigation in the shift from *Z Cars* to *Softly, Softly* and on to *Softly, Softly Taskforce.* What the new series offered was a closed unit of characters who would appear regularly enough to develop into individual characters against a background of the drama of serious crime. It should be remembered that the concept of 'serious crime' had assumed particular connotations by the early 1970s: it referred to crimes involving large amounts of money and large amounts of violence and usually both. *The Sweeney* legitimated the transition to violence as part of the routine of police work by locating the fiction within the framework of that section of the police force most likely to deal with violence in the course of its work. The Flying Squad was in retrospect an ideal vehicle for this fictional representation both in terms of the internal logistics of the genre and the concerns of the law and order debate being conducted beyond the series.

The Sweeney marked a distinct move away from the earlier police series, not just in terms of the stylistic conventions, but because of its attitude towards crime. An important element of the police series prior to the 1970s had been the sense of social conscience that the series had portrayed. Quite often the crime which formed the subject matter for an evening's episode would be treated in complex ways, considering the underlying causes of the action, the criminal's individual problems as well as the police response which was deemed to be most appropriate. *Z Cars*'s origins in a drama-documentary series of police interrogation techniques often revealed itself in the treatment given to problems such as shoplifters and the well-being of hoboes. *Dixon of Dock Green* is still remembered for George Dixon's 'Evening all' and opening and closing monologues which outlined and underlined the moral dimensions of that night's story, even though these were dropped from the later series. They spoke of a sense of community which informed the concern about crime, represented as a neighbourly interest in something which could affect each and every one of the audience. The policemen/heroes were friendly types, an image captured in the opening sequence of *The Blue Lamp* where a pedestrian is seen approaching a policeman and asking for directions. As Walker pointed out, Regan is not that sort of policeman. The spirit of co-operation and optimism which the shared values of *Dixon of Dock Green* suggest is replaced by a world-weary cynicism in *The Sweeney*. Dixon was an integral part of his 'manor' and the patrol cars became an important landmark in *Z Cars's* Newtown. The London of *The Sweeney* is not like that and the policeman no longer enjoys any sense of belonging.

This alienation is expressed in a speech Regan made in an episode called 'Abduction' (transmitted 27 March 1975). Things do not always go smoothly for Regan and this particular day was no exception. He tells his driver:

> I sometimes hate this bastard place. It's a bloody holiday camp for thieves and weirdoes . . . all the rubbish. You age prematurely trying to sort some of them out. Try and protect the public and all they do is call you 'fascist'. You nail a villain and some ponced-up, pinstriped, Hampstead barrister screws it up like an old fag packet on a point of procedure and then pops off for a game of squash and a glass of Madeira. . . . He's taking home thirty grand a year and we can just about afford ten days in Eastbourne and a second hand car. . . . No, it is all bloody wrong my son.

These sentiments could not have been thought within the structure of *Dixon of Dock Green* but flow 'naturally' from the construction of *The Sweeney*. Regan does his job to put villains away where they can do no more harm to society. His motivation is to stop the country being swamped by the crime wave. Unlike Dixon he has no time for contemplation about the outcome of a particular case because there is another one to attend to, and then another and another.

This transformation is vitally important in understanding the new police series which followed *The Sweeney* in the mid-1970s.

The crime series of the 1960s developed a set of concepts about crime which had been cast in the period of post-war reconstruction. Crime was thought, though important, to be only a passing problem which would disappear, or at least return to acceptable levels as society returned to an orderly routine following the disruption of the war. Crime was to be tackled co-operatively, with the police as one party in the concerted effort (Clarke 1983). In the late 1960s, these attitutudes were attacked from many sides. The crime rate did not return to 'normal' and periodically, as they were constructed, new 'crime waves' swept the country, with the popular press fanning the flames of concern. One of the causes of concern was the so-called permissiveness of the 1960s and the threat that this posed to our way of life as it had been known for generations. The 'soft' options on crime and punishment were vigorously attacked and a lack of discipline throughout society was frequently bemoaned. Crime became not so much a problem for the community but was represented as threatening the very existence of that community. It was becoming a problem truly recognizable as one of 'law and order'. The question had become, how could law be enforced and order maintained?

In the theatre of politics these issues were brought together in the 1970 general election by the manifesto of the Conservative Party and their subsequent actions when they formed the new government. Heath followed President Nixon's lead in claiming to speak for the silent majority of decent, law-abiding citizens and promised not to allow the dangers of American-style crime to infect the streets of this country. The Heath government took recourse to the law as a means of confronting a range of situations from student protest to industrial action. This extension of the role of the state led to what the authors of *Policing the Crisis* called the 'exceptional state' (Hall *et al.* 1978) – 'exceptional' precisely because the power of the state which had remained so effectively concealed was being unmasked to shore up the position of the ruling bloc threatened from so many quarters it did not know what else to do. The old systems of policing were being challenged by the new role which the ever-increasing legislation was thrusting upon the police and new systems of policing were being developed to deal with this new emphasis. The importance of public co-operation was not denied but was made one part of the policing process as a bifurcation took place within the force. Ideas of 'community policing' gained favour to meet certain 'local difficulties' but alongside this work, more and more police were being trained in crowd and riot control. Counter-insurgency measures were openly discussed and joint operations between the police and the army were organized.

The Sweeney was a child of its time but this is not to say that the series simply reflected the public debates about crime and the changes in policing practice which were taking place. In no way should it be thought that the series even attempted to reflect these changes. The process, as Voloshinov correctly observed, is not one of reflection but of refraction (Voloshinov 1973). It is not possible to understand the series without some understanding of the conditions of its production, but these conditions are not sufficient to explain the particular form of the series as it was broadcast. The problem of the relationship between the fictional and what it portrays is particularly acute in the police series, where the referent is so clearly present in the world outside the series. However, all too often the criteria of reality imposed to assess the fiction are based on only a partial knowledge of that reality. Hence, with the police series, the authenticity of the series may actually be judged against the fictional presentation of the police in other series, the well-publicized views of certain leading police officers and the new reports – themselves constructed – of police actions. Only a very small minority of the audience for *The Sweeney* will have any direct knowledge of the Flying Squad or that kind of police work. The image which is finally presented in the series takes some of the public knowledge about the police, carefully selected to deny the 'outrageous', and refracts this through the medium of the generic conventions which are themselves subject to change (Barthes 1976).

In this way the 1970s could give rise to police series which, at one and the same time, eulogized the police for the effectiveness of their efforts in the war against crime and raised issues about police wrong-doing which, according to some right-wing critics, could have undermined public confidence in the police force. It is noticeable, however, that the police wrong-doing complained of consists mainly of bad language, the slightly over-zealous use of violence, searching premises without a proper warrant and so on. The more serious claims which were levelled against the police during the same period are excluded – for instance, no one dealt with racism within the police force, no one dealt with

deaths in police custody. Generic conventions which sensation-
alize the presentation of police practices do not extend to the
presentation of such damaging and fundamental issues. The
action may focus on car chases and shoot-outs rather than
writing up reports, more time can be spent on actual arrests than
on the collection of evidence but the amount of critical material
is severely limited (Keating 1978). The good guys have borrowed
from the tough guy's wardrobe but have left the bad guys' clothes
on the peg. What we witness is, in fact, an inflection of the moral
domain of the hero rather than a shift in the moral basis of the
series and the genre.

AUTHORITARIANISM WITH A SMILE

Before looking in detail at any material from *The Sweeney*, it is
important to consider the character of Jack Regan and to
compare this with earlier characterizations of policemen.What
the inflection of the moral domain produces is not a complete
transformation of the character, but rather a character with a
difference, a harder edge than any previously found in the series.
George Dixon is the archetype of the British television character.
Dixon was one of the earliest policemen to be seen on British
television and the series ran for so long that the character had an
influence on other series at least until 1976 when it went off the
air. I suspect that the influence of *Dixon of Dock Green* has
lasted longer than the series itself, as the Dixon character has
become a part of the popular folklore. Indeed the *Financial
Times* (28 July 1981) headlined a review of policing methods
after the summer riots of 1981 – 'We can't leave it to old George
any more'.

   George Dixon created the classic standards that the police were
supposed to embody when they were established as 'citizens in
uniform'. He was a constant good example, displaying civilized
behaviour at all times. We saw him at home, coping admirably
with the routine domestic tribulations which befall all of us and
he even found time to sing in the police choir. We saw a man
with true local knowledge of the streets and of the people, even
going so far as being on speaking terms with most of them. He
was always correctly attired, properly dressed, his uniform spot-
less. Above all, George Dixon was honest. Any thought of
corruption was impossible where he was concerned. He was a

man of integrity who would not have devalued himself or the force he was serving by bringing the possibility of dishonour to the uniform. He belongd to a generation that had lived through the war and thus recognized the need for discipline, both within himself and within the force. The world Dixon inhabited in Dock Green was presented as being profoundly ordered and orderly – a world where the police uniform itself deserved respect but where the individual bearer of that uniform could earn personal respect by living up to the ideals of public service. Throughout his career Dixon did that and much more, fully justifying the decision to reincarnate him after his untimely death in his filmic debut. I have argued that in many respects he was too good to be true and, as the series progressed, it became increasingly clear that Dixon was a product of a world that was in the process of ceasing to exist. He personified the world which many people in the 1970s were complaining was being eroded by the tide of permissiveness which was sweeping the country. When Jack Warner, the actor who had played Dixon, died on 25 May 1981, the BBC repeated an episode of *Dixon of Dock Green* as a tribute to him. It was a particularly appropriate episode as it focused on the allegations of corruption against an ambitious young policeman. Dixon was always cast in a paternal role to the new recruits and championed PC Warren's innocence through-out the enquiry into his activities. At the end of the investigation it was found that the allegations were unfounded but, although his name had been cleared Warren presented his resignation. Dixon asked him for his reasons:

> *Warren* When I joined the force, my friends thought I was mad. But then there was all that stuff about a career in the police force and once I was on the beat I said to myself, 'yes, this is worth doing'. Not that I meant to pad the streets for long. Commissioner of Police one day, that was me.

> *Dixon* Could be. Though I do happen to think any job in the force is worth doing.

> *Warren* Yes, I know. Oh I'd have settled in the end for whatever came my way.

> *Dixon* Why quit now? Your'e a good copper. We can't afford to lose men like you.

Warren Because there are some things I just can't take.

Dixon   Look, we're a disciplined force, any raw recruit knows that. We've got to be.

Warren Does that include being put under suspicion on the strength of an anonymous letter? Does it include having your room searched and your private papers gone through without permission? Does it include being required to explain your personal bank account and being suspected of taking bribes if you don't? No, not me. I'll do my job as a policeman to the best of my ability but I am still a human being in my own right. I joined because I wanted to. A fine uniform, and quarters or rent allowance in lieu doesn't turn me into a bonded slave. I've too much pride for that.

Dixon   Well, as it happens, Len, I've got quite a bit of pride myself. All the years I've spent as a copper, I think every minute has been worth it. Oh, the police force isn't perfect. It can't be, its manned by ordinary men. I know we talk about red tape and frustration when a villain goes free and the harm done by the occasional bent copper. But for all the criticism the police are there to protect the public and that's what we do. We curb violence. We do our best to deal with villains who want to prey on society. I've been proud to have been a part of that. It's been my life for a long time now and I don't regret any of it.

It was this ideal image and associated sentimentalism of character which many of the subsequent writers attempted to get away from in their scripts. Yet, underneath the hard-hitting veneer of the new characters, a substantial element of Dixon remained.

There is no time here to list all the characters who attempted to develop the Dixon style of character. Some were more like Dixon – like Gideon of *Gideon's Way* and Lockhart of *No Hiding Place* – than others – most memorably Barlow. However, even when we look closely at the Regan character, we can see the 'Dixon tradition' is still present. Several of the peripheral characteristics have changed: Regan is divorced rather than widowed; he does not have any permanent family home but lives in an untidy bedsit; he is not always polite to his superior officers or to the public. Within the narrative of the series these changes are explained and woven into the development of the action in such a way that they become naturalized. Once they become an accepted part of the narrative format they cease to challenge the central notions of the policeman's character. We know Regan is honest and incorruptible. We know Regan is firm and fair. We know, above all else, that he is working to protect the public from the villains who would prey on society. What we see is thus a continuity of the core values and this can be seen to perform two functions as we analyse the police series. One is to link the police heroes across time and reinforce the trust placed in the police as the upholders of the law and the maintainers of order. The other is to establish a link between the series themselves to maintain the parameters of the genre.

Early studies of the genre worked on the iconography of content, stressing the audience's recognition of the essential feature of the type (Ryall 1978). This led to work on the western, the gangster movies, horror films and musicals which identified the disparate imagery of the films. Subsequently this was refined to include the specific filmic conventions of each genre as well as their specific imagery. However, these definitions by content are tautologous and do not serve to take the analysis beyond an initial classification. For instance, in looking at the gangster movies, McArthur (1972) devotes a great deal of time to the importance of the gun. Kitses (1969), looking at the western, also spends time elaborating the importance of the gun. The two are making slightly different points which cannot be supported simply by showing how these genres use different weapons in different physical locations. Indeed, for the analysis we would have to point at the significant absence of guns from the British series for many years if we were going to unpack the significance of weapons in the British context. It is how the presence or absence of the weapons is constructed within the narrative which is crucial to the development of the argument, and the analysis of this setting requires that the focus of attention be shifted from the iconographic to the narrative. What this means for the practice of generic criticism is that more attention has to be given to the clustering of ideological elements with each genre, thus locating the difference betwen genres not at the level of iconographic content but at the deeper structural level of ideology. This is the view Neale (1980) elaborates in his monograph on *Genre* with an argument which is premised on a notion of narrative as a 'process of transformation of the balance of elements that constitute its pretext'.   Neale construes narrative as a process through which an initial equilibrium is disturbed – dispersed in Neale's term – leading to an eventual resolution which seeks a refiguration of the elements into a new equilibrium. Neale makes two intersting points about the basic model:

> The first is that the 'elements' in question, their equilibrium and disequilibrium, their order/disorder, are not simply reducible to the signified components of a given narrative situation, nor are they solely the product of the narrative considered as a single discourse or discursive structure. Rather they are signifiers articulated in a narrative process which is simultaneously that of the inscription of a number of discourses, and that of the modification, restructuration and transformation they each undergo as a result of their interaction. The second point following from this is that disequilibrium, order and disorder are essentially a function of the relations of coherence between the discourses involved, of the compatibilities and contradition which exists between them.
>
> (Neale 1980: 20)

Genres, for Neale, are therefore to be read through the presentation of elements and the specific clustering of these elements. The relations of coherence, compatibility and contradiction which exist between the character of Dixon and the character of Regan are an example of the development of a genre through the transformation of the constituent elements.

The elements which typify the police series of the 1970s become clear if we consider the structure for *The Sweeney*. The original story-line concerned the struggle between two gangs – one from south of the Thames and the other from north of the Thames – for the supremacy of the criminal underworld in London. When one of Regan's squad gets a hint of what is happening, he is killed, bringing Regan's full attention to the investigation. His motivation owes as much to a sense of revenge as it does to any legalistic notion of justice. The narrative uncovers a cluster of four elements which define the parameters for the series.

The threat of crime

We are presented with a world of rival gangs committed to the ruthless eradication of any competition. As the story unwinds, we see that the situation is worse than we were led to suspect. The members of one gang actually murder their own leader because they have received a better offer from the rival gang leader. It is the threat to society which this attitude, signifies that Regan and Carter act to protect us, the audience, from. This profession of violence legitimates the violence of *The Sweeney*. The sense of threat is heightened by the stark contrast of their own immediate interests and the human face of the heroes who, even in the pilot episode, are presented as more rounded characters. Regan arrests Dale, the villain responsible for killing the policeman and his former boss, after a tense confrontation in a disused warehouse. Carter covers Dale with one gun as Dale's three thugs all hold their guns on Regan. By suggesting that the three can save themselves by not shooting, Regan is able to persuade them to leave the building. Once they have gone, Regan tells Dale that he wants their full names and we know that they will be arrested later. In the process of asking the questions Regan hits Dale several times. The last scene ends with them sprawled across the bonnet of Dale's limousine where Regan sees the road tax disc on the windscreen. He tells Dale 'This stinking heap was licensed to March. It's April the 20th. I'll have you for that an' all.' This touch of humour helps to defuse the tension and shows Regan to be more than the violent automatons that the villains represent.

The family

The human side of Regan is picked up again in the way the programme handles the presentation of the family. Regan has been married and has one daughter. This is made clear to the viewer when Regan receives a message to call on his ex-wife. The opening sequence of the scene where they meet puts their relationship into sharp focus:

> *Kate* You're late. I kept Susie up to seven thirty. She was so excited. She thought she was going to see her dad. Poor kid fell asleep on the couch. I had to put her to bed. Why can't you ever be on time for us?

> *Jack* I'm on an important case. There's a young copper . . .
>
> *Kate* Look I'm not interested any more in your silly cases and
> your stupid criminals.

Regan never had any time for his wife or family, his work always
had to come first – a point Regan makes to the newly married
Carter who complains that this wife will nag him for working
with Regan rather than in a routine job where he could keep
reasonable hours. 'You're not a nine to five man. Over there
sitting behind a desk, swigging tea all day and waiting to get
home to the roses. You're like me, you're a copper.'

Regan has sacrificed his personal family for the greater good of
us all. The same problem arises in any relationship he could
have. The series uses women's attitudes towards Regan to define
and reinforce the complete demarcation between what is
presented as the masculine world, the world of work, as it is
inscribed within *The Sweeney* and the feminine obsession with
the domestic – that which is not contained within the definition
of 'work'.

Rule breaking

Regan transgresses the moral code of society but within strictly
contained limits. He is moderately permissive but heterosexual.
He is a moderately heavy drinker but not an alcoholic. The same
is true of his attitude towards police work. His view is that the
only good rule is one which allows him to catch criminals. When
Carter asked him whether he thought breaking into a club where
they might find some crucial evidence was a 'good idea', Regan
replied: 'I think it is a good idea, yes.' Cause if I don't sort this
out in the next twelve hours before they get their Cowley enquiry
organized, I'm out of the force for good. Now if you don't see it
that way, then on your bike and out of my way.' He is against
bureaucratic structures which would clip his freedom of action.

This rule-bending covers minor indiscretions, like breaking
and entering of premises and using weapons without the proper
authorization. All of this is of no consequence in the quest for the
villain. The final sequence of the programme has Carter saying
to Regan: 'Got away with it again, didn't you?' Regan replies,
'Ah don't you start! "Got away with it." I got the bastard who did

it': this is the total and only explanation of his actions which is necessary in terms of the world constructed in the series.

Individualism

This strand is inextricably linked with Regan's stance against bureaucratic restrictions. The contrast comes out in the sense of frustration that his superiors feel in dealing with him and wanting to put him on disciplinary charges:

> *Maynon* It will not stop Regan. Twenty years ago, he would have been a perfect cop in the days of the individualists. Now he's out on a limb. I sometimes wonder if these ideas are for the best.
>
> *Haskins* I think so, sir.
>
> *Maynon* Ok bring him in. Put him on suspension with full pay.
>
> *Haskins* Right, sir.
>
> *Maynon* By the way I think he's right . . .

Regan's position is secured by his record of successful cases and, of course, he was right, but it is this individualism which sets him apart from the rest of the force. He could have gone through the correct procedures and arrived at the same conclusion but, by cutting corners, he achieves the results more quickly.

The Sweeney did not present a romantic notion of policing in the way that *Dixon of Dock Green* had done, but even without the anachronistic sentimentality, it still offers a powerful moral. The consensus no longer guarantees the police force the co-operation of the public but the police series underline repeatedly that any sensible person would help the police. Regan explains the situation to an ex-member of one of the gangs in this way:

> Detective Inspector Regan, Flying Squad. Now you work for Mallory so you know the score. I want to ask you some questions. You don't want to answer them. So, up front, I'll lay it on. This is a colleague of mine, he hits people. Isn't that right, colleague?

The answers are obtained, even if certain threats have to be made to elicit the information. We cannot expect the police to behave like perfect gentlemen because they are presented as the front line soldiers in the war against crime and not merely the keepers of the Queen's Peace.

The generic specificity of the police series in the 1970s owes much to the way that the attempt to confront contemporary situations was situated within a framework set by the earlier series. Overthrowing the stylistic conventions of the earlier series was not enough to allow series like *The Sweeney* and *Target* to escape from the overwhelming moral certainties of the genre and which had been constructed within the previous series. It is possible to see how these series help to construct the understanding of the law and order issue through portraying fictional resolutions to what become ever more familiar problems. Each episode poses a threat anew, each episode provides a restoration of the equilibrium within the established framework.

Attempts have been made to operate outside this framework, particularly in the serial format. Freed of the constraints of the series conventions both *Law and Order* and *Out* challenged the pattern of presentation by concentrating on the corruption of the police. These serials were condemned for overemphasizing the extent and scope of corruption and the Metropolitan Police withdrew all co-operation with series made by the BBC. Even within these serials, the power of the genre and the institutional practices which facilitate the production of series held the serials within their parameters. The police are still seen to restore the equilibrium by their positive intervention and even their corruption is portrayed as motivated by an underlying desire to stamp out crime.

The 1970s have themselves been superseded by a return to a more orderly, gentler world of crime in series like *Juliet Bravo*, *The Gentle Touch* and *The Bill* (Clarke 1983). The first two of these series featured women in senior positions and used this device to look at the world of crime from what is presented as a new perspective. The 'feminine' viewpoint allows the return of the social conscience into the series, creating an angle of interest. In fact what was produced is the re-creation of the earlier presentation, previously seen in the late 1960s episodes of *Z Cars*, *No Hiding Place* and other such series. The use of women in key roles defuses the presentation of violence by overlaying and legitimizing a caring dimension to the work of the police officer.

In this change a transformation in the genre is accomplished, not in the change of character but through the reordering of the ideological elements. Of the elements outlined above, these series retain the central ideological values and core concerns as we can see.

The threat of crime

In these series the crime has been reduced in scale, although both *The Gentle Touch* and *The Bill* do have the remit to enter into the realm of serious crime. However, the return to the routine and mundane crimes of everyday life do not make the threat any the less and in fact make the portrayal more immediate to the viewing public. What the shift does address directly is the question of violence, which had attracted a great deal of criticism to the police series and which has been largely removed in these series. It is a sanitized world, where violence is recognized as a natural part of the world but does not dominate the presentation of conflict.

The family

The two series featuring women were particularly strong on this theme, finding the domestic situations of the leading characters irresistible and devoting far more script time to the problems than in the pevious male series. There have been two *Juliet Bravos* – the name representing the character's radio call sign and not the Inspector's name – who have been portrayed first, with Jean Darblay as having a husband who finds her career success threatening but no children, and then with Kate Longton, who had no family at all. This lack in both characters was the cause for much comment and speculation in the series. In *The Gentle Touch*, the subject was approached rather differently. Maggie Forbes was a police officer married to another police officer who was killed and left her with her career and her teenage son to look after. Here the presence of the son was used to dramatize the conflict of priority which working mothers face when confronted with a demanding job. The tension here was a heightened version of that constructed by Regan's absence from home in *The Sweeney*.

Rule breaking

There is far less of the overt rule breaking in the new series, with
a greater emphasis on due process and proper procedure. Again
this reflects some of the criticisms levelled at the 'action series' for
the image they constructed of the police as little better than the
villains. This element is used to good effect in *The Bill* to
distinguish between the two different camps within the Sun Hill
station – the uniformed officers who follow the book and the CID
officers who need the convictions.

Individualism

This is probably the most interesting of the elements which have
been rearticulated in the new series. On one level the individualism of the earlier series is still there, with very strong central
characters taking the initiative in the narrative. The emphasis on
individual traits, the domestic situations and the career pro-
gression of the main characters – especially the female characters
– presents a different picture of individualism to that developed
in *The Sweeney*. Where Regan's was an isolation, the emphasis
on individualism in the more recent series has focused on the
individual within the context of the supportive team which
makes the successful operation of the police station possible.

The Bill demonstrates this most effectively, with a return to the
fictional roots of the police series at a small London police
station and the construction of a realistic environment for the
routine police drama. The early promotional material stressed
this authenticity:

> The local police officer was impressed. Put a young copper in
> Sun Hill Police Station, he said, and his only doubt would be
> which nick it was. There's the front counter, parade room,
> charge room, cells, CID, Offices, Showers . . .
> But then he would notice cameras on the stairs – and
> smoked salmon being served in the canteen.
> Sun Hill is a former factory in London's East End, stripped
> out and refurbished by Thames Television as the setting for
> Tuesday's new ITV series *The Bill*.
> It's different from most other police series. There's a gritty
> realism about it. Shot on location in the East End, with a fine
> – but as yet almost unknown – cast, it is, says producer

Michael Chapman, 'about the police being policemen rather than investigators in someone else's crime story'.

Eric Richard plays Sgt Bob Cryer, the station officer, fifteen years in the job and a father figure to the young bobbies. He has a crusty relationship with the local CID, headed by tough young Det. Insp. Galloway who is played by John Salthouse.

'Galloway just believes in nicking people if they've broken the law,' says Salthouse. 'If it means bending a few rules that's what he'll do. There isn't much difference between him and some of the villains.'

Salthouse gained first hand experience for the role, going the rounds with a detective inspector at a North London police station. 'Policemen see all the bad things in society. Yet somehow they have to get through the day,' says Salthouse. 'That's what we're trying to show – how it affects the policeman as a person.'

(*TV Times*, 13–19 October 1984)

It will be seen that there is, in fact, nothing new in this change of format which makes if different from the earlier series, rather than from the series which were on in 1984. This presentation of policemen as people with problems evokes the anti-sentimentalism which characterized the *Z Cars* initiative at the BBC. The format is remarkably familiar and therefore arguably welcome. It retains enough of the drama of the major crimes, with the CID section located within the same building, and by interweaving story lines – similar to the five story narrative developed by *Hill Street Blues* in the American context – allowing for both sides of the police role to be depicted. The core values, the continuity referred to earlier, remain. There is no challenge to the central thrust of the police series, portraying the Sun Hill station as honest, hardworking, diligent but troubled officers. It is gritty realism to depict Sgt Bob Cryer as short tempered because he has toothache, but it hardly challenges the generic conventions.

Perhaps the most significant challenge to the ideological presentation of the police has been the re-emergence of an alternative form of the genre or a different genre entirely with the return to the police procedural. New series have been ousted in favour of longer explorations of a single case investigation. Often drawn from novels, these serials have given the thinking policeman a new lease of life. Morse, Dalglish and Wexford have all been introduced to television audiences and have broadened the appeal they held for devotees of the literature. In these longer adaptations there is a chance to develop character and plot beyond the confines of a 55-minute episode. This is the classic mystery story with the policeman as hero, where the interest lies in the unravelling of complicated crime and the pleasure is in the ingenuity of the solution. There are different conventions at play in these works but they do not escape the parameters of the police genre and, indeed, the integrity of the central characters does much to restore faith in the police procedures.

As this brief analysis has attempted to show, the transformation of the genre is the product of the social forces of production shaping the clustering of the elements. It is important not to isolate the moment of fictional representation from the rest of the lived world. The political forces of society cannot be disentangled from this nexus, the dramas are enacted within the structured ideological field of society. The police series do have a role in shaping the consensus, which is not a simple entity but a complex set of matrices, and it is that role which is important here. It is not that the police series are partisan in any straightforward sense but that they are contained within the mode of reality of the state. As such they constitute one of the sites on which ideological struggle can take place and in which the cultural formation can be shaped. However, as this article has attempted to show, the continuities which are generated within this process are as important to the understanding of each specific moment of ideological production as are any changes within the genres.

REFERENCES

Barthes, R. (1976) *Mythologies*, St. Albans: Paladin.
Cameron, I. (1975) *Crime Films*, London: Hamlyn.
Clarke, A. (1983) 'Holding the blue lamp', *Crime and Social Justice*, 19.
Clarke, A. (1986) 'This is not the boy scouts: Television police series and definitions of law and order,' in Bennett, T., Mercer, C. and Woollacott, J. *Popular Culture and Social Relations*, Milton Keynes: Open University Press.
Clarke, A. (1983) 'An Interview with the Chinese Detective', *Marxism Today*, October.
Financial Times 28 July 1981.

Hall, S., Critcher, C., Jefferson, T., Clarke, J. and Roberts, B. (1978) *Policing the Crisis: Mugging, the State and Law and Order*, London: Macmillan.

Hall, S. (1977) 'Culture, the media and the ideological effect', in J. Curran, M. Gurevitch and J. Woollacott (eds) *Mass Communication and Society*, London: Edward Arnold.

Keating, H. R. F. (ed.) (1978) *Crimewriters*, London: BBC Publications.

Kerr, P. (1981) 'Watching the detectives', *Prime Time* 1.

Kitses, T. (1969) *Horizons West*, London: Secker & Warburg.

McArthur, C. (1972) *Underworld USA*, London: Secker & Warburg.

Neale, S. (1980) *Genre*, London: British Film Institute.

Ryall, T. (1978) *BFI Teachers' Study Guide: Gangster Film*, London: British Film Institute.

Staig, L. and Williams, T. (1985) *Italian Western: The Opera of Violence*, London: Lorimar.

Voloshinov, V. (1973) *Marxism and the Philosophy of Language*, New York: Seminar Press.

Walker, F. (1977) 'It's The Sweeney', *Fiesta* II (6).

Wicking, C. and Vahimagi, T. (1979) *The American Vein*, London: Talisman Books.

Chapter 10

You've never had it so silly
The politics of British satirical comedy from *Beyond the Fringe* to *Spitting Image*

Stephen Wagg

Well, I used to be disgusted
But now I try to be amused.

(Elvis Costello, 'Red Shoes')

People who are sad
Sometimes they wear a frown
And people who are kings
Sometimes they wear a crown
But all the people who don't fit
Get the only fun they get
From people putting people down
People putting people down.

(John Prine, 'People Putting People Down')

Anthony Wedgwood Benn MP spent much of Saturday 28 September 1963 in Bridlington on Labour Party business but, as he recorded in his diary,

I dashed back in time to watch That Was The Week That Was, which returned to TV tonight. It was savage and brilliant in parts, and the room was packed with Labour leaders and journalists. Not a single anti-Labour joke was made and even I wondered if it had gone too far.

(Benn 1988: 65)

Benn's reaction to 'TW3', BBC television's late night satirical programme, first broadcast in 1962, was a typical one in the Labour Party and on the British left: the show, and the 'satire boom' of which it appeared to be a part, was 'on their side' and against the Conservative government. But for how long could they get away with it? However, a meeting a year later with *That*

Was The Week . . .'s producer, Ned Sherrin, brought Benn to a more sober judgement:

> I felt like a wet blanket and I sensed an enormously powerful anti-political feeling. It wasn't anti-political in the way that CND or the real left is anti-political. It was anti-political in a scornful and contemptuous way.
>
> (Benn 1988: 138)

This article aims, essentially, to probe these two reactions to British 'satire' by looking at the origin and development of British satirical comedy and trying thereby to make sense of its place in Britain's political and popular culture. There will be special consideration of TV programmes such as the afore-mentioned *That Was The Week That Was*, *Monty Python's Flying Circus* and *Spitting Image*, and the satirical magazine *Private Eye*.

Broadly speaking, it will argue that this form of comedy is born of, and expresses, important changes in the dominant values of British society in the post-war period. These changes have seen the rise of what are now variously described as the values of 'late capitalism', 'consumer capitalism' or – most commonly now, perhaps – 'postmodernism'. The principal thrust of the comedy has, I believe, been toward an elevation of the *private* sphere of individual activities and decision-making at the expense of the *public* realm of parliamentary and 'party political' deliberation.

THIS IS A SEND UP

'Satire', as such, is, of course, nothing new. The word itself dates from the early sixteenth century and its meaning – the ridicule of prevailing vices and their perpetrators – has survived intact. There have, moreover, been times in British history when a strong tradition of satire at the expense of the monarch and other eminent statespeople has been established – notable in the eighteenth and early nineteenth centuries, through street theatre and the 'pauper press'. What seems to me to distinguish modern satire from earlier versions is its apparent emergence from *within* the culture of the dominant social classes (as a minor 'revolt of the privileged'), its firm and enduring place there, and its subsequent dissemination, via the mass media, into popular culture. This dissemination began in the early 1960s but, given the political and broadcasting conventions of the 1950s, would have been unthinkable much earlier.

Although comedy had been part of the 'light entertainment' provision of the BBC from its earliest days (Briggs 1985: 69) the tone and subject matter of this comedy was severely restricted. This policy of restriction was explicitly reaffirmed in 1949 in a 'Green Book' issued to all comedy writers and producers. This booklet was apparently written with the working-class comedian, Max Miller, in mind. Miller was known for his suggestiveness and had reputedly uttered a sexual double entendre during a live broadcast from the Holborn Empire in 1940. The prohibitions now set out were wide-ranging: there were to be no jokes about lavatories, effeminacy in men, honeymoon couples, lodgers, commercial travellers, marital infidelity. . . . Jokes about religion were specifically forbidden, as, significantly in this context, were comic references to politicians or political institutions (Took 1981: 86–91).

Some people detected a mild subversiveness in the popular radio comedy programme *ITMA* which ran from 1939 to 1949 and provided, according to a *Guardian* correspondent, 'a laughing criticism of the mysterious "them" who rule our fortunes' (Briggs 1985: 253). But, while *ITMA* had merely availed itself of notions, popular especially in the early period of World War Two, of the meddling 'men from the Ministry', *The Goon Show* (first broadcast in 1951 as *Those Crazy People, The Goons*) was more self-consciously politically satirical. *The Goon Show* was sanctioned at the BBC in the face of considerable opposition. Its creator, Spike Milligan, its other main players, Harry Secombe and Peter Sellers, and the BBC producer who championed it, Dennis Main Wilson, all came from lower-middle-class backgrounds and lacked the elite university education which would spawn so many 'satirical' comedians in later years. Innocent as it may seem to many ears in the 1990s, *The Goon Show*, with its carefree surrealism and succession of 'silly voices', was seen at the time as subversive – by its more reluctant patrons at the BBC, and by Milligan himself. Not only was *The Goon Show* subversive of adult conventions (grown men behaving like children), it was also, some thought, blatantly disrespectful to authority and the British Establishment. A *Goons* producer, Peter Eton, was, for example, reprimanded on separate occasions for the award to a fictitious character, 'Major Denis Bloodnok', of an OBE 'for emptying dustbins in the heat of battle' in one episode, and the imitation of the Queen's voice trying to shoo some pigeons out of Trafalgar Square in another (Milligan 1974: 10). Milligan, the son of a British Army sergeant major and a veteran of the North African campaign, whose humour expressed the sense of grievance against authority felt by many British service people in the 1940s, was well aware of the subversive thrust of his comedy:

> Essentially it is critical comedy. It is against bureaucracy, and on the side of human beings. Its starting point is one man shouting gibberish in the face of authority, and proving by fabricated insanity that nothing could be as mad as what passes for ordinary living.
>
> (Draper *et al.* 1976: 21)

And, within this madness that passed for ordinary living, Milligan took special inspiration from the world of politics.

'I got my influences from the members of parliament making fools of themselves', he said. 'We were trying to break out into satire. We were ripe for it. Peter [Sellers] could do any voice of any politician in the land – the Queen included. That made us lethal. They [BBC management] were all frightened for their fucking little jobs. We were ready to break out – we could have beaten [Beyond] the Fringe by ten years' (Scudamore 1987).

However, Milligan and the Goons had a clear and strong influence on the young, elite comedians of Cambridge and Oxford universities, whose patterns of humour were, in any event, in the process of changing. This particularly applies to Cambridge, whose Footlights Club had provided a steady trickle of recruits to the entertainment world since its foundation in 1883. For much of its history Footlight members had been known for their beer drinking, their rowing and their lack of political sophistication. Women were not allowed to take part in Footlights productions until 1959 (despite brief aberrations in 1932 and 1957) and were only admitted to club membership in 1964. The annual Footlights revue had invariably been a light and self-referential affair in which young men in boaters and striped blazers sang songs and dispensed jokes about punts, proctors and hangovers. References to politics of any kind had been rare: a lighthearted send-up of Fabian socialism in 1910 and sporadic, fearful references to the spread of Bolshevism during the 1920s (Hewison 1984). Impatience with this style was evident, however, during the 1950s and a decisive break was made in 1959 with a show called *The Last Laugh*, the theme of which was imminent nuclear disaster. This revue was directed by John Bird and strongly featured Peter Cook as both writer and performer. Eleanor Bron, another member of the cast, recalled: 'There really was great anger, they really were politically aware' (Hewison 1984: 124). It's the nature, though, of this anger which seems to me most important in the understanding of this revue and much of the 'undergraduate humour' that has followed it.

From accounts of it, *The Last Laugh*, like much subsequent 'satire', did in some measure express a radical political disgust, but principally on issues which 'cut across party boundaries' and which did not, on the face of it, relate to the economic organization of society: nuclear weapons, foxhunting and, importantly, notions of 'the meritocracy' were early examples. But another political strand seems to me discernible in the work of this generation of Cambridge satirists which has effectively been a paradigm for 'satirical' or 'undergraduate' comedy since 1959/60. This strand variously expresses the view that the world of politics and public life *per se* is necessarily open to ridicule. Central to this view is the notion, extensively explored in the work of Erving Goffman, of *performance*: through performance the public world (of goods, services, politics, etc.) is mediated to the private one via the advertisement, the party political broadcast, and so on. The ideology acknowledges the difference between 'image' and 'reality', but gives equal validity to each. The art of the new Oxbridge comedians says of public life that 'it's all a game', reducible to the posturings of so many public figures.

For many of the individuals propounding this new comedy, it may be that 'satire' provided an emotional insulation from many matters – poverty, nuclear weapons and so on – too vexatious to contemplate: all such matters were assimilable to the new ideology – they were all symptomatic of the mess created for 'us' by 'politicians'. But these 'Goffmanesque' values are identifiable, it seems to me, with a number of groups in British society in the 1950s – notably cultural liberals and young entrepreneurs associated with media and impression management (advertising, public relations, commercial broadcasting – ITV, Radio Caroline, etc. – the pop music industry, and so on). Many of

the younger members of these groups were seeeking, and seeking
to promote, freedom and fun in the private realm and adopting,
in the public sphere, a greater instrumentalism and other-
directedness, commensurate with an economy increasingly based
on mass media and mass consumption (Gouldner 1972: 378–90;
Hall and Jefferson 1976: 57–71). Politics, according to these
emergent values, was seen as an intrusion into the lives of
(usually grudging) 'ordinary people'. This intrusion was growing, due to the expansion of television set ownership during the
late 1950s and early 1960s, and was sanctioned by a public service
tradition in broadcasting which many now thought to be
outmoded. Many undergraduates at Oxford and Cambridge
during this period felt that politicians shouldn't be taken so
seriously. Some of these undergraduates would carry these
assumptions into the world of comedy; others would import the
same assumptions into the world of politics itself, where it was
wholly marriageable with the neo-liberal philosophies of the late
1970s and 1980s that sought to diminish 'big government' and get
it 'off the backs of the people'. For instance, Geoffrey Pattie, one
of the cast of the anti-nuclear Footlights show *The Last Laugh*,
went on to become a Conservative MP and Minister of State for
Defence Procurement in 1983. One sketch in *The Last Laugh*
presented House of Commons Question Time as a TV quiz: this
seems to have been one of the first examples of comedy effecting a
symbolic collision between politics and entertainment, high
culture and media culture.

Peter Cook, the principal writer on *The Last Laugh* and the
most prominent Cambridge comedian of the time, joined with a
Cambridge graduate, Jonathan Miller, and two Oxford
University writer-performers, Alan Bennett and Dudley Moore,
to perform a show of sketches on the fringe of the Edinburgh
Festival in 1960. This show, entitled *Beyond the Fringe*, marked
the entry of 'satire' into popular consciousness. One of its most
celebrated sketches, *TV PM*, was a lampoon by Cook of the
Prime Minister of the time, Harold Macmillan. In the sketch a
distinctly doddery Macmillan talks vaguely about recent talks he
has had with the German foreign minister, whose name he has
now forgotten, and the American president. He then produces a
letter he has received from an elderly lady in Scotland complaining about her own poverty and asking what the government
proposes to do about it. He responds:

Well, let me say right away, Mrs McFarlane – as one Scottish old age pensioner to another – be of good cheer. There are many people in this country today who are far worse off than yourself. And it is the policy of the Conservative Party to see that this position is maintained.

(Bennett *et al.* 1987: 55)

In another sketch, Alan Bennett, as a government Civil Defence official assures the audience that any nuclear attack by Britain must be authorized by the Prime Minister ('And Mr Macmillan will say "yes" – or "no" – as the mood takes him'). Moreover, should Macmillan be out at the time, the decision will be taken by his wife, Lady Dorothy (ibid.: 81).

There were, of course, different ways of making sense, politically, of *Beyond the Fringe*. Clearly, some of the material would have pleased socialists and nuclear disarmers. Just as clearly, those steeped in the public service tradition of politics were affronted: Michael Frayn, for example, recalls a young Conservative responding the *TV PM* sketch with a stunted 'I say! This is supposed to be the Prime Minister' (Bennett *et al.* 1987: 7). Cultural critic Kenneth Tynan, for the left of centre, pronounced the show 'anti-reactionary without being progressive' (*Observer*, 14 May 1961; quoted in Wilmut 1980: 17).

The performers themselves, on the other hand, had no political consciousness, nor affiliation, nor thought-out position to speak of. 'None of us', reflected Miller later, 'approached the world with a satirical indignation' (Wilmut 1987: 17). Cook, the dominant member of the group, having 'moved to the left from my very solid Nazi position at the age of sixteen' (ibid.: 6), nevertheless had no genuine quarrel with the Conservative Prime Minister: 'My impersonation of Macmillan was in fact extremely affectionate – I was a great Macmillan fan' (ibid.: 18). (Similarly, William Rushton, another of the now proliferating Macmillan impersonators, commented later: 'I did do it quite well . . . so I'm very grateful to the old bugger . . . but then I had voted for him, so I think he owed me something!) (ibid.: 64). Cook went on in October 1961 to found *The Establishment*, a satirical nightclub in Soho where the apparent political confusion of the new humour was compounded. 'What really annoyed people', noticed Cook,

were attacks on the liberal left. If there *were* sacred cows at that time, they weren't Macmillan, or the Church – the real sacred cows, to some people, were ladies like Pat Arrowsmith [a leading member of CND]. If *The Establishment* did an attack on Pat Arrowsmith (worthy though her thinking might be), people used to get physically violent.

(Wilmut 1987: 55)

Thus to its public, still trying to make political sense of it, the new satire appeared to express a leftish critique of society's ills. However, to many of its practitioners, a political figure or cause, though worthy, could none the less invite attack on the elusive ground that it might 'to some people' represent a 'sacred cow'. 'Satire' seemed therefore to represent nothing so much as a fear of politics, of confronting social issues, of 'taking things too seriously'. This anxiety, and the accompanying political ambiguity of 'satire', are well illustrated by the progress of the magazine *Private Eye*.

'THE SWINERIES OF PUBLIC LIFE' : POLITICS, THE PRIVATE AND *PRIVATE EYE*

Private Eye is a magazine composed of spoof current affairs coverage, cartoons and 'inside stories'. It was founded in 1961 by a coterie of young upper- and upper-middle-class males. Several of these had been pupils together at Shrewsbury, one of the nine most socially prestigious private schools in Britain, in the early 1950s. These were Richard Ingrams, the son of a merchant banker; Paul Foot, the son of an ambassador and a member of an eminent political family in the West Country; Christopher Booker; and William Rushton. Ingrams and Foot had gone on to Oxford University, where they had worked on an undergraduate journal called *Parson's Pleasure* which, in Ingrams's words, had been 'entirely given over to savage insults and abuse of everyone in the university' (Ingrams 1971: 7). Later they, along with Rushton and fellow-undergraduates Andrew Osmond and Peter Usborne, worked on another humorous university magazine called *Mesopotamia*, which was risqué (proctors complained about a number of double entendres) but apparently apolitical. *Private Eye*, conceived soon after the group left Oxford, was a conscious attempt to keep 'Mespot', and the privileged, carefree social world which nurtured such enterprises, alive in the minds of its contributors. As Osmond put it: 'We decided that if we could live the way we had lived at Oxford we would have found supreme bliss' (Marnham 1983: 29).

The logic of this aspiration, at an editorial level, was to treat politics and 'public life' as an intolerable invasion of privacy, and this – although life at the *Eye* has never been quite so straightforward – has remained the magazine's guiding principle. Similarly, early issues of *Private Eye* were sold largely within the social milieu of its authors: the 'South Kensington coffee bar strip', with its high concentration of young people from private school and 'Oxbridge' backgrounds. As at Oxford, women were involved in the magazine's sales (posters, leaflets) and production (stapling) but not in the writing of it; virtually all the *Eye*'s writers, throughout its life, have been male.

The first years of *Private Eye* coincided with the end of a long period of Conservative government in Britain: the latter phase of Harold Macmillan's premiership, the brief tenure of Lord Hume, and the narrow victory of Labour under Harold Wilson in the general election of 1964. The *Eye*, under the editorship of Richard Ingrams, treated Macmillan with much derision, both as a politician and as a person. For instance, when in 1963 it was claimed that Macmillan had personally prevented R.A. Butler from succeeding him, the *Eye* ran a cover photograph of Macmillan and his wife sitting on a park bench, with the caption:

> In the autumn tranquillity of his days while the golden leaves fall silently to the ground an old man, his faithful wife by his side, sits peacefully in the park happy in the knowledge of a lifetime's work well done, a country served and an old colleague stabbed ruthlessly in the back.
>
> (*Private Eye* 49, 1 November 1963)

On other occasions they speculated as to whether the mange in Macmillan's moustache would spread to his brain (quoted in Seymour-Ure 1974: 240) and asked 'What's Macmillan like in bed?' (A cartoon overleaf shows Macmillan sitting up in bed, wearing a night cap, with the caption 'Much the same as everyone else, old cock!') (reproduced in Ingrams 1971: 63–4). Other leading Tory politicians received similar treatment: R.A. Butler was called 'a flabby faced old coward' for not opposing the

Commonwealth Immigration Act of 1962 (Ingrams 1971: 47); the magazine played a leading role in provoking the resignation of War Minister John Profumo in 1963; and, in 1964, readers were invited to send in for their own 'Stuff Your Own Quintin Hogg Cushion Kit'. (Marnham 1983: 98–100). When Home succeeded Macmillan in October 1963 *Private Eye* announced the death of the Conservative Party (Ingrams 1971: 9).

These comic assaults were widely perceived – not least by some of the people who made them – to be 'from the left'. This perception was based partly on the simple observation that the politicians being attacked were Conservatives, and partly on the belief that patricians like Macmillan and Home represented an ossified class structure, founded on privilege. Ingrams wrote later: 'The government ranks were thick with Earls and Marquesses . . . and it was obvious that Macmillan revelled in this anachronistic state of affairs, even boasting at one point that his powers of patronage made all those years of reading Trollope seem worth while' (Ingrams 1971: 12). Others, however, were not convinced that *Private Eye* was 'left wing' – Kenneth Tynan, for example, delivered the celebrated reproof, 'When are you going to get a point of view?', to which the magazine's principals replied that 'they were prepared to agree on the need for a more democratic educational system' (Marnham 1983: 49). However, when Labour came to power in 1964, committed *inter alia* to comprehensive education, the *Eye*'s cover photograph was of the Queen's speech to the House of Lords [setting out government policy] with the Queen saying '. . . and I hope you realize I didn't write this crap' (*Private Eye* 75, 30 October 1964). Ingrams subsequently claimed to have been disillusioned progressively with Wilson's Labour Party and not to have rejected them finally until 1968, when the *Eye*, predictably perhaps, published the party's obituary (Ingrams 1971: 19). Nevertheless Wilson, along with all other prominent politicians, appears to have been pilloried by *Private Eye* throughout the period of his prominence. The *Eye* has seldom, if ever, explicitly endorsed a political cause.

At an individual level, *Private Eye* has in general been more diverse politically than all this might suggest: Booker and Rushton, for example, were both associated with the Liberal Party in the early 1960s; Paul Foot, author of a series of exposés published in the *Eye*, is, by contrast, a long-standing member of the (Trotskyite) Socialist Workers' Party; Auberon Waugh, another frequent contributor, is known as the maverick of the far right. What has united them, apart from the particularistic attachments of friendship and common social background, is a shared belief in the *culpability of public figures.* Thereafter they divide, in the words of the *Eye*'s biographer Patrick Marnham, into 'those who want to rebuild the world and those who want to laugh at it' (Marnham 1983: 117). Thus, Booker's Liberalism, with its plague-on-both-your-houses view of the major political parties, Foot's socialism, with its inherent suspicion of political and economic elites, and Waugh's world-weary distaste for politicians as a social category have all been assimilable to the *Eye*'s editorial ethos. The beliefs of Waugh and Ingrams were apparently rooted in Christianity (Waugh is a Roman Catholic and Ingrams a member of the Church of England) and their 'iconoclasm' therefore extends only to the secular world which, being profane, should not have icons in the first place. In the traditional world view of the high church English gentleman, the realms of economics and politics might be seen as 'fallen' and inhabited by bounders, whose pursuit and exercise of earthly power is futile. In this perspective, the private world of family and faith is exalted and the world of public affairs discounted. The right-wing journalist and critic Bernard Levin once observed that the 'savage sanity' of *Private Eye* was a 'just counterpart to the swineries of public life', to which Ingrams replied, 'What happens when Levin is among the swine?' Even friends of Ingrams have been attacked in the magazine 'once they ventured too far into the public arena' (Marnham 1983).

But, for much of its life, *Private Eye* has also been at pains to censure *private* behaviour of which its principal contributors disapproved. This applied particularly to the 'counter-culture' of the mid-1960s: 'Booker remembers how much they wanted to distance themselves from the trendy sixties which they were considered to be a part of' (Marnham 1983: 41). Ingrams wrote of 'the trendies currently bemused by the so-called Underground Press and the cult of Revolution and Pot' (Ingrams 1971: 22). He has also frequently expressed his disapproval of homosexuality and the *Eye* popularized the word 'poove' (reputed to have been coined by Jeremy Geidt, a performer at the *Establishment* club) – issue no. 23 parodied the Cuban missile crisis of 1962 by claiming to have uncovered a plot by Cuba 'to flood the USA with pooves'.

In issue no. 465 it was asserted that Earl Mountbatten had been 'a raging queen'.

Private Eye long ago established itself in British popular culture. By the early 1980s it had a circulation of 190,000. Its mixture of mockery of public figures, parody of other media – notably newspapers – and investigative journalism has not changed substantially. It has retained strong Establishment connections and approval. Peter Usborne, for example, worked for a time in the Foreign Office, before returning to the *Eye*. He recalled at his interview at the FO: 'As I walked in [the interview panel] all turned up a copy of *Private Eye* and said "Are you responsible for this?" and tittered. I knew then I was in' (Marnham 1983: 35). The *Eye*'s financial column, 'Slicker', is said to be required reading in City institutions. The magazine's originators have now been replaced by younger, career satirists and their mockery of political and other public events further routinized. In 1986 Ingrams passed the editorship to Ian Hislop, an Oxford graduate, who had made his name at the *Eye* with a parody of the *Observer magazine* feature 'A Room of My Own'. In it an IRA hunger striker in the Maze prison described the excrement on the walls of his cell as a 'decoration that has cost me next to nothing'.

THAT WAS THE WEEK THAT WAS: 'SERIOUSLY, THOUGH, YOU'RE DOING A GRAND JOB'

That Was The Week That Was was a late night television show first broadcast by the BBC in 1962. It consisted of comic sketches, songs and monologues which reflected irreverently on the political events of the preceding week and it marked the official entry of 'satire' into popular mass media culture. The programme emerged out of the BBC's Current Affairs Department, rather than Light Entertainment (whose Head professed himself ashamed of the show) and thus reflected changing conceptions of *politics* and *public service*, rather than of comedy *per se*.

The immediate inspiration for 'TW3' was *Beyond the Fringe* and the recent trends in Oxbridge comedy which younger BBC producers and executives had witnessed first hand, as undergraduates. Indeed, a member of the cast of *Beyond the Fringe*, Jonathan Miller, was for a time given a spot on the current affairs

TV programme *Tonight*. These developments expressed a new ideology of the broadcasting of politics wherein the Pomposity-of-Politicians-Must-be-Pricked. In this ideology, the public world must make concessions to the private one, as is argued in a memo written by Donald Baverstock, the BBC's Assistant Controller of Programmes at the time:

> Late on Saturday night people are more aware of being persons and less of being citizens than at any other time of the week. It is, therefore, the best time to hang contemporary philosophy on the hook in the hall, to relieve the pressure of earnest concern and goodwill which presses down on us throughout the rest of the week. To abandon what Mary McCarthy calls 'the slow drip of cant'.
>
> (Quoted in Milne 1988: 32)

Similarly, years later, the Head of Talks and Current Affairs at the BBC, Grace Wyndham Goldie, would later describe 'TW3' as 'private fun' shared 'with a mass public' (Goldie 1977: 235). The show was firmly rooted in the new Oxbridge culture of satire: its producer, Ned Sherrin, had known Alasdair Milne, the editor, at Oxford; the programme's presenter was David Frost, who had appeared in the Footlights revue at Cambridge the previous year; Christopher Booker was one of the show's chief writers. *That Was The Week* . . . expressed much the same angry scepticism of politicians as *Private Eye*, and the importation of this scepticism into broadcasting was the cause of some disquiet in political circles. Since the principal focus of the satire was government ministers, and since the Conservative Party was in office, the programme appeared to be anti-Conservative: even Richard Ingrams suggested that it 'blatantly defied the Corporation's obligation to be fair and provide balance' (Ingrams 1971: 11). A number of senior Tories complained, but the perplexed response of the Postmaster General, Reginald Bevins – 'I am going to do something about it' – drew a quick reproof from the publicity-conscious Macmillan: a note on his desk reading simply 'Oh, no you're not' (quoted in Tracey 1983: 207). Similarly, the BBC's Director-General, the liberal Sir Hugh Greene, who had strongly endorsed the idea of the programme, sent word to the cast that 'I take my hat off to them' (ibid.: 210).

'TW3' closed in December 1963 with an estimated audience of 11 million. Greene took the view that a further series in 1964 – an election year – would invite the accusation that the BBC was siding with Labour. There was little doubt in the minds of the programme-makers, however, that *That Was The Week* . . . met the BBC's requirement, under its charter, to show political balance. Milne, for example, argued years later that it had been 'balanced' by other, more sober, current affairs output (Milne 1988: 42) and that, in any event, Labour politicians, as well as Tories, had been frequently lampooned on the show: Greene once suggested that the writers 'lay off George Brown [Deputy Leader of the Labour Party in 1963] for the time being'. Indeed, one of 'TW3's most remembered items, and the one to draw the biggest public furore, was a soliloquy written by Booker for Frost, expressing the anti-whoever's-in-charge ethos of *Private Eye* and characterizing the coming election between Sir Alec Douglas-Home's Conservatives and the Labour Party led by Harold Wilson as a contest of 'Dull Alec versus Smart Alec' (Wilmut 1980: 70–1). Moreover, the programme signed off in December 1963 with a What-They-Said/What-They-Meant sketch which charged the Conservatives, Labour *and* the Liberal Party with deception. They also paid a fulsome tribute to the assassinated President Kennedy, whose image of youthful idealism and vigour they appeared to take at face value. This was important as a rare statement of the positive dimension of the *Private Eye* paradigm: if Macmillan equalled old equalled mangy moustache equalled privilege equalled bad then, logically, Kennedy equalled young equalled handsome equalled democratic equalled good.

But where 'TW3' does seem to have departed from the dyspeptic iconoclasm of *Private Eye* is in its cultural politics, which were more coherent and progressive than those of the *Eye*. This, again, was in keeping with Greene's interpretation of 'balance' which was that its charter bound the BBC to be neutral in matters of *party* politics, but not on issues like racism, which, he argued, was quite simply wrong and should be treated as such. Thus, in the spring of 1963, *That Was The Week* . . . recorded a most swingeing satiric assault of US racism, following the murder by the Ku Klux Klan of a young civil rights sympathizer in Mississippi. In it Millicent Martin, dressed as Uncle Sam, sang a parody of 'I Wanna Go Back to Mississippi', accompanied by the George Mitchell Singers, blacked up to make it a simultaneous mockery of the BBC's own *Black and White Minstrel Show*. In

Mississippi, they chorused, 'we hate all the darkies and the Catholics and the Jews'. Similarly, 'TW3' scorned the prejudice and stereotyping which surrounded homosexuality: one monologue in 1963, spoken by Kenneth Cope, told of the 'twilight world of the heterosexual' and another ridiculed the prevailing attitudes to homosexuality in high places which had allegedly made it possible for the civil servant John Vassall to be blackmailed into espionage.

I'd like now to look at the infusion of Oxbridge-derived satirical strains into popular comedy.

'SOCIETY IS TO BLAME' : *MONTY PYTHON* AND THE POLITICS OF SILLINESS

The fundamental importance of 'satire' to broadcasters – the BBC, in the first instance – was that it promised access to certain audiences: the educated, liberal middle class and, in particular, the young. This consideration began increasingly to exercise the minds of comedy programme-makers and the BBC Light Entertainment department, for one, stepped up its recruitment of people from Oxbridge revues, as writers and producers (Hewison 1984: 143). Here, unlike with 'TW3', they would no longer be confined to generating comic adjuncts to current affairs reportage. A group of Cambridge graduates collaborated as writers and performers, most notably on *I'm Sorry I'll Read That Again*, a surreal radio comedy (partly inspired by Milligan) that began in 1964. The apparent popularity of this programme with children alerted other broadcasters to the audience possibilities of the new Oxbridge comedy – as, for example, with *Do Not Adjust Your Set*, an early evening TV show for the young, commissioned in 1967 by the ITV company Associated Redifussion with the remit of not 'talking down' to children (Wilmut 1980: 181). Veterans of Oxbridge revue were also employed as writers for mainstream comedians and they contributed in some numbers to BBC's *The Frost Report* (1966-7), which marked David Frost's translation as a comedy presenter to prime time television. They were conscious, though, as Graham Chapman recalled, 'that some of the items that we knew were funny would not get done because it was felt that they were too rude or too silly' (quoted in Perry 1983: 106). Something more 'adult' and uninhibited was therefore attempted in *At Last the 1948 Show*, also made in 1967 by Rediffusion but only partially networked by ITV. Then, in 1969, the BBC convened a meeting of the leading Oxbridge comedy writers to form *Monty Python's Flying Circus*. Although the writer-performers of *Monty Python* were annoyed at their initial billing as 'satirical' by *Radio Times* (Hewison 1981: 17), the work of the Python team became the most lasting and significant contribution of the Oxbridge 'satire movement' to popular media culture.

The point about *Python* is that it represents a *social* critique and is not narrowly concerned with politics or politicians. The six creators of the show were all noticeably *petit bourgeois* in origin: the sons, respectively, of a clerk in an engineering works, a bank clerk, a travelling salesman, a police inspector, an insurance salesman and an airman. With the exception of the American cartoonist, Terry Gilliam, most of the others had grown up in suburbia and attended grammar, or minor private, schools. Their upbringing had in general been strict according to the prevailing values of the lower middle class during the 1940s and 1950s. Michael Palin, for instance, recalled:

> our sort of reaction was against a . . . rather stifling world. It was not necessarily oppressive. It didn't hurt us. It wasn't unpleasant. It wasn't unkind. It was just very, very, conventional.
>
> (BBC 1, *Omnibus*, 'Life of Python' 1990)

Palin spent much time at the home of his friend, a doctor's son, which had a 'more easy-going regime' (Perry 1983: 47); Graham Chapman, in 1969 an undeclared homosexual and alcoholic, strongly resented the narrow-mindedness of his parents (Chapman *et al.* 1980:41); John Cleese recollected in 1974: 'I never had a bike. My parents thought I might hurt myself' (*Daily Telegraph*, 21 June 1974, quoted in Thompson 1984: 9). Apart from Gilliam, who had experience of journalism and advertising, and Chapman, who had practised briefly as a doctor, none of 'the Pythons' had seen much of the world outside home, school, elite university and comedy writing. None of them had any conspicuous political affiliation, nor was there 'at any time a conscious decision to challenge convention' (Hewison 1981: 15). But *Python* was distinctly less other-directed than the authors' previous work: what went into the show was not material for an imagined mass audience so much as material which amused the writers themselves. (The *actual*   audience hovered initially between 1 and 3 million.)

Python was sketch based, the sketches moving arbitrarily from one to the next and interspersed with Gilliam's surreal animations. The sketches in large part represent a comedic tirade against lower-middle-class culture: Freemasons hop along a city street with their trousers around their ankles; the dinner-jacketed President of the Society for Putting Things on Top of Other Things congratulates his members on a good year, but warns against complacency; a police inspector is unable to remember the word 'burglary' and insists instead that he is investigating a 'Burnley'; an I-Know-My-Rights stereotype in a plastic mac angrily demands a licence for his pet halibut. . . . Similarly, those elements in the class structure which have traditionally been the focus of *petit bourgeois* respect and/or aspiration – the Royal Family, the upper classes, the professions – take their place in a grotesquerie of Dummy Princess Margarets, Pantomime Dukes of Kent, Upper-Class Twits, doctors in search of rich patients, male judges wearing women's underwear, City gents advocating greed and flogging (round at their place) and stockbrokers still failing, after much explanation, to comprehend the concept of charity.

A strong strain of cruelty runs through *Monty Python* and much of it is located in the female characters, most of whom are played by 'the Pythons' in drag: a woman contestant in a TV quiz programme, who doesn't like 'darkies', wins a blow on the head; another middle-aged woman, accompanied by her friend 'Mrs Niggerbaiter', treats her son like a recalcitrant child even though he is, apparently, the Minister for Overseas Development; knitting ladies guard a nuclear submarine; a Somerset landlady applies lard to her cat's boil, oblivious to Hitler and Himmler, wearing a full Nazi regalia, plotting in her dining room to take Stalingrad; members of the Batley Townswomen's Guild re-enact the Battle of Pearl Harbour. . . . Women were thus often portrayed as reactionary and repressive creatures, holding screeching dominion over the domestic sphere. One of the team, Eric Idle, later reflected that the show 'mocks all the authority figures. Including mothers. Especially mothers' (BBC 1, *Omnibus* 1990). Nor was this implied attitude to women lost on female contemporaries: Miriam Margolyes, who had been at Cambridge with Cleese, Chapman and Eric Idle recalled 'I loathed them and they loathed me . . . they're not actually interested in women. They play all the women's parts, and they play them in bold caricature' (quoted in Banks and Swift 1987: 190). Chapman, for one, acknowledged this and, in 1972, in an interview with *Gay News*, a magazine he helped to finance, he said:

> Women are very, very oppressed. They are certainly not equal human beings at the moment, and that is *very* unfortunate. It's particularly unfortunate for us, because we all have mothers, and our mothers, in the position of being oppressed, in turn oppress us, push us with all kinds of views we shouldn't really hold. In fact, I think mothers as such, as produced by society, are probably responsible for most of the wars we've ever had. Because they teach us to be so butch. . . . Maybe . . . you shouldn't treat children as being different sexes at all . . . because children aren't different sexes, and neither, for that matter, are adults. . . . On the whole women are conservative in every way, politically too. I'm very pro-women's lib, I really am, 'cos that would be homosexual liberation as well.
>
> (*Gay News* 4, quoted in Thompson 1984:16)

Much of Python as a media phenomenon (encompassing both the comedic imagery and ideas of the show itself and the public statements of the cast) can thus be read as an extension of the counter culture of the mid-1960s – an oblique demand for sexual and personal liberation by emotionally stunted, if highly educated, young middle-class males, symbolically wrenching their own umbilical cords and exhorting others to do the same.

But there is also an implied politics of culture to set beside the politics of the personal. Time and again, in *Monty Python*, elite, high culture marries, or collides, with banal mass culture: in one spoof TV show contestants have to summarize seven works of Marcel Proust in fifteen seconds each; in another, questions on football and pop music are put to Karl Marx, Lenin, Mao Zedong and Che Guevara; *Wuthering Heights* is performed in semaphore, *Julius Caesar* in morse code . . . and so on. Doubtless this, like all 'texts', will have been read differently by different sections of the audience: for example, those with little knowledge of the novelists, philosophers or political theorists featured in these sketches might nevertheless appreciate the mockery of popular TV formats; those with higher education, on the other hand, might enjoy better the apparent subversion of high cultural icons. From within their own subculture of Oxbridge 'satire', this strain in Python comedy provoked accusations of 'intellectualism' – most notably from Jonathan Miller and Alan Bennett (Wilmut 1980: 216–17). But this comedy could reasonably be said to express an alienation from *both* cultures quite equally and, indeed, could be seen as an implied call for a more satisfying *popular* culture. After all, each 'Python' has continued to work in popular culture (TV and film comedy, comic books, children's fiction, humorous training films, travel documentaries), the only contribution to traditional high culture being Terry Jones's book *Chaucer's Knight* (Jones 1980), which he hoped would be 'accessible to ordinary people' (quoted in Thompson 1984: 20). It's also worth noting that one of Python's most damning parodies of mass culture – in which the compère of a TV show called *Prejudice* asks viewers to send in insulting names for the Belgians – was effectively realized when, during the 'Sheep Meat' dispute of 1982, the *Sun* newspaper invited readers to contribute derogatory names for the French.

Monty Python also conveys much of the same fear of politics which underlies earlier Oxbridge 'satire'. Politicians in *Python* are among the principal bearers of life's absurdities and pomposities. Often in bowler hats (already an anachronism for British politics in the late 1960s) they are portrayed: presiding over the Ministry of Silly Walks; performing striptease; falling through the earth's crust during a party political broadcast . . . the Minister for Home Affairs, male but in a woman's evening gown, debates issues with a small puddle of brown liquid; the Silly Party holds Leicester, and takes Luton (surprising the pundits, who had it down as a constituency where many people weren't a bit silly). Politicians are seldom named; they simply have their place in a gallery of *petit bourgeois* caricatures. Chapman, in particular, expressed a profound loathing of politicians and, as a token of this loathing, once went to speak to the Cambridge University students' union ('where their up-and-coming politicians go to speak') dressed as a carrot:

And when it was my turn to make a speech, I said nothing. . . .

And that was my comment on the whole bloody business of
people standing up and debating, trying to be clever, and
eventually becoming politicians – fucking mess, they're a load
of bloody idiots, and none of them have any social conscience.
(*Gay News* 4, 1972, quoted in Thompson 1984:34)

Clearly, though, there were political differences within the
Python group which were experienced by individual members
essentially as clashes between the inbred mentalities of Oxford
and Cambridge universities, respectively (Perry 1983: 84, 92, 148).
In practice, this meant 'the Cambridge contribution would be
verbal, logical, literate, with absurdism arising from the commonplace', while the Oxford graduates, Palin and Jones, were
'more visual and romantically inventive' (Perry 1983: 148). These
differences shaded into more straightforwardly political ones – as
between a right-wing anarchist/nihilist resolve to make jokes
about anything at all and a more restrained, in part socialist,
desire to mock only certain things. The famed undertaker sketch,
broadcast in 1970 and never repeated, is a case in point. In the
sketch, written by Cleese and Chapman, a man, bearing his dead
mother in a sack, discusses with an undertaker the possibility of
eating her, with vegetables and french fries. Again, it can be read
in different ways: as a mockery of mother-fixation, of death, of
'good taste' and censorship. The broadcasting of the sketch had
to be negotiated with the BBC's Head of Comedy and, indeed,
within the group, Idle, Palin and Jones are said, initially, to have
been shocked by it (Hewison 1981: 19–20). Ultimately, the libertarian, Why Not? ethos prevailed.

Perhaps oddly, in view of the thrust of his comedy, Cleese in
1971 persuaded Chapman, Jones and Palin to make 'Who's
There?', an instructional film about canvassing, for the Labour
Party. Later, however, clear political differences were apparent
within 'Python'. This seems at least partly to have been bound
up with the growing commercialization and internationalization
of the Python phenomenon. The company Python Productions
was formed in 1970 and was followed by books, LP records, full
length feature films, coupled with the sale by the BBC of *Monty
Python's Flying Circus* episodes to foreign TV networks and,
latterly, the issue of Monty Python videos. The marketing and
export of British irony and iconoclastic irreverence became, and
has remained, surprisingly lucrative. Initially through touring

and then with their films, 'the Pythons' found that they could successfully outrage Middle Canada, Middle America and Middle Norway, as well as Middle England – while simultaneously conquering the markets of the young and the educated in each country. Just as, in the words of Dick Hebdige, in chap. 13 in this book, Britain became noted in post-imperial popular culture for having the best Gender Benders (Bowie, Boy George, etc.), *Python* established her as having the best Piss Takers. The first two original *Monty Python* feature films were financed by pop stars, members of a new bourgeois elite, with its roots in the counter culture. *Monty Python and the Holy Grail* (1974), funded by members of Pink Floyd and Led Zeppelin, was seen by a million cinema-goers in France alone and *Life of Brian* (1979), sustained in production by George Harrison of the Beatles, 1½ million in the same country (Grantham 1989). *Brian* was seen in sixteen countries during its first year of release. During the progress of *Python* toward the status of licensed International Piss Takers, Cleese, more than any of the others an autonomous figure-in-his-own-right in popular culture, sought to reaffirm the position of the group as seeking to laugh at the world, rather than to remake it, a position variously marriageable with the ideas of the political centre and the neo-liberal right. He spoke of the need to make fun of the left as well as the right, and this is clearly evidenced in the *Life of Brian*, which grossed 75 million dollars between 1979 and 1983. In *Brian* the Judean People's Front squabbles pointlessly with the People's Front of Judea. Cleese plays Reg, the caricature of an ideologically hidebound revolutionary, who initiates the now famous 'What have the Romans done for us?' dialogue, in which his colleagues suggest to him that Roman imperial occupation has brought a lot of public benefits to Judea (Chapman *et al.* 1979). In 1983 Cleese told *The Times* that, unlike left-wing comedy film-makers, 'the Python people, I think, really enjoy life and also see how absurd it is' (10 June). Later the same year he informed the same newspaper of the need to have discipline in life and boundaries to kerb the ego: 'Cleese', wrote the reporter, 'sees a parallel with the Labour Party, which he used to support before he saw them as chickening out and mollycoddling their supporters and the unions' (28 September). By 1987, Cleese was reminiscing, again in *The Times* (12 December), about 'left-wing views' among the Pythons in which business was regarded as a negative activity. . . . I was never against business but I was against certain ways of carrying on business. The main thing is people's attitude to authority. I always felt that authority was not necessarily a bad thing. I now think it can be an absolutely excellent thing. I'm interested in making fun of authority that's exercised badly.

Chapman, years earlier, affirmed a more libertarian position, declaring himself 'against any organization, communist, capitalist or religious that pretends to know best' (Chapman 1980: 117) and, in 1989, Idle reflected with some pride that during 'the years in which [Python] flourished it was no longer possible to take any party seriously. . . . I think Python shows a healthy comtempt for both left and right' (*New Statesman and Society*, 29 September).

Only Jones has tried to read Python from outside the paradigm of anti-political iconoclasm in which Oxbridge satirical comedy has grown:

Today's comedians are much more politically aware. The only real tangible effect of Python that I really heard of was in the seventies when a friend teaching in a comprehensive said she had noticed a big difference in the way boys showed off. Instead of being macho they would be silly and their antics would be more verbal.

'For me', he commented in 1989, now taking a more leftish view, 'Python would have a different line if it started up today under Thatcher' (*New Statesman and Society*, 29 September).

'IF WE ALL SPIT TOGETHER, WE'LL DROWN THE BASTARDS': THE POLITICS OF *SPITTING IMAGE*

With the accumulated irreverence of *That Was the Week. . . , Private Eye* and *Monty Python*, satire became *work*, simply. A freer market in comedy had been established and a place in that market identified where an audience was game for jokes at the expense of politicians and famous personalities, risqué sketches about social mores and tongue-in-cheek treatment of current affairs. *Not the Nine O'Clock News*, put out by the BBC in four series between 1978 and 1982, represents a formula, based on a variety of previously successful satirical elements: sketches, media spoofs and current news photographs with subversive captions (a huge congregation of Muslims is shown, for example, with the commentary: 'And the search goes on for the Ayatollah Khomeini's contact lens') commissioned from a large team of writers, performed by actors and presided over by two producers, one from Comedy (John Lloyd) and one from Current Affairs (Sean Hardie). Lloyd and two of the leading actors, Rowan Atkinson and Griff Rhys Jones were Oxbridge educated, as was Tony Hendra, originator of the show's name and a contemporary at Cambridge of Cleese and Chapman.

Hendra and Lloyd were also founders of *Spitting Image*, first shown by Central Television in 1984 and the most significant popular cultural phenomenon to emanate in the 1980s from what was now a thriving cottage industry: the satire business. Surprisingly, though, despite becoming the most full-blooded expression yet of the by now familiar anti-political iconoclasm, *Spitting Image* was a site of some struggle, with a more explicit difference in political aims and philosophy between its contributors than on other satirical enterprises.

The puppets for *Spitting Image* sketches were created by Peter Fluck and Roger Law, both of whom have described themselves as being 'on the left'. Law had been associated with the Establishment Club in the 1960s, but had also been a member of the Communist Party and had done work for *Newsline*, the newspaper of the Workers' Revolutionary Party: 'I have a lot of time for parties like that. I think they're very important for educating people – especially working people – in what capitalist society is all about.' Fluck and Law wanted the person writing scripts for their puppets 'to be someone in tune with their own ideas, some way left of left' (Chester 1986: 8,11). From the beginning, though, their perspective clashed with others in the team devising the show. For example, Martin Lambie-Nairn, a graphic artist at London Weekend Television, who is generally credited with the original idea for the programme, was a born-again Christian, expressing a world-weary disgust for the shallowness of politicians he had met in ITV studios. His view, reminiscent of *Private Eye*'s, implicitly opposed the assimilation of politics into the publicity process, turning politicians into role-distanced performers. The approach of Tony Hendra, by contrast, fully embraced the notion of publicity, arguing that the programme should trawl the waters of media fame, drawing on

'forms of television and film, *apart* from the news' and avail itself
of 'an almost inexhaustible supply of distinguished idiots' from
left, right, centre, royalty, showbusiness (ibid.: 13,19). This was
close to the ethos of the US TV show *Saturday Night Live*, with
which Hendra had been associated and through which famous
people were subjected to a semi-official media lampoon. Often
artists appeared on the programme in person to show that they
Didn't Take Themselves Too Seriously. The show was very
popular with US college students and, as *Spitting Image* was to
become, an important adjunct to the publicity process itself.

The early puppet caricatures on *Spitting Image* reflected a
partial acceptance of the Hendra approach, including politicians
both domestic (Michael Foot, Ian Paisley) and foreign (Reagan,
Gadaffi, Khomeini) as well as a few sportspeople (for instance,
John McEnroe) and showbusiness figures (Mick Jagger, Joan
Collins). But unfavourable reaction to the first series – particularly in the press, where the 'populars' were hostile and the
'qualities' disappointed – led to creative adjustments. New,
specialist comedy writers, Rob Grant and Doug Naylor, who
were uncomfortable with 'satire', were brought into a writing
team which already included Ian Hislop and Rob Newman of
Private Eye. There would be 'less politics (and less anti-right
stuff where we do politics at all) . . . [and] . . . far more quickies'
so that the puppet-makers now had to meet

> a demand for caricatures of people who meant little, or
> nothing, to them. All their experience in caricature had been
> of 'attacking' politicians and public figures. It was hard to
> muster the same feeling when devising models of some of the
> more soft-centred entertainers and media personalities who
> now appeared on the order list.
>
> (Chester 1986: 76,85)

Thereafter the programme-makers aimed for a 50/50 split between
politicians and people from showbusiness or sport, but there
continued to be friction about 'how much politics' to do. Issues
were not always resolved at the expense of the left: in 1985, when
Lloyd as producer suggested that in a sketch about the miners'
strike the puppet of miners' leader Arthur Scargill should be
treated with the programme's routine derogation, Fluck and Law
successfully objected that this would be to trivialize the miners
themselves (Chester 1986: 87). This unusual, and apparently

arbitrary departure from the dominant ideology of British satirical comedy brings the ideology itself into sharper focus: in satire,
as a rule, *all* public figures have been open to ridicule, regardless
of cause of constituency. The decision on Scargill momentarily
waived this assumption but, in reality, all politicians and public
figures portrayed in *Spitting Image* could claim that they have
followers who are being trivialized. Despite setbacks and com-
promises, Roger Law has claimed a radical role for *Spitting
Image*:

> If you don't like what public figures are doing, and you've got
> absolutely no way of changing anything, it helps to slag them
> off. Saatchi and Saatchi are doing the opposite to us. People
> say we're too savage but you never hear of anyone going to
> Saatchi and Saatchi to complain that they're grossly
> benevolent.
>
> (Chester 1986: 117)

In practice, however, and in general, *Spitting Image* is no more
selective in its choice of public figures than *Private Eye*. Moreover, today's politicians are in the being-famous business, the
first maxim of which is that there is no such thing as bad
publicity: it's all good, whether it's dispensed by satirists or
advertising agencies. Politicians across the parliamentary political spectrum are said to enjoy it (Chester 1986: 138–40) and the
younger ones to see the inclusion of a puppet bearing their own
likeness as a sign that they are now established.

Spitting Image is, first and foremost, a successful commercial
operation with an annual turnover in 1986 of £2 million. It was
originally financed by Central Television with this sort of
development in mind, the company taking 25 per cent of any
profits from merchandising and first refusal on any film. *Spitting Image* has a TV audience of over 6 million and a market for
goods which mock the famous: books, videos, records and T
shirts bearing the suggestion that 'If we all spit together we'll
drown the bastards'. The puppets also hire out for public
appearances. The fee for this is in some cases higher than that
charged by the 'real' personalities they represent.

THE MEANING OF LIFE AND SATIRICAL COMEDY. PART ONE: SATIRICAL COMEDY

In conclusion, a number of points can sensibly be made about the popular cultural legacy of the British 'satire boom' and its aftermath.

First, Colin Seymour-Ure, in his study of *Private Eye* (Seymour-Ure 1974: 240–64), argues an essentially functionalist case for British satire, suggesting that it fulfils the historical role of the Fool at a royal court – a licensed jester pointing up the difference between the formalities of government and the human frailty of the governors. There is much in this but, whereas a great deal of what the Fool said was for private consumption of the powerful, 'satirical' comedy became popular culture, disseminated – in the case of the BBC – by a prestigious public institution to a mass audience. The Fool-ishness, clearly generated and generalized from within the culture of the elite, resonated with, and legitimated, a longer standing popular distaste for politicians, both within the working class and among the 'angry ratepayer' elements of the lower-middle-class suburbs. Thus it has helped to make scorn for politicians, and impatience with politics, semi-official.

Second, this is not, of course, confined to Britain. There has, for example, been much speculation in France recently on the influence of the TV programme *Le Bébête Show*, the French equivalent of *Spitting Image*: many argue that 'its picture of the political establishment as a barmy, brawling, corrupt but closely knit gang' has helped to promote and deepen the apathy of French voters (*Observer*, 5 March 1989). But many view 'satire' within a paradigm of *British* ethnicity. John Connor, for instance, wrote of *Monty Python* in 1989: 'The real secret of Python wasn't their surrealism – it's the fact that they were the first to articulate the madness of the British, and in particular the English. Margaret Thatcher could have been created by Python' (*Guardian*, 6 October 1989). This is almost certainly intended to mean that Thatcher represented the narrow-minded, *petit bourgeois* English bigot that Python had been trying to subvert, but it seems to me that Python, and the other 'satirists', also helped to invent what became known as Thatcher*ism*.

'Satire' has played its part in the promotion of a freer market in political-comic ideas, and in the erosion of many of the caste-like elements in British political culture. The holders of high office today receive a measure of routinized disrespect (and almost nothing of what could be called deference) from the media. This in turn has helped to redefine the boundaries of citizenship, moving them subtly away from public service toward the private domain of consumption. For instance, political parties no longer have privileged access to television: their party political broadcasts, previously shown on all channels simultaneously, now compete with other programmes for viewers' attention. So the world of public affairs has no moral priority and anyone who believes, for example, that 'politicians are all a waste of time' is provided for.

Scepticism about particular politicians can be found in all social groups and is compatible with all political positions. But the problem, of course, is that 'politics' encompasses not only political processes and the machinations of politicians, but also the exercise of power and the whole gamut of human exploitations, with which politicians in some way engage. So a rejection of politicians which equates them with 'politics' effects what Zygmunt Bauman calls 'the exit of human concerns from politics'. This, Bauman suggests, was at the heart of Thatcherite politics:

> Thatcher's government . . . responds to the resistance of local and group interests by casting such interests off the limits of the political agenda. It offers the public a massive programme of *buying oneself out*, singly or severally, from politics: of making politics irrelevant to the pursuit of individual or collective goals and ideas. This dismantling of effective citizenship is presented as the triumph of freedom: as liberation. What makes such presentation credible is the parallel reduction of political power to the role of a purely constraining force, and an emphatic surrender of its *enabling* function. Politics means now taxes ('less money in your pocket'), petty regulations ('no freedom of choice'), and official secrets. Politics is not where you invest your hopes. Life is elsewhere. Politics is a nuisance. The less of it, the better.
>
> (Bauman 1988: 37)

At the time of writing this new 'citizenship' is said to be central to the deliberations of Conservative Party tacticians as they struggle to fashion a philosophy (provisionally called 'Majorism') for the present Prime Minister. It will be based, it is said, on the idea of 'value for money from the public services'.

Third, 'satire' has also provided an emotional and ideological antidote to visible injustice. 'Satire' emerged and grew over the same period as the electronic mass media proliferated in capacity and outlets. Since the 1960s comparatively few people in western societies could escape TV film of starving African infants, grinding poverty in British inner cities, brutish dictatorships in the Third World. But the fruits of the 'satire boom' have helped the satirists themselves and many western consumers shrug off any guilt they may have felt about enjoying themselves, simply by asserting the across-the-board absurdity of it all. Thus it underwrites the apparently powerful paradox in the calculations of contemporary voters of 'private affluence and public squalor' (Crewe 1987:7). John Cleese, the richest and most celebrated figure to emerge from British 'satire', represents the new, consummated politics of irony. Wealthy from his work as a film-maker, Cleese now hires out, expensively, as an actor in commercials. Corporations want him as a means of access to certain audiences, part of whose culture is irony. The mode of the commercial is therefore parodic. In 1990, for instance, Cleese was recruited to film an advertisement for Schweppes tonic water. The ad had been devised by Saatchi and Saatchi, lately image-makers to the Conservative Party, and was to be shot in the Virgin Islands.

> The company was keen to get him because of his huge international reputation, particularly in America. Saatchi's account manager Gareth Coombes says Cleese was central to the campaign, built around his reputation as the king of intelligent comedy. The soft drinks commercials were just asking to be parodied.
>
> (*Today*, 4 July 1990)

Cleese is much in demand as an ironist-for-commercials ('Those awfully nice Sony people') and so are many other 'satirical' and 'alternative' comedians. Irony flatters the consumer by anticipating any resistance on their part and by implying that the advertisers don't take themselves, or the advertisement, seriously. And, for Cleese, the fact that he is being paid a reputed one-quarter of a million pounds for a few days' filming on a poverty-stricken Caribbean island should not be taken seriously either because, although it is happening, it is happening in the public world:

> It's a mad, crazy world. I make no attempt to change it. I accept it for what it is and the fact is you make money from commercials. But the audience is intelligent. I don't think they are in danger of buying something they don't want because of me.
>
> (*Today*, 4 July 1990)

Thus, for Cleese, 'the world' (i.e. the *public* world) is mad; the individual, inhabiting a more private sphere, is 'intelligent'. The problems of this private sphere, unlike those of the public world, are seen as tractable: hence the psychiatric help in dealing with family life that Cleese has sought to offer (Skynner and Cleese 1983).

Auberon Waugh, long-time stalwart of *Private Eye*, has struggled to a similar clarity of self-awareness in his work: praised in *The Independent on Sunday* for 'blow[ing] the raspberry of gaiety in the face of a *Guardian*-grey world', he told his admiring interviewer, 'I'm just not prepared to be agonized by all the suffering in the world. There's no *point* in the world if we've all got to suffer with the suffering, because the whole point is that while some people suffer, others don't' (Lynn Barber interview, 17 February 1991).

Not everyone, of course, would be so uncompromising in their political use of 'satire': not everyone would see it as a pretext for ignoring injustice. After all, every year a cadre of satirists performs the *Secret Policeman* revue, in aid of *Amnesty International*, the politically liberal organization that monitors repressive government activity around the world. But, in this context, the main popular cultural inheritance of 'satire' is *Comic Relief*. The logic of such enterprises, wherein people wear red noses and sit in baths full of baked beans for twenty-four hours, in aid of the starving of the Third World, is, at root, the same as Cleese's. We should not ask why the poor have no food, because we know: it's because we live in a 'mad, crazy world'. The only refuge from this mad world is the private sphere of rationality, inhabited by intelligent consumers. Through *Comic Relief* these consumers are in large numbers persuaded to help the victims of the world's madness by being sponsored in a day's craziness of their own. Thus 'satire', in a symbolic way, replaces history; and, in the ultimate irony, western hedonism is mobilized in aid of the world's poor.

NOTE

I'd like to acknowledge the advice of Dominic Strinati and John Williams in the preparation of this essay, and to thank Felicity Peadon for library help.

REFERENCES

Banks, Morwenna and Swift, Amanda (1987) *The Joke's on Us: Women in Comedy from Music Hall to the Present*, London: Pandora.

Bauman, Zygmunt (1988) 'Britain's exit from politics', *New Statesman and Society*, 29 July: 34–8.

Benn, Tony (1988) *Out of the Wilderness: Diaries 1963–7*, London: Arrow Books.

Bennett, Alan *et al.* (1987) *The Complete Beyond the Fringe*, ed. Roger Wilmut, London: Methuen.

Briggs, Asa (1985) *The BBC. The First Fifty Years*, Oxford: Oxford University Press.

Chapman, Graham *et al.* (1979) *The Life of Brian*, London: Eyre Methuen.

Chapman, Graham *et al.* (1980) *A Liar's Autobiography Volume VII*, London: Eyre Methuen.

Chester, Lewis (1986) *Tooth and Claw: The Inside Story of Spitting Image*, London: Faber & Faber.

Crewe, Ivor (1987) 'Why Mrs Thatcher was returned with a landslide', *Social Studies Review* 3 (1), September: 2–14.

Draper, Alfred with Austin, John and Edgington, Harry (1976) *The Story of The Goons*, London: Everest Books.

Gouldner, Alvin W. (1972) *The Coming Crisis of Western Sociology*, London: Heinemann.

Grantham, Bill (1989) 'Monty in Montmartre', *Listener*, 28 September: 36.

Hall, Stuart and Jefferson, Tony, eds (1976) *Resistance Through Rituals*, London: Hutchinson.

Hewison, Robert (1981) *Monty Python: The Case Against*, London: Eyre Methuen.

Hewison, Robert (1984) *Footlights! A Hundred Years of Cambridge Comedy*, London: Methuen.

Ingrams, Richard, ed. (1971) *The Life and Times of Private Eye*, Harmondsworth: Penguin.

Jones, Terry (1980) *Chaucer's Knight – The Portrait of a Mediaeval Mercenary*, London: Weidenfeld & Nicolson.

Marnham, Patrick (1983) *The Private Eye Story: The First 21 Years*, London: Fontana/Collins.

Milligan, Spike (1974) *The Book of the Goons*, London: Robson Books.
Milne, Alasdair (1988) *DG: The Memoirs of a British Broadcaster*, London: Hodder & Stoughton.
Perry, George (1983) *Life of Python*, London: Pavilion/Michael Joseph.
Scudamore, Pauline (1987) *Spike Milligan: A Biography*, London: Grafton Books.
Seymour-Ure, Colin (1974) 'Private Eye: the politics of the Fool', in C. Seymour-Ure *The Political Impact of the Mass Media*, London: Constable: 240-64.
Skynner, Robin and Cleese, John (1983) *Families and How To Survive Them*, London: Methuen.
Thompson, John O. (ed.) (1984) *Monty Python: The Complete and Utter Theory of the Grotesque*, London: British Film Institute.
Took, Barry (1981) *Laughter in the Air: An Informal History of British Radio Comedy*, London: Robson Books/BBC.
Tracey, Michael (1983) *A Variety of Lives: A Biography of Sir Hugh Greene*, London: The Bodley Head.
Wilmut, Roger (1980) *From Fringe to Flying Circus*, London: Eyre Methuen.
Wilmut, Roger (1987) Introduction to Alan Bennett *et al. The Complete Beyond the Fringe*, London: Methuen.
Wyndham Goldie, Grace (1977) *Facing the Nation: Television and Politics 1936-76*, London: The Bodley Head.

Chapter 11

A 'divine gift to inspire'?
Popular cultural representation, nationhood and the British monarchy

Rosalind Brunt

In world terms, hereditary monarchies are a declining breed – variously exiled, assassinated or nicely pensioned off throughout the twentieth century. But in Britain, far from disappearing, the monarchy has never been so popular. It is therefore worth considering how a country that prides itself on its democratic institutions still retains such an obvious political anachronism and one that has secured both the affection and esteem of the British people.

The British monarchy's popularity is frequently attested in both public surveys and personal testimony. For instance, in a detailed Gallup Poll published in December 1988, 82 per cent of adult Britons said they favoured the monarchy in its present form in preference to an elected head of state. Furthermore, 48 per cent of respondents felt the Queen should have more power to influence affairs of state, compared with 40 per cent who felt her influence was about right and only 9 per cent who felt it should be less. Asked what was their 'strongest feeling for the Royal Family', exactly half the sample replied 'respect', followed by 'admiration' and 'indifference' at 20 per cent each (*Daily Telegraph*, 28 December 1988).

We also know from the testimony of both everyday conversation and media stories what an important part royalty play in the lives of British citizens. Meeting any member of the Royal Family, or even being 'in the presence', is an event to be recalled in full detail as a life-enhancing moment. There are, of course, many currents of anti-monarchical opinion and no citizen can be unaware of 'the case against' in terms of wealth and inherited privilege. But what is striking about any expression of republican sentiment is that it remains at the level of moaning and takes no organizational form. Of all the established institutions of the British state, the monarchy is unique in its immunity from contemporary political dissent. When most of the rest of the world has long gone republican, there is no anti-royalist movement of any significant size in Britain and the abolition of the monarchy appears as neither an important nor even an achievable demand of any progressive party manifesto. So how to account for this degree of success – and what does the monarchy's popular appeal tell us about ourselves, the British people, and where we think we're going?

In attempting an explanation, I'm going to consider the Royal Family in terms of 'representation' in both its cultural and political senses. That is, what meanings, values and images does the monarchy embody – and how are these communicated to us, particularly via the mass media? And then, who do the Royal Family speak for? On whose behalf, in whose interest, do they act? This double sense of 'representation' is central to any consideration of royalty because it could be said that the increase in their popularity is in direct relationship to a decline in their actual power.

As a modern constitutional monarchy, there is little the Royal Family can 'do' to us politically. The few royal prerogatives that remain have only been exercised by the present Queen as a result of 'advice' from government circles. What the Queen can do on her own initiative in terms of running the country is circumscribed and entirely negligible. Unlike the government of the day, the Royal Family can't impinge on our daily conduct and all the ways in which we make a living. But precisely because they matter to us so little at the material level, it's important to take their popularity seriously at the level of representation. For, in my view, how the monarchy operates today is through the exercise of considerable 'ideological' power. It works with clusters of symbols that function, not as free-floating ideas, but as effective expressions of value, contributing to how we make sense of our everyday lives and what beliefs we have about future possibilities.

So thinking what it is the Royal Family represents is hardly a trivial question. In the first place, while the Queen herself cannot directly affect us, most of the institutions in Britain which *can* derive their ultimate legitimacy from royalty: they function *in the name of* the Queen. So the Queen 'opens' parliament, gives 'royal assent' to its legislation, 'defends' the faith, 'upholds' the judiciary and is the very 'fount' of honour. The government and the opposition parties, the education inspectorate, the armed services are all 'Her Majesty's'. The national anthem makes no mention of an actual nation but asks God to save our gracious Queen and let her reign long over us. And the British passport, that proof of both personal identity and citizenship, issues the opening proclamation beneath the heraldic lion and unicorn: 'Her Britannic Majesty's Principal Secretary of State for Foreign and Commonwealth Affairs Requests and requires in the Name of Her Majesty all those whom it may concern to allow the bearer to pass freely. . .'

Without having a choice in the matter, all British, and many Commonwealth citizens are implicated in 'Her Majesty'. And the process of naming is also an act of belonging. Our very identities as 'subjects' of the Queen are keyed into the institutions of state and given a sense of national belonging. Whatever our personal opinions about the Royal Family, we are socially placed and put in a national context: to be British is to belong to the Queen's domain, that United 'Kingdom' of Great Britain and Northern Ireland.

But national identity is not only a matter of what is imposed on us. Citizens also come to inhabit their nationhood by actively contributing to its formation and reproduction. It is through such intensely personal attitudes as 'national pride', 'national guilt' and 'patriotism' that the individual is linked to the collective entity of nation. While each nation exists as a real geographical space and set of legal institutions, its citizens relate to it also in terms of what Benedict Anderson (1983) has called 'an imagined community' that represents shared values, meanings and aspirations. The historical composition of the United Kingdom, based as it is on an often uneasy amalgam of nations and peoples and the imperial dominance of one nation, England, makes any conception of national identity a particularly pro-blematic one, involving competing world views. In this situa-tion, the notion of 'Britishness' as mediated through an appar-ently non-political monarchy, offers a powerfully unifying myth of nationhood.

In a recent survey which examined British attitudes in an international context, more than half the Britons polled agreed they were 'very proud' of their country (compared to one-fifth of West Germans) and by far the greatest source of national pride was the monarchy (the first choice of one-third of respondents and included in the lists of two-thirds). After the monarchy, at 37 per cent of responses, came scientific achievements (22 per cent); health and welfare (16 per cent); parliament (8 per cent); sporting achievements (5 per cent) and the arts at 3 per cent. Hardly registering, and at rock bottom, came pride in Britain's economic achievements (for West Germany their economy came number two, after pride in the post-war constitution, the Basic Law) (Jowell 1989).

It would be useful to kncw in more detail what specific examples respondents had in mind for these ratings. Of the achievements that pertain more directly to material well-being, I suspect that only 'health and welfare' is seen in terms of the twentieth century and the post-war creation of the National Health Service, whereas most of the others belong to a vague sense of national heritage, way back in Britain's past. Beliefs in 'the Mother of Parliaments' or 'the fairness of British justice' are buried in popular memory as sources of national pride. But in present day conditions they relate to institutions that are at best often regarded with cynicism if not openly contested. So, apart from the monarchy, the categories that make us 'very proud' to be British begin to look rather insubstantial.

The list would probably look even thinner if the question had been posed thus: 'What is it that Britain currently does best in the world?' and the answers had been given in terms of what 'everyone' knows. We British have – what do we say? – the best ballroom dancers, middle-distance runners, actors, broadcasting system, youth culture and rock music in the world. We did have Torvill and Dean, Sebastian Coe, Bobby Charlton – and in 1966 we won the World Cup against West Germany. . .

The Best of British is a fast-dwindling list, not least in the area of sport and among the national games 'we gave the world'. This means that each of our 'best' categories has to carry a heavier load of Britishness with every event and appearance. So thank goodness for the big state occasions, which no other country can do like the British, for nowhere else boasts the Royal Family and such pageantry and tradition. Moreover, the Royal Family is better equipped to carry British pride because they rely, not on transitory merit, but on heredity.

Nothing could be more indicative of the country's dramatic post-war decline as a world power than that any litany of the Best of British should contain, apart from references to a battered National Health Service, nothing of any political or economic significance. The main claims to any British primacy in the world appear to rest in the sphere of the cultural and concern ceremony, style, spectacle. Indeed, it's as if the cultural sphere is having to act as the last consolation for imperialist losses. And given that the Royal Family form, by virtue of reproducing themselves, the only enduring category of Britishness, they bear the full weight of the question: if they no longer existed, what would still be great about Britain?

The requirement that royalty overcompensate for national inadequacy and highlight Britishness at its cultural best was what made the wedding of Prince Charles and Lady Diana Spencer such a popular spectacle in 1981. It also offered a view of Britishness intended for export as well as home consumption. In particular, the wedding was addressed to the USA with the message that although it long ago superceded Britain as the major imperialist power, Nancy Reagan could never outshine the Queen and had been invited to the ceremony only as an upstart commoner. Besides, everyone knows that Americans are more royalist than the British. And from the great height of their hegemony, the American media were happy to collude with this quirky consolatory myth of the British.

As this was the wedding that made Britain, if only for a day, 'great again', it also had the power as a 'fairytale romance' to act as a unifying balm to the nation. The ceremony came in the immediate aftermath of widespread urban unrest in Britain and was represented as a celebration that cut across all conflict to connect with an image of Britain as a united nation. As the *Sunday Times* said of the vast crowd that walked down the Mall towards Buckingham Palace:

> Only the Victory Parade and the Coronations of 1937 and 1953 have witnessed crowds as dense as this. In spite of fears in an age that has grown used to bitterness, riots and mindless assassination, the people of Britain and many visitors to London from abroad gave the world a visible demonstration of the power of a great royal event to unite a nation. In a sense it was a wedding to which we were all invited.

The invitation to participate in both the greatness and unity of Britain via the monarchy can only operate at the ceremonial and symbolic plane. For when the crowd disperses, real troubles start up again. But, through the spectacular events they perform, the Royal Family represent some kind of aspiration for a myth of nationhood that could reverse decline and overcome social division.

The Royal Family's capacity to offer this kind of magical transcendence derives from the roles they play in Britain's pageant of Living History. The story of the monarchy is commonly understood to parallel that of 'our island race', whereby the genius of both the British and their monarchy is said to lie in their particular ability to be adaptable and stable at the same time.

This is also how official discourse sees it. Locating the history of the present Queen, the government's Central Office of Information handbook on the monarchy says:

> The development of the monarchy during the Queen's reign is only the most recent example of its long evolution in the light of changing circumstances. It is the oldest secular institution in Britain, going back to at least the ninth century. The Queen can trace her descent from King Egbert who united all England under his sovereignty in 829. The monarchy antedates Parliament by four centuries, and the law courts by three. Its continuity has been broken only once (during the republic under Cromwell from 1649 to 1660). There have been interruptions in the direct line of succession, but the hereditary principle has always been preserved.
>
> (Central Office of Information, 1981)

The version of history which equates Britain with the lives and times of its kings and queens literally brackets off any inconvenient discontinuities like a monarch beheaded and has the effect of undermining any alternative versions of people's history 'from below' which place emphasis on resistance and conflict. Instead it offers reassurance. Orthodox history tells the British that, like our monarchy, we have minor hiccups but basically we go on reproducing our true nature, the timeless essence of stability. Thus in the year of the Falklands War the Queen chose to broadcast her Christmas message from the very room where the first Queen Elizabeth had sent forth her navy to fight the Spanish Armada. Four centuries later, Britons were once again celebrating our bulldog determination to ward off invaders and never never to be slaves.

It is particularly at moments of national crisis that the destinies of both monarchy and Britain are linked together to guarantee a reassuring continuity. Take, for example, the media coverage of the Queen's sixtieth birthday in April 1986. This came in the immediate aftermath of her Prime Minister's decision to let President Reagan use British bases to bomb Libyan targets. The news showed a massively intensified security operation mounted on the royal route, but also the Queen's manifest determination to carry on as usual without obvious additional protection and to participate in the familiar rituals of church and state – Windsor Chapel ceremony and Buckingham Palace appearances.

And once again the media took the opportunity to plug the Queen's own biography into key moments of national history, particularly those of the Second World War. So the images replayed: the two princesses on *Children's Hour* encouraging evacuees; the King and Queen in the blitzed East End; Elizabeth in uniform changing a wheel; the Royal Family and Prime Minister Churchill on the Palace balcony on VE Day; enter the gallant naval officer, Philip. . . . One by one these images of Britain's last finest hour, mediated through its still living royal embodiment, were dusted down and restored after Margaret Thatcher had dramatically exposed present day political subservience. For a moment it was possible to believe that Our Island History, reduced to the role of Yankee aircraft carrier and nuclear target, had been a bad dream after all.

These birthday celebrations were a striking instance of the extent to which the monarchy has become almost the sole prop and mainstay of national identity. They also indicated a new level of affection for the Queen herself. She had chosen the occasion to present her newly engaged son, Prince Andrew, and his future wife, Sarah Ferguson, to the celebrating crowds and together they collected armfuls of flowers, including daffodils, from a huge contingent of schoolchildren who processed down the Mall with a specially written birthday song: 'With all our love, Good in ev'rything.' As the press headlines put it next day, 'Bloomin' Marvellous! Well Done, Ma'am! Many Daffy Returns!'

But what constitutes the special marvel of the modern monarchy is that it no longer rests on just one person but depends on a whole dynastic family being constantly on public display. In being the focus of mass affection, the monarchy offers itself as the only British institution literally able to reproduce itself and carry on through the generations because, as George VI observed: 'We are the Family Firm.'

The significance of the monarchy functioning as a family is what Walter Bagehot, author of *The English Constitution* (1867), defined as its major advantage over any republican apparatus. Having a family to head up a state, he said, rendered it 'intelligible' to the people. Whereas the appeal of a republic was abstract, coldly 'rational' and basically 'uninteresting', a family on the throne . . . brings down the pride of sovereignty to the level of petty life'. It offers 'nice and pretty events' based on an easily comprehensible 'humanity' and invites a direct emotional response from the citizenry.

What Bagehot was highlighting as a new feature of monarchy constructed in Victoria's reign would now be described as 'human interest value'. Having a Royal Family creates a means of identification between subjects and monarchy that is, in every sense, familiar. We know where we are with the Royal Family because of our own experience of everyday family life. On this basis it is possible to identify with the monarchy through 'family likenesses' recognizing the ways in which individual members of the Royal Family conform to cultural stereotypes like bossy sister, black sheep, mother's boy, wayward aunt, and become involved in generational behaviour that's labelled 'sowing your wild oats', 'settling down' or 'getting too old for it'.

The process of familiar identification heightens the sense of the Royal Family as being 'just like us', like all Britain's families. It is the sentiment which the British tabloid and magazine press most regularly draws on in its royal representations – as on the cover of a Christmas edition of the *TV Times* which featured the Prince of Wales's family round the Christmas tree, as if they happened to be any young couple just called 'Charles and Diana' with their first baby. The coloured drawing was captioned: 'Welcome home, *everyone*, to a right royal Christmas.' The media association of royalty with Christmas has become ritualized through the regular Christmas broadcast which started with George V's radio message to Britain and the Empire in 1932 and is now addressed to Britain and the Commonwealth by the present Queen, also on television and in colour, and often accompanied by 'home movie' and travelogue pictures of other members of the family.

Such identificaion also implies an identity of interests: what it is assumed 'we all' share in common. Hence the appeal of any 'right royal' Christmas, birthday or wedding derives from the role all such events are assumed to play in everybody's family life as rites of passage and social markers of personal memory. As Bagehot put if, 'A princely wedding is the brilliant edition of a universal fact and as such it rivets mankind.' On such occasions we come together as a nation of normal families, and Britain, through its monarchy, becomes The Family of families.

But, of course, how this happens is because the Windsors are not *only* normal and really 'just like you and me'. They must also be special, unique, indeed sacred; invested with the names of Highness, Majesty and Defender of the Faith; appointed, anointed, even, to reign over us by the Grace of God. In a predominantly secular society these terms, if taken literally, are clearly anachronistic. Although the majority of the population retain a belief in an ultimate creator, they are not regular observers of the faith which the Queen defends, while increasingly vocal minorities observe a variety of other faiths of both Christian and non-Christian denominations. But, at another level, the bestowal of special royal names is an expression of the belief that for anyone to be a worthy object of identification they must be both 'just like us' while at the same time remaining as unlike us as possible.

This double dialectic of likeness and unlikeness is the way any media-promoted star system now operates and has been most manifest in the coverage, throughout the 1980s of the Princess of Wales. She is promoted as both 'the Number One Superstar of the World' and as 'an ordinary working mum' who 'slips round the corner to Sainsbury's when she can'. In this combination, Diana has featured ever since her engagement to Charles as 'main attraction' covergirl for European and American news magazines and for the whole range of British women's magazines, as well as being the promotional inspiration behind the burgeoning market of fanzines and partworks like *Young Royals, The Royal Family* and *Majesty*.

The new intensity of national and international coverage in the 1980s has led many commentators to say that the Royal Family have become the stars in their own soap opera (Coward

1984; Simmonds 1984). But although it is true that they share the same 'star' appeal in their capacity to represent both the ordinarily familiar and the extraordinarily remote, the Royal Family is also special in a different way from the stars of film and television.

The specialness of stars is often described as 'charisma', a term that has passed from Weberian sociology into everday speech to name some exceptional quality that is regarded as incomprehensibly 'other'. Stars are 'charismatic' because they have that extra something that all can recognize but none can define. As media stars, the Royal Family become invested with this sort of charisma; but they also get the nearest of any institution in modern times to the original magical and religious meaning of the term as 'the divine gift to inspire'. This is the definition developed by Weber in his examination of different types of legitimate authority. 'Charismatic authority', he suggested, rested on 'devotion to the specific and exceptional sanctity, heroism or exemplary character of an individual person, and of the normative patterns or order revealed or ordained by him' (Weber 1964: 328).

According to this definition of charisma, Princess Diana is special in a way that Joan Collins or Elizabeth Taylor, say, could never be. Take, for instance, the coded, but nevertheless explicit, concern around Diana's presumed premarital virginity. Besides the usual expressions of prurience, the media were also articulating a public belief that whatever might be acceptable sexual behaviour for other modern young women, or indeed Hollywood stars, when it came to a future Queen of England it was fundamentally important that she be 'undefiled' by any commoner male if she was to 'bear the child of a future King'.

Modern monarchy is required to rest on a higher moral plane than its subjects because it is examplifying values that many people may no longer see as relevant to their own lives but still wish to see maintained as the natural order of the British Way of Life. The monarchy repeatedly demonstrates its resilience and staying power by mastering the knack of constant adaptation to modern circumstances while upholding continuity and apparently ancient tradition. So when the Princess Royal announced her separation from her husband after a sixteen-year marriage that had started out as another 'fairytale romance', the media produced marriage counsellors to pronounce the break-up merely typical of the state of much modern marriage while at the same time expressing considerable concern about its effect on the 'mystique' of royalty. The BBC's *Today* radio programme led with the news and made its central question: 'But what about the *aura* of Royalty? Would that have been affected in any way?' And subsequent discussions in both news broadcasts and the quality press returned to Walter Bagehot to offer reflection based on his authoritative statement that, 'When there is a select committee on the Queen, the charm of royalty will be gone. Its mystery is its life. We must not let in daylight upon magic.'

In the realm of the magical monarchy there is always the problem of steering some middle course between the extreme dangers of being either too common or too remote, too formal/ informal, too distant/close. When television and film cameras entered Westminster Abbey to record the Coronation in 1953; when the first 'insider' television film, *Royal Family* was made in 1969; when the royal 'walkabout' was introduced in 1973; when the younger royals participated in the television game show *It's a Knockout* in 1987 – the fear was always that too much public exposure would diminish the magic, that the monarchy would be revealed as just too ordinary to maintain its mystique.

The fact that the British monarchy is still being invested with the qualities of the divine and the sacred is what makes it, according to Tom Nairn's book of the same title, *The Enchanted Glass* for the magical kingdom called 'Ukania'. For Nairn, the popularity of the modern monarchy, far from being the passive product of media hype or the star system, derives its power from plugging into the national psyche and offering the mesmerising fascination of 'the glamour of backwardness' (Nairn 1988).

As I have argued, what 'The Enchanted Glass' of royalty reflects are those symbols of nationhood which appeal to deeply atavistic longings for a great and united nation, a sense of harmony in national heritage and a belief in the stability and continuity of family life. If these are some of the values and traditions that account for the popularity of the Royal Family in cultural terms, we also need to address what they represent politically. That is how do we, as the subjects of monarchy, see ourselves reflected in the mirror? How is it, for instance, that the interests of the monarchy and of the people appear identical and that monarchy comes to speak on our behalf?

To start with Bagehot's evocation of the 'nice and pretty events' with which monarchy is associated. These are enjoyable and cheerful occasions; people are making an effort to be pleasant and everyone has the aim of the event 'going well' and being a collective success; moreover, anyone participating in a royal event will be made 'special' by it and rewarded by a type of charismatic authority that appears to want nothing in return, like a vote or an increase in productivity. This is why people always describe their encounters with royalty in such effusive and reverent terms – even when they can recall very little of what was actually said (Reynolds 1989). It also explains why royalty features so regularly as 'the good news' tag of daily current affairs programmes, keeping viewers sitting through 'the bad news' with the promise of uplift at the end. Even dreaming about the Royal Family appears to be a widespread phenomenon and, as the researcher Brian Masters discovered, the most common theme for fantasy is 'the day I had tea with the Queen' (Masters 1972).

The capacity of royalty to bestow recognition and reward on all sectors of society is what makes them appear to be 'on our side' in a way that others claiming legitimate authority do not. In particular the Royal Family are counterposed to 'the politicians' who, in the commonsense view of politics are 'just as bad as each other when it comes down to it and only out for number one'. By contrast, members of the Royal Family are understood to be, apart from one or two assumed 'drones', hard working, conscientious and caring, and only wanting the best for us all. Disillusionment with 'the politicians' contributes to the belief that it is the monarchy which best embodies aspiration for the national good.

Throughout the 1980s, this public perception of a monarchy operating somehow 'against politics' to represent the nation's best interests has been heightened both by the new role of the Prince of Wales as a moral commentator on public affairs and by the apparent concern expressed by the Queen about the direction taken by the Conservative administration. The media have been crucial here in the construction of appropriate royal personas and, in Prince Charles's case, allowing him a platform to put his views directly to the public.

In 1988 Prince Charles appeared in two significant BBC programmes. The first was on the flagship current affairs programme, *Panorama*. The special report was entitled 'Prince of Conscience', an accurate indication of the particular role Charles has chosen for himself as heir to the throne. It examined his increasing involvement with problems of the environment, inner city decay and unemployment. In the film he warily acknowledged his obvious difference and distance from the lives of his disadvantaged subjects-to-be but also spoke of his 'effort to put myself in their position'. As he had explained in a previous radio interview: 'Clearly it would be much easier to lead a quiet life. I don't need to do all this. It's just that I feel strongly about a lot of these things. If you go round the country in my position – I've learned a lot, I've listened, I've looked a lot – you can't just sit there and do nothing about it.' On the same *Panorama* programme the former Chairman of the Conservative Party, Norman Tebbit, expressed the fear that the Prince of Wales was possibly exceeding his constitutional role and might one day 'go too far' and start advocating 'socialist solutions'. But it was clear from opinion polls conducted in the 1980s that Charles's self-chosen role commanded widespread public approval – and especially because it was understood as a moral, humane intervention and not a political one.

The popularity of the Prince's opinions and his reputation as a spokesman for the nation was most clearly demonstrated in November 1988 at the time of his fortieth birthday celebrations. Here was a man now readied by destiny and dynasty to be a worthy king: 'God Bless the Prince of Wales!' (*Sunday Express*) and 'Britain's verdict on Charles at 40: fit to be King NOW!' (*Sunday Mirror*). The occasion of these editoral paeans was the BBC's *Omnibus* programme, written and narrated by Charles. Although ostensibly confined to the subject of architecture, it included the Prince's meditation on the relationship between God and 'Man' and was actually entitled 'A Vision of Britain'. In the course of the programme the Prince assumed a wide historical range of royal personas. These included the eighteenth-century patrician Whig (referring to his own enlightened landowning activities in the Duchy of Cornwall); nineteenth-century industrial philanthropist, in the line of Queen Victoria's husband, Prince Albert (asking why more modern developers couldn't behave like the old civic capitalists of Glasgow and Birmingham); and twentieth-century supporter of grassroots activists and local pressure groups demanding planning regulations as a basic democratic right.

The huge public response to the programme indicated that Charles's 'vision' could be interpreted in terms of a populism that was as much progressive as reactionary. It demonstrated the extent to which anyone can, as the old joke about women's magazines had it, 'knit their own Royal Family'. The programme displayed the Prince chatting most amiably, listening most intently, to women and men of all classes and British regions: 'one of us' but, more than that, 'on our side'.

Opinion polls commissioned by newspapers in the wake of the programme demonstrated that an overwhelming majority were in favour of Prince Charles 'speaking up'. Against whom or what it was unclear, but *for* whom there was no doubt. As letters to BBC Radio's current affairs programme *PM* put it: 'He speaks for the people'; and 'Thank God for Prince Charles', because he had the courage to 'speak on all matters relating to the nature of man. . . . Oh that we had more of his calibre in the House of Commons!' Such letters echoed the unanimous verdict of the press that 'Britain is backing Charles' (*Sunday Mirror*); 'The Crusader Prince' who 'speaks like the ordinary bloke in the street' (*News of the World*); so 'Let the once despised masses take up the Prince's cry!' (*Sunday Express*).

The language of these tabloid rallying cries is obviously over the top and, at first sight, dramatically at odds with that other tabloid stance towards royalty, the 'who do they think they are?' approach, whereby royal figures are clearly identified with their objective class positions as aristocrats and then invested with the accompanying moralistic epithets of being effete, odd and useless. Indeed, the fortieth birthday tabloid apotheosis involved a wholesale rewriting and reappraisal of the Prince, for the prevailing image created by the popular press in the preceding year had been of an eccentric aristocrat, quite out of touch with the lives of his future subjects and stuck in a marriage 'exposed' as a typically dynastic one of convenience rather than romantic love. While his wife was photographed consorting with 'eligible bachelors', her ageing fogey husband was represented as 'talking to flowers', led into the Kalahari desert and Jungian mysticism by the philosopher Laurens van der Post, and then appearing washed up on a barren Scottish island. 'Hermit Charles plants spuds on remote isle' said the *Sun*, summing up the heir's dilemmas in the notorious headline: 'A LOON AGAIN!'

However, such explicitly knocking copy always invites its opposite, including the charge, from other media, of betraying the British virtue of fair play on the spurious but widely believed grounds that 'Royalty cannot answer back'. Besides, a press so dependent on the continual flow of royal stories has no interest in being seriously anti-monarchical. Badmouthing members of the Royal Family has more to do with the wish of a deeply conservative press to maintain an image of apparent freedom and independence and thereby strengthen its contact with its readers, for such stories articulate what Richard Hoggart has called 'the aggressive plain man's stance' evoking a deeply felt sense of class envy that is commonplace in everyday grumbling about the Royal Family (Hoggart 1958). But while it may express real anger and frustration, class envy does not imply a political perspective based on class and does not suggest other possibilities or invite further questions about monarchy.

So 'who do they think they are?' never becomes 'what on earth do we need them for?' And the pendulum swing of the royal tabloid narrative happily reverts to the more familiar deferential stance that implies excessive loyalty and devotion to the royal 'cause'. This is similarly unquestioning because, as in the case of the Prince's fortieth birthday celebrations, it never asks what it is that royalty could actually *do* to effect change in Britain. But precisely because these questions are never posed and precisely to the extent that, however privileged, the Prince *is* powerless in this situation, he appears much more appealing, in the figure of some reborn Lionheart, than real world politics and elected politicians whose policies do have some material purchase on the world.

Deference to royalty is actually not that distinct from the aggressive tabloid mode in that both are based on what Hoggart describes as 'a scepticism without tension', a populist knowingness about the world which leads to self-protective but ultimately powerless cynicism (Hoggart 1958). The appeal of the deferential approach is that it articulates a populist disillusion and frustration with the world of 'politics'. The extent of alienation is indicated by the transformation of Charles into something predemocratic, an almost feudal concept of kingship whereby the monarch is on the side of the common people against all comers, from robber baron to foreign 'infidel'.

Unlike Prince Charles, the Queen *as* queen, and one who is continually and cautiously mindful of her place as constitutional monarch, chooses not to 'speak out', or to use the media as an open platform for her views – apart from her broadcast Christmas messages to Britain and the Commonwealth. Instead, through her advisers, press office and her own speeches, she arranges elaborately coded signals for letting it be known that she is 'concerned' about particular situations. In the 1980s these were notably about the Prime Minister's and President Reagan's various underminings of the Commonwealth, such as the invasion of Grenada and the issue of South African sanctions; the use of British bases for the American bombing of Libya and the social divisiveness of the miners' strike.

What was happening throughout this period was that government and monarchy, and specifically the figures of the Queen and the Prime Minister, Margaret Thatcher, were being seen as emblems of polar opposition. In the popular imagination, they were widely assumed to be personal rivals, engaged in a sort of moral battle for the British soul – to the extent that each was assumed to want the stately trappings of the other.

Thus in caricature and cartoons, Margaret Thatcher was frequently presented as trying to outroyal the royals, if not indeed achieve the status of Absolute Monarch. Hence the routine plot of the popular puppet review show, ITV's *Spitting Image*, which regularly featured members of the Royal Family planning how to get rid of the Prime Minister. On the other hand, the Queen, along with Prince Charles, was being viewed in the role of champion of her people; a member of the Establishment, of course, and admittedly one of Them, but nevertheless, at the same time, somehow on the side of Us. This feeling was most poignantly expressed when representatives of the Women Against Pit Closures movement came to Buckingham Palace with a petition for the Queen at the height of the miners' strike in the mid-1980s. They were appealing to a monarch known to have a degreee of sympathy with their situation to, in some indefinable way, 'do' something. For if the Queen of England could not help, then who was left who could?.

But the fact that the Queen is quite beside the point when it comes to real social and economic change is what is most problematic about the Royal Family's representative status. In my view, the recent symbolic confrontation between unpopular administration and popular monarchy is part of a wider crisis of cultural and political representation. Because what is happening when hereditary and non-elected figures come to stand in for the national identity and popular will is that this prevents the development of other representational forms to do with citizenship and popular sovereignty. For if it is primarily or exclusively the Royal Family who represent the people of Britain, then it becomes difficult to think in terms of an alternative concept of 'the people'.

In so far as ideologies are never simply ideas in people's heads but are indeed the myths we live by and which contribute to our sense of self and self-worth, then I think it actually matters that the British have no real identity as 'we the people' but continue to consign ourselves to a subordinated position as 'subjects' of the Queen (Althusser 1971). Not that we see it that way; the commonsense view is that the British are freer than their monarch; we can go anywhere we please without a police escort and 'I wouldn't have her job for the world!' In this way we happily consent to the monarch's continuing to act on our behalf. But the very popularity of present day monarchy is also how we, the British, tell ourselves that we're not quite ready for self-government yet.

REFERENCES

Althusser, L.(1971) 'Ideology and ideological state apparatuses', in his *Lenin and Philosophy and Other Essays*, London; New Left Books (for a discussion of the position of 'subjects').

Anderson, B. (1983) *Imagined Communities*, London; Verso.

Central Office of Information (1981) *The Monarchy in Britain*, London: HMSO.

Coward, Rosalind (1984) 'The royals', in her *Female Desire: Women's Sexuality Today*, London: Paladin.

Hoggart, R. (1958) *The Uses of Literacy*, Harmondsworth: Penguin.

Jowell, R. *et al.* (eds) (1989) *British Social Attitudes, Special International Report*, Aldershot: Gower.

Masters, B. (1972) *Dreams about HM the Queen*, London: Blond & Briggs.

Nairn, T. (1988) *The Enchanted Glass: Britain and its Monarchy*, London: Radius.

Reynolds, Gillian (1989) 'She smiled at me!', *Listener*, 12 December (an account of the BBC *Forty Minutes* documentary, 'The Day I Met the Queen').

Simmonds, Diana (1984) *Princess Di, the National Dish: The Making of a Media Star*, London: Pluto Press.

Weber, M. (1964) *The Theory of Social and Economic Organization*, London: Collier-Macmillan.

Chapter 12

Shock waves
The authoritative response to popular music

John Street

There is a story told about post-war popular music: first it was shocking, then it was subversive, and now it is respectable. We can include a real princess in this tale, Princess Michael of Kent, who remarked: 'Dreary, conventional people looked at the pop industry in a different way after Live Aid. It has got a different image now' (*Daily Mail* 28 June 1986). It is a familiar story, but is it a true one?

Certainly, public perceptions of pop have changed. We only have to compare the virtual canonization of Bob Geldof and the sanctification of Band Aid with the time, thirty years earlier, when rock music was a cause of outrage and moral indignation. Then, church leaders, politicians and other guardians of public morality argued that young people would be corrupted by listening to Elvis Presley or Bill Haley.

This neatly rounded story, however, only reveals a partial truth. Despite the warm afterglow of Live Aid, pop stars have not been fully embraced by the moral guardians. The same tabloids that had called for a Nobel peace prize for Geldof were later to persecute Elton John and Boy George for their alleged sexual and other habits. When the US rappers, the Beastie Boys, threatened to bring a 20-foot inflatable penis (part of their stage show) to Britain in 1987, they managed to inspire a familiar outburst of tabloid panic. The *Daily Mirror* claimed that the Home Secretary was going to ban them. (He didn't.) Albert Goldman's prurient biography of John Lennon served only to reinforce doubts about the acceptability of rock musicians. And then, in 1988–9, the popular press and (less popular) politicians discover the acid house party. As thousands of young people gather in fields, warehouses and deserted airfields all over Britain to have a good time (and make a few clever entrepreneurs very rich), the police start setting up road-blocks to prevent the events, encouraged by MPs like Graham Bright who initiate legal barriers to the parties. As Steve Redhead comments, 'The media story of Acid House shows that it is not so much a case of back to the future, as forward to the past' (Redhead 1990: 6).

But even the revised story does not end here. Just as pop musicians are being reviled again, there is a twist to the tale and they are acclaimed as conscientious citizens. They tour the globe for Amnesty International, visit the Soviet Union for Greenpeace, and perform for Nelson Mandela and against the poll tax. So whatever story is to be told about pop's reception, it does not have a simple plot. Maybe it has no plot at all. There is, after all, a temptation to dismiss all such reactions to rock as the ravings of reactionaries or the delusions of faddists.

This essay is an attempt to uncover the reality behind these competing interpretations. How should we regard the Establishment's reaction to pop? Was there good cause to be frightened – is pop ever dangerous? My answer is a hesitant and qualified 'yes'. I agree with Robert Hewison when he writes: 'It is true that rock 'n' roll has not led to revolution, but the fact that revolt *did* become a style . . . does not diminish the genuine effect that style had on the culture which contained it' (1988: 62).

The shifts in pop's public treatment reveal a common assumption: that pop has power. The argument is over whether that power is used for good or evil. In many ways, it is a theological debate. We are dealing with perceptions of the music, the way it is analysed and interpreted, and not necessarily with its real impact. None the less, these perceptions, I want to suggest, do display something interesting about the changing character of post-war British popular culture and its relationship to the surrounding political structures. My assumption is that the significance of popular music is related to, but not exclusively determined by, its social context, and that pop works by reflecting and shaping the relations within the society. The reaction provoked by pop, therefore, was part of its style – just as the outrage was part of the Establishment's style.

My aim here is to look more closely at the terms and form in which reaction came, whether from the 'political Establishment' of politicians, church leaders, etc. or from the musical Establishment of the pop press. In an attempt to make this potentially long-winded and unwieldy project more manageable, my focus is on four moments in pop's history:

1956–7: Bill Haley, Elvis Presley and the emergence of rock 'n' roll in Britain.

1965:   The Beatles and their award of the MBE by Prime Minister Harold Wilson.

1976–7: The Sex Pistols and the banning of 'Anarchy in the UK'.

1985:   Live Aid.

These moments each represent a time when reactions to pop were sharply focused. They are not necessarily key moments in the history of pop itself.

1956–7

The release of the film *Rock Around the Clock* in 1956 provoked rock's first shock wave. Cinema seats, it was reported, were torn up in celebration of the film's rock'n'roll soundtrack. Anthony Bicat described the times: 'In Manchester, after showing *Rock Around the Clock,* ten youths were fined for insulting behaviour when they left the cinema. "Rhythm-crazed" youngsters, after they had seen the film, held up traffic for half an hour and trampled in the flower beds in the municipal garden. In Blackburn the Watch Committee banned the film. . . . In Croydon the police cleared the Davis Theatre on Sunday of jiving youngsters' (Bicat 1970: 324–5). The announcement of a tour by Bill Haley and the Comets, to capitalize on the film's success, further fuelled the moral panic. Local authorities withdrew permission for concerts to be held in their dance halls and cinemas. This was not a simple matter of anti-Americanism. Britain's skiffle star, Lonnie Donegan, was caught up in the reaction; he was thought 'unsuitable' for Swansea Hall. Tommy Steele, then a rising pop star, was not allowed to play Portsmouth on a Sunday.

Lt-Col. Marcus Lipton, Labour Member of Parliament for Brixton, demanded that the Conservative Home Secretary ban indecent records. He sent copies of offensive songs – Stan Freberg's 'John and Marsha' and Mary Bryant's 'Don't Touch Me Nylon' – to the Home Office. In the typical fashion of such things, the newspapers had been instrumental in spurring

Lipton into action. They claimed that the Public Morality Council had received complaints about the songs, and that the Moral Welfare Council of the Church of England were concerned about the harm they might do (*Melody Maker*, 30th June 1956: 4). The Revd Albert Carter of the Pentecostal church, Nottingham, warned that 'Rock'n'roll is a revival of devil dancing . . . the same sort of thing that is done in black magic ritual'. The music threatened, it seemed, to provoke lawlessness, impair nervous stability and destroy the sanctity of marriage.

The BBC, less noisily, developed its own response to the emerging musical fashion. It deployed aesthetic and moral judgements. Some records were banned on the grounds that they were unsuitable for a family audience. In 1957, for example, the Vipers' 'Maggie May' was proscribed for its suggestive content. Other records suffered through a different measure of taste. Hotted-up versions of classical pieces were deemed equally unsavoury. Such music was thought to offend against aesthetic as well as moral sensibilities.

How do we make sense of these reactions? There are different elements involved. At one level, there is racism. There may not have been the crude outbursts of the Klu Klux Klan or of people like Asa Carter, secretary of North Alabama's White Citizens Council, who condemned rock'n'roll' as a means of 'pulling down the white man to the level of the negro. . . . It is part of a plot to undermine the morals of the youth of our nation. It is sexualistic, unmoralistic and the best way to bring people of both races together' (*Melody Maker*, 12 May 1956: 7). (This was meant as a criticism.) But while there may have been no concerted racist political response, prejudice was evident. Two Nigerian students were refused entry to the Victoria Dance Hall in Cardiff. The club operated a rule which stated that 'only when accompanied by a partner would coloured people be allowed on the floor' (ibid., 6 October 1956: 2).

More commonly, the reaction to the music was couched in moral terms. The music was offensive to parents and was alleged to encourage wayward behaviour in their children. The singing of rock'n'roll' songs was interpreted by the police as 'ranting and raving'; audiences were seen as problems of social control. A magistrate, sentencing a fan for disorderly behaviour after a screening of *Rock Around the Clock*, said to the defendant: 'You have had your fun and now you have to pay for it.' He added, 'We are getting rather tired of rowdyism' (Martin and Segrave, 1988: 35, 33). There was little talk of pop's political subversiveness.

The BBC's own concern seemed to stem mostly from the criteria, established by Lord Reith, for good music broadcasting. Writing in 1924, the Director-General had defined the value of broadcast music: 'It forms a pleasing and unobtrusive background to the ordinary pursuits and employments of evening.' This was not intended to rule out eclecticism, but the emphasis was on the need 'to transmit as much music as possible which, while perfectly good, should also be quite popular, easily understood and assimilated, or capable of being understood and assimilated' (Reith 1924: 173–5). Writing in the 1930s, the radio critic Sydney Moseley remarked that 'Broadcasting House has not "cheapened" music; it has not degraded, but uplifted popular taste' (1935: 125). Music policy was designed, therefore, to enlighten, provided that, in the words of Asa Briggs, it did not offend (1985: 249). The idea of what would offend was itself shaped by the notion of how, when and where people listened, and indeed about who 'the people' were. According to Simon Frith (1983), the BBC imagined the people as family groups gathered around the fireplace, enjoying 'the pleasures of the hearth'. The BBC approach to pop was, then, a combination of moral paternalism and aesthetics. Taste and behaviour were linked to form 'light entertainment'. Whatever criticisms might be made of this approach – and the BBC did nothing to promote rock 'n' roll – it did at least allow for a more considered and subtle response to new musical forms than could be found in parliament, the pulpit or the press. By the same token, we should be wary of painting too lurid a picture of responses outside the BBC. The reaction was often based on little more than the outbursts of certain individuals. The music press, on the other hand, might have been thought a natural ally of rock 'n' roll'. It wasn't.

Rock 'n' roll upset the journalists on *Melody Maker* almost as much as it upset MPs and church people. In the early 1950s, *MM* defined good popular music as jazz, and it was not going to give up this claim easily.

The mistrust of rock took a variety of forms, but what distinguished it from Establishment criticisms was its emphasis on the aesthetics of popular music. The dance band leader Jack Payne, for example, simply objected to singing. 'There must be a saturation point,' he announced. 'Surely the public itself will tire of its monotonous diet of singers, singers – and more singers?' ('Swan song for pop singers', *MM*, 21 April 1956). Steve Race was more direct in his criticism: 'Viewed as a social phenomenon', he wrote, 'the current craze for rock 'n' roll material is one of the most terrifying things ever to happen to popular music.' Using words that were to be repeated ten years later in attacks on the Beatles, Race referred 'to the cheap, nasty lyrics' (*MM*, 5 May 1956: 5).

Even where jazz critics used the language of morality, their concern remained with the sound and style of the music. Morality acts as a code for authenticity, for the truthful expression which jazz is held to represent. Steve Race wrote of rock 'n' roll as 'a monstrous threat, both to the moral acceptance and the artistic emancipation of jazz'. Explaining the popularity of this apparently unappealing music, Race put the blame on 'American industry' and 'the gimlet-eyed men of commerce' (*MM*, 5 May 1956: 5). Another *MM* stalwart, Tony Brown, spread the blame more widely, putting it on democracy and populist politics: 'It is one of the embarrassments of democracy that it is the age of the common man. The achievement of fame in popular music today demands a rabble rousing technique' (*MM*, 21 July 1956: 3).

Such attacks, with their explicitly political gloss, were concerned to defend jazz and to make the case for its authentic voice, against the 'commercialism' of rock 'n' roll. They saw mass consumption as manipulative and debased (a theme that was to reappear in the 1960s and 1970s in defence of 'progressive rock').

Often, the reality turned out to be at odds with the Establishment's expectations. Bill Haley was reluctant to accept the label 'rebel'; and his concerts, despite the expectations, caused no riots. As Nik Cohn explained, 'Instead of a space age rocker, all arrogant and mean and huge, he turned out to be a back-dated vaudeville act' (Cohn 1970: 21). There is a further irony in the fact that the new pop performers were worried about the worthiness of their art and the fears that their performances provoked. A festival of rock 'n' roll bands was organized in 1957 to provide support for Hungary. The singer Eve Boswell donated the royalties of her *Sugar and Spice* LP to the Lord Mayor's Hungary Relief Fund (*MM*, 17 November 1956: 14,20). Like

Live Aid, such gestures helped to establish an air of worthiness about rock.

It is important not to inflate the claims made for rock's actual ability to shock. Although there were people who were genuinely disturbed by what they saw and heard, they tended to sit on the periphery of the surrounding cultural and political edifice. Perhaps more significantly, we need to be aware of the very different types and sources of criticism that greeted rock ' n ' roll, extending from *Melody Maker*'s jazz aesthetics to the moral hysteria of churchmen.

1965

Although *Melody Maker* had scorned rock ' n ' roll in the 1950s, by the 1960s it had become entranced. A front page editorial in March 1965 demanded that 'The Beatles should be nationally honoured. Britain should demonstrate its pride in the four young musicians who have broken all pop records, to become the biggest pop phenomenon in history.' *MM*'s wish was granted in June when the Beatles were awarded the MBE in the Queen's Birthday Honours list (on the recommendation of Prime Minister Harold Wilson).

The announcement was met with derision and protest in some quarters, and the press made much of the news that previous recipients of the MBE were threatening to return their medals. *Melody Maker* had no time for such people. The editor described the protestors as 'adults who ought to know better' or as 'reactionary old fuddy duddies'. Such people, *MM* went on, should realize that 'the Beatles have waved the British flag all round the world. They have raised the standard of popular music. Immeasurably' (*MM*, 19 June 1965).

But while the first impression was that the paper gave unconditional support for The Beatles and pop, note the tone and the terms. The defence of the Beatles was, in some ways, the other side of Steve Race's condemnation of rock 'n' roll in the 1950s. Just as Race had attacked rock for the threat it posed to the quality of jazz, so the *MM* defended the Beatles for raising the quality of popular music. The paper was worried about the respectability of pop, displaying the same anxiety that Race had shown for the fate of authentic jazz. This concern was translated into a claim for the music's artistic merit. In doing this,

Melody Maker joined with the trend among 'serious' music critics, writers like the *Observer*'s Tony Palmer, *The Times*'s William Mann and Wilfrid Mellers. Writing in 1967, Mellers, a Professor of Music, said that 'the melodic, rhythmic and harmonic texture of the Beatles' songs is itself primitive; at least it has more in common with conventions of late medieval and early Renaissance music than it has with the harmonic conventions of the eighteenth century and after.' He then goes on to analyse 'She Loves You' in terms of its pentatonic opening and an 'Aeolian C which veers towards E Flat' (Eisen 1969: 182). Such accounts of the Beatles were clearly intended to incorporate them into established critical canons and criteria of good music. Tony Palmer claimed Lennon and McCartney as the true heirs of Schubert, not of Chuck Berry. If the standards were not set by the established traditions of classical music, then literary values came into play. D.G. Bridson, an influential and innovative radio producer at the BBC, explained his use of folk and blues on the Third programme: 'When I first heard modern American folk-singing during the war, I realized how truly it stemmed from the sung poetry of the past' (Bridson 1971: 222). The Beatles' respectability was confirmed politically by the fact that Conservative candidates in elections were urged to mention the group as often as possible. As early in their career as March 1964, the Beatles were being entertained by the senior members of Brasenose College, Oxford (Norman 1981: 227); Princess Margaret attended the première of *Help!* Even the Rolling Stones were accorded such respect. In 1965, Viscount Massereene and Ferrand had taken a paternal interest in the band, albeit for questionable motives. Using the House of Lords as his platform, the Viscount protested at the ban imposed on the group by the Musicians' Union which prevented them from playing in South Africa (*The Times*, 19 November 1965: 6). A group of Liverpool Labour MPs tabled a motion in parliament which drew attention to 'the great good and happiness that the Beatles have brought to millions throughout the world and furthermore being the first entertainment group that has captured the American market and brought in its wake great commercial advantage in dollar earnings to this country' (quoted in *The Times*, 16 June 1965). Support did not just come from the left. As President of the Board of Trade, Edward Heath had reportedly believed that the Beatles 'saved the British corduroy industry' (*The Times*, 19 June 1965: 6).

But if this is looking too cosy, what of the row over the MBEs? Surely this was a sign that the Beatles had not been properly accepted? It is true that 10 Downing Street received some mail about the award and that the critics outnumbered the supporters two to one. However, the total number of letters was to be counted in scores not hundreds; and it transpired that several of the critical correspondents turned out to be fans of other bands which, in the writer's opinion, had been unjustly overlooked by Her Majesty (*The Times*, 17 June 1965: 6).

It is true that the columns of *The Times* carried a mildly hot exchange about the rights and wrongs of rewarding the Beatles. It is noticeable, though, that the Beatles formed a focus for a more general series of concerns about who and what deserved such honours. A former RAF squadron leader, Mr Paul Pearson, voiced the general line of attack when he wrote, 'I feel that when people like the Beatles are given the MBE the whole thing becomes debased and cheapened' (*The Times*, 15 June 1965: 12). Colonel F.W. Wagg resigned from his local Labour Party and cancelled a £12,000 bequest to the party. But even amid the noise and the impression of Downing Street swimming in a sea of discarded MBEs, the reality turned out – again – to be rather different. By mid-June only one MBE had been returned (*The Times*, 17 June 1965: 6).

If anything, the complaints of the left were loudest. For Tony Benn, Wilson's gesture did not make practical political sense. He recorded in his dairy: 'the plain truth is that the Beatles have done more for the royal family by accepting MBEs than the royal family have done for the Beatles by giving them. . . . I think Harold Wilson makes the most appalling mistake if he thinks that in this way he can buy popularity, for he is ultimately bolstering a force that is an enemy of his political stand' (Benn 1987: 273). Other left critics took a more lofty line. Writing for the *New Statesman* in the days before his paternalist Fabian socialism became paternalist High Toryism, Paul Johnson railed against the Beatles. In his now famous piece, 'The menace of Beatlism', Johnson focused his anger on William Deedes who, in 1964, was a member of the Tory Cabinet. Deedes had rashly welcomed the Beatles: 'They herald a cultural movement among the young which may become part of the history of our time. . . . For those with eyes to see it, something important and heartening is happening. The young are rejecting some of the sloppy standards of their elders.' This was too much for Johnson. Deedes's praise was a sign of the moral bankruptcy of the Conservative Party. The Beatles were, after all, the 'apotheosis of inanity', and should not be granted ' a respectable veneer of academic scholarship. . . by grown men'. The Beatles' music was, said Johnson, 'the monotonous braying of savage instruments'. (In the *Daily Mirror*, Cassandra had described the Beatles 'as unskilled as a quartet of chimps tarring a back fence' (Smith 1975: 167).) Johnson's most vicious onslaught, however, was reserved for youth and the cult of youth. Watching a TV pop show audience, his eyes fell upon a terrible sight: 'What a bottomless chasm of vacuity they reveal! The huge faces, bloated with cheap confectionery and smeared with chain-store make-up, the open, sagging mouths and glazed eyes, the hands mindlessly drumming in time to the music, the broken stiletto heels, the shoddy, stereotyped "with it" clothes.' What Johnson thought he saw was 'a generation enslaved by a commercial machine', 'young girls, hardly any more than sixteen, dressed as adults and lined up as fodder for exploitation'. Johnson's only reassurance was the thought that not all teenagers shared a love for the Beatles (there are those, like Johnson himself, who devote their youth to the study of, and delight in, the works of Beethoven, Wagner and Debussy). The Beatle fan was, after all, only the 'least fortunate of their generation, the dull, the idle, the failures'.

Johnson was not the only – or the last – left voice decrying popular music. The debate, as we shall see, still rages over the same issue of whether or not pop is just a form of mass exploitation. But not everyone on the left took Johnson's line or adopted his bombastic tone. Some of the more interesting contributions to the debate were to be read in the pages of *New Left Review* in the 1960s. The issue here was the case against popular music made by Adorno in the 1940s. Alan Beckett (1966) attacked Adorno's blanket condemnation of popular music. Adorno, argued Beckett, failed to distinguish between types of pop music (especially the different jazz traditions). Adorno's critique was, therefore, incapable of appreciating the qualities achieved by, say, Ray Charles or the Beatles who had created innovative music through the fusion of different styles without becoming 'contaminated' by eclecticism; they had, thus, remained authentic. Beckett's defence of rock, therefore, used a similar critical language to defend rock as writers like Race in the 1950s had used to attack it. They cherished a picture of a genuine (authentic or uncontaminated) musical form, and they saw this purity as depending upon freedom from commercialism. In this attitude could be read, among other things, an elitism and desire for 'the real thing' which as Simon Frith (1988a) has observed, is characteristic of male, middle-class suburban attitudes to popular music.

All the readings of, and reactions to, popular music have to be located in a wider social context. The language of authenticity used by the critics can be seen as a code for their relationship to the music, which in turn was linked to wider political interests. The idea of 'authenticity' was itself constructed through and against the competing claims made for the importance of popular music by political and musical commentators. For the left and the pop journalists, we have to understand, in Frith's words, 'the strange fear of being inauthentic' (1988a: 22). For the rest, we have to understand the threat of the 'authenticity', the base passions, which they detected in the music of, and the audiences for, the Beatles. The power to shock is precisely the ability to touch such fears.

But not everyone was prepared to concede that pop had any significance for good or bad. Elsewhere in the political Establishment, away from these debates and away from the noise of outraged military gentlemen, there were those prepared to argue that pop was of little importance either way. This was the tone taken by William Rees-Mogg who, as editor of *The Times*, attacked the decision to imprison Mick Jagger and Keith Richard on drug offences; he argued that the sentences were a gross over-reaction. Rees-Mogg likened pop stars to bright butterflies; and the implication was that while we might temporarily be mesmerized by the beauty and success of pop stars, they did not represent any threat. The *Daily Express* displayed a similar attitude. Although it carried attacks on drug-taking, it also gave space to those who argued that drug users were 'in search of an awareness and breadth of experience they do not believe they can achieve under normal circumstances'. The *Express* may not have been enamoured of hippies, but it did not condemn them either. They were acknowledged to have a certain style that 'allowed William

Hickey to link the aristocracy of pop with the pop of his more conventional champagne acquaintances' (Smith 1975: 167).

Such a relaxed attitude was not, however, a sign of the complete incorporation of pop. Punk provided an excuse for the script to be rerun and for battle to be resumed over the idea of authenticity, itself once more linked to the ability to shock. This time, though, shock techniques were exploited by all sides; they became part of sales techniques.

1976–7

With its three chords and furious beat, punk made a tremendous noise. That was the point. Punk was the shock effect in action. Its images, targets and rhetoric were all designed to challenge and oppose existing musical and social conventions. The use of the swastika and songs like the Sex Pistols' 'Holidays in the Sun' (which referred to the Nazi death camp at Belsen) were clearly meant to offend. And if no one had reacted, the performers and entrepreneurs of the fledgling independent record labels would have been disappointed. The Sex Pistols, the Clash, the Damned, X-Ray Spex set out to shock. There were similarities with 1956–7 and the birth of rock 'n' roll, but the differences are almost more important. This time the musicians and their mentors knew the story. Not only did they know rock's history, they had also been to art school, and they understood the *theory* as well. They had read or heard about the French Situationists who had developed the idea of the disruptive political power of the public 'spectacle'. Punk culture had been developed in the late 1960s and – even though they renounced and hated hippies and hippy music – it believed that music mattered politically. What differentiated them from their predecessors was their awareness that they were part of the music business and that money and hype were inextricably part of their art.

This knowingness did seem to extend to the Establishment which dutifully played its part in punk's plan. Just as with rock 'n' roll, punk upset the pop Establishment quite as much as the political Establishment. The editor of *Music Week* announced that punk rock was 'unconcerned with musical competence' (quoted in Martin and Segrave 1988: 224). Phil Collins saw only 'a lack of talent'; Dave Dee, then an A & R executive at WEA, could not see it going any further, a view shared by his opposite

number at CBS who wrote it off as another fad. Over at the
Sunday Times, Derek Jewell welcomed punk as 'the latest
musical garbage' (all quoted in Coon 1982: 3). Like their 1950s
predecessors, several local authorities decided to ban punk
concerts from their halls. A voice from the 1950s could be heard
again in parliament speaking on the same topic as before.
Marcus Lipton MP warned that punk was 'a commercial exploitation of sex and depravity'. The Chair of the GLC's Art
Committee, Bernard Brooks-Partridge, said: 'I think the Sex
Pistols are absolutely bloody revolting . . . there are two members
of this authority, Mr John Branagan of the Labour Party and
myself, who would do anything they could within the law to stop
them ever appearing in London again' (Coon 1982: 126).

Punk's desire to offend did not stop at upsetting 'adults'; it was
also directed against the rock music Establishment. Much of
punk's anger, its driving force, was directed against the excesses
of Elton John, Led Zepplin and Pink Floyd (see Laing 1985:
chap. 1). Itself a reaction against some of the political worthiness
of 1960s rock, early 1970s music celebrated the extremes of
showbiz glitziness. The stars, staggering about on platform boots
and wearing gold lamé costumes, performed in huge arenas.
Being rich and living in grand mansions was no longer a rock
star's guilty secret, it was a crucial part of their image. Mick
Jagger played host to Princess Margaret backstage at Earls Court.

The cleverness of the punks was not matched by any novelty on
the part of their opponents. Politicians, the media and record
companies all contributed to the impression that punk was
subversive. The most dramatic demonstration of this was the Sex
Pistols' appearance on the *Today* show. Under provocation from
their host, Bill Grundy, the Pistols obliged by swearing. The
papers duly responded with shock and, in turn, the group's
record company, EMI, began to reconsider its investment. Only
The Times, it seemed, could distance itself sufficiently from the
phenomenon to acknowledge that the Sex Pistols' skill lay in a
talent for 'outrage, anarchy and behaviour calculated to disgust
and shock' (quoted in Martin and Segrave 1988: 225).

Punk came to be an object of tabloid fascination, and with the
increasing publicity fans and musicians were attacked physically.
There were fights in the King's Road (although these remained
on a small scale). When the Sex Pistols released their first album
in 1977, there was an unsuccessful attempt to prosecute the group

for the use of the word 'bollocks' on the cover (Chambers 1985: 177). The BBC and other radio stations dutifully banned almost all the Sex Pistols' singles, ensuring respectable sales for each of them.

In some ways, defenders of punk in the pop press were as deluded as the opponents. They were tempted to see punk as a reincarnation of the spirit of the 1960s dressed in the musical language of 1950s rock 'n' roll. Caroline Coon, writing *Melody Maker*'s first major piece on punk, reported that 'rock was no longer showbiz pop. It was once more a way of life. And adults hated it' (1982: 12).

A more clear-eyed interpretation of punk's effect and approach is offered by Dave Laing. For him, the reaction to punk was a deliberate component of the musical form. Many punk songs, he writes, 'were aimed at "them", targets outside the subculture, in such a way that the shock-effect of the impact on "them" was an essential part of a song's success. That is, it was vital that the import of the lyrics, their message, was communicated to the target, because the outrage and shock thus generated (and the awareness of it) was part of the punk discourse itself. . . . Punk was not separate from mainstream morality and culture, but symbiotic with it' (1985: 125). Whatever the rhetoric, punk was not so much a subculture or counter culture, but a parasite upon mainstream culture. It both learnt from, and taught, the existing dominant forms of popular culture. The tabloid press and punk taught each other the commercial value of the shock effect.

While its targets were fairly clear, punk was not defined by a single style of shock. Laing distinguished between the local and the structural shock techniques (1985: 79), the former being confined to single gestures – an offensive song title, a tasteless cover; the latter being concerned to effect a more complete disruption – a deliberately unconventional musical technique in which the conventions of playing and consuming music are unsettlingly altered. There are intriguing political implications of this. Songs of conventional political opposition relied on remaining within accepted codes of address and performance to convey their message. Where no such straightforward political ambitions exist, musical codes can be called into question and broken, thereby denying 'the listener an easily recognizable position or identity' (ibid.: 131).

The reaction to punk, however, overlooked these distinctions, choosing instead to see it as either subversive or threatening. Such interpretations rested, once again, on the language of authenticity. The separation of punk from glitter rock was premised on some idea of the former's authenticity and the latter's artificiality. Punk was the genuine article, it had stripped away the packaging, the showbiz fripperies and the pretensions of stadium rock. It had recovered rock's roots. This reading fits the patterns of rock criticism that have accompanied each shock wave. And, each time, it looks less and less convincing not just because of the limited scale of the reaction but also because of the assumptions of the argument. Was punk any more 'authentic' or 'subversive' than glitter? Was Establishment outrage proof of punk's power?

What is interesting is why this idea of rock as a subversive, subcultural force seems so implausible now. Perhaps, as Green of Scritti Politti reflected, it was destined for a quick death: 'I mean, going down to the Electric Ballroom and hitting empty film cans and scratching a guitar, playing this jittering, apologetic half-reggae and singing about hegemony while putting in as many discords as you could was probably doomed to failure' (Rimmer 1985: 18). As Simon Frith writes: 'The rock era . . . turned out to be a by-way in the development of twentieth-century popular music, rather than, as we thought at the time, any kind of mass-cultural revolution' (1988a: 1). Part of the evidence for this can be seen in the way that TV and press reaction to punk was not simply innocent outrage. Being shocked made good commercial sense. It helped to sell newspapers, for example. 'Shocking revelations' about pop performers became a source of news – the more shocking the better. The popular press learnt the lessons of punk, and in doing so ensured the incorporation of popular music into the mainstream mass market. Any doubts to the contrary were eliminated by Live Aid.

1985: LIVE AID AND AFTER

Boy George, Cliff Richard, Elton John and Bob Geldof, the Housemartins, and a few more besides, have all been subjected to salacious examination by the tabloid press – that is, when they were not being fêted for their generous works for a variety of good causes. The reaction has had little to do with their music. The targets of press venom are there because they – like the actors in soap operas – are now part of the world of entertainment. They are not representatives of a youth culture or subculture. They are now participants in the mainstream of popular culture. They may not be the direct equivalents of Max Bygraves, but they are close.

This shift is not a matter of another loss of 'authenticity', or of another capitulation to commercialism. It is a sign that pop has acquired a new populist version of 'authenticity'. Pop stars are now supposed to represent the way we all are. This move is driven by the changing political economy of the communications industry. Live Aid was, in one way, a symbol of the commercial importance of rock as a device for delivering consumers to markets. Pepsi sponsored Live Aid, just as in 1988 Reebok sponsored an Amnesty International tour by Bruce Springsteen and others.

Live Aid rejected the oppositional rhetoric that fuelled the mythology of 1960s and 1970s festivals. It was just another spectacle, on a par with a royal wedding. (It is perhaps worth noting that, despite the noise and fury that surrounded them, the pop festivals of previous eras were relatively uneventful affairs. Michael Clarke's *The Politics of Pop Festivals* (1982) shows that the events were accommodated by the existing political channels.) Live Aid's very lack of controversy and disruption worried rock critics (Marcus 1985). The question was about how to link the politics (worthy but naive) to the music (banal but popular). Woodstock formed an implicit – and sometimes explicit – backdrop. There was no radical opposition to existing structures, and nothing, besides Geldof's swearing, to shock. For the committed rock critic, Live Aid seemed to confirm that rock's politics had finally collapsed into style. Politics was just a fashion accessory. Against such arguments is the view that politics and style are not opposites, and that Live Aid contributed positively to pop's political power (Hebdige 1988: 217–18).

Another version of these arguments accompanied the emergence of the Beastie Boys in 1987. These white boy rappers divided those who saw them as a subversive parody of adolescent male culture from those who condemned them for their puerile sexism. While the topics change, the underlying concern remains. Does the music authentically represent political reality? But what is interesting is how redundant such questions have come to seem. As the pop press is dominated by *Q* at the older end of the market and by *Smash Hits* at the younger end, the issue of authenticity becomes irrelevant. These magazines, geared to readers who consume pop without the musical–political paraphernalia, are not interested in the need to be *really* in touch, to be part of an exclusive cult. Authenticity in this context is merely a sales pitch. It only acts as a code for marketing 'serious' popular music, from 'world music' to the folksy sounds of Tanita Tikaram and Paul Simon. In the same way, shock techniques are now largely devices for selling mass circulation papers. To observe such trends, though, should not commit us to elegiac reminiscences about the decline of pop. Rather, it calls for a reassessment of that past and the role of 'shock' in it.

WHERE DO WE GO FROM HERE?

It is possible to read my account of pop's history as a crude exercise in revisionism, an attempt to suggest that pop has always been trivial and inconsequential. I want, in this last section, to make a quite different case, to argue that pop's sounds and images do have the power to shock, and that the reaction of the musical and political Establishment was not entirely misconceived. The point is that, while the air of panic and outrage was both exaggerated and an over-reaction, there was a persistent concern on the part of the industry and the media to control and manage the consumption of popular music and, at the same time, a resistance to this control by audiences and performers. The shock waves have tended to obscure these underlying themes.

Not all Establishments are malign

The BBC's role in the shaping and distribution of popular music has been more ambiguous than is often allowed. There is a school of thought which sees its role as wholly negative. The corporation is portrayed as bringing the dead weight of bureaucracy and political conservatism down upon the neck of popular music. Radio 1, by this account, becomes a pale version of the pirate ships it replaced. The BBC then re-established its monopoly power, and implemented a policy of lowest common denominator populism, combined with a pathological fear of giving offence to either its audience or its political masters. Such thoughts lie behind criticism of the BBC's scheduling and its use of playlists (and other devices which work against eclecticism) and its censorship of records.

Although there may be some truth in criticisms of this type, they tend to rest on unwarranted assumptions about the benefits of the pirates and/or non-centralized broadcast structures. It is worth bearing in mind the arguments of Tony Benn when he, as Postmaster General in the mid 1960s, initiated the government's campaign against the pirate stations. 'These pirates', he said, 'are interfering by stealing wavelengths. . . . They are also stealing the copyright of all the records they broadcast and are thus stealing the work of those who make the records and the legitimate business claims of those who manufacture them' (*The Times*, 17 March 1965: 5). Furthermore, when compared to the so-called independent stations, the BBC may have enjoyed greater autonomy and less commercial pressure than its rivals. It is the BBC that has afforded a place for John Peel. And without Peel the much-vaunted innovation of the independent sector might never have begun. It is also possible to argue that Radio 2, much decried for its music and its ageing disc jockeys, actually offers an opening for a genuine popular culture, one which 'people themselves produce rather than what centralized media produce for them' (Dyer 1986). The scheduling policy of the pop video cable television channel MTV and the new independent commercial radio service Radio, Radio, both of which are commercially driven and designed to deliver audiences to advertisers (not to aid musical appreciation), does not suggest that variety is a logical entailment of freedom from the state and public corporation bureaucracy (see also Frith 1988b: 3).

It is important, therefore, to distinguish, first, between the factions within 'the Establishment' and, second between the types of reaction. It is not altogether clear that the pop press did more to promote rock than did the BBC to suppress it. Certainly, if we are to examine the role of the BBC or the press, we need to look at more than the public face of 'shock'.

The censorship that can't be seen

Often the records which are banned sell very well, because of (not despite) their treatment. The Sex Pistols and Frankie Goes to Hollywood had no real reason to complain. The true losers are those who suffer a more insidious form of surveillance, by which their music is effectively censored, but there are no censors and no blacklist. This is the fate of much black music. The under-representation of black musicians and their exploitation are persistent features of popular music. In the pop press and in broadcasting, a set of values and arguments operate which in their effect (if not always their intention) exclude black music from the so-called mainstream of popular music. This derives from the way black music is organized and delivered for consumption. It is, for example, a commonplace of broadcasting that certain types of music do not sound 'right' on daytime radio. This argument has been used against many types of black music. There have been, of course, the odd rap, reggae or funk hit, but they have generally been accorded the status of a 'novelty' item, rather than as a typical element of pop radio. As Simon Jones (1988) observes, 'For many radio producers, reggae's perceived lack of harmony and unsophisticated musical arrangements failed to measure up to the standards of white pop, while its overtly political or sexual lyrics were regarded as "unsuitable" for mainstream programming.' Derek Chinnery, Head of Radio 1 in 1976, offered this excuse: 'There doesn't seem to be much of a national demand for reggae. . . . And of course there's an awful lot of reggae that's simply not suitable for Radio 1. Some of them have strong political content while others are just poor quality records' (Jones 1988: 81-2). A similar note has been struck by Chinnery's successor, Johnny Beerling, who said of dance club records: 'They don't generally sound good on the radio, particularly on AM; they're repetitious, low on the melody line' (Martin 1985). The 'lack' of a national demand may say more about the organization of the charts and the BBC's dependence on them than about the popularity of reggae.

There is a sense in which the argument – that the music does not sound right – is correct. Rap does not fit easily into the Simon Bates morning show on Radio 1. But why? The format of daytime shows is organized to produce a particular mood and mode of address, both of which are defined in terms of a type of music. A set of criteria, albeit disguised as the commonsense and culture of the BBC, are employed to identify the acceptability of certain sounds. The effect is to make legitimate the criticism of black music that 'it all sounds the same'. Such criteria can have the same effect on late night, alternative broadcasting (black acts rarely featured on the Janice Long show). Black music is given a separate show instead – and is scheduled for a time, at the weekend, when listening figures are low.

Institutionalized censorship of this type is different from that practised by commercially driven broadcasting like MTV. Here the criterion for selection entails producing audiences for markets and advertisers. It works in large part through existing patterns of taste. It makes no pretence to educate, unlike public institutions like the BBC which can at least aspire to such goals.

It is different, too, from the way in which rock writers have created meanings around forms of music, although these have also worked against the status of black music. Earlier generations of rock writers used to deploy the idea of 'authenticity' to distinguish between types of black and white music. Janis Joplin's career traded on such criteria: she was seen to represent the 'true' sound of soul; her crying and shouting were, it was said, the direct expression of her feelings. The rougher sounds of Stax were favoured over the more subtle, less raucous virtues of Tamla Motown. Tamla's singers used their voices and lyrics to convey emotion indirectly, whereas Stax's artists translated emotion into sound more explicitly – compare Smokey Robinson to Wilson Pickett. Today, similar judgements can be detected in the celebration of 'world music' which is presented as more exotic or more natural than western music.

The point is not to claim that there is a complete edifice of racist institutions, although there is an element of truth to such a portrayal. Rather, it is to suggest that the ways in which institutions react to popular music cannot be read off explicit public pronouncements, and that there is an official secrecy, disguised as commonsense, in the way black pop is managed. Public shock may distract attention from systematic processes managing and producing pop. Besides, shock may serve as a deliberate device in the promotion, rather than denial, of pop.

Shock as a sales technique

By the 1960s, pop entrepreneurs had learnt that moral outrage had its uses. The outcry that greeted the Rolling Stones' second album, released in January 1965, owed little to either the music or to the group's behaviour. It was generated almost entirely by the sleeve notes written by the group's manager, Andrew Loog Oldham: 'Cast deep into your pockets for loot to buy this disc of groovies and fancy words. If you don't have the bread, see that blind man, knock him on the head, steal his wallet and lo and behold, you have the loot. If you put in the boot, good. Another one sold.' Decca, the Stones' record company (willing agents, it seems, in this ruse – 'a giggle', they called it), received a number of complaints as a result. The record was withdrawn, although not before Lord Conesford, a Conservative peer, had called for the Director of Public Prosecutions to investigate the case. The Home Office, however, treated the matter lightly. Lord Stonham replied to his fellow peer, 'If it is any consolation to the noble lord, research I made at the weekend supports the view that even when they are intelligible the words of a pop song are not considered important and teenagers have even less regard for the blurb on the envelope [sic]' (*The Times*, 17 March 1965: 5). None of this did any harm to the Stones' career.

Oldham's example was followed. The Move attracted attention to themselves by producing postcards of the Prime Minister, Harold Wilson, in the nude. Just to make sure they were noticed the cards were delivered to 10 Downing Street. Malcolm McLaren was just another student of the art of shocking, developing his skills with the Sex Pistols and later BowWowWow.

While these deliberate attempts to shock were cynical exercises in manipulation, it is wrong to dismiss them completely – if only because they worked. People were shocked and people were impressed. The skill and imagination behind the shocks indicated a real understanding of the way fans and others thought about the world.

Rock music really did disturb people, its noise and its images did jar against their sense of how things should be ordered. Were it not so, then it is unlikely that it would have made some people so rich, nor would so much time and resources have been devoted to organizing it. Nor, paradoxically, would it now feature as a standard device for supporting worthy causes and mass marketing consumer products. Tennents lager announced in September 1988 that it was putting over £1 million into sponsoring rock music in Scotland. As one of the people behind such sponsorship deals remarked, 'Rock 'n' roll music is the common denominator of 12 to 34 year olds and it's a wonderful way to target young people' (Sandall 1988). The tempting conclusion is that sponsorship, in the words of the manager of Dire Straits, has made 'music very safe at the moment, very corporate. . . . The element of rebelliousness is missing.'

What is important, though, is that this 'rebelliousness' is not to be set *against* pop's commercialism but *with* it. While the moments which this chapter has picked out can be seen as purely cultural events, they have also to be explained by reference to the economic fortunes of the record industry. Rock 'n' roll cannot be separated from the emergence of a relatively autonomous youth market, just as punk has to be linked to a slump in the profitability of the record business, and just as Live Aid has to be connected to the global market for pop. Pop's changing infrastructure does not remove its power to offend, as the acid house party testifies. What matters, though, is that such reactions are now part of the business of recycling pop and its history. The sound of moral outrage has a different tone this time around. It has a familiar ring, simply because it recalls a vaguely remembered earlier era. The 'shock value' can no longer be an innocent feature of pop's pleasures; instead, it is an established part of the new politics of popular culture. Shock techniques, by definition, always have a limited life – what shocks today will be conventional tomorrow. This wisdom is now, though, the commercial commonsense of advertisers and newspaper editors, who borrow from yesterday's shock to sell today's convention.

Meanwhile, musicians and audiences explore another version of pop's ability to shock. They delight in the construction of differences in daily choices and fantasies, and in sharing and distorting the memories of pop's history. Seeing such a culture as 'authentic' may be pointless; seeing it as shocking is the point, because sometimes the differences being discovered work against the dead weight of unsurprising, commonsensical convention.

NOTE

My thanks to Simon Frith, Dominic Strinati and Steve Wagg for doing what they could for this chapter.

REFERENCES

Beckett, Alan (1966) 'Popular music', *New Left Review* 39 September/October: 87–90.
Benn, Tony (1987) *Out of the Wilderness. Diaries 1963-67*, London: Hutchinson.

Bicat, Anthony (1970) 'Fifties children: sixties people', in V. Bogdanor and R. Skidelsky (eds) *The Age of Affluence 1951-1964*, London: Macmillan.

Bridson, D. G. (1971) *Prospero and Aerial*, London: Victor Gollancz.

Briggs, Asa (1985) *The BBC: The First Fifty Years*, London: Macmillan.

Chambers, Iain (1985) *Urban Rhythms: Pop Music and Popular Culture*, London: Macmillan.

Clarke, Michael (1982) *The Politics of Pop Festivals*, London: Junction.

Cohn, Nik (1970) *AWopBopALooBopAWopBamBoom*, London: Paladin.

Coon, Caroline (1982) *1988: The New Wave Punk Rock Explosion*, London : Omnibus.

Dyer, Richard (1986) 'Opening up the airwaves', *Marxism Today*, May: 40–1.

Eisen, Jonathan (1969) *The Age of Rock*, New York: Vintage.

Frith, Simon (1983) 'Pleasures of the hearth', *Formations of Pleasure*, London: Routledge & Kegan Paul: 101-23.

Frith, Simon (1988a) 'Playing with real feeling: making sense of jazz in Britain', *New Formations* 4 (Spring): 7-24.

Frith, Simon (1988b) *Music for Pleasure*, Oxford: Polity.

Hebdige, Dick (1988) *Hiding in the Light*, London: Routledge.

Hewison, Robert (1988) *Too Much*, London: Methuen.

Johnson, Paul (1964) 'The menace of Beatlism', *New Statesman*, 28 February: 326-7.

Jones, Simon (1988) *Black Culture, White Youth*, London: Macmillan.

Laing, Dave (1985) *One Chord Wonders*, Milton Keynes: Open University Press.

Marcus, Greil (1985) *Rock for Ethiopia*, IASPM Working Paper, also included in Angela McRobbie (ed.) *Zoot Suits and Second-Hand Dresses*, London: Macmillan: chap. 22.

Martin, Gavin (1985) 'Air head', *New Musical Express*, 16 November 1985.

Martin, Linda and Segrave, Kerry (1988) *Anti-Rock: The Opposition to Rock 'n' Roll*, Hamden, Connecticut: Shoe String Press.

Moseley, Sydney (1935) *Broadcasting in My Time*, London: Rich & Cowan.

Norman, Philip (1981) *Shout: The True Story of the Beatles*, London: Elm Tree.

Redhead, Steve (1990) *The End-of-the-century Party*, Manchester: Manchester University Press.

Reith, Lord (1924) *Broadcast over Britain*, London: Hodder & Stoughton.

Rimmer, Dave (1985) *Like Punk Never Happened*, London: Faber.

Sandall, Robert (1988) 'Watch this Space' *Q*, October: 40-6.

Smith, A. C. H. (1975) *Paper Voices*, London: Chatto & Windus.

Chapter 13

Digging for Britain
An excavation in seven parts

Dick Hebdige

We want . . . a nation at ease with itself.

(John Major)

A national culture is not a folk lore, nor an abstract populism that believes it can discover a people's true nature. A national culture is the whole body of efforts made by a people in the sphere of thought to describe, justify and praise the action through which that people has created itself and keeps itself in existence.

(Frantz Fanon)

Perhaps, instead of thinking of identity as an accomplished fact, which the new cultural practices then represent, we should think, instead, of identity as a 'production' which is never complete, always in process, and always constituted with, not outside, representation.

(Stuart Hall)

The essay reprinted below entitled 'Digging for Britain' (elsewhere referred to as DFB) was first published in the catalogue for *The British Edge*, an exhibition and events programme, mounted in the autumn of 1987 at the Institute of Contemporary Art, Boston, Massachussets.[1] DFB looks at how different, often contradictory myths of 'Britishness' are constructed, lived and represented in contemporary British society, how they circulate as sounds and images, signs and narratives in popular culture, and how they themselves are regularly used in various combinations to 'interpellate' (call up and hold in place) different 'imaginary communities' (Anderson 1983) round the larger image of the nation or the 'national interest'. The Thatcher years saw a particular investment in a set of images and myths designed to 'put the "Great" back into Great Britain again' (to quote a 1980s Tory Party campaign slogan). The ideas of British 'grit' and rugged island independence, of Britain as a nation of 'hardworking, home-loving ordinary people' were regularly invoked to secure popular support for the Thatcherite project of 'regressive modernization' (Hall and Jacques 1985). This project entailed the selective appropriation of elements of national 'heritage' (e.g. Victorian entrepreneurial values) which were summoned up to lay to rest the more recent ghosts of post-war consensus politics, welfarism and 1960s libertarianism while, at the same time, selected British institutions (e.g. local government, the health service, education) were opened up to 'free market forces'.

DFB was written when that project was beginning to appear immune to effective opposition, when Thatcher herself, about to embark on a third term in office, looked virtually invincible. In other words, it was written (just) before Black Monday in October 1987, when the value of shares held on the London stock exchange suffered a sudden, massive drop, before the recession which presaged the demise (or at least mutation) of the legendary power-dressing yuppy. It was written before the art market crash and the fall of design entrepreneurs like George Davies and Terence Conran, before what the *Guardian* reporting on the 'spectacularly messy collapse' in September 1990 of the Michael Peters Design Group (responsible for styling Bang & Olufson TV sets, Nat West reports, the new Heinz baked beans label, Smile stamps, the Powergen logo, the Tory Torch of Freedom logo), described as 'the growing line of fallen 1980s icons from the polluting of Perrier and fall of filofax to the slump of the Saatchis' (*Guardian*, 10 September 1990). DFB was written before the 'caring' 1990s and another (Gulf) War, before incessant skiing trips together with another increase in the money awarded the Royal Family precipitated, for a few months in 1991, an alleged decline in their popularity at home, unrivalled in the second Elizabethan age. It was written, finally, long before the grumbling anti-European animus of the Bruges group conspired at last with soaring interest rates, high inflation and the poll tax to get Mrs Thatcher ousted from office at the hands of her own party in mid-November 1990. There is a sense in which DFB reads like a text rescued from a lost world. In a way the problem of unplanned obsolescence dogged the essay from day one and the limited generalizability of the material and insights containted therein indicates, perhaps, how much of enduring value may be lost to sociology in an 'excavation' of popular culture which substitues a 'fascination' with contingent, surface forms for the traditional toils of the 'depth model' and deep structural analysis.

It is, then, not the purpose of these prefatory remarks to make any claims for the intrinsic value of the essay, still less to present it as an examplar of what postmodernism can do for the study of popular culture. On the contrary, it may well serve to deter those who might otherwise be tempted to experiment with modes of data-presentation. Certainly parts of the essay look to me now – as they will, no doubt, to any future readers – as portentous, dated and overdressed as the rock music video clips discussed inside them. And no matter how many arguments are produced for the aestheticization of theory, such arguments fail to make writing that at times resembles the verbal equivalent of dry ice in an old Ultravox video any more acceptable or easy to read. Instead of seeking to recover or redeem the original intentions, the aims of this introduction are threefold: (1) to situate the essay in some kind of historical and epistemological context; (2) to consider some of the problems posed by its interpretive and presentational 'take' on contemporary cultural issues; and (3) to explicate what I regard to be the key assumptions and positions which lie, for the most part buried and unstated, in both the essay and the strategy which 'speaks' it.

In the first instance, the original (US public arts) context for which DFB was written accounts for some, at least, of the essay's substantive concerns – for example, the references to British heritage and English romanticism, the focus on contemporary British design and, specifically, on the mediated aesthetics of UK youth culture in the 1980s. It explains perhaps why much of the 'popular culture' examined here (documentary and independent film and video; avant-garde design; fine art; Indi pop, etc.) hardly seems to qualify as 'popular' at all. That context also helps to explain (if not to excuse) the peculiarities of style and present-ation. I opted in the essay for a polyvocal, image-centred approach partly because I knew from experience that such an approach would be more amenable than a conventionally argued 'thesis' to the kind of mixed media presentation – incorporating video, audiotape, slides and 'live' commentary – I wanted to give in lieu of the critic's conventional 'paper' in the lecture series accompanying the exhibition (see p. 325). Of course, the transgressions of academic codes of detachment, consistent 'voice' and so on were not just expedient but rather formed part of that more general questioning of the established forms and functions of institutionalized critique identified by the late 1980s with postmodernism.

A postmodern (or alternatively 'New Times') (Hall and Jacques 1990) problematic drew the essay together at another level round a number of themes: the nation as 'imaginary community', the decline of national sovereignty and national autonomy, the contradictory dynamics of globalization and localization, the imbrication of culture, technology and economics, the place of consumption in the construction of social identities, the reversibility of centre – margin oppositions, the stress on fragmentation and difference, surface and style, the strategic invocation of memory and the past, the emergence of 'new (black British) ethnicities' (see note 3 of main essay). Needless to say, many of these issues have been more fully elaborated and more competently theorized elsewhere and by others, not least in the interval between the original publication and this reprint.

It is worth reviewing briefly some of the theoretical advances accomplished in recent years round at least one of the essay's central points of focus – the ethnicity/identity axis. The last few years have seen an explosion of discourse round cultural identity, an explosion which Kobena Mercer, through a combination of astute social-historical/political analysis and a sustained deconstruction of 'the *trope* of race',[2] links suggestively to the 'crisis of political agency' afflicting the left in the post-1968 period – a crisis which Mercer argues became particularly acute in the Thatcher era. Drawing on the insights of, among others, Gramsci, Laclau and Mouffe, Mercer confronts the full implications of a 'relational' view of both identity *and* hegemonic struggle without retreating back into either 'ethnic absolutism'[3] or the utopian rhetoric of 'rainbow alliance(s)'. Instead he concentrates on the sheer *difficulty* of 'learning to live with difference', on the ambivalent potentialities of a 'politics of identity' in postmodern, postindustrial, postcolonial societies like the contemporary UK – a politics of identity which he contrasts with the emancipatory and essentialist 'identity politics' left over from the 'counter culture' of the 1960s. In much the same vein and working with a similar set of critical resources (here in the context of an analysis of Caribbean hybridity), Stuart Hall has usefully distinguished two influential though not entirely commensurable models of identity which operate across the blurred boundaries of cultural studies and cultural politics today. The first defines cultural identity in terms of one shared culture rooted in, and guaranteed by, a common historical experience. In this version, the

> 'oneness', underlying all the other, more superficial differences, is the truth, the essence, of 'Caribbeanness' of the black experience. It is this identity which a Caribbean or black diaspora must discover, excavate, bring to light and express through . . . representation.
>
> (Hall 1991)

By way of contrast, the second model presents identity as an always open-ended process of becoming, conditioned by the 'positions of enunciation' available at any one moment to historically and socially situated subjects. Here identity is theorized as

> constituted not outside but within representation . . . not as a second-hand mirror held up to reflect what already exists, but as that form of representation which is able to constitute us as new kinds of subjects, and thereby enables us to discover places from which to speak.
>
> (Hall 1991)

These contributions both clarify and complexify the issues at stake in any discussion of national or ethnic identity without closing off in advance the strategies and choices likely to emerge from such discussion. In comparison, the 'Digging for Britain' piece may appear to readers in the 1990s as both too simple-minded, too limited in terms of its political imagination and too elaborate, too stuffed with irrelevant detail. As the title, perhaps, suggests, it straddles the two versions of identity distinguished by Hall and remains half stuck inside an earlier set of questions (concerning roots and authenticity, the location of the *real* subcultural resistance to official, i.e. ideological 'lies'), and half aware that there are other questions to be framed once the decision is made to confront head on the challenge of the contingent character of human agency and historical change. Unfortunately, all too often, the old questions win through. At certain key points in DFB, cultural politics threaten to degenerate into a Manichean opposition between rebellious goodies and Establishment baddies, as Lawrence Grossberg has pointed out in his critique of the essay:

> Power, however dispersed, is always articulated (in DFB) into a struggle between the popular – represented by London's street-styled and economically marginalized male youth and the (evil) other of Thatcherism and official culture. Culture is differentiated according to a single dichotomous vision of contemporary Britain and of the possibilities of British identity. . . . There is an assumed necessary correspondence between social position, lived experience, cultural practice and political significance.
>
> (Grossberg 1988)

Such a reductive view of what Grossberg more adequately figures as the 'continuous "war of position" dispersed across the entire terrain of social and cultural life' suggests, as he indicates in his critique, that the more urgent lessons of postmodernism have hardly been assimilated here (Grossberg 1988). None the less, while DFB may look out of place in the present collection, it's clear enough where it *does* fit in those debates on popular culture, 'ethnicity' and national identity which constitute some of the most powerful vectors in (British) cultural studies today.

But the form of the essay is, as they used to say, 'something else'. Justifications for a 'narrative poetics' within the social sciences have been put forward intermittently since the earliest attempts to legitimate and codify qualitative method. The recent work of Clifford, Marcus and others (Clifford and Marcus 1986; Clifford 1988) which seeks to deconstruct anthropology's colonial inheritance and to integrate 'the poetics and politics of ethnography' embodies a thorough investigation of the relevant issues, especially when read alongside Clifford Geertz's powerful defence of the anthropological project (Geertz 1988). Closer to home, the confidence with which the critic can pronounce from a safe distance on the 'meaning' of contemporary cultural 'forms' has been shaken for at least two decades now by the 'discursive turn'[4] in cultural studies, taken to accomodate the now-familiar series of European theory imports (semiotics, poststructuralism, etc.). The challenge to the truth claims of what Mercer calls the 'Big Picture' theories[5] like Marxism have been highlighted over the same period by the 'acknowledgement of the *plural* sources of antagonism' which heralded the arrival of 'new' social movements and new political demands. And the steady stream of criticism which, since the late 1950s, sought to promote the academic study of popular culture has turned into a flood thirty years on as the key concepts used to define the 'postmodern condition' – eclecticism (Lyotard), simulation (Baudrillard), indifference (Grossberg), de-differentiation (Lash), recoding (Foster), pastiche (Jameson), weak thought (Vattimo), etc. – have begun to circulate and, in the process, to accelerate the 'implosion' (Baudrillard) of the analytical hierarchies and binary oppositions (base *v.* superstructure; high *v.* low; minority *v.* mass) which used to underwrite the study of contemporary culture in humanities and social science departments in past decades.

It is not just that, as Steven Connor puts it, cultural critics today 'unabashedly bring to bear on (popular culture) the same degree of theoretical sophistication as they would bring to any high cultural artefact' (Connor 1989). As Connor himself goes on to indicate in his comprehensive review of postmodernist culture, for many of us this expansion of both the legitimated field of study and the 'means of dissemination' (e.g. audiovisual technologies) modifies the terms of critical engagement in such a way and to such an extent that the old contract governing the relations between readers and texts, between audiences, critics and their objects of study have to be radically redrawn. To take just one example, the postmodern pedagogy of people like Gregory Ulmer, Gavriel Salomon and Genevieve Jacquinot builds on the work, of among others, Barthes, Derrida and Walter Ong,[6] takes implosion as a starting point rather than a source of lamentation and seeks to 'provide an educational discourse for an age of video' – one which Ulmer suggests should prioritize 'a shift away from the exclusive domination of mind . . . to a mode that includes the body' (Ulmer 1985, 1989). Elsewhere, in an attempt to respond constructively to the new conditions under which signs, information, knowledges circulate today, I have argued (Hebdige 1988) that there are positive benefits to be derived from 'the splintering of the masterly overview and the totalizing aspiration' and that the cultivation of a more relaxed ('critical but credulous') disposition on the part of the critic is not incompatible with either rigour or reponsibility in an epoch characterized by Barbara Hernnstein-Smith as 'the age of value without truth-value' (Smith 1988). If the 'price paid by a powerful rationality is a terrific limitation in the object it manages to see and talk about' (G. Vattimo quoted in Chambers 1990), then the proliferation of objects and our possible relations to them and with them promised in postmodern philosophy and postmodernist critical practice might also license 'a productive blurring of the line between fiction and critique, a blurring, too, of origins and roles in such a way that no single author can lord it over the world of the text (or, it goes without saying, the text of the world)' (Hebdige 1988).

All these factors, pressures and decentring moves helped in different ways to determine the style of presentation chosen for the 'Digging' essay. I set out to suspend a 'constellation' of ideas and images of British identity in a 'textile' web of associations which would in turn, I hoped, be more flexible, more open-ended, more *dialogical*, to use Mikhail Bakhtin's term, than the conceptual frameworks generally preferred in academic or analytical work on contemporary culture. The essay was, in this way, an attempt, following Walter Benjamin's famous analogy, to 'excavate' rather than to explicate the contested ground of British cultural identity in the late 1980s via a series of competing and contingently related images and narratives of nation. Those images and narratives had to be plural enough to demonstrate that, as Bruce Ferguson puts it, 'the nation is an impossible name, an incorrigible sign', that 'repressions (are) necessary to produce a unified image' (Ferguson 1991) and that there is a cost that accrues from that repression.

This last point leads us back to the conjunctural analysis of the crisis of the Thatcherite formation with which I opened these remarks because it is somewhere here in the gap between the image, the act of utterance and the repression which makes them both possible that the essay's stylistic 'strangeness' and the substantive issue of identity (and difference) come together. To sum up: instead of laying out 'arguments' in a more or less linear fashion, the idea was to subject hegemonic constructions of 'Britishness' and 'national heritage', specifically those foregrounded in Thatcherism, to a kind of immanent critique by using anecdotes, metaphors, collage and quotation in ways that would expose to view the edgy ambivalence of the figure of the 'British edge' itself. For a moment's reflection reveals at least two opposed 'readings' of that metaphor (which is presumably why the curators chose it as a title in the first place): (1) Britain's putative 'edge' over its competitors in what were, at the time of writing in late 1987, the still burgeoning advertising, marketing and design sectors, the British 'lead' in certain areas of finance, retail and the culture industries (e.g. the British 'invasion' of American MTV in the mid-1980s); and (2) the British 'edge' as in the repressed or excluded margin, the unincorporated remainder automatically produced in exclusive definitions of nationhood and national belonging, e.g. the threatening others alluded to in Powell's 'rivers of blood' speech in 1968[7] or in Thatcher's 'enemies within' speech. To turn the metaphor one last time, it is tempting to suggest that the Thatcherite bloc, centred at the point where these two lines of antagonism intersect, was torn apart in late 1990 by spiralling inflation and interest rates and global recession which removed the first 'edge' altogether and by the Ridley–Thatcher 'wrecking' stance on 1992 which left Britain (at least the increasingly centralized province of 'little England') hanging off the edge of the new federal Europe.

NOTES

1 The ICA programme aimed to showcase innovative new work in contemporary British art and culture and included gallery installations by artists Tim Head, Hannah Collins, David Mach, Mary Kelly, Victor Burgin, Edward Allington and Narrative Architecture Today (NATO); screenings of independent film and video (including work by Derek Jarman, Sally Potter, George Barber and Isaac Julien), a series of music events at a local night club (performances by Smiley Culture, Mark Stewart and the Mafia, Wire and the Wolfgang Press) and lectures by visiting artists and critics.
2 K. Mercer in L. Grossberg *et al.* (eds) (1992) and in J. Rutherford (ed.) (1991). See also A. Gramsci (1972); E. Laclau and C. Mouffe (1985); E. Laclau (1991).
3 See P. Gilroy in L. Grossberg *et al.* (eds) (1992) for an impressive critique of the uses to which the '*trope* of race' has been put in Anglo-American cultural studies. Gilroy's essay takes a longer historical view than Mercer's and includes an examination of the metaphors of migration rooted in the experience and memory of slavery.
4 See S. Hall in L. Grossberg *et al.* (eds) (1992) for an account of these accommodations.

5 K. Mercer in L. Grossberg *et al.* (eds) (1992).
6 See C. and D. Parr (1991), G. Ulmer (1985 and 1989), G. Salomon (1981) and D. Hebdige (1991).
7 K. Mercer in L. Grossberg *et al.* (eds) (1992).

REFERENCES

Anderson, B. (1983) *Imaginary Communities*, London: Verso.
Chambers, I. (1990) *Border Dialogues*, London: Routledge.
Clifford, J. (1988) *The Predicament of Culture: Twentieth-century Ethnography, Literature and Art*, Cambridge, Mass.: Harvard University Press.
Clifford, J. and Marcus, G. (eds) (1986) *Writing Culture: The Poetics and Politics of Ethnography*, Berkeley: University of California Press.
Connor, S. (1989) *Postmodernist Culture: An Introduction to Theories of the Contemporary*, Oxford: Basil Blackwell.
Ferguson, B. (1991) 'Un-natural acts and tongue ties', in *Un-natural Traces: Contemporary Art from Canada*, London: Barbican Art Gallery.
Geertz, C. (1988) *Works and Lives: The Anthropologist as Author*, Stanford: Stanford University Press.
Gilroy, P. (1992) 'Cultural Studies and ethnic absolutism', in L. Grossberg *et al.* (eds) *Cultural Studies*, London: Routledge.
Gramsci, A. (1972) *The Prison Notebooks*, London: Lawrence & Wishart.
Grossberg, L. (1988) *It's a Sin: Essays on Postmodernism, Politics and Culture*, Sydney: Institute of Fine Art, University of Sydney.
Grossberg, L. *et al.* (eds) (1992) *Cultural Studies*, London: Routledge:
Hall, S. (1991) 'Cultural identity and diaspora', in J. Rutherford (ed.) *Identity*, London: Verso.
Hall, S. (1992) 'Cultural studies and its theoretical legacies' in L. Grossberg, op. cit.
Hall, S. and Jacques, M. (eds) *The Politics of Thatcherism*, London: Lawrence & Wishart, in conjunction with *Marxism Today*.
Hall, S. and Jacques, M. (eds) (1990) *New Times: The Changing Face of Politics in the 1990s*, London: Lawrence & Wishart, in conjunction with *Marxism Today*.
Hebdige, D. (1988) *Hiding in the Light: On Images and Things*, London: Routledge/Comedia.
Hebdige, D. (1991) 'What is soul?', in A. M. Olson *et al.* (eds) *Video Icons and Values*, Albany: State University of New York.
Laclau, E. (1991) *New Reflections on the Revolution of Our Time*, London: Verso.
Laclau, E. and Mouffe, C. (1985) *Hegemony and Socialist Strategy*, London: Verso.
Mercer, K. (1991) 'Welcome to the jungle: identity and diversity in postmodern politics', in J. Rutherford (ed.) *Identity*, London: Verso.
Mercer, K. (1992) ' "1968": periodizing postmodern politics and identity', in L. Grossberg, op. cit.

Olson, A. M. *et al.* (1991) *Video Icons and Values*, Albany: State University of New York.
Parr, C. and D. (1991) 'Afterword: beyond lamentation', in A. M. Olson, op. cit.
Rutherford, J. (ed.) (1991) *Identity*, London: Verso.
Salomon, G. (1981) *Communication and Education: Social and Psychological Interactions*, London: Sage.
Smith, B. H. (1988) 'Value without truth-value', in J. Fekete (ed.) *Life after Postmodernism*, Basingstoke: Macmillan.
Ulmer, G. (1985) *Applied Grammatology: Post(e)-Pedagogy from Jacques Derrida to Joseph Beuys*, Baltimore: Johns Hopkins University Press.
Ulmer, G. (1989) *Teletheory*, London: Routledge.

Digging for Britain:
An excavation in seven parts

Dig! Dig! Dig! And your muscles wiill grow big.
Keep on pushing in the spade!
Never mind the worms
Just ignore the squirms
And when your back aches laugh with glee
And keep on diggin'
Till we give our foes a wiggin
Dig! Dig! Dig! to Victory.
(Ministry of Food jingle to promote the 1943 Home Front
  nutritional self-sufficiency campaign, 'Digging for Victory')

. . . true, for successful excavators, a plan is needed. Yet no less
indispensable is the cautious probing of the space in the dark
loam, and it is to cheat oneself of the richest prize to preserve
as a record merely the inventory of one's own discoveries, and
not this dark joy of the place of the finding itself. Fruitless
searching is as much a part of this as succeeding, and
consequently remembrance must not proceed in the manner of
a narrative or still less that of report, but must, in the strictest
epic and rhapsodic manner, assay its spade in ever-new places,
and in the old ones delve to ever deeper layers.
(Walter Benjamin, 'A Berlin chronicle' from *One Way Street*
                                                    (1940))

To write in general terms about the 'British edge' is fraught with
risk. When words like 'nation', 'culture' and 'identity' are placed
together, historiography has a tendency to degenerate into fairy
tale and narrative; multi- and multiply contested traditions to
congeal into *the* singular 'Great Tradition': a set of lifeless
monuments authored by 'Great Men'. Walter Benjamin's metaphor of 'excavation' provides an alternative model of history
writing. His preferred methods for drawing up the stuff of
history to the surface through an attention precisely to the detail
are well known – his reasoned preference for pastiche, quotation,
aphorism over linear 'reconstructions'; his preference, too, for
'exhibiting' the relations in which particular phenomena are
embedded rather than 'explaining' their imagined origins.

Benjamin was always reluctant to subsume individual phenomena under general concepts and advocated that the writer
should cultivate a sensitivity both to the uniqueness, importance
and complexity of individual detail ('the fragment is the gateway
to the whole') and to the invisible networks of relations – what he
called the 'constellations' – in which they were embedded, drawn
together and made meaningful. He felt himself drawn irresistibly
by the incandescence of the particular, drawn back again and
again to 'this dark joy of the place of the finding itself'.

Taking Benjamin's metaphor and his method as a model in
this essay, I shall try to dig for Britain – to explore some of the
rich, heterogeneous (and contradictory) connotations surrounding terms like 'national identity', 'British culture', the 'British
edge', and by sifting through the relics that are turned up as we
cut back and forth between different geological strata, different
points in time. Some 'places' will possess a particular intensity
and power (1940: time of war; 1977: time of punk; 1987: time of
writing) – they provide the temporal co-ordinates through which
the excavation can be guided and directed. This dig has been
undertaken not as an attempt to recover some lost substantial
unity ('England, my England') – the fragments dispersed
throughout the different layers are unlikely to be parts of the
same, single object. Instead it will be conducted in the spirit of
the seance as a convocation of bits and pieces of the past (the
national past, the personal past), as a procession, first and
foremost, of images of Britain, for as Benjamin puts it:

> To articulate the past historically does not mean to recognize
> it 'the way it really was' (Ranke). It means to seize hold of a
> memory as it flashes up at a moment of danger.[1]

ENGLAND, YOUR ENGLANDS

The year 1940 was one such moment. In his essay, 'England, your
England', George Orwell sought to capture the English 'character' in a series of vivid, fragmentary insights:

> One has only to look at their methods of town-planning and
> water-supply, their obstinate clinging to everything that is out
> of date and a nuisance, a spelling system that defies analysis
> and a system of weights and measures that is intelligible only
> to the compilers of arithmetic books, to see how little they care

about mere efficiency. . . . Another English characteristic . . . is the addiction to hobbies and spare-time occupations, the *privateness* of English life. We are a nation of flower lovers . . . of stamp-collectors, pigeon-fanciers, amateur carpenters, coupon-snippers, darts-players, crossword-puzzle fans. All the culture that is most truly native centres round things which even when they are communal are not official – the pub, the football match, the back garden, the fireside and the 'nice cup of tea'. The liberty of the individual is still believed in, almost as in the nineteenth century. But this has nothing to do with economic liberty, the right to exploit others for profit. It is the liberty to have a home of your own, to do what you like in your spare time, to choose your own amusements instead of having them chosen from above . . . it is obvious, of course, that even this purely private liberty is a lost cause. Like all other modern peoples, the English are in the process of being numbered, labelled, conscripted, 'co-ordinated'. But the pull of their impulses is in the other direction, and the kind of regimentation that can be imposed on them will be modified in consequence.

(George Orwell, 'England, your England' (1940))

Orwell's passionate and controversial eulogy to the 'ordinariness' of the 'British working people' was written in the aftermath of Dunkirk, just before the bombs began to rain on Britain's cities. The portrait, even now, can strike a chord. It is conditioned by Orwell's almost palpable affection for the ordinary and the unremarkable wherever he encountered them surviving against all the odds, although the poignancy of that emotion was no doubt heightened for Orwell, writing in 1940, with the Germans apparently about to invade. Many of the defining qualities of that Britishness, more accurately that Englishness, which Orwell singles out in contrast to the cold 'realism', the mindless, mass somnabulism of the 'truly modern men, the Nazis and the Fascists'[2] could be used to trace out the eccentric contours of the 'national character' today: the 'privateness', the hobbies, the insular, parochial preoccupations. Such is the nature of national stereotypes. They are infinitely flexible forms of wishful thinking. The quest for a German or Japanese 'essence', a wild, sadistic, wayward gene 'responsible' for Auschwitz or the River Kwai is surely, we know now, futile. No such gene, no such

essence exists: those of us *Schuldig geboren*, born guilty and born
late, find it hard to place much faith in the authority of words
like 'race', in the permanence or plausibility of single definitions
of 'Destiny' or 'Nation'.

For much has changed in England in 1987 after over forty years
of imperial decay, industrial disaster, the ill-directed lurch and
stumble of a hotch-potch mixed economy, after the bungle of
Suez, the tatty dumbshow of the King's Road, and the 'swinging
sixties', after the Stones and the yuppies and the Sex Pistols, after
soccer hooliganism and the massacre at the Heysel football
stadium in 1984, above all, after eight years of Mrs Thatcher's
iron tillage, the soil of Nation and the 'British character' are
barely recognizable. The ground is still more or less the same –
Orwell would no doubt have identified the various mineral
constituents: the granite-like persistence of social class, the rock-
like insularity, the bloody-minded sticking to feet and yards and
inches when the rest of the world has long ago gone metric. But
though the ground remains the same, the landscape has
transformed: all changed . . . changed utterly.

In 1940, it was still possible in times of crisis to call up in both
senses – to enlist for national service and to interpellate as loyal
subjects of the Crown – a more or less (racially and, in the
broadest sense culturally) homogeneous 'community' of 'decent,
fair-minded' Britons.[3] (A larger 'commonwealth' was called up,
too, beyond national and racial boundaries.) A British Nation
could be forged, despite the persistence of the deepest class
divisions in the western world ('England is the most class-ridden
country under the sun' – Orwell). A community of interest could
be welded together around words like 'liberty', 'democracy',
'natural justice', around what Thomas Carlyle once called a
native 'hatred of disorder, a hatred of injustice which is the worst
disorder'.[4] This mythical but mobilizable Nation (mobilizable
indeed because mythical) – the sentimental heart of a vast
financial and commercial cartel called the British Empire – has
been replaced in the 1980s by Mrs Thatcher's vision of a
'property-owning democracy' and an 'enterprise culture', a
dream which is no more real, no more imaginary, and perhaps,
in the long run, no less politically effective than that other,
earlier, picture postcard construction of the decent, jackboot-
hating British type. Mrs Thatcher's Nation is composed of
different stuff. It is populated by a different 'People'. It is full of

early risers and hard workers who can think for themselves without big bully trades unions ('Rise early, work late, strike oil – that's the only strike worth having!' was an early 1980s Thatcher slogan). Mrs Thatcher's Nation comprises, most of all, family people mortgaged and industrious, an army of smiling shop assistants led by intrepid 'go-getters' pulled up by their bootstraps from the ranks. Its higher echelons are occupied not by 'faceless bureaucrats' or a faded, fopperish gentry but by a hard-eyed meritocracy of 'self-made businessfolk' toiling seven days a week in the burgeoning service, finance and communications sectors – a People with a portfolio of shares under its arm (this, after all, to use another Thatcher catchphrase, is 'popular capitalism') – shares acquired in the recent flotations on the stock market of formerly nationalized industries: British Telecom, North Sea Oil, British Gas, British Airways.

Against this Nation (for identities require differences) are ranked the Enemies Without and Within:[5] outside the gates, the swarthy terrorists, the PLO and IRA, the 'Argies' and the Reds; inside, sliding like an asp across Britannia's milk-white bosom, the trade unions, the agitators, the wastrels, the 'scroungers', the 'moaning minnies', the 'do-gooders' and the 'loony left', the unassimilable ethnic minorities too insignificant in number to be worth courting for a vote, the out of work 'who simply don't want to work'.

The New Albion – UK Inc. – was declared officially open for business one morning in October 1986 on the day of the so-called 'Big Bang' when, as a part of the general process of institutional overhaul, 'rationalization' and removal of controls on the free play of market forces – a process which Mrs Thatcher has recently dubbed her 'cultural revolution' – the City of London abolished the traditional demarcation between jobbers and brokers. On that day British share-dealing went 'on-line' and the stock exchange was thrown wide open to the international markets of a world *sans frontières, sans temps* – where money circulates three months in advance around commodities which may never exist in the real world but which function as signs in a game called the 'futures market'; in a placeless world of capital cities where nations exist only as currency prices, where dealers hang all day on the end of a telephone wire with one eye on the VDU of a computer terminal; in a timeless world where fortunes can be made and blipped away again in a fraction of a nanosecond.

And in the meantime, down on Planet Earth, the British bobby, that no less mythical embodiment of mild English manners, courtesy and commonsense – a figure that Orwell, himself a sometime member of the Imperial Indian Police, would certainly have recognized – has been replaced by a growing army of specially trained, highly paid, frequently armed professionals deploying in the routine policing of industrial disputes and multi-racial riots on the mainland, surveillance and crowd control techniques perfected in the war in Northern Ireland.

For nations and identities are delicate, resilient things. Neither purely organic, nor directly imposed, neither simply invented nor stumbled upon, they are substantial apparitions. And national identities especially so. They are, in essence, multiply-contested invocations, snatched attempts to solve what Patrick Wright calls the vexed 'question of historicity, of cultural authenticity and security in the face of change'.[6]

VISIONS OF THE DAUGHTERS OF ALBION
(*Spare Time* (1939))

I load the video machine with a cassette of a 1939 documentary film. (It is sometimes claimed that Britain has the highest *per capita* ownership of VCRs in the world.) The film, directed by Humphrey Jennings, is called *Spare Time*. It is permeated with the kind of openly avowed curiosity about and affection for the 'British working people' that gave so much of the documentary output of that decade from the photo-weeklies to the English journeys of Priestley and Orwell to the work of Tom Harrisson's *Mass Observation Unit*[7] its peculiar flavour – at once pungent and cloying – that unmistakable mixture of the patronizing, the heartfelt and the voyeuristic which speaks not just of *times* past but of a superseded social order – a disintegrated or at the very least severely damaged caste. All this is tempered in this particular case by Jennings's surrealist eye, the gentle, probing lyricism which makes his films so memorable.

Over footage of flickering industrial landscapes, a voice addresses the world in the clipped patrician accent which is the trademark of the films produced under the aegis of John Grierson at the Empire Marketing Board and the GPO: 'This is a film about the way people spend their spare time in three separate industries: steel, cotton and coal. Between work and sleep comes the time we call our own. What do we do with it?' Orwell's England of hobbyists, darts-players, brass-band enthusiasts, pigeon-fanciers and ballroom-dancers rolls by on a grey stream of images and old popular music. In the centre of this stream, for me at least, a stone, a startling *punctum*,[8] an interruption of the flow.

The section on cotton opens onto a dingy recreation ground flanked by the squat terraced houses typical of northern industrial towns before the war. Out of the damp, freckly fog produced through the unfortunate conjunction of the original atmospheric conditions and deteriorated film stock, a little troupe of child gazzoo-players marches grimly into frame led by a bandleader waving a short baton. The camera closes in on an adolescent boy, his long pale face bereft of any vestige of expression beyond the hideous, awkward *consciouness* of adolescence (this is long before adolescence had acquired its mystique, long before James Dean and *Catcher in the Rye*).

The boy holds up an illegible placard and our attention is directed to the baton bearer. Dressed like his charges in a tailored mock-military uniform with billowing sleeves and pinched-in cuffs made of Widow Twankey satin[9] he turns his back to the camera to oversee the raising of Albion: a little girl in a cut-down sheet wearing a miniature fireman's helmet is hoisted aloft by four stern-faced boys.

The band strikes up with 'Rule Britannia'. The little symbol stands for a moment facing the camera, wobbling slightly on her boards, Britannia's shield (a round cake-tin lid with a Union Jack painted on it) on one arm, an aluminium foil trident in the other. A row of dark chimney pots frame her burnished head as a flag flaps softly in the foreground and the conductor's arms wave off and into the opening bars of the battle hymn with the crisp, fluttering movements popularized by Geraldo, Joe Loss and all the other 1930s danceband leaders. A tiny tot – younger than the others – the band mascot? – grimaces at the camera, her satin cap cocked at a cute angle like Shirley Temple on *The Good Ship Lollipop*. The gazzoos pipe out the marching song of the British Empire: 'Rule Britannia'.

Played as the composer no doubt intended it to be played by a military brass band, the song is redolent of stone lions and solemn state occasions. It is a paean to the indomitable British

spirit. It celebrates the fierce defence of individual liberty con-
jured up by Magna Carta enshrined (or so the story goes) in
British law. Its lyrics commemorate 900 years of freedom from
foreign dictatorships ('Britons never, never, never shall be
slaves'); the bullish, bulldoggish (soon to be Churchillian)
independence of a rugged island race. It reiterates the pledge to
retain naval supremacy at all costs: 'Britannia rules the waves.'

All this pomp and circumstance, all this history made suddenly bizarre, domesticated, brought down to size by a group of
children blowing in unison into the manufactured equivalent of
a tissue paper and comb. With grave inscrutable expressions, a
row of girls, swaying slightly in time to the music, blow little
trills at the end of each line (at one point 'Rule Britannia'
threatens to merge imperceptibly with the old music hall favourite, 'I'm forever blowing bubbles'). With the gravity born of
concentration, the children are decorating, embellishing the
original tune. They are 'yiddling' – jazzing up the authorized
version. The gazzoo band are embroidering their own gaudy
motifs on the red, white and blue – motifs woven out of the
bandleader's imagination, but derived in essence from Hollywood, from Busby Berkeley musicals, from photographs of
American marching bands, from the stylistic flourishes of American popular songs, from the group dynamics of *Snow White and
the Seven Dwarfs*. The New Jerusalem is here proclaimed among
England's dark satanic mills in warbling glissandos by a shining
host of pinched-faced Seraphim. The Countenance Divine which
shines forth upon the assembled throng from behind the bandleader's shoulder is – unmistakably – Walt Disney's.

The original motivation for this patriotic display – a motivation which is anyway obscured by the English drizzle, by the
blank delivery and the deadpan expressions, by the passage of
time and the images blurred by that passage – doesn't really
matter. The question of a satirical intention as far as Humphrey
Jennings is concerned is neither here nor there (though we can
surely discount such an intention on the part of the band itself).
The solemn observance of Empire Day in the schools even of my
childhood in the 1950s, and the provenance of the 'organized
youth', the patriotic aftermath of the British forces' derring-do at
Mafeking and Bloemfontein,[10] would seem to indicate that this is
a straightforward affirmation of loyalty to the Crown; an oath of
fealty, albeit one expressed in the 'Americanized' accent so typical

of a certain kind of British popular culture then as now). The intention is obscure, perhaps irrelevant.

But the kitsch – of course – the pathos make us smile. Fifty years on, the performance evokes a 'tender feeling'.[11] We are moved by the campy contrast between what we see and what we hear, between all that visible effort (the uniforms, the military postures, the needle-browed concentration) and what it actually achieves – the funny strangulated noise that crackles on the soundtrack. We are moved by the sad-sweet innocence, the quaintness of which is compounded by age – by *our* age (these grave little children), by the age in which we live (these ancient children) in a cotton town before the war, before Hiroshima, before the ignominious bundling off the stage of history of the straight-backed British Empire, before the 'birth of the teenager' and the final death-throes of King Cotton before, above all, the treachery of video (treacherous this taking out of time of the original event, the original film watched at a distance on my Japanese Sony TV, paused, re-viewed on fast-forward fifty years on in the middle of the 1980s and another recession).

Whatever the intention, a transformation has none the less occurred.

In this casual comedy, the monarch too has resigned his part.
He, too, has been changed in his turn.
All changed, changed utterly.
A terrible beauty is born:
His Majesty, King George VI is wearing Mickey Mouse ears.[12]

AUGURIES OF INNOCENCE (sounding out new Britains)

Albion: Britain (Pliny) from Latin: *albus* white, the allusion being to the white cliffs of Dover.

Keep our Empire undismembered
Guide our Forces by Thy Hand,
Gallant blacks from far Jamaica,
Honduras and Togoland;
Protect them Lord in all their fights,
And, even more, protect the whites.

Think of what our Nation stands for,
Books from Boots and country lanes,

Free speech, free passes, class distinction
Democracy and proper drains.
Lord, put beneath Thy special care
One-eighty-nine Cadogan Square.
(John Betjeman, 'In Westminster Abbey' (1940))

I have spoken all the while of 'the nation', 'England', as
though 45 million souls could somehow be treated as a unit.
But is not England notoriously two nations, the rich and the
poor? Dare one pretend that there is anything in common
between people with 100,000 pounds a year and people with
one pound a week? And even Welsh and Scottish readers are
likely to have been offended because I have used the word
'England' more often than 'Britain', as though the whole
population dwelled in London and the Home Counties and
neither north nor west possessed a culture of its own. . . . A
Scotsman, for instance, does not thank you if you call him an
Englishman. You can see the hesitation we feel on this point
by the fact that we call our islands by no less than six different
names: England, Britain, Great Britain, the British Isles, the
United Kingdom and, in very exalted moments, Albion.'
(George Orwell, 'England, your England' (1940))

Those whom the gods wish to destroy they first make mad. We
must be mad, literally mad, to be permitting the annual
inflow of some 50,000 dependents, who are for the most part
the material of the future growth of the immigrant-descended
population. It is like watching a nation busily engaged in
heaping up its own funeral pyre. So insane are we that we
actually permit unmarried persons to immigrate for the
purpose of founding a family with spouses and fiancées whom
they have never seen. As I look ahead, I am filled with
foreboding. Like the Roman, I seem to see 'the River Tiber
foaming with much blood'. That tragic and intractable phenomenon which we watch with horror on the other side of the
Atlantic, but which there is interwoven with the history and
existence of the States itself, is coming upon us here by our
own volition and neglect.
(Enoch Powell, Birmingham address, 20 April 1968)

The West Indian or Asian does not by being born in England

become an Englishman. In law he is a United Kingdom
citizen, by birth in fact he is a West Indian or Asian still.

(Enoch Powell, speech to the London Rotary Club,
Eastbourne, November 1968)

The question mark which hangs over the 'united' in United
Kingdom has been highlighted in the post-war period through
that process of entropy which Tom Nairn has dubbed 'the break-
up of Britain'. In Nairn's account, the dominance of England
(the 'incubator of capitalism') – of English rule and Westminster
– within the British Isles has been challenged by the emergence in
the 1970s of Welsh and Scottish nationalism (in the latter case
fuelled, by North Sea oil), by the deliberate accentuation of Celtic
'differentiae' and the resuscitation of the formerly 'dead' or
'dying' Gaelic languages, by the 'Troubles' in Northern Ireland,
and the controversy surrounding Britain's membership of the
European community.[13]

In the ten years or so since Nairn's book was first published,
the stark division between the prosperous south and the
deindustrialized, impoverished north – made most bitterly apparent in the year-long miners' strikes – has been stretched and
deepened into a gulf during the Thatcher years. And Enoch
Powell's brooding rhetoric condemning the 'betrayal of the
nation' by Westminster, the 'swamping' of British singularity by
successive waves of alien (i.e. non-European) immigration
threads darkly underneath the public discourse of national
decline – a stream of oratory 'flowing like the Tiber with much
blood', it soaks through to the surface of the speeches made on
the appropriate occasions – in the wake of a riot, on the eve of an
election – by right-minded politicians to colour their pronouncements on the 'crisis', 'national identity', endangered 'birthright'.

But there are, of course, other stories, other histories. On the
other side of the imperialist imaginary, beyond the nostalgia for
the stable and the fixed, new identities, new communities are
being formed which can't be reduced to the old frameworks of
class or returned to the social and ideological locations guaranteed by traditional party politics in Britain.

'The place of the finding itself' can be quite to one side of the
centre, in an overlooked corner or right beneath our feet in, for
instance, the domain of the 'trivial' and the 'popular'.

To strike the spade again into some already well-turned soil, punk has often been cited as a terminus or starting point in chronological accounts of the relationship between post-war British popular music, popular culture and design. The auguries – the visual and aural 'noise' that signalled punk's arrival – have been interpreted and reinterpreted. They have been 'read' as a direct reflection or expression of adolescent anomie, unemployment, 'identity crisis' (dole queue rock); as symptoms of a further decline in traditional familial values, a collapse of social, sexual and sartorial norms, as prognostics of the 'death of meaning' or the 'waning of affect' (Fredric Jameson); as evidence of the art school's influence on the British pop scene (Simon Frith), as an ironic commentary on the rhetoric of crisis (clothes for Britain to go down the drain in – what Phil Cohen calls 'Storm and Dress Theory'), as a deconstruction of the languages of rock and teen rebellion (Dave Laing), as critical modernism for the masses (Greil Marcus, Iain Chambers), as the inspired creation – through bricolage, parody and dreamwork – of a cohort of entrepreneurs, musicians, designers and stylists, as a disaffected 'subculture's' 'resistance' to the lies of consensus politics (Dick Hebdige).[14] On the one hand the lyrics and the looks of punk music and fashions topicalized the themes of 'youth unemployment', 'urban crisis', 'national decline' – themes which were generalized as the recession deepened during the next decade, especially when the pressure points in the inner cities erupted in the youth riots of 1981 and 1985. On the other hand, punk's visual and musical hyperboles helped to boost the British textile and design industries, put Britain (or at least London) back on the international fashion map, led to a (temporary) boom in independent record production and marked the beginning of a long-term (re)visualization of popular music which spread from poster and record sleeve design to the massive investment in video promotions which was to pave the way for the 'second British invasion' of the US charts after MTV was set up in the early 1980s.

But punk also inaugurated in earnest the long retreat from the phallocentric codes of 'cock rock'[15] and the rediscovery of other (more or less marginalized) musics – bebop, cool jazz, swing, r & b, salsa, reggae, funk, blues and the 1940s/1950s 'torch singing'. It marked the beginning of a long-term questioning of the mythologies of technique, originality, genre boundaries and authorship in pop and rock which was eventually to lead to the invention of new musics – electro pop, MC reggae, rap, jazz funk, etc. These new or transfigured musical languages have been used by performers and 'fans' alike to contest the given constructions of masculinity and femininity available within the wider culture and to articulate less monotonously phallic and/or heterosexual structures of desire (e.g. the music and performance styles of the Slits, the Au Pairs, Carmen, Sade, Alison Moyet, Culture Club, Bronski Beat, and the Communards, Frankie Goes to Hollywood, the Smiths).

A moratorium was also held in British punk on questions of race, ethnicity, nation. Not only did this involve refusals of the ideal of a *united* nation in songs like 'White Riot' (the Clash) and 'Anarchy in the UK' (the Sex Pistols) and the negative 'white noise' of hardcore and later Oi (early 1980s neo-skinhead 'music'). There were also attempts actively to erode internal racial – ethnic divisions in Britain and within the punk movement itself, both through explicit interventions like Rock against Racism (RAR) and Two Tone and through the creation of hybrid musics which integrated or spliced together black and white musical forms. RAR – set up by music journalists, designers, performers, record business personnel – together with the Anti-Nazi League – a broad, non-aligned pressure group headed by political, sports and showbusiness figures – set out to mobilize a popular front against the threatened resurgence in the late 1970s of racist political parties like the National Front (NF). Using the demotic forms of the rock concert, the poster, the magazine (*Temporary Hoarding*) and the slogan (e.g. NF = No Fun), RAR activists sought to shift the emergent structure of feeling inscribed within punk away from the nihilism and racism of some elements in punk itself towards the left-libertarian multiculturalism which was being simultaneously promoted by the *New Musical Express* – at that time Britain's leading music paper.[16]

Less overtly 'political' and interventionist in tone, less didactic in character, Two Tone was a loose confederation of music groups (the Specials, the Beat, the Selector, Madness) from diverse racial–ethnic backgrounds, who set out to produce a fusion of white (punk) and black (reggae) British musical traditions by developing a contemporary version of 1960s Jamaican ska (a forerunner of reggae). This transmogrified ska – more congenial, accessible and easily danced to than punk, less exclusive, separatist and turned in upon itself than 'heavy' roots reggae –

provided a vehicle designed literally to move the audience through dance into a new kind of British territory, a new multicultural space, an organic bonding of signs and bodies. Here through the forging of a series of formal and informal, aesthetic and experiential 'fits', an affective alliance was offered as the ground on which organic solidarity could develop between disaffected black and white youths – a solidarity, the authenticity of which was guaranteed by the 'rootedness' of the Two Tone musicians themselves in the Ghost Town of the inner city.

This forging of affective alliances through the invocation of a specific mix of signs and rhythms has always functioned as a vital strategy within black music creating, as Paul Gilroy has forcefully argued,[17] a diasporan identity among the black urban dispossessed, an identity which can be mobilized to abolish geographical distances and the systematic mystification of a shared history and common interests. In Britain, from the 1960s onwards, reggae music, transmitted through channels embedded deep in the black community, has offered a powerful bass line against 'Babylon pressure'. The sound systems – the mobile reggae discos with their own deejays, emcees ('microphone chanters'), their 'specials' and 'dub plates' (specially recorded rhythms 'owned' by the system), their own local followings – are networks of live wires and speakers. They call up (assemble and service) particular 'communities' wherever they are plugged in and played. Hip hop, funk and 'wild style' have functioned in a similar way in the 1980s. These forms and the cultural and commercial institutions which support them have worked to forge a community beyond the constricting 'arboreal' logic of race and 'roots'.[18]

The affective alliances created through rap and hip hop – through what might sound on first hearing like a deconstructed (schizophrenic/schizogenic) collage of broken, stuttering and fragmented noise binds together black and white youths historically and geographically dispersed, dispossessed, divided against each other as the modern western empires implode into their metropolitan centres, Afrika Bambaata's Zulu Nation (a British chapter was formed in 1984 under the auspices of MC Spyrock at WLR, a London pirate radio station) is rapped up in a tradition which valorizes verbal and physical dexterity and which is, according to Bambaata and James Brown[19] overtly pledged to the sublimation of fight into dance, of conflict into contest, of desperation into style and a sense of self-respect. The definite contours of race – the topography of skin – begins to be rubbed away in the mosaic – musics and found sounds of Banbaata who dissolves continents and categories as he mixes punk with funk, a snatch of a Monkees' melody with a quote from Beethoven, a Keith Richards' guitar riff, the theme from *The Munsters* or *The Pink Panther* centring these sounds around a solid bass line laid down originally by Chic, the US disco band.[20] The earthbound logic of 'national' and 'ethnic' cultures is further disordered by the tape-deck tourism of Malcom McLaren who fuses opera and rap, Zulu, Latin and Burundi rhythms of Appalachian hillbilly music. As rhythms, melodies and harmonies are borrowed, worked with, quoted and returned to the air waves new connections are made, new 'communités' made possible both within and beyond the confines of race and nation.

Now with that fusion of Indian and Pakistani folk forms and western popular music sometimes referred to as 'Indi pop', a novel British – Asian (more accurately British – South Asian) cultural identity has begun to form and find its voice – an identity uniquely adapted to local conditions, attuned to the diverse, often conflicting experiences of parents who emigrated from the subcontinent and from Kenya and Uganda in the 1960s and their children born and brought up in Britain. The answer once again is in the mix – the blend in Bangra music of Punjabi rhythms, the electronic instrumentation and production values of the western popular music industry and performance styles gleaned partly from domestic video viewings of imported Indian musicals, partly from the onstage poses of western 'stars' like Boy George, Madonna, Elvis Presley. Bangra and Indi pop, the vibrant trademark of a growing number of second generation British Asians, is played across the gaps and tensions not just between the 'home' and the 'host culture', with their different languages, behavioural norms, belief systems and cuisines, not just between *two* cultures (the 'traditional' east, the 'permissive' or 'progressive' west) but between many *different* South Asian cultures, between the multiple boundaries which for centuries have marked off different religions, castes, ethnic traditions within a 'community' which appears deceptively homogeneous only when viewed from the outside.

If, as Prabhu Guptara has recently put it, the place called 'India' is a British creation, if 'Kashmir in the north, Kerela in the south, Gujarat in the west, and Mizoram in the east have nothing in common except that they were all conquered by the British at some stage and made independent together',[21] if the concept of 'nation' seems meaningless when applied to a vast expanse of territory whose people, according to the last census, speak more than a thousand different languages, then a new pan-Asian/British community is being brought together *in the face of* the increasingly racist proscriptions which have motivated official definitions of British citizenship and British culture for centuries – explicitly so since the 1960s when Enoch Powell made his ominous intervention in the politics of race in Britain – proscriptions which have found their way directly onto the statute book in the form of racist legislation like the Nationality Act of 1981.

As Tamil refugees strip in protest at the threat of deportation on the tarmac at Heathrow Airport, as visa restrictions determine entry to Britain on the grounds of race and consign black and brown peoples to second-class status within the Commonwealth, as Bengali residents are subjected to routine racist attacks on the streets and housing estates of east London and Bradford, a brighter blurring of the old divisive ethnic and religious lines which set, for instance, Muslim against Hindu, Hindu against Sikh, seems about to occur in the dancehalls and ballrooms of Britain's cities hired out for Bangra nights by Asian promoters and attended by contingents from most of the major 'Asian' communities now established in Britain. Another new territory is opened up here: a positive assertion of another non-white *British* presence.

The miscegenation of sounds and images originating in quite separate ethnic contexts heralds the emergence, then, of new native styles, incipient social identities. In the mid-1980s, in fast style reggae (reggae's response to the call of black American rap), a new generation of young black British MCs like Smiley Culture, Lady Di, Lorna Gee and Tipper Irie began talking their way beyond 'Africa' and the retrospective destiny of Rasta into a new British space, affirming hybrid identities formed out of the conjunction of Caribbean and indigenous traditions, forms and idioms. In Smiley Culture's 'Cockney Translation' (1984), for instance, the dense and overgrown interiors, the echoing spaces and weird effects of dub reggae have been flattened down beneath the light, tight beat pushed out by a drum machine. Over this rhythm punctuated by gleeful snatches of brass, Smiley Culture

(David Emmanuel) reels off the rap, alternating lines of cockney rhyming patter and Caribbean patois, exchanging identities like masks:

> 11,10,9,8,7,6,5,4,3,2,1
> It's Smiley Culture with the mike in a me hand
> Me come to teach you right and not the wrong
> In a de Cockney translation.
>
> Cockney have names like Terry, Arthur and Del-Boy
> We have names like Winston, Lloyd and Leroy,
> We bawl out YOW! While cockneys say Oi!
> What Cockney calla Jacks, we call a Blue Bwoy
> Say Cockney have mates while we have spar
> Cockney live in a drum while we live in a yard
> Rope chain and choparita me say cockney call tom
> Say cockney say Old Bill, We say dutty Babylon
> In a de cockney translation
> In a de cockney traslation.[22]

For young blacks in Britain in the wake of the riots in Brixton and at Broadwater Farm, liable to negative coverage in the press and on TV (where they figure predominantly as victims, culprits, unemployment figures, 'immigration' figures), subject to aggressive and intensive policing, such a blatant assertion of the rights to be a black Londoner, to be both black and British have political bite – this is an identity traced out along a special jagged kind of 'British edge'.

The 'casual' style of dress which since the early to mid 1980s has functioned as a uniform for 'streetwise' inner city youth of whatever ethnic origin represents a similar appropriation – this time of the signs of 'quality', 'distinction', (international) 'class'. The various combinations of expensive designer label sportswear (Sergio Tacchini tracksuits, Adidas running shoes, Lacoste and Christian Dior shirts, etc.) are at once a repudiation of the rhetoric of wasted youth and of subcultural 'costume' for 'good, (classical) clothes'. The casual fashions euphemize the joblessness or irregular employment by converting 'casual' work in the 'black economy' into a comfortable and affluent 'casual *style*'. They swap enforced 'idleness' for a 'life of leisure'. The casual style asserts the right to be relaxed, at *home* on Britain's windy streets instead of yearning back to an imaginary homeland in

Africa, the Caribbean, India, Pakistan, Cyprus, 'Albion'. The casual look displaces attention away from the question of ethnic origin onto the question of how to build affinities on a shared cultural and aesthetic ground. It is focused on a set of common preferences rooted in the experience of the contemporary realities of city life. A community of taste can thus be formed that smudges ethnic lines. In the culture of the 'casuals' of the British (or is it just the English?) inner city in the 1980s, the question of roots and 'breeding' – of where a person 'comes from' – fades into insignificance before the altogether more *soluble* question of the pedigree of his or her clothes . . . (designer label roots).

This is the generation which in the different (though by no means unrelated) institutional sites of independent film and video production – funded by organizations like the British Film Institute, Channel 4 and the left-led inner city education authorities – is finding a distinctive voice and vision for black Britons – a vision and a voice which challenge the established fixings of both 'black politics' and 'black film'. Young black intellectuals working together in the new film and video collectives (e.g. SANKOFA, CEDDO, the Black Audiovisual Collective) are disrupting the image-flow, smudging the line which separates the two dominant image strands of the black communities which are relayed through the British press and TV – troublesome blacks (the riots) and fun-loving blacks (the grinning dance of carnival). In films like *Handsworth Song* and *Territories*, the film-makers use everything at their disposal – the words of Fanon, Foucault, C.L.R. James, TV news footage, didactic voice-over, interviews and found sound, the dislocated ghostly echoes of dub reggae, the scattergun of rap – in order to assert the fact of difference, to articulate new relations to the body, subjectivity, politics, to make fresh connections between another set of bodies, another set of histories – to open up the 'territories of race . . . of class . . . or sexuality'.[23] Deconstruction here takes a different turn as it moves outside the gallery, the academy, the library to mobilize the *crucial* forms of lived experience and resistance embedded in the streets, the shops and clubs of urban life. Deconstruction here is *used* publicly to cut across the categories of 'body' and 'critique', the 'intellectual' and the 'masses', 'Them' and 'Us' – to bring into being a new eroticized body of critique, a sensuous and pointed logic – and to bring it to *bear* on the situation, to make the crisis *speak*.

> Curses, says the Proverb, are like chickens, they return always home.
>
> (Thomas Carlyle, 'The Irish', 1839)

For the British Empire has folded in upon itself and the chickens have come home. And as the pressure in the cities continues to mount, the old unities have shattered: the ideal of a national culture transcending its regional components and of a racially proscribed 'British' identity consistent and unchanging from one decade to the next – these fantasies have started cracking at the seams. More and more people are growing up feeling, to use Colin MacInnes's phrase, 'english half-english'.

> There's no such thing as 'England' any more . . . welcome to India brothers! This is the Caribbean! . . . Nigeria! . . . There is no England, man. This is what is coming. Balsall Heath is the centre of the melting pot, 'cos all I ever see when I go out is half-Arab, half-Pakistani, half-Jamaican, half-Scottish, half-Irish, I know 'cos I am (half Scottish/half Irish) . . . who am I? . . .Tell me who do I belong to? They criticize me, the good old England. Alright, where do I belong? You know I was brought up with blacks, Pakistanis, Africans, Asians, everything, you name it . . . who do I belong to? . . . I'm just a broad person. The earth is mine . . . you know we was not born in Jamaica . . . we was not born in 'England'. We were born here, man. It's our right. That's the way I see it. That's the way I deal with it.
>
> (Jo Jo, a white reggae fan, interviewed in Birmingham's Balsall Heath, one of the oldest areas of black settlement in Britain)[24]

AMERICA A PROPHECY (Levi Jeans, Coca Cola, Men from Mars)

I switch from video to broadcast TV: on *Dallas*, JR is about to be shot in the back. Later on I might catch an episode of *Hill Street Blues* or *St Elsewhere*, a news item on Irangate or the sudden death of Andy Warhol, or a situation comedy like *Cheers* or *Taxi*.

It was estimated as long ago as 1973 that 50 per cent of the world's screen time was taken up with American films, and that American-made programmes accounted for more than 20 per cent of total TV transmission time in western Europe; that

20–25 per cent of British manufacturing output was American controlled and that eight of the leading advertising agencies in the UK were owned by American companies.[25] Developments in broadcasting in the last fifteen years – developments which range from deregulation and the privatization of national TV networks to the rise of cable and satellite technologies and the growth of multinational communication conglomerates – have undoubtedly led to increased American penetration of international image markets (though the Japanese are beginning to fight back, apparently, with cartoons pitched at south east Asian markets). In 1982, Mattelart, Mattelart and Delcourt (1986) estimated that over 80 per cent of all imported programmes shown on Italian TV were American, that the distribution of Latin American films had actually declined in Spanish-speaking countries since the 1970s, that 61 per cent of the feature films programmed on Spanish TV were American in origin, that between 1975 and 1980 Britain lost half its internal market in film to US-based companies and that national production fell from 41 to 20 per cent.[26] A brief boom in mainstream British film production in the early 1980s was halted due to a lack of adequate capitalization, and the removal by the Chancellor of a 'favourable tax environment' for the industry. As a result, another cohort of British film-makers have 'defected' to Hollywood.

The shared language, the strategic links and military commitments within the NATO alliance and the common cultural and historical heritage binding Britain to the States seem likely further to accentuate these trends in future years. In 1986 the spacious, centrally located, newly opened Boilerhouse Gallery in the Victoria and Albert Museum in South Kensington was given over to an exhibition (sponsored by the Conran Foundation) celebrating a hundred years of Coca Cola entitled *Coca Cola: Designing a Megabrand*.

I switch to Channel 4 and tune in to an old *Twilight Zone* double bill. The first *Twilight Zone* story concerns a man who travels back and forth in time. . . .

There is a break for ads. The gleaming flank of a chrome-encrusted car glides up to the entrance of a 'typical' age-of-affluence US laundromat as Marvin Gaye's voice opens out into the refrain from the mid-1960s Motown hit, 'I Heard it through the Grapevine'. We are back in the pastiche (timeless) 1950s of the latest string of Levi TV ads made for the British style and fashion-conscious *Face*-reading market(s) where, in the Old Edward Hopper Laundromat on 501 Street, a 1980s hunk with a Tony Curtis hairstyle (Nick Kamen, model-turned-pop-star-pin-up) strips off his T shirt and his jeans before placing them in a 'classical' front-loading washing machine (baring his boxer shorts in the process), and sitting down in a nonchalant narcissistic daze on the laundromat bench alongside a cast of 1950s 'American' stereotypes who could serve as stand-ins for the figures in a Duane Hanson exhibition (giggling pony-tailed bobby-soxers, chewing fat guy with hamburger, mortified blue stocking with glasses, etc.).

The Levi logo fades and we are back into the second story from the *Twilight Zone*. In this episode a three-armed martian, a scout for an invading force, is prevented from taking over a small American town by the owner of a soda fountain who removes his cap in the final shot to reveal a third eye in the middle of his forehead – Venus has already invaded.

THE PROVERBS OF HELL (British designers on design)

> Without Contraries there is no progression. Attraction and Repulsion, Reason and Energy, Love and Hate, are necessary to Human existence.
>
> From these contraries spring what the religious call Good and Evil. Good is the passive that obeys Reason. Evil is the active spring from Energy.
>
> Good is Heaven. Evil is Hell.
>
> As I was walking among the fires of hell, delighted with the enjoyments of Genius; which to Angels look like torment and insanity, I collected some of their Proverbs: thinking that as the sayings used in a nation mark its character, so the Proverbs of Hell, shew the nature of Infernal wisdom.
>
> (William Blake, *The Marriage of Heaven and Hell* (1793))

The Proverbs[27]

> 'If people can't make a stand, they can at least wear one.'
> (Katherine Hamnett, fashion designer, on her designer-slogan
> T shirts)

> 'Destroy, Disorder and Disorientate.'

(The 3D label of fashion designers John Richmond and Marie
Cornejo. The woven labels also include quotes from the work
of the Italian Marxist theorist, Antonio Gramsci)

'Cash from Chaos.'
(Malcolm McLaren, sound designer, concept and product
packager (1979))

'What's interesting about England right now is that there's a
definite movement to get involved with the Third World: to
wear an African dress, and put it with a Dominican hat, throw
in some Peruvian beads and wear make-up like one of the
tribes in New Guinea – simply because we have to go even
further to demonstrate that we want to get out of this island
mentality, this village we live in, and relate ourselves to those
taboos and magical things we believe we've lost'
(Malcolm McLaren, interviewed in *The Face* (1983))

'You can't touch the foundation of the Establishment. It
changes its clothes as fast as you can cut them up. If you are a
radical, it's only a matter of time before you are automatically
accepted – that's provided you don't go bankrupt.'
(Neville Brody, typographer, graphic artist record sleeve and
magazine designer (1986)

'We have put together a design environment for Duran Duran.
. . . To us Duran Duran are ICI or Kodak.'
(Malcolm Garrett of Assorted Images, record sleeve designer
(1985))

'Barbie takes a trip round nature's cosmic curves.'
(Title of the 1985 fashion collection of Bodymap (Steve
Stewart and David Hollah), with textiles based on computer
graphics courtesy of Hilde Smith, self-styled 'surface-pattern
designer'.)

. . . sometimes it's just tacky parody.'
(Vivienne Westwood, fashion designer, on 'Street Fashion')

'although it's a Fourth-World economy, it's a first-rate
culture.'
(Daniel Weill, 'product' designer, on Britain (1986))

JERUSALEM: EMANATIONS OF THE GIANT ALBION
(Of Piracy and Jungloid Roots)

> Tyger, Tyger burning bright
> In the forest of the night;
> What immortal hand or eye,
> Could frame thy fearful symmetry?
>
> When the stars threw down their spears
> And water'd heaven with their tears;
> Did he smile his work to see?
> Did he who made the Lamb make thee?
> (William Blake, 'The Tyger' (1794))

The British edge is in fashion, in record work, it's not in fine art, it's not in film. British film hasn't progressed in the last twenty years. If they change the formula it doesn't sell. The British edge is in TV commercials and pop videos – in the really upmarket promos for established acts and the really cheap ones where they go for maximum impact with special effects and animation. The Americans come back now and then with a killer. They've got exceptional talent there but it's in smaller numbers than in Britain. Design is run like a business there and they do know how to run it. It's not like that in Britain. Design is not what I'd call an adult business over here. It's not taken seriously. But the standards are higher here than in the States, the general level of the work, the energy, the ideas, the willingness to risk. I honestly believe you could group a pile of (design) people together in London and they would kill anybody.

> (Dave Richardson, founder of
> Shoot That Tiger design agency)

In 1982, Margaret Thatcher presided over a series of seminars held at Downing Street devoted to the subject of British design. Four years later, for the first time in British business history, a handful of the largest design practices went public on the stock market. Interior designers Sir Terence Conran and Rodney Fitch; the advertising magnates, Saatchi and Saatchi, and the fashion designer, Stephen Marks, are now among the hundred richest people in the UK, beneficiaries in large part of the decade-long retail boom for which they are also partially – directly or indirectly – responsible.[28] The phenomenal growth rates enjoyed by these companies (a symptom of the 1980s 'takeover fever' that has gripped the business community from New York to London, from Boessky to Sanders) may or may not be reliable indicators of the long-term financial viability of large-scale design practices in Britain. We can only wait and see. But as the vaunted transformation of the British high street proceeds apace, there are signs of a slight faltering of momentum – the queue of mega-clients is shortening as the corporate giants and nationwide chain stores receive their total image overhauls. Growth at the top end can also lead to the imposition of monolithic house-styles which stifle diversity. All too often the packaging of product lines descends into designer cliché. All too often the 'revolution' in shop interiors means the installation of standardized fittings: the creation of the 'Americanized' postmodern space that Jameson describes in which consumers drift like the zombies in George Romero's *Dawn of the Dead* from atrium through galleria to the shop-within-a-shop. The refurbished Debenhams in London's Oxford Street or the recently opened Dôme cocktail bar in Islington could be sited in any capital city anywhere in the western world. The effacement of regional *differentiae* beneath the hyper-deluxe chic which has become synonymous in some quarters with the very word 'design' forms part of that englobement of the real by uniform 'solutions' underpinned by uniform exchange values, part of the urgent onward march of commodification into every corner of civil society which Marx discerned a century ago as he sat in the British Museum in the heart of London writing *Capital*.

But 'development' itself is fraught with contradictions. It can meander as it marches and – once again – in British design it is in the margins not the mainstreams, in the 'ephemeral' areas of graphics, fashion, music and video production, the experimental work in interiors, in the product prototypes and Heath Robinson-like follies of subindustrial design that the crucial 'edge' in British design culture is most startlingly encountered.

In the years at least since punk there is in the more vivid output of the smaller studios a shared reliance in the design process on intuition, serendipity, obsession, a parody of 'English' empirical method – a working-out from the material rather than working-down from some pre-given master plan. From Vivienne

Westwood's Appalachian Buffalo Girl fashions, her outlaw, pirate and witch couture, to Jamie Reid's situationist-inspired graphics, from Hilde Smith's computer-simulating textile designs to Neville Brody's trademark typefaces and Nigel Coates's dream-like 'narrative' interiors, from the 'Mad Max of product design' (Ron Arad) to the 'King of the Cubist kitchen conversation' (Michael Graves) we find the same blurring of the lines between genres and categories, high and low forms, fine art and popular culture, pure and applied arts, the same questioning of the functions and formulas of design, the same impatience with fixity, with the established wisdoms and certainties of art and design lore. And always there is an absence of straight lines linking cause to effect: the logic of catastrophe and surprise is everywhere paramount. On the pages of stylezines like *The Face* and *I-D*, the 'laws' of layout and 'good' typography are laid waste as grids are abandoned, as colour bars and registration marks – the invisible 'backstage' tools of conventional design practice – are brought forward and incorporated into the final design, as photographs are stretched and blurred and 'swished' across the glass of the photocopy machine, as incommensurable typefaces are mixed and new, scarcely legible ones invented. In the clothes of Westwood and Bodymap, classical scale and structure are collapsed into outlandish asymmetrical shapes. The rules of couture and modernist functionalism are systematically broken as holes and gashes interrupt the 'line', as silks and man-made fibres fight it out on the happy battlefield of the restructured body. In the record sleeve designs of the late Barney Bubbles, and of the newer studios – XL, Assorted iMaGes, Shoot That Tiger, Town & Country Planning – every available image source is raided from the authorized histories of art and design to comic books and car manual illustrations, from Renaissance perspective to the grotesque, from the Bauhaus to Walt Disney, from Rodchenko and Lissitsky to de Stijl, from Spencer's *Pioneers of Modern Typography* to socialist realism to Hollywood and beyond.

The vision is hallucinogenic and excessive. Disturbingly, there is plenty of evidence of formal education of one kind or another, evidence of what the French sociologist, Pierre Bourdieu, calls 'cultural capital', but there is nothing scholarly or bookish about the way this knowledge is held and deployed. In fact there is something decidedly unhinged about it. Britannia here appears as a psychotic baglady shuffling through a ruined city muttering to herself, her bags stuffed with old books, rusting heirlooms, priceless paintings.

The British edge is 'ex-centric' in a very 'English' way. It is quite unlike its Milanese equivalent. The genius of Italian design stems from the ease of access enjoyed by Italian designers to what is, perhaps, the richest visual heritage in western Europe, from a culture steeped in a tradition of 'extravagant' expenditure and overt displays of solvency that goes back to the Medicis if not to Imperial Rome. ('Italy . . . (has) . . . a different mentality, as a country, it's used to a weak currency and that's encouraged the idea that money should be spent and enjoyed': Lynne Wilson, British designer resident in Milan.[29]) Italian designers can draw on a vast reserve of artisanal and craft skills which have survived into the late twentieth centuty because industrialization in Italy came comparatively late and because, outside the major cities, large-scale industrial production is only precariously established and has left the infrastructure of small craft workshops relatively untouched. (When Bertolucci sought to recreate the Emperor's palace in Peking for his recent film *The Last Emperor* he had to fly in the craftsmen from Florence and Sienna to do the necessary restorations because the appropriate native skills and specialist knowledge had been wiped out during the Cultural Revolution.)

No such advantages are there to be exploited by the designer working in Britain, the land of Oliver Cromwell, Samuel Arkwright, James Watt and the 'threadbare ethic'[30] where the early lead in industrial output effectively destroyed the craft base (the post 1960s Anglo-craft 'revival' is still tinged with a nostalgia for the rustic and the anti-urban which has roots stretching back via the ruralistic painters and the hippies to Cobbett and Constable). And in Britain the designer has to contend with the obdurate lingering residues of an Anglo-Saxon puritanism that can still dictate that furniture for instance, should come thirty-seventh in the list of the average English person's spending priorities.[31] So NATO (Narrative Architecture Today) and Ron Arad are not like Memphis, the Italian design group who work with vernacular 1950s formica motifs which they 'redeem' by 'elevating' the colour scheme (from lurid primaries to 'tasteful' pastels) and the materials used (mixing plastic and marble, etc.).

There isn't the same sense of archness, the same relaxed bending of the rules, the same *disciplined* (controlled) use of metaphor and irony – the hallmarks which distinguish 'quality' Milanese design – in the work of Arad and Coates, Fred Baier and Daniel Weill [for disciplined metaphor, e.g. Memphis = ancient Egyptian capital (primitivism + the cradle of classical western civilization) *and* the home town of Elvis Presley (primitivism + the cradle of post-war western civilization.)] Logic only figures as a half-remembered ghost in the soft machine of British avant-garde design – the connections for the most part are somatic. Everyday objects suffer a sea-change as contraries are merged, forms and functions transposed to produce the kinds of thing we encounter during sleep: a classless class of impractical, impossible objects: deflated plastic chairs, a hi-fi system encased in blocks of broken concrete (Arad), spindly 1950s bentwood furniture upholstered in wetsuit rubber (Baier), a Radio Bag comprising functioning components suspended in a transparent plastic bag with flexible PVC speakers (Weill). The authority and linearity of History, the exteriority of Tradition give way to personalized reverie and remembrance: in Nigel Coates's interiors, decay is designed in as a resonant factor. In his design for the Metropole restaurant in Tokyo in 1986, for instance, he created a dreamscape of 'europe', a 'europe' half forgotten, half destroyed. Beneath a ceiling festooned like a pirate ship or Ship of Fools with billowing drapes he integrated found objects and contemporary features, an Embassy flagpole, a revolving globe, classical statuary, old clocks, specially commissioned murals, doors taken from an old London hotel. Empty space is used here as a landing pad for ghostly presences: a seance is convened of auratic objects which bear with them the traces of their earlier contexts and uses, their other former lives.

For the past is inescapable. It runs like Carlyle's chickens always *home*, back into the present moment. The world of culture as seen from the British edge is the 'civilized world' viewed at twilight from the other side of the British Empire, from the wild side of sobriety, order and the 'rational'. It is civilization viewed from a tropic, a jungloid place where nothing quite adds up any more. Frith and Horne may be right: the vitality and unpredictability of British pop culture may say more about the British higher education system than it does in any direct way about the class system, the mythological 'streets' or some general *Zeitgeist* of the past. It may, as Frith and Horne suggest, stem from the sudden mind-boggling exposure of untrained youth to

Big Ideas in the ramshackle hothouse of the Great British art school rather than from the mysteriously authored emanations of Blake's 'Great Albion'.[32]

It's in the interlinked fields of music and fashion that the 'killing combination' of piracy and jungloid roots in the production of British popular culture has attracted most attention and interest internationally. While the popular music business has always relied on the profitable alignment of 'attractive' or 'arresting' sounds and images, there has, in the last few decades, been an investment on an unprecedented scale in the development of audiovisual technologies and marketing techniques designed to make such an alignment more profitable and secure. Britain is the home of the pop video and the pop video is an undecidable (ideal) commodity: neither 'pure entertainment' nor 'straightforward promotion', it is a commodity in its own right (i.e. it's sold in shops), designed to sell another commodity (the band, the clothes, the image, the attitudes they're designed to 'represent'), to 'tell' – often through non-linear narrational devices – an image, not a story: the image of the group. Ideally from a marketing viewpoint, pop video turns in such a way that the image and the sound, the video and the record chase after each other (i.e. sell each other) in a double helix which seems to promise cash for all concerned. Furthermore it functions as raw material for broadcast (e.g. MTV). There is no doubt a tangled, contradictory dynamic dictating the leap into music visualization but the more immediate economic pressures seem clear enough: the decline in record sales worldwide, the fragmentation of markets, the collapse of any kind of unitary youth market.

The post-punk fragmentation of music markets, the displacement of attention (and energy and capital resources) away from the constructed sound to the constructed look (especially pronounced in the last few years with the decline in new musical ideas on the British pop and rock scenes) and the creation of more flexible, aggressive and ingenious marketing strategies – these trends are perhaps most advanced in Britain. The 'postmodern' implications of these developments have been explored suggestively at length elsewhere.[33] To sum up, it is argued that as vinyl begins competing with less palpably *material* audio technologies (CD, audio tape, etc.) (and, in the latter case, less controllable ones) and as the studio takes over from the stage as the primary production site, sound recording is freed from the moral obligation of (high) 'fidelity', to 'live' (where the living human voice and instrumental virtuosity convey 'presence', where the proscenium arch and the spotlit stage confer a priest-like authority on the performer). Sound itself is freed from the restrictions of time and the contiguous magic of the single session – as the music is broken down into independently recorded sections, assembled on a multitrack mixer, stretched and 'sculptured' by audio engineers. Sound begins to lose its priority, becoming just one designed element in a totally designed pack-age composed of both aural signals and visual signs, 'concepts', postures, 'lifestyles'. The record – the thing itself – the hard, black, brittle vinyl, the circle of frozen sounds – dematerializes. It melts and bends in the era of the floppy disc and the flexi-disc, the tape deck and the personalized portable stereo. And it is *rematerialized* (1) as image: as a 'bag' (record sleeve), a video, magazine advertisements, TV commercials, point of sale 3D installations, a 'picture disc' (on a picture disc, a star's face is inscribed on the record itself); and (2) as an image-thing-to-be-identified-with-and-identified-by (the record-as-thing now has what record executives call 'cultural utility': it has an 'expressive' value in the first instance not in the last (subcultural) moment of 'appropriation' (i.e. the 'expressive' component – the mark of difference that signals the 'sub' in subculture – is designed in, not projected in by people on 'the street'). 'It says who you are – like fashion shoes, a Big Mac, or a Sony Walkman' (Paul Walton). The apotheosis of this process of de- and rematerialization occurs in hip hop where the 'finished product' is opened up again and the record-object is turned into a percussive instrument to be handled, 'scratched' and mixed with quotes from other records by the hip hop deejays who skip between multiple turntables to produce fresh 'one off' aural compositions 'live'. (A similar 'deconsecration' of the finished product occurs in reggae in 'versioning' which has been institutionalized in popular music in the form of dub club and guest 'mixes', and 9- and 12-inch versions of the same record.)

New job categories have been created within the British music/fashion/video industries to accommodate and facilitate these changes. 'Concept packagers' and 'style and image engineers' work alongside 'sound designers' to unleash sound-and-image kits on a primed and stimulated market.

The selling of Frankie Goes to Hollywood marks out one kind

of limit to promotion. This was state-of-the-art music business packaging: a detective story (the mystery: who or what is/are 'Frankie'?) which unfolded in a series of tantalizing stages: (1) pre-planned orchestration of media interest/outrage; (2) selection of key signifiers (leather, S & M, 'the gay club', boxy suits, Holly's face, 'hardcore' amyl nitrate disco rhythms); (3) mobilization of 'shock' and 'censure' (record and video BBC bannings); (4) remixing of the original cut in new formats (several 12-inch versions of the same number, each reissued in a different (collectable) 'bag'); (5) promotion of the ethos of promotion-for-promotion's sake, packaging as Art. The *Welcome to the Pleasure Dome* album (1984) came complete with quotations from Coleridge, Baudelaire, Barthes and Nietzsche. An advertising mock-up on the inner sleeve of the fold-out cover offered, in addition, Baudelaire socks and Nietzsche T shirts available by mail order.

But any notional benefits derived from native packaging and promotional expertise are overshadowed by Britain's poor industrial performance. London in the 1980s may qualify as one of the world's leading advertising and media production centres (hosting, for example, the two principal international TV news agencies, WTN and Visnews), but Britain remains unable to compete with its industrial competitors in the design and construction of communications hardware. Britain's long-lost manufacturing edge (forfeited a century ago to Germany and the USA) has been even further eroded in the post-war years. Explanations for Britain's postimperial, postindustrial decline are, of course, various though the well-worn metaphors of illness and old age – metaphors which first gained a wide currency in the 'angry' 1950s continue to naturalize and strenthen perceptions of national decline.[34]

It is often claimed, for instance, that native traditions of workmanship have been finished off in the past three decades by the 'British disease' (which is variously diagnosed as over-cautious patterns of business investment, undercapitalized industry and research, inefficient, short-sighted management, decrepit plant and work practices, a non-vocationally-oriented education system and/or a 'lazy', 'greedy', untrained or – alternatively – inappropriately trained workforce). What survived of native manufacturing after the pre-war depression, German bombing and a combination of the ailments listed above has been further decimated by the 'hollowing out' of the industrial base as investments are shifted into the finance and service sectors, as research and development are moved overseas, as British 'manufacturing' comes increasingly to turn on the assembly of prepackaged components produced at low cost for low wages in Taiwan, Japan or South Korea.[35] In this elegy to England's lost prestige and power, Britain 'colonized', in the words of Tony Benn '(by) . . . the Common Market, the Pentagon, the IMF and the multinationals'[36] becomes just one more staging post on the circuits (of money, resources, goods and services) owned, organized and overseen from elsewhere.

THE SICK ROSE ('The Queen is Dead' (1986))

O Rose thou art sick.
The invisible worm,
That flies in the night
In the howling storm:

Has found out thy bed
Of crimson joy:
And his dark secret love
Does thy life destroy.

(William Blake, 'The Sick Rose' (1794))

I push the eject button, take out the *Spare Time* tape and load in Derek Jarman's video promo for the Smiths, 'The Queen is Dead' made in 1986. The tape opens with old black and white footage of a cathedral spire. It seems a lot has changed in fifty years, not least the consciousness of time itself: the past has become a reservoir of signifiers to be tapped, consumed, recycled like the London water supply.) On the soundtrack a chorus of young voices sing lines from some forgotten (playground?) song. The cathedral image is replaced by colour film of a group of unkempt children, blinking in the sunlight. As the drums crash into the opening bars of 'The Queen is Dead', the camera is bundled along behind a young 'boy' dressed in the archaic costume of a 1950s childhood, the short trousers, and 'short back and sides' haircut designed to mark the 'hims' off from the 'hers'. . . . The hairstyle, humiliating sign – in the sideburned 1950s of *my* youth – of the impotence of little boys to resist the will of parents, teachers, barbers – is now in the late 1980s eminently fashionable with young people of both genders (nowadays it functions to detach 'youth' from its fixings in the 'swinging', 'liberated', sexed and 'sex mad' 1960s)[37].

In a series of jump cuts synchronized to the beat of the drums, we see the 'boy' spray-painting the song's title along the broken wall that marks the boundary of an abandoned industrial estate. A close-up reveals that the 'boy' is a young woman and as the 4/4 rock beat calls the (camera) shots, we are taken on a ride at breakneck speed through a disorienting image-montage: rings of fire alternate with a spiralling red rose, a yellow sunflower, a child's xylophone, a red guitar that spins in the centre of the frame. A man, stripped to the waist, cracks eggs on his head; a woman, stripped to the waist, walks towards a tower block, and unfurls a Union Jack in its shadow. Image is laid upon image in a series of superimpositions so dense and excessive that the single lines of (cinematic) narrative – the this-then-this-then-this of plot and story – dissolve into the synchronicities of video and computer-generated effects. Metonymy, and repetition impose instead different kind of order: a royal crown revolves across the screen over a still of Buckingham Palace. Postcard shots of Westminster Bridge and the Houses of Parliament frame a filmed sequence of a quiet suburban street, its mock Tudor frontages bathed in bright sunlight. This sequence in turn is laid against a rapid black and white collage of sharp images of office blocks. Skyscrapered modernity, the International Style and 'zany' 1960s poses clash against the cozy pebble-dash of the typically English semi-detached home – the suburban Betjeman 'cottage' of the 1930s-built commuter belts that still encircle London.

Through it all, a single image-figure dances: the statue of Eros detached by some editor's scissors from its moorings in the granite steps at Piccadilly Circus. It flies across the image-flow, this emblem of desire, appearing at different points as photographed monument; as free 'floating signifier'; as the mascot perched on the bonnet of a Rolls-Royce car; as a parodic incarnation of one of Yeats's 'cocks of Hades'[38] in the image of a crouching, crowing boy dressed in chicken feather wings. As the singer's voice loops crazily round the helter-skelter lyrics, a row of little girls, rescued from some ancient 1930s film clip, dance in a line, their identical dresses with neat velvet collars, their uniformly bobbed hair swaying to the beat. 'Blood-begotten spirits', they dance, these ancient children, round and round the rings of fire, dying, as the tape turns, 'into a dance', into 'an agony of flame that cannot singe a sleeve': 'So ashamed to discover,' (wails Morrissey, the 'vocalist') 'That I'm the eighteenth pale descendant of some old queen or other'.[39]

What I'm watching here is a different kind of royal wedding video: the marriage of two queens – Widow Twankey, the traditional pantomime dame, and Queen Elizabeth II. And with this merger, this blending-in of 'high' and 'low', the reconciliation of all contraries in magic, the fusion of the sexes in the image of the superhuman form of Eros.

> Before me floats an image, man or shade,
> Shade more than man, more image than a shade;
> . . . I hail the superhuman,
> I call it death-in-life and life-in-death.

wrote William Butler Yeats – Dublin-born and schooled in London – as he sailed off to Byzantium.[40]

> God save the Queen
> She ain't a human being.
> There ain't no future in England's dreaming.[41]

sang London-Irish John Lydon (Johnny Rotten of the Sex Pistols) forty years later, as he sailed off for Hollywood (via New York City).

The allegory on which both song and video (and Sex Pistol song) are based is as transparent as it is clichéd. The same allegory has been set to work repeatedly in the post-war British cinema in the 'grotesque (sur)realism' of films like *The Ruling Class, O Lucky Man!, Britannia Hospital* and Jarman's own feature, *Jubilee*.[42] The allegorizing is 'camp', the debunking intention self-consciously 'critical' and 'anti-patriotic'. It sets out to expose the vanity of national pretensions to either 'unity' or 'greatness' by celebrating the repressed or excluded social, sexual and semantic margins – the bits that do not fit into the preferred narratives of Englishness. In this 'end-of-England' allegory the signifiers of national pride, consensus and heritage are decomposed and ironized. *Eros* substitutes for *logos*, 'crisis' for 'homeland'. Here among the 'liberal', 'left' or 'non-aligned', 'anarchic' or just plain 'alienated' British arts intelligentsia, the Queen indeed is dead: a victim of deconstruction along with the mythically unified 'straight and narrow' community she notionally represents.[43]

And yet, twenty years after the collapse of the British Empire, the Queen is still head of State in eighteen countries. And if *popularity* and media-generated interest are anything to go by, then the Queen, the Royal Family, the office of the monarchy itself and the order and continuity it supposedly guarantees and represents are very much alive in 1987. Fifty years after the Abdication Crisis, popular support for and interest in the monarchy has probably never been stronger in Great Britain, the republican impulse never so weak. It is, for instance, a significant and telling irony that one of the factors contributing to EMI's decision to terminate their contract with the Sex Pistols in 1977 was the response of the women workers at the record pressing plant, shocked and offended by Jamie Reid's 'customized' version of Sir Cecil Beaton's famous portrait of the Queen emblazoned on the cover of the 'No Future' single. The women refused to pack vinyl in a sleeve consisting of an image of Elizabeth II with her eyes and mouth striped out with the black bars which conventionally connote 'criminal anonymity'. In prophetic anticipation of the born-again royalism of the British working class in the 1980s, the gut reaction against art school punk and and anti-monarchist visual 'noise' came from the shopfloor rather than – as the Sex Pistols's publicists would have it – from the offices of the fusty old 'Establishment'.

During this decade we have had two royal weddings watched 'live' via satellite by millions worldwide.

> 'The Royals' is the longest-running soap opera in Britain. . . . We have become just as intimate with the doings of the folk from Buckingham Palace as we have with the folk from Southfork Ranch.[44]

In 1982, all the Queen's forces and all the Queen's men – the special police unit guarding Buckingham Palace, headed at the time by Commander Michael Trestrail (who in another 'scandal' was forced to resign the same summer over revelations concerning his relationship with a male prostitute) – failed to prevent a mentally disturbed commoner called Michael Fagan from breaking into the Queen's bedroom one spring morning intent on talking through his domestic problems with Her Majesty.

No more poignant indication of the charmed life of the monarchy in England in 1980s could be found than in this strange, pathetic meeting in the grey-lit dawn between a fifty-six-year-old woman caught between her dreams and Great Affairs of State and her distressed, dishevelled subject. At around 7.00 a.m., Her Majesty's eyes opened to see, silhouetted at the window, the diminutive figure of Mr Fagan, who sat unshaven on the edge of the bed, asking in a north London accent not for a fortune in jewels or the release of imprisoned terrorists, not for a united Ireland, a change in England's obsolete licensing laws or a helicopter to the airport, not even for a date with Jody Foster, but for a 'bit of a chat' and a 'light' for his 'fag'.

The centuries of sporting links between landed aristocrats and the 'criminal classes', the centuries which saw the maturation of what Gareth Stedman Jones has called that 'affinity of outlook between the "top and bottom drawer" against the "kill joys" in between' [45] the forces, contradictions and chances that have combined to produce the uniquely *British* compromise, that affective alliance between what Malcom McLaren calls 'a corrupt and faded aristocracy' and a 'brutalized proletariat' converge in the crepuscular dawn of the morning above the bed in a room in the Queen's largest London residence.

In March 1987 Michael Shea, the Queen's secretary for the past nine years, resigned. (He had been brought over from the British Information Service in New York after his 'brilliant' handling of the Royal Bicentennial Tour.) More than any other individual, Shea is probably responsible for the buoyant state of the monarchy in Britain today. He was the man who modernized the Royal image, who 'professionalized' media access (giving the go-ahead for relaxed *vérité*-style documentaries, cosy fireside chats between Royals and TV 'personalities'). He was the man who stage-managed 'State Occasions' for the benefit of the cameras,[46] who allegedly leaked news of the controversial rift[47] between Buckingham Palace and Downing Street and who once in an indiscreet moment disclosed to a Canadian journalist that the Queen's nickname among Palace staff was 'Miss Piggy' (from *The Muppet Show*). In March, Shea left the Royal service to take up a PR job with the Anglo-American multinational conglomerate, Hanson Trust, for three times his former salary.

It would be fitting, as Mr Shea ascends the steps of Concorde to take up his new job, for the surviving members of the original Lancashire cotton-mill gazzoo band to be reassembled on the tarmac to pipe him out with an appropriate medley of mid-Atlantic tunes: Walt Disney's 'When You Wish Upon A Star', perhaps, or William Blake's 'Jerusalem', played not as Blake himself intended, as a battle cry, a ringing call to build the Holy City here and now on England's 'green and pleasant land' but as a hymn to resignation, a looney toon, a lullaby to Britain.

NOTES AND REFERENCES

This essay was first commissioned by the Institute of Contemporary Art, Boston, Massachusetts, USA. The author wishes to acknowledge the support offered by the Institute for this work.
1 Walter Benjamin (1973) *Illuminations*, London: Fontana.
2 George Orwell, 'England, your England' (itself a parodic reference to D. H. Lawrence's 'England, My England') in F. Kermode *et al.* (eds) (1973) *The Oxford Anthology of English Literature. Vol. 2: 1880- The Present*, Oxford: Oxford University Press.
3 For the debate on populism and nationalism in Britain, see for instance, S. Hall and M. Jacques (1983) *The Politics of Thatcherism*, London: Lawrence & Wishart with *Marxism Today*; J. Donald *et al.* (eds) *Formations of Nation and People*, London: Routledge & Kegan Paul. M. Langlan and B. Schwartz (eds) (1985) *Crises in the British State 1880-1930*, London: Hutchinson; B. Schwartz 'Conservatism, nationalism and imperialism' in J. Donald and S. Hall (eds) (1986) *Politics and Ideology*, Milton Keynes: Open University Press; Martin Wiener (1985) *English Culture and the Decline of the Industrial Spirit*, Harmondsworth: Penguin; Benedict Anderson (1982) *Imagined Communities*, London: Verso.

Since writing this essay the critical literature on national and ethnic cultural identity has been greatly expanded. See, among others, D. Morley and K. Robbins, 'Spaces of identity', *Screen* 30 (4) Autumn 1989 and 'No place like *Heimat*: images of home(land) in European culture', *New Formations* 12, Winter 1990; I. Chambers (1990) *Border Dialogues*, London: Comedia/Routledge, which not only provides an overview of recent debates on 'Englishness' but also offers in its probing of the 'ground' of postmodernity a more lucid and concise rationale for the eccentric form of this present essay than I could myself provide. Also there is a great deal of recently published, critically innovative and politically suggestive work which sets out to deconstruct colonial discourse and the *tropes* of 'race'. See, for instance, Gayatri Chakravorty Spivak (1987) *In Other Worlds*, London: Methuen, and (1990) *The Post-Colonial Critic: Interviews, Strategies, Dialogues*, London: Routledge; H. K. Bhabha (1990) *Narration and Nationalism*, London: Routledge; also 'The other question: difference, discrimination and the discourse of colonialism', in F. Barker *et al.* (eds) (1986) *Literature, Politics and Theory*, London: Methuen; 'The commitment to theory', *New Formations* 5, 1988; and 'Of mimicry and man: the ambivalence of colonial discourse', in J. Donald and S. Hall (eds), op. cit.

K. Mercer, 'Black hair style/politics', *New Formations* 3, 1987 and '"1968": periodizing postmodern politics and identity' in L. Grossberg *et al.* (eds) (1992) *Cultural Studies*, London: Routledge. Also P. Gilroy (1987) *There Ain't No Black in the Union Jack*, London: Hutchinson, and 'Cultural studies and ethnic absolutism' in L. Grossberg, op. cit., (1992). Finally D. Webster (1988) *Looka Yonder*, London: Comedia/Routledge is wholeheartedly recommended for its scholarly and readable exploration of the impact of the 'imaginary America of populist culture' on British and European taste formations and cultural identities.

4 Thomas Carlyle (1839) 'The Irish' in *Chartism*, London: Chapman and Hall, 1858.

5 The phrase 'enemies within' was first used by Thatcher during the miners' strike in 1984 to distinguish internal from external threats to national security. All the other terms which appear in quotation marks elsewhere in this sentence – 'scroungers' etc. – are taken from 'Thatcherite discourse' (i.e. either from personal statements made by the Prime Minister or from Thatcherite press editorials, publicity campaigns, etc.).

6 P. Wright (1987) *On Living in an Old Country: The National Past in Contemporary Britain*, London: Verso.

7 See for example, J. B. Priestley (1934) *An English Journey*, London: Heinemann and Victor Gollancz; G. Orwell (1937) *The Road to Wigan Pier*; Tom Harrisson (1978) *Living through the Blitz*, Harmondsworth: Penguin; A. Calder and D. Sheridan (eds) (1985) *Speak for Yourself: Mass Observation Anthology 1937-1949* Oxford: Oxford University Press; M. Jennings (ed.) *Humphrey Jennings: Filmmaker, Painter, Poet*, London: BFI; F. Hardy (ed.) *Grierson on Documentary*, London: Faber & Faber.

8 For the distinction between *studium* and *punctum*, see R. Barthes (1981) *Camera Lucida*, New York: Hill & Wang:

> The *studium* is that very field of unconcerned desire . . . of inconsequential taste. . . . (That element of the photograph) . . . which will disturb the *studium* I shall call . . . the *punctum* for punctum is also: sting, speck, cut, little hole – and also a cast of the dice. A photograph's *punctum* is that accident which pricks me (but also bruises me, is poignant to me).

Barthes develops a similar topology of reader-text 'intensities' with regard to film in 'The third meaning', in S. Heath (ed.) *Image – Music – Text*, Harmondsworth: Penguin.

9 Widow Twankey is a pantomime 'dame', traditionally played as a comic grotesque by a female impersonator. For the history of cross-dressing in pantomime and elsewhere see P. Ackroyd (1979) *Dressing Up: Tranvestism and Drag: The History of an Obsession*, London: Thames & Hudson.

10 The Boy Scout movement was formed by Baden-Powell after the Boer War. The poor physical condition and listlessness of young urban working-class recruits to the forces was regarded as a factor in the

British defeat and as a long-term threat to the survival and strength of the Nation, the Empire, hence the 'race'. See, for instance R. S. S. Baden-Powell (1909) *Scouting for Boys: A Handbook for Instruction in Good Citizenship*, London: Scout Association; J. Springhall (1974) *Coming of Age: Adolescence in Britain, 1860 - 1960*, London: Gill & Macmillan; G. Pearson (1983) *Hooligan: A Haunt of Respectable Fears*, London: Macmillan; M. Blanch (1979) 'Imperialism, nationalism and organized youth', in J. Clarke *et al.* (eds) *Working Class Culture: Studies in History and Theory*, London: Hutchinson.

11 'Camp taste is, above all, a mode of enjoyment, of appreciation - not judgement. . . . Camp taste is a kind of love, love for human nature. It relishes rather than judges the little triumphs and awkward intensities of "character". . . . Camp taste identifies with what it is enjoying. People who share this sensibility are not laughing at the thing they label as "camp", they're enjoying it. Camp is a tender feeling'. (S. Sontag (1966) 'Notes on camp', *Against Interpretation*, New York: Farrar, Straus & Giroux).

12 These lines are a travesty of the following lines from W.B. Yeats's poem 'Easter 1916', written in September 1916 to honour what Maud Gonne called the 'tragic dignity' of the martyrs of the failed rebellion of 24-29 April, organized in Dublin against the English by the Irish Republican Brotherhood:

This other man I had dreamed
A drunken, vainglorious lout.
He had done most bitter wrong
To some who are near my heart.
Yet I number him in the song;
He, too, has resigned his part
In the casual comedy;
He, too, has been changed in his turn.
Transformed utterly:
A terrible beauty is born.

The original reference is to Major John MacBride, estranged husband of Maude Gonne, hence - as far, at least, as Yeats was concerned - a former rival in love.

13 T. Nairn (1977) *The Break-Up of Britain*, London: Verso.

14 For instance, F. Jameson (1984) 'Postmodernism or the cultural logic of late capital', *New Left Review* 146 (July–August); S. Frith (1983) *South Effects: Youth, Leisure and the Politics of Rock*, London: Constable, and with H. Horne (1986) *Art into Pop*, London: Methuen; G. Marcus (1989) *Lipstick Traces; A Secret History of the 20th Century*, London: Secker & Warburg; I. Chambers (1985) *Popular Culture; The Metropolitan Experience*, London: Methuen; D. Laing (1985) *One Chord Wonders*, Milton Keynes: Open University Press; D. Hebdige (1979) *Subculture: The Meaning of Style*, London: Methuen.

15 See S. Frith and A. McRobbie (1978-9) 'Rock and sexuality', *Screen Education* 29 for the distinction between 'cock rock' and 'teenybop'.

16 See P. Gilroy (1987) op. cit.; D. Widgery (1986) *Beating Time: Riot'n'
Race 'n' Rock 'n' Roll*, London: Chatto & Windus; D. Hebdige (1987)
Cut 'n' Mix: Culture, Identity and Caribbean Music, London:
Comedia/Routledge; and (1988) *Hiding in the Light: On Images and
Things*, London: Comedia/Routledge. This section includes
passages drawn directly from this last book (212–15).

17 P. Gilroy (1937) op. cit.

18 I have tried to develop these arguments further in two articles: 'After
the masses', *Marxism Today*, January 1989 reprinted in S. Hall and
M. Jacques (eds) (1990) *New Times: The Changing Face of Politics in
the 1990s*, London: Lawrence & Wishart with *Marxism Today*, and
'Fax to the future', *Marxism Today*, January 1990.

19 See Gilroy (1987) op. cit. and D. Toop (1984) *The Rap Attack:
African Jive to New York Hip Hop*, London: Pluto. Also Hebdige
(1987) and (1988) op. cit.

20 See Toop (1984) op. cit.

21 Prabhu Guptara, 'Look who's winning the glittering English prizes',
Evening Standard, 2 February 1987.

22 Smiley Culture, 'Cockney Translation' (Fashion, 1984).

23 *Territories* (1985) (SANKOFA Black Film and Video collective),
directed by I. Julien. But also *The Passion of Remembrance* (1987)
and *Looking for Langston* (1990) and *Young Soul Rebels* to be
released in 1991) by the same director. Also *Expeditions* (1983) and
Handsworth Songs (1985) (Black Audio Film Collective). For parallel
developments in fine art see, for example, *Third Text* 8/9 (Autumn/
Winter 1989 Special Issue), 'The other story: AfroAsian artists in
postwar Britain'. For debates around the new black British films,
their relations in both popular cinema and 'new ethnicities', see K.
Mercer (ed.) (1988) *Black Film, British Cinema*, London: Institute of
Contemporary Arts, especially the essays by Mercer, Hall,
Williamson and – for sharply distinguished reponses to the new
Black avant garde – the exchanges between Rushdie, Hall and Howe.
For a further critique of the place of black experimental film within
both modernism and black 'vernacular' culture, see P. Gilroy (1989)
'Cruciality and the frog's perspective: an agenda of difficulties for the
black arts movement in Britain', *Art & Text* 32 (Autumn). See also the
work by Cornel West both on black British cinema and the work of
Spike Lee.

24 See S. Jones (1987) *White Youth and Jamaican Popular Culture*,
Basingstoke: Macmillan. Also Hebdige (1987) op. cit.

25 See C. W. E. Bigsby (ed.) (1975) *Superculture: American Popular
Culture and Europe*, Bowling Green: Bowling Green University
Press; But see also D. Webster (1988) op. cit. D. Morley and D.
Robbins (1989) and (1990) op. cit. for updates on Americanization
and European culture(s).

26 A. Mattelart, F. Mattelart and D. Delcourt (1986) *International Image
Markets*, London: Comedia.

27 Most of the 'proverbs' have been taken from C. McDermott (1987)

Street Style: British Design in the 1980s, London: Design Council.
28 ibid. and J. Thackara and S. Jane (1986) *New British Design*, London: Thames & Hudson.
29 C. McDermott (1987) op. cit.
30 ibid.
31 ibid.
32 S. Frith and H. Horne (1986) op. cit.
33 See, for instance, I. Chambers (1985) and (1990) op. cit.; also (1987) 'The obscured metropolis', *Cultural Studies* 1 (1) January, London: Methuen.
34 Listen, for instance to Jimmy Porter in J. Osborne's (1956) *Look Back in Anger* or read the tirades delivered by Osborne, Lindsay Anderson and Kenneth Tynan against English conservatism, anti-modernism and colonial atavism (e.g. the Suez debacle) published in their (1957) *Declaration*, London: MacGibbon & Kee.
35 These loosely and polemically argued points bear little relation to the more ambitiously (and competently) theorized analyses of 'post-Fordism' and 'disorganized capitalism' developed by Robin Murray, Scott Lash and John Urry. For examples of this work see, for instance, S. Hall and M. Jacques (eds) (1990) op. cit. See also P. Hirst's critique of 'postFordism' in the same volume. In addition, see R. Murray (1988) 'Life after Henry Ford', *Marxism Today* , October; S. Lash and J. Urry (1987) *The End of Organized Capitalism*, Cambridge: Polity Press. Further see D. Harvey (1989) *The Condition of Postmodernity*, Oxford: Basil Blackwell, for a comprehensive account of 'flexible accumulation' and the spatial implications of the new modes of capitalist finance, production, distribution and exchange. Also debates in *Marxism Today* on the political dimensions of the new 'global - local nexus'; E. Soja (1989) *Postmodern Geographies*, London: Verso; D. Massey (1984) *Spatial Divisions of Labour: Social Structures and the Geography of Production*, London: Macmillan; and (1989) 'Subjects in space', *New Formations* 11, (Summer).
36 T. Benn (1981) 'Britain is a colony', *New Socialist* 1 (October). For a critique of hard left anti-Americanism, see especially D. Webster (1988) op. cit., chap. 7 and Conclusion.
37 Another historical irony: 1960s styles are again back in fashion in the 'rave' culture of the early 1990s. Many of the angst-ridden white 'indie' bands who modelled their image and vocal style on Morrissey and the Smiths switched in the late 1980s/early 1990s to the black-influenced 'dance music' styles derived from black American house music and the so-called 'Manchester sound'.
38 The reference comes from W. B. Yeats's poem, 'Byzantium' (1930) which builds on the earlier poem, 'Sailing to Byzantium'. Yeats's late romanticism, his interest in the esoteric tradition, in the occult image of the 'gyre' and the 'shade', 'dreaming back' or unwinding its natural life through an unravelling swathe of images, all seem apposite here. The fascination with the textures of 'Englishness', the Proustian attention to conjuring up (or with) the past, the preciosity

and mysticism evident in the output of both Jarman and Morrissey all suggest that they might qualify for membership of an English equivalent of Yeats's 'Celtic Twilight' circle. The 'evocation' of Jarman's film I attempt here 'diverts' lines taken from stanzas 2 to 4 of that poem, especially the fourth:

> At midnight on the Emperor's pavement flit
> Flames that no faggot feeds, not steel has lit,
> Nor storm disturbs, flames begotten of flame,
> Where blood-begotten spirits come
> And all complexities of fury leave,
> Dying into a dance,
> An agony of trance,
> An agony of flame that cannot singe a sleeve.

39 The Smiths, 'The Queen is Dead' (Rough Trade, 1986).
40 W. B. Yeats, 'Byzantium' (1930), stanza 2. See note 38 above.
41 The Sex Pistols, 'God Save the Queen (No Future)' (Virgin, 1978).
42 Certain of the more recent crop of British movies (e.g. Jarman's own *The Last of England* as well as *Business as Usual, Eat the Rich, Empire State* and *Sammy and Rosie Get Laid*, most of which were released after this text was first published) extend the same basic imagery and build upon the same allegory. They all evoke the 'sense of an ending' (of the truth-value or plausibility) of the dominant national myths.
43 I want to distinguish my attempt to characterize the 'anti-nationalist', 'anti-normative' political and aesthetic tendencies in recent independent British films from the kind of vitriolic dismissal meted out by a right-wing historian like Norman Stone who, in the *Sunday Times*, 10 January 1988, wrote off all the films mentioned in the last note (along with *My Beautiful Launderette*) as 'tawdry, ragged, rancidly provincial . . . semi-educated ambitious mediocrities (which were) overcompeting in a declining market, suffering from bouts of muddled creativity, waiting in line to catch public or semi-public money while dreaming of revolting sensationalism'. (See 'Through a lens darkly' reprinted in Mercer (ed.) (1988) op. cit. 23.) I direct my criticisms exclusively at the institutionalized nature of the 'symbolism' employed in many of these films, at the overpolarized vision of cultural and political conflict encoded therein and the likely impact of both these 'predictabilities' on the extent and degree of genuine audience 'engagement' with the 'issues' supposedly raised within the films. For the rest, I am aware that most of Stone's comments ('tawdry . . . provincial . . . muddled . . . sensational', etc.) could (and no doubt would) be applied with equal venom to this essay.
44 R. Coward (1984) 'The royals', in her *Female Desire*, London: Paladin.
45 Gareth Stedman Jones (1982) 'Working-class culture and working-class politics in London, 1870–1890: notes on the remaking of a working class', in B. Waites (ed.) *Popular Culture: Past and Present,*

London: Croom Helm.

46 For the extent of routine collusion/alignment of interests between Buckingham Palace and the media during the royal wedding, see for instance, D. Dayan and E. Katz (1985) 'Electronic ceremonies', in M. Blonsky (ed.) *On Signs*, Oxford: Basil Blackwell.

47 On 20 July 1986 a report appeared in the *Sunday Times* that the Queen was concerned about the Thatcher government's socially divisive policies, its handling of the miners' strike and the implications for the future of the Commonwealth of the government's refusal to impose sanctions on South Africa. Hugo Young points out in his book on Thatcher (1989) *One of Us*, London: Macmillan, that 'this story turned out, on inspection, to be almost entirely false' and that the telling differences between the two women were primarily ones 'of style and feel' rather than substantive opinion. Towards the end of her reign, Mrs Thatcher proclaimed her identity of outlook with the monarch by adopting the 'royal We', so that when her daughter-in-law gave birth to an heir in 1989, Thatcher announced the transformation in her status with the words: 'We are a grandmother.'

Index